*Imperial Subjects*

A book in the series
LATIN AMERICA OTHERWISE:
LANGUAGES, EMPIRES, NATIONS

Series editors:
*Walter D. Mignolo, Duke University*
*Irene Silverblatt, Duke University*
*Sonia Saldívar-Hull, University of Texas, San Antonio*

ABOUT THE SERIES

*Latin America Otherwise: Languages, Empires, Nations* is a critical series. It aims to explore the emergence and consequences of concepts used to define "Latin America" while at the same time exploring the broad interplay of political, economic, and cultural practices that have shaped Latin American worlds. Latin America, at the crossroads of competing imperial designs and local responses, has been construed as a geocultural and geopolitical entity since the nineteenth century. This series provides a starting point to redefine Latin America as a configuration of political, linguistic, cultural, and economic intersections that demands a continuous reappraisal of the role of the Americas in history, and of the ongoing process of globalization and the relocation of people and cultures that have characterized Latin America's experience. *Latin America Otherwise: Languages, Empires, Nations* is a forum that confronts established geocultural constructions, rethinks area studies and disciplinary boundaries, assesses convictions of the academy and of public policy, and correspondingly demands that the practices through which we produce knowledge and understanding about and from Latin America be subject to rigorous and critical scrutiny.

When can a subject be described as imperial and when as colonial? Imperial subjects seem to emerge from imperial identifications, such as the Spanish use of "Indian" to label the diverse people of Anahuac, Tawantinsuyu, and Abya-Yala. Descriptions of subjects as colonial imply new conditions of existence for people under imperial rule. In the sixteenth century, new identities emerged as traditional subjects, changing geo-political demarcations, and racism in the form of imperial hierarchies imposed over ethnic formations, came together.

This collection of essays offers a splendid map of identity formation at the intersection of imperial rule, colonial administration, the invention of "Indians," and the emergence of a new ethno-class, the Creole. The foreword by Irene Silverblatt and the introduction by Andrew B. Fisher and Matthew D. O'Hara lay the foundation for this exploration of the interconnected subjects of race and identity in colonial Latin America.

*❖I❖I❖I❖*

# Imperial Subjects

*❖I❖I❖I❖*

RACE AND IDENTITY IN

COLONIAL LATIN AMERICA

Andrew B. Fisher and Matthew D. O'Hara, eds.

*Foreword by Irene Silverblatt*

Duke University Press

Durham and London 2009

Printed in the United States of America on
acid-free paper ∞

Designed by Heather Hensley

Typeset in Whitman by Keystone Typesetting, Inc.

Library of Congress Cataloging-in-Publication
Data appear on the last printed page of this book.

Duke University Press gratefully acknowledges
the support of the Program for Cultural
Cooperation between Spain's Ministry of Culture
and United States Universities, which provided
funds toward the production of this book.

A. B. F.

*For Debbie and Gabriel*

M. D. O.

*For Sue, Maeve, Bridgid, and Farrin*

# Contents

# Foreword

Taken collectively the chapters in this volume make a strong statement about the relevance of identity to the study of the Iberian (mostly Spanish) colonial world. They also make a strong case for a particular view of identity—one that understands the concept as fluid, malleable, yet constrained; one that understands identity as being born out of a dynamic between individuals and the givens of cultural and political life—the relations of being—through which humans make themselves and succeeding conditions of experience. That is, they insist on studying identity in history.

And that history was quite extraordinary, for Spanish colonialism was coterminous with the initial processes of European state making. The sixteenth and seventeenth centuries, witnessing profound transformations in political and economic life, spawned nothing less than a cultural revolution—or, better said, a revolution in the possible ways of being human. This was a revolution of identities—a revolution of social selves, of social relations, and of social understandings; this was the cultural revolution behind the making of the emerging modern world.

One of the emerging modern world's signature behaviors was to embed economic and political authority into a radical cultural design. Spanish political and economic dominion was charted through a novel trio of human beings—*español, indio,* and *negro* (to be expanded as the categories proved insufficient)—each with a publicly conferred configuration of obligations and possibilities. These categories contributed to the ambience of political culture through which human beings, in daily living, gave meaning to themselves and their lives. Taken as a whole, the essays here explore how structures of colonial rule were transformed into venues of lived experience, were transformed into identities.

In the colonial world, aspects of identity were in dialogue with categories of rule—the categories through which the Crown governed its population. Institutions of political and religious life—the bureaucracies of church and state—circumscribed individuals by placing them in colonialism's definitional boxes. Although these categories were implanted into the sinews of living, state and religious institutions did not have the only say—or even the final say. These categories were frames of cultural possibility; but it was individuals, in history, living through social relations, that made them into structures of experience.

I stress again the importance of seeing these chapters as part of a whole, more comprehensive project. The kind of wide-ranging lens provided by this volume points to the analytical advantage of abstractions like "identity" and "race" but it also lays bare their limits. If one of the messages of this volume is the importance of studying identity dialectally, as a dynamic relation between a subject and the social forms and practices of a given milieu, another is the importance of history, of exploring identity in terms of the context through which identities are created, transformed, and maintained. We can draw lessons about the nature of identity—or, better, of identities—only by analyzing their varieties over lifetimes, over decades, and over geographies. Then we can see how relations of power, in a variety of spheres, tinge the air in which identities breathe.

If we are to think about race and identity not as things but as processes of living, a turn to Iberian colonialism is particularly helpful. One reason is that the first waves of colonialism inaugurated the global, racialized categories of humanity with which we are only too familiar today. We are forced to recognize that these divisions had a historical genesis and that their construction was party to the politics making the modern world and its illusions.

Western mythology, described by Fernando Coronil as "occidentalism," masked the roots of Western nation building in global politics. Contrary to common understandings, the modern world, from its inception, was transnational in scope and hierarchical in structure. These characteristics are evident in the categories of Spanish colonialism, constructed to politically order the newly globalized humanity. Notions of "Spanishness" were emerging in Europe at the same time that colonizers were civilizing Indians, enslaving Africans, and distinguishing themselves from the lower orders of Indians and blacks by calling one another "Spanish." Exploring Spanish expansion allows us to better grasp the significance of colonialism to what we call "modernity" as well as the antagonistic social relationships—racialized relationships—at its core.

Bureaucrats control knowledge, and, as social analysts have pointed out, this authority is a source of their power. But many colonial bureaucrats dominated a special kind of knowledge: they could determine the most profound of societal truths—membership in a human community. Seventeenth-century functionaries inherited a world whose humanity was increasingly understood in racialized, colonially driven terms. With the authority to determine the categorical "box" in which human beings were placed, officials played a significant (if unwitting) role in deepening and consolidating race-thinking as a way of life. In their bureaucratic practices, officials were specifying the very terms of social experience: the terms by which the world was to be judged and the terms framing any individual's social truth. Essays in this volume shed light on this process of identity-naming and, taken collectively, they locate identity in history, by highlighting the interaction of identity with structures of power.

Administrators in Spain and Spain's colonies used a particular race-thinking notion to shape and calibrate the "natural order" of political life. They argued that blood carried stains, and that stains could determine character traits, intelligence, political rights, and economic possibilities. The notion of blood purity was first elaborated in Europe, where it was used to separate Old Christians from Spain's New Christians—women and men of Jewish and Muslim origin whose ancestors had converted to Christianity. New Christians carried stained blood and, consequently, were perceived as a potential danger to official life. Conquistadores brought the curse of New Christians, the concept of stained blood (*mancha*), to the Americas. Bureaucrats were obliged to indicate the "race" and blood purity of everyone brought before them; their records give us a ringside view of the New Christian dilemma in the New World. Authorities in the Americas were vexed by such blood-related questions as Was the blood stain of Europe's New Christians the same as the blood stain of Indians or blacks? Were such stains indelible? Could baptism override them? Were all stains equal? When bureaucrats and their colleagues responded to these issues in their daily chores of statecraft, they helped make race into a calculable thing. They were also imbuing "race" with very modern, often state-related, confusions—of nation and religion, culture and genes, color and ability.

The essays in this rich and varied collection point to the confused, overlapping, and muddied dimensions of identitymaking in the Spanish colonial world; they point to the dialectic conjoining public dimensions of colonial order, expressed through cultural designs, and the ways that human beings, born into this world, gave meaning to, made sense of, and in the process (unwittingly) put their stamp on the racialized orders of colonial life. By providing us with abundant examples—crossing boundaries of time and geography—they give us a perspective on the broad historical processes, mixing cultural forms and political ordering, that have shaped not only the Spanish colonial world but so much of modern experience.

Thus, domination, in its many forms, was overlaid on a radical, cultural map of social being; moreover, the exploitative social relations girding this global cultural map were hidden behind a semblance of categorical "race" things.

*Irene Silverblatt*

# Acknowledgments

Edited volumes are by definition a collective effort, yet this project owes an especially great debt to others. Well before the project's inception, our advisers and fellow graduate students at the University of California, San Diego, greatly influenced our thinking about Latin American history, its changing historiography on race and identity, and the place of analytic frameworks in historical interpretation. In particular, we wish to express our gratitude to our graduate mentors, Eric Van Young and Dain Borges.

In 2004–2005, we began a series of informal conversations stemming from our surprise that topics as central to the field of colonial Latin American history as race and identity had not been the subject of a book such as this one (with the exception of some well-known but rather dated syntheses published several decades ago). Holed up in a hotel room in downtown Seattle during the American Historical Association's annual meeting, we outlined a plan for bringing such a volume to fruition in the hope of offering not only a representative sampling of current scholarship but also an anticipation of the field's future direction. The result of those initial musings is this book.

Academic folklore abounds with ominous tales of edited book projects that never quite got off the ground or were mired for years somewhere in the middle of the editorial process, consuming in the process the life-blood of those foolhardy enough to take on the helm. We are glad to report that our experience could not have been more different. Above all, we have our contributors to thank for the project's success. Their intelligent, crisp, and (almost always!) timely drafts filled our journey with a deep sense of scholarly purpose. Likewise, the encouragement and support that we received at Duke University Press from Valerie Millholland and Miriam Angress made the editorial process a breeze. Irene Silverblatt and Doug Cope also merit a special note of gratitude for their support and enthusiasm for the project while it was still at its conceptual stage.

As editors, we were privileged to orchestrate a series of cordial yet lively exchanges of ideas among such an exemplary group of scholars. We believe the work as a whole benefited from the cross-pollination that occurred through the circulation of early versions of the book's chapters. Our own introductory essay certainly improved thanks to the insights of a number of the volume's contributors, as well as those of our friend and colleague Javier Villa-Flores. On behalf of everyone involved in the project, we would also like to thank the three anonymous reviewers who offered feedback for how to strengthen the internal cohesion and interpretative force of the final product.

Last, we would not have found the time to complete this project had it not been for the generous support offered by our home institutions and a number of external grants over the course of several years. In particular, Andrew Fisher thanks Carleton College for an extended leave from teaching and the Center for U.S.–Mexican Studies at the University of California, San Diego. For his part, Matt O'Hara thanks the History Department and the Division of Humanities at the University of California at Santa Cruz, the History Department at New Mexico State University, the National Endowment for the Humanities, the Newberry Library, and the Rockefeller Foundation.

*A.B.F., Northfield, Minnesota*
*M.D.O., Santa Cruz, California*

ANDREW B. FISHER AND MATTHEW D. O'HARA

# Introduction

*Racial Identities and Their Interpreters in Colonial Latin America*

We are informed that it is extremely inconvenient for the welfare and good of the Indian natives of those provinces that mulattoes, mestizos, and Negroes circulate in their company, because in addition to the fact that they treat them badly and use them as servants, they teach them their evil customs and habits of laziness and also certain errors and vices that tend to corrupt and hinder the objectives that we desire for the salvation of the said Indians' souls, and that they live in an orderly society.
~Philip II to the Royal Audiencia of Panamá, 1578

All Indian women are deceitful, lustful, thieving, disobedient, and above all, great whores. . . . They prefer to live as concubines of the Spaniards, and on occasion with black and mulatto men, than marry an Indian commoner.
~Felipe Guaman Poma de Ayala to Philip III, 1615

In today's parlance, the New World has lost most of its value as a historically useful term. Critics most commonly point out that what Columbus "discovered" was not new to the millions of indigenous people whose ancestors had lived in the western hemisphere for millennia prior to 1492. To question the novelty of the "New World" is no longer a radical critique but a baseline assumption. The more significant conceptual problem is that the term privileges a precise (even pristine) condition captured at a particular moment in time. Precontact America was not, after all, populated by timeless societies beyond the bounds of history, nor was there a clear and universal endpoint for the many repercussions unleashed on what would become the Atlantic world in the aftermath of 1492. The colonial societies that coalesced in early Latin America, in other words, remained ever-changing and multiple new worlds that could be just as alien to indigenous people as they were for European and African newcomers.[1] Seemingly impersonal historical forces—such as the introduction and spread of Hispanic culture and Catholicism, mercantile capitalism, and the transatlantic slave trade, among others—certainly played an important role in the shaping of these societies, and as a consequence they helped create the opportunities, resources, perils, and limitations the people of early Latin America faced on a daily basis. But, as the contributors to this volume show, colonial reality was also formed by the cumulative effect of an infinite number of interactions, both mundane and extraordinary, among Spain's and Portugal's diverse set of imperial subjects. While historians can readily discern evidence of the material forces that shaped the colonial experience—where people worked, the goods they consumed, and the taxes they paid—it is often more difficult to assess affective experience, such as how historical actors understood their sense of self or their attachment to a place or community. At its core, this volume seeks to unlock this fundamental question of how Iberian settlers, African slaves, Native Americans, and their multiethnic progeny understood who they were as individuals, as members of various communities, and ultimately as imperial subjects. More specifically, it explores the relationship between colonial ideologies of difference and the identities historical actors presented, performed, and defended in their interactions with one another and the representatives of the twin bastions of imperial rule, the Crown and the Church. It is an attempt to understand the inseparable bond between public and private realities.

While the question of identity may appear to be an intrinsically personal inquiry, it carries a political dimension that relates directly to the nature of Iberian imperialism. That is, although it has long been asserted that Spanish and Portuguese colonization tolerated racial miscegenation to a degree unimaginable in the British (and to a lesser extent, French) worlds, the Iberian project in the Americas rested on the presumption of a long-term, discernible boundary between the colonizers and the colonized that reflected a sliding scale of inferiority among subsets of the Crown's vassals.[2] Royal jurists and advisors thus justified empire in part by appealing to their nations' historic mission to bring civilization and the Catholic faith to a heathen and barbaric indigenous population. In exchange for these benefits, the newly ascribed "Indians" were expected to offer their fealty, labor, and tribute to the monarch and his representatives. In Spanish America, this reciprocal relationship, summarized in Karen Caplan's chapter in this volume, went further, by offering a modicum of protection to these new subjects as legal minors of the Crown. Reality, though, often diverged dramatically from the espoused ideal, particularly in the early colonial period, prompting the introduction of African slaves to the colonies so as to spare the rapidly declining indigenous population from the severest form of exploitation. Consigned to the status of chattel and a life of grueling labor, Africans and their American-born descendants did not initially enjoy a paternalistic connection to the Crown. Nevertheless, as the chapters by Dantas, Díaz, and Twinam in this volume attest, free and enslaved blacks, as they became familiar with Hispanic culture and Iberian law, began to assert an identity as imperial subjects entitled to rights, honors, and privileges that colonial society did not readily concede to those associated with the stigma of slavery and an inferior racial status.

Despite this ideological premise, colonial realities often required transgressing boundaries of difference. Early on, for instance, Spanish and Portuguese men learned that securing power and economic resources was made easier through marriages, or more commonly informal liaisons, with the daughters of indigenous rulers.[3] In some instances, the Crown even encouraged such strategies in the belief that Spanish traits could "redeem" Indian ones in the resulting progeny.[4] More mundane demographic forces yielded similar though largely unintended outcomes. For one, the dearth of Spanish and Portuguese women, particularly in the early years of colonization, induced all sorts of male settlers to seek out temporary or permanent relations of varying degrees of coercion with indigenous women that went well beyond the scope of strategic elite unions.[5] An even more skewed and longer-lasting gender imbalance among African slaves—exacerbated by competition between black men and white owners for enslaved female companions—also led to high rates of exogamy among this group. Iberian law, which considered a child's civil status inherited from the mother, further encouraged enslaved black men to seek out Indian and mestiza wives. In all these instances, it was not immediately clear how the resulting children were to be characterized, although many were probably automatically accorded their mother's status given the absence of an acknowledged (or even known) father. Children born from indigenous mothers and notable Spanish fathers constituted the most noteworthy exception, since they frequently gained honorary membership in the "superior" group. In time, however, new intermediate categories (for example, mestizo and mulatto) emerged to address the liminal status of interracial children. The elite viewed these groups with suspicion and distaste, especially as their numbers grew. The fact that these unions occurred outside the bounds of Christian matrimony, and among lower-status individuals, only contributed to the belief that racially heterogeneous individuals lacked honor and legitimacy and possibly carried the stain of black ancestry.[6] Racial ambiguity, in sum, has deep roots in Latin American history that have been informed by unequal relations of power across group boundaries and gender lines.

Given these entrenched ideological assumptions about the colonial order, it is no wonder that the state and those groups with an interest in the status quo viewed with suspicion and hostility any challenges to the fixed and "natural" boundaries between different sorts of people. These attitudes were perhaps best embodied by the so-called Two Republic system of Spanish America, a sprawling collection of royal legislation, local administrative policies, and informal practices, through which Spanish colonizers attempted to separate native peoples from other colonial subjects. These included restrictions against non-Indians living in Indian towns, distinct systems of religious administration for native peoples, and separate juridical institutions for Indians and non-Indians. While historians now recognize that the Two Republics composed a "system" only as a theoretical abstraction, and even then an imperfect one, the on-again off-again efforts to resurrect it betrayed a long-term Iberian preoccupation with social mixture. Therefore, consternation over intermingling, whether of a linguistic, residential, or sexual manner, such as that registered in Philip II's *auto* cited above, was a constant motif voiced by imperial spokesmen in Iberia and the Americas throughout the duration of colonial rule.[7] Hostility toward the crossing of perceived racial boundaries was not an imperial monopoly, however. Members of the indigenous elite, such as Felipe Guaman Poma, could also be critical of a world perceived as "upside-down," especially as it related to the erosion of their own class and gender privileges.[8] For such individuals, cultural and ethnic diversity were phenomena to be reversed rather than embraced. Elite and state preoccupations aside, the colonial societies that emerged in Latin America were increasingly characterized by fluidity and creativity that could not be bounded by mandate or social taboo. Clumsy efforts to classify racial and ethnic diversity, such as the Spanish *sistema de castas*, which comprised a series of elaborate social categories based primarily on an individual's descent and lineage, may have allayed a few colonists but the finer granularities of social categorization often held little significance in daily life.[9]

In light of these Iberian preoccupations about social difference, historians of the Americas have long recognized that the physical encounters that began in the late fifteenth century between Europeans, Africans, and Amerindians were also encounters of the mind, whereby preexisting cognitive frameworks for interpreting social difference came into contact, often violently, and as a result changed irrevocably. Not surprisingly, European ideas about the Americas and its inhabitants tend to receive the most attention, since they form the lion's share of the historical record on the topic.[10] Many colonists, theologians, and jurists interpreted the early Latin American reality through the prism of an Iberian tradition that crystallized over centuries of interaction and conflict among Christians, Muslims, and Jews. While all three faiths ultimately traced their origins to the patriarch Abraham, an ideology of purity of blood (*limpieza de sangre*) gradually coalesced, which posited that fundamental, even if intangible, differences divided the members of the three religious communities, and that one generation passed down these qualities to the next. These ideas were fully formed by the advent of Iberian oceanic expansion and thus played a critical role in shaping attitudes toward difference and the guiding spirit of colonial law (perhaps most visibly in the concept of distinct Indian and Spanish "republics"). Indeed, such concepts continued to inform twentieth-century debates regarding the nature and origins of Spanish nationalism.[11]

How these inchoate ideas about difference reassembled into colonial (and later modern) notions of racial disparity has generated a great deal of interest among historians. One important facet of this inquiry concerns the question of the relative importance of racial ideas in the development of African slavery in the Americas. While the prominent West Indian historian Eric Williams posited in the 1940s that the enslavement of Africans rested initially on economic considerations (that is, African slaves were the cheapest option available to planters), with beliefs in

racial inferiority coming later, more recent studies have argued that prej-
udicial images of blacks had a much longer genealogy among western
Europeans than previously thought. That the enslavement of other more
readily available Europeans was never pursued as a viable option by
imperial powers further suggests that the path toward African slavery was
indeed informed as much by emerging ideas of group difference in Europe as it was by impersonal market forces.[12] By the 1960s, Marxist-
inspired scholars began to formulate explanations of the origins of racial
categorization that extended well beyond the topic of slavery.[13] These
historians and social scientists sought to identify a correlation between
the development of racial ideology and a wider array of coercive labor
practices in the Americas that developed on the heels of European expansion and what some consider a nascent capitalist world economy. In the
words of Immanuel Wallerstein, race (and racism) thus became "the
expression, the promoter, and the consequence of the geographical con-
centrations associated with the axial division of labor" that reflected a
global hierarchy of different structures of production.[14] Challenges to
Wallerstein's world-system approach, partly shaped by similar responses
to earlier dependency theory, raised significant questions concerning
whether early Latin American economic and social reality fit models of
peripheral capitalism, but even critics generally agreed that comparable
forces contributed to the formation of enduring racial ideologies. The
historian Steve J. Stern, himself a critic of Wallerstein's model, thus
concluded in his study of early Peruvian society that "colonialism created
'Indians,' and defined them as "an inferior, degraded race." By this statement Stern described not just an elite ideological formulation but rather a
set of circumstances—poverty, exploitation, and an internalization of the
colonial norm—that shaped the lives of native peoples and informed their
very understanding of their place in the imposed colonial order.[15]

While these questions remain largely with us, a more fundamental
point to take from this rich body of work is that racial discourse has
always been a product of specific cultural and historical contexts. Perhaps
most obviously, to equate Iberian obsession over blood purity with nine-
teenth- and twentieth-century theories of race would risk obscuring more
than it illuminates.[16] Even fairly "obvious" markers of difference, such as
phenotype, map out in extraordinarily different ways across time and
space. To be labeled black, for instance, in the U.S. South during the

height of Jim Crow involved a different set of criteria than, say, those deemed most relevant in contemporary (let alone colonial) Brazil. Recognizing the perils of applying a term like race, so hopelessly entangled in nineteenth- and twentieth-century resonances, to early-modern Latin America highlights a critical set of theoretical and methodological conundrums. At the heart of the matter is the question of terminology. Namely, historians must grapple with how to translate into modern meaning and parlance the elaborate system of nomenclature that developed to signify difference in colonial Latin America. That the meaning of this vocabulary shifted across time and space only complicates an already thorny predicament. To cite just one example, colonial law in Spanish America referenced categories such as "Indian" (*indio*) and "black" (*negro*) so frequently and reflexively as to suggest that jurists and others understood these terms as effective generalizations that could render a semblance of order to an admittedly more complex social reality. But, which factors were the most crucial in assigning particular people or groups to a given category? As David Tavárez's chapter on the Mexican Inquisition demonstrates, the answer often proved far from straightforward for officials, let alone other subjects.

Apart from their individual meanings, the problem of translation complicates efforts to interpret the ideologies behind colonial terminology. To return to the previous example, should these legal abstractions and formulations about phenotype and descent be understood as the expressions of a "racial" ideology, or something quite different? Or, to express the corollary, did historical actors understand the differences between themselves and others as something akin to modern-day notions of race? For a variety of reasons, which we explore in greater detail below, historians have increasingly answered no to both questions. This response is partly due to a growing appreciation of how historical actors understood difference in the distant past, but it also relates to changing academic sensibilities toward the categories we use when interpreting and describing that history. Let us tackle the latter question first. The debunking of race as a scientific discourse during the course of the twentieth century led many in the academic community to shift discussion of social difference to the analytic categories of ethnicity or identity, terms that are perceived as more value-free, or at least more clearly divorced from the eugenics nightmare that culminated in the Nazi movement and the Holocaust.

Identity, in particular, has proven to be especially alluring to Latin Americanists given contemporary developments and preoccupations. Academics have been keen to examine, for example, the impact of the current phase of globalization on the region and the attendant proliferation of "hybrid" cultures that presumably transcend national identities and boundaries. The dramatic reshaping of Latin America's post–Cold War political landscape away from class-based organization and mobilization toward an explicitly ethnic struggle centered on the demands for a plurinational state has also contributed to this shift within the academy.[17]

Of course, as with any analytic category, ethnicity and identity are imperfect tools. Even more so than the modern notion of race, their intellectual genealogies are distinct from the ideological milieu of early Latin America that they purport to describe and explain.[18] Perhaps the most critical concern alleged by critics, though, is that both terms, again like race, cannot be defined with sufficient precision, a point we will return to momentarily. Indeed, the fact that, as Peter Wade has shown, indigenous groups have long been studied in terms of ethnicity and blacks in terms of race (under the erroneous assumption that the former status is defined by fluid cultural signifiers and the latter by more fixed phenotypical ones) only highlights the treacherous waters any poorly conceived categorization can stir up.[19] On the other hand, they do offer a decided advantage over their predecessor in that they signal more clearly the situational and constructed nature of self and group formation that race, with all its associations with fixed and "natural" qualities, is less capable of managing. In other words, ethnicity and identity are most commonly used today to stress the cognitive and cultural dimensions behind the construction of difference (and sameness), a proposition more difficult for an overtly biologically determinative model of race.[20]

We caution, however, against misconstruing this constructed quality as intrinsically artificial or necessarily intentional. Identities are performed before others, but this social dimension does not deny the importance of other private (even subconscious) aspects formed a priori through socialization and key formative experiences in an individual's life.[21] Critics notwithstanding, we would further suggest that a basic typological difference exists between the two terms that informs our decision to favor identity over ethnicity in this volume. Whereas scholars tend to use ethnicity when describing the relational aspect of intergroup dynamics (to paraphrase Fredrik Barth, how culture shapes a "them" that helps to define an "us"), identity more commonly connotes a multinodal approach to the construction of personhood that recognizes no primary factor.[22] This is a tremendous aid, for it makes explicit recent critiques of older approaches to the study of race. That is, rather than considering race (or its usual attendants, class and gender) as independent variables, a multinodular model of identity recognizes upfront that all three are universal and dependent variables that intersect and interact with one another.[23] How all these variables are articulated, contested, and enforced, therefore, allows us "to move beyond the recuperation of the historical (and often heroicized) experiences of supposedly marginal groups to establishing how central these categories are to the construction of power (whether political or economic or cultural), meaning and identities at every level of Latin American society."[24]

Along with the related matters of terminology and meaning, the study of identity runs up against a second major theoretical and methodological hurdle. Specifically, how can historians capture the voice and *mentalité* of the colonial subaltern? This problem, of course, is not unique to this field of inquiry. Any project purporting to embrace a "history from below" must confront the question of sources. Granted, all sources must be treated critically, but particular caution must be exercised in those cases where the available documentation is largely texts produced in a setting of unequal power. Reconstituting the "soft tissue" of culture and cognition from the partial and fossilized remains of the historical record is difficult enough to do for the literate and elite strata of colonial society; achieving the same goal for the nonelite, who were often illiterate and thus less likely to have a semblance of their voice recorded for later study, is made that much more difficult.[25] Moreover, for those imperial subjects who drew from a cultural heritage distinct from the dominant Hispanic one (early postcontact indigenous groups are perhaps the most frequently studied) there are the additional challenges of determining how internally defined and colonial markers of differences interacted with one another, and how their use varied depending upon the intended audience.[26] Stated more simply, how are we to understand what subalterns meant when they employed the discourse of difference in reference to themselves and others?

Let us take these interrelated concerns one at a time, starting with the question of how to impute the normative meanings of colonial classifications of difference. The initial forays by historians into this question focused mostly on identifying the relevant vocabulary and its internal logic. Relying on elite discourse recorded in government decrees (including those against intermixture, such as our first epigraph) and other bureaucratic documentation where attempts at racial categorization were recorded (such as census reports), these pioneering studies traced the evolution of a nomenclature intended to capture the growing demographic complexity of colonial society (most famously embodied in the Spanish sistema de castas). Examining casta categories primarily from a juridical perspective, it is not surprising perhaps that these studies tended, intentionally or not, to favor the elite perspective informed by their sources. The racial or caste-based terminology was thus believed to map out, at least in broad strokes, a social reality, namely a "pigmentocracy" or hierarchy of color that structured colonial societies, most visible through the lens of labor.[27] In essence, ideologies of difference confirmed what historians already suspected about early Latin America: that European- and American-born whites monopolized the upper echelon of society through their positions as officials, merchants, and mine and landowners, while those enjoying partial white ancestry inhabited an intermediate position of employment and status, and blacks or Indians (depending on the specific region) occupied the bottom rung as base labor.[28] That is not to suggest, however, that these early scholars failed to recognize that their sources were fraught with peril. Gonzalo Aguirre Beltrán's seminal study, published in 1946, of New Spain's black population, for instance, acknowledged quite clearly that the caste system was ultimately an elite construction that often left officials at a loss as to how to apply such a blunt tool to the enormously complicated cultural and biological intermixture that characterized colonial society. Scholars also recognized early on that colonial racial ideologies rested on a fragile demographic reality that only grew more complicated over time, a situation that facilitated the phenomenon of "passing" by which individuals "moved" from one porous racial grouping to another.[29] In a remarkably prescient article published in 1966, one of the leading figures of the field, Magnus Mörner, highlighted many of these critical points, perhaps none more fundamental than that colonial texts "provide a classification that is already as much socially as racially determined." He also called for historians to pay greater attention to how the caste system evolved over time, and how closely its terminology coincided with economic criteria (in other words, the trappings of class).[30]

Over the next decade or so, understanding of the meaning and function of racial terminology grew as a result of the kind of work that Mörner had suggested. Often buttressing their claims with sophisticated quantitative analysis of census and parish records (the latter usually providing demographic information captured at key moments in the life cycle, especially baptisms, marriages, and burials), scholars reached differing conclusions regarding the nature of social stratification in colonial Latin America. Simplifying the contours of the debate somewhat, some understood a given individual's position within the social hierarchy (reflected in his or her range of available occupations and the possibility of social mobility) as determined principally by some sort of juridical status (variously defined as estate, race, or caste) while others stressed the growing importance of economic criteria (in shorthand, class) by the late colonial period. The latter group thus emphasized a degree of upward and downward mobility as the colonial market matured and expanded, a development that individuals from the former camp did not deny, although they questioned the market's ability to override the racial dynamics of social stratification.[31] Perhaps fittingly, mestizos occupied the most ambiguous socioeconomic position, exhibiting no one dominant occupational pattern in some areas, a conclusion others reached more controversially for mulattoes and creoles, as well.[32]

Admittedly, these studies, and the debate more generally, focused primarily on late-colonial urban areas (principally the cities of New Spain, no less), raising questions as to whether their findings were applicable to rural settings, earlier periods, or even to cities of other regions.[33] Nevertheless, this vein of research led historians to stress even more than before the potential flexibility of colonial racial categories and the only partial correspondence of caste categories to other markers of social status, such as occupation and wealth. In response, some turned to the concept of "social race," or the colonial term *calidad* (as do many of our authors) to capture the multiple factors beyond phenotype (for example, occupation, reputation, language abilities, dress) that qualified an otherwise straightforward "racial" classification.[34] Stated simply, social categories such as indio, negro, or mestizo did not always mean the same thing in different social and institutional settings, over the duration of an individual's life, let alone across generations. In an influential study, Patricia Seed concluded that such instances of "racial variability" most commonly involved individuals of multiracial descent (more specifically, mestizos and *castizos*) who held occupations at variance with ingrained assumptions concerning their "group's" place in the colonial economic structure. "The reality of social race," in other words, "was formed by the intersection of the division of labor and the cognitive system of racial labels."[35]

To survey the ground so far covered, we have seen that studying social categories is inherently diachronic (and historical) rather than synchronic (and static). This is true even for case studies with a relatively short periodization, since diachronic comparison is implicit in the analysis of identity formation and boundary definition. In the abstract, such a model of social identity implies some degree of dynamism and agency, that is, some mechanism for historical actors or other forces to change over time the meaning of social nomenclature. Nonetheless, both the earlier studies of caste and more recent and primarily quantitative critiques of that literature did not adequately conceptualize change over time (examining on the one hand, legal codes and decrees that suggested a somewhat timeless caste system and, on the other hand, using sophisticated studies of census records to debunk these earlier claims). The two competing methods functioned as snapshots in time, or in some cases, snapshots over time. They offered empirically rich and insightful analyses of social structures and demographic patterns, yet they did not tackle the way that the interaction of subjects with colonial institutions could produce new meanings for social identities or alter existing ones.

By the 1990s, the class versus caste debate began to make way for new approaches to the study of colonial racial ideologies. Monographic studies reinforced many of the previous findings that emphasized the class dynamic of racial identities, although their focus still remained largely on late-colonial urban settings, and quite often their conclusions were different. For example, Douglas Cope's study of seventeenth-century Mexico City found that racial passing was not a critical concern (or a practical goal) for the plebeian poor whose daily lives more often centered on securing physical and economic survival. Moreover, although colonial categories of difference did map onto the poor's social and kinship networks, *grosso modo*, the principal source of colonial control rested more on vertical networks of patronage than horizontal racial divisions.[36] These conclusions cast critical light on many of the assumptions in previous analyses of the caste system, which tended to emphasize its preventive role (keeping nonelite from passing into a "higher" racial status) and the means of subverting subaltern collective acts of resistance.[37] Cope's book was thus particularly influential in that it shifted focus from elite constructions of difference to plebeian reception and understanding of racial terminology.[38] Similar studies of popular notions of difference, and subaltern manipulations of elite ideology, have suggested promising new directions for a cultural analysis of what was beginning to look like an exhausted line of inquiry. In the words of one practitioner, the key is to consider racial categories "as more a discursive resource than reflective of a self-evident structure of society . . . rais[ing] the possibility that so-called 'loose' and apparently contradictory uses of the categories make political if not descriptive sense as people placed each other in situations of everyday life."[39] In a similar manner, some recent work has emphasized how gender and caste differentiation formed part of the same process, while others have explored more fully the colonial state's role in the construction of a racial discourse that trumped previous markers of difference (including those of religion, culture, and origin).[40] All these approaches are helping to move the field beyond debates over how reliable colonial categories of difference were in describing early Latin American society, instead placing greater emphasis on the social construction of these group categories.

In a postmodern academic world—one in which the Enlightenment's essentialist notion of an autonomous human subject has been replaced with a view that emphasizes the construction of identity—it is not altogether surprising that historians have taken a renewed interest in the agency of the subaltern and their ability to recast colonial normative racial ascriptions. But this is not to argue that systems of categorization were trivial and unrelated to the lives of the individuals they purported to describe. Indeed, even casual observers of Latin American history are struck by the pervasive and long-term use of vocabularies of social and cultural difference. Throughout the colonial era legal and social structures buttressed formal terms of difference, giving these categories practical meanings and material consequences. Studies of social identities, therefore, must also take into account the factors (be they social, cultural, economic, political) that provided categories of social difference a force and solidity, reproduced the terms over time, and influenced the behavior of historical actors.[41]

Considering these factors together, we are faced with the old social-scientific problem of relating agency to structure and understanding their dynamic relationship in time. A constructionist interpretation of personhood may place too much stock in the ability of individuals and groups to shape their identities, but the necessary response requires more than a simple reminder of the constraints on human creativity. Rather, to borrow from Eric Wolf's recent critique of anthropology, it involves paying greater attention "to how . . . [historical actors] mobilize, shape, and reshape cultural repertoires and are shaped by them in turn; how . . . [they] shape and reshape their self-images to elicit participation and commitment and are themselves shaped by these representations; how . . . [they] mobilize and deploy resources but do not do this 'just as they please,' either in the course of mobilization or in the wake of the effects they so create."[42] As the critique relates to colonial Latin America, scholars have become increasingly aware of how the production and contestation of social categories took place within a broader context of unequal power, particularly as embodied and expressed through colonial institutions.[43] Perhaps the richest body of scholarship has debunked the presumed total destruction of pre-Hispanic social structure and culture following the conquest and identified the responses of many indigenous people to the demands of a new colonial order.[44] The study of colonial Latin America's black population has confronted similar issues, examining the significance of racial designations and cultural change over significant spans of time.[45]

In sum, then, recent historical scholarship has underlined the degree to which imperial subjects played a hand in shaping the meaning of colonial racial discourse. Due to the nature of the available sources, such investigations must rely overwhelmingly on the political and public dimensions of identity. Keeping in mind that these texts often emerge from a context of unequal power, even repression and violence, this remains a dialogue rather than a soliloquy. Royal and Church officials may have been responsible for articulating and enforcing the norms of colonial behavior and thought, but they never governed passive human objects. Rather, colonial mandates, rulings, and legislation worked in conjunction with the actual exercise and negotiation of power between individual officials and a bewildering array of social actors. The identities of imperial subjects evolved not just in a macro sense, that is, as they changed across large swaths of territory and blocs of time, but in countless brief interactions, through the constant interplay between *internalized* understandings of self and group association and *externalized* social norms and categories. But how might one approach the study of this complex, pliant and seemingly elusive concept?

*The Identity Nexus: Social Categories and Self-Understandings*

The essays collected here support this more nuanced view of colonial practice and its relationship to social identities. As the book's contributors demonstrate, the lived experience of social categories rarely fits comfortably within normative models, and most individuals' life experiences could not easily be subsumed under a single identity—be it an ethnic, gender, or racial one. The hybridity so often noted by contemporary observers may have its own modern-day flavors and influences, but it was always a critical element of Latin American society and culture.[46] Thus, if we define social hybridity as a creative fusion of categories and self-understandings that were previously thought to be distinct, it is clearly not a product of the recent past but was present to varying degrees throughout the colonial period. But while such dynamics are recognized by historians and supported by empirical research, they have not been well integrated into a methodology for the study of identity.

The study of identity formation in colonial Latin America thus presents a methodological challenge, but also an exciting opportunity. On the one hand, the historical distance between our contemporary selves and the social actors we study limits the kinds of questions that we can ask of the past. Most importantly, the passage of experience through a fragmented historical record, and one that is primarily textual, mediates our access to the thoughts and emotions—the very subjectivity—of colonial subjects.[47] On the other hand, because social hybridity and mestizaje were so prominent in Latin America's colonial experience and drew so much commentary from contemporaries, commentary that was both mundane and learned, Latin America's colonial past provides an ideal historical laboratory to study identification. Moreover, with the ability to examine large blocks of experience and time, historians are well equipped to study topics that tend to change at a very measured and subtle rate, such as social identification. Taken together the two sides of this methodological coin—our limited and textually mediated knowledge of the past, but a past that is unusually verbose on the subject of identity—force historians of colonial Latin America to approach social identities with a healthy dose of caution. In practice, this means that historians often confront interpretive roadblocks and are expected to tease meaning out of incomplete documents or to reconstruct the past from sources that address one's analytic interests only tangentially. While such methodological issues are dilemmas for historians of all time periods—those studying the ancient, the modern, and everything in between—we suggest that a more explicit engagement with recent identity theory might make them a bit less painful for colonial historians.

As we have noted, one of the theoretical points of consensus in recent work on social difference is that identity is the result of a process that should not, and indeed cannot, be analyzed solely in terms of its constituent ethnic, racial, or gendered parts. Beginning most clearly with the writings of the Norwegian anthropologist Fredrik Barth, theorists of social identity began to shift their attention away from the ostensible "substance" of race and ethnicity and toward the processes that gave meaning to racial and ethnic categories, examining how social groups and identifications come into and out of existence. For Barth, the cultural "content" that supposedly defined ethnic groups—things like language use, style of dress, ritual practices, and so on—are in fact the product of boundary definition between social groups, rather than the root causes of group differentiation. Instead of some kind of deep, cultural *Urstoff* that was thought to differentiate one ethnic group from another, Barth argued that ethnic identities come into being through a process of group interaction and boundary definition. Boundary definition determines the importance of cultural contents as markers of social difference. As ethnic boundaries are defined, according to Barth, certain traits are emphasized as markers of group difference, while others are set to the side. By offering a theory to explain ethnic formation, rather than a descriptive anthropology of preexisting ethnic groups, Barth's work pointed out the possibility and in fact the probability of ethnic fluidity—the meaning of ethnic identities and even the existence of the groups they purport to represent should be expected to change over time.[48]

Other theorists of identity have extended and critiqued the work of Barth in important ways, providing new insights into the processual ontology of identity. The relationship of individuals to collective identities has been an especially important line of inquiry. The sociologist Richard Jenkins emphasizes the inseparability of the individual and the collective in the process of identification. Following Barth, Jenkins notes that if the collective does not exist outside the process of boundary definition, then the student of identity must pay close attention to the choices and behaviors of the embodied individuals engaged in boundary definition, the social actors building and mending the fences of social difference. Jenkins's work suggests, in turn, that social identities arise from the feedback between individual behavior and the meanings derived from that behavior.[49]

But if social identities—both those of collectives and individuals—do not exist outside the actions and behaviors of embodied subjects, how are we to explain the emergence of collective identities out of a diverse group of individuals? Put simply, how do collectivities cohere? What is the social glue that creates a sense of groupness, a sense of "us" versus "them"? The anthropologist Anthony Cohen's early work addressed these problems by analyzing the substance of group boundaries, which he found to be essentially symbolic. Markers of group difference, Cohen pointed out, are effective because individuals routinely impute different meanings to them, enabling a sense of "groupness" without "sameness," that is to say, a collectivity with real meaning for its members despite difference and inequality within the group. Symbols mark community boundaries so well, Cohen suggested, because they are polyvalent and allow each member of a community to interpret them in different ways. Markers of group difference do not project a singular message of exclusion and inclusion but are in fact receptive to the many meanings that individuals choose to attach to them. Cohen's insights help to explain how communities that are internally heterogeneous and socially stratified tend to cohere around key symbols of collective identity during times of "external" social stress. The difference between the "internal" and "external" construction of community has also been the subject of important work by colonial and nineteenth-century historians of Latin America and reminds us to avoid facile ascriptions of group identity to the diverse historical actors that we are studying. Collectively, such work demonstrates that community solidarity was often fleeting and contingent, and rarely timeless or predictable.[50]

The work of Barth, especially, has come under some criticism for overemphasizing how difference and boundary definition foster group identity. Critiques in this vein have pointed out different ways of group making, where the shared experiences and practices of the collective are the primary engine of solidarity. In such cases, actions that are "internal" to the collective are of utmost importance. Vered Amit characterizes these as "relational" or "network" identities. "These are forms of community," Amit continues, "which are conceptualized first and foremost by reference to what is held in common by members rather than in terms of oppositional categories between insiders and outsiders . . . What matters most, therefore, is what 'we' have shared, not the boundary dividing 'us' from 'them.'"[51]

Even in these critiques, however, it is clear that sociological and anthropological study of ethnicity and identity has undergone a fundamental shift. The *process* of identity formation is now placed at the center of the research agenda.[52] This reorientation of the field also provides historians a useful starting point for investigating social identities. First, analytic attention is now focused squarely on the actions and understandings of individual historical actors—rather than ethnic groups, caste categories, or other collective identifications that one encounters in the records of the colonial Americas. Analyzing the motivations and behaviors of living and breathing historical actors helps one resist the temptations of analytic "groupism" or "the tendency to treat groups as substantial entities to which interests and agency can be imputed."[53] Similarly, it reminds one to pay close attention to the power and limits of individual agency. To what degree are individuals constrained by the social identities they encounter in the world? How are those identities reshaped by actions of individuals?

Second, students of social difference—implicitly in some cases, explicitly in the work of Cohen and others—now pay more attention to the meaning of social identities. At about the time that Barth's work began to influence American anthropologists, this analytic shift toward meaning took place explicitly and much more prominently in the work of Clifford Geertz, symbolic anthropology in general, and eventually in the "cultural turn" among historians. As Geertz famously proclaimed, the study of culture is "not an experimental science in search of law but an interpretive one in search of meaning."[54] As the Geertzian agenda became the mainstream, the individual moved to the center of our understanding of culture, as the agent responsible for interpreting culture and infusing it with meaning. Cohen offers, "We have to come to see culture as the outcome and product of social interaction, or, to put it another way, to see people as active in the creation of culture, rather than passive in receiving it."[55]

In sum, the study of social identities has evolved in three fundamental ways: it now focuses on the process of identity formation; it pays special attention to how the individual shapes identifications; and it examines closely the relationship of external categorization to individual self-understanding. These methodological changes hold important implications for historians of identity. They suggest, above all, that historians must reject the analytic groupism referred to above. Racial categories, caste labels, and other social identifications that pepper the archives of colonial Latin America cannot be studied as disembodied historical actors. Despite the apparent resilience and permanence of such categories, identification takes place at the moment when an individual interacts on a cognitive level with some external, publicly available system of social categories and symbols.[56]

Despite these theoretical advances, the very distinct meanings of identity (categorization and self-understanding) are not always acknowledged by researchers, who sometimes use the term to mean the former, sometimes the latter, sometimes both, and sometimes other things entirely.[57] Coupled with an explosion in "identity studies" in recent years, the slippery use of identity as an analytic concept has led to critiques that question the use of the term altogether. Rogers Brubaker and Frederick Cooper offer the gloomiest assessment, detailing the term's many and sometimes contradictory meanings. Because identity is so multivalent, they argue, and does not clearly distinguish between the processes of categorization and self-understanding, the term should be jettisoned in favor of a more precise nomenclature.[58]

While we agree that it is essential to recognize the differences between external and internal forms of identification, and a more exact vocabulary might help some studies from wandering down the path of analytic fuzziness, we are hesitant to discard the term "identity" altogether. Breaking the subject of identity into a number of apparently more precise labels is at times critical, as Brubaker and Cooper point out, but at others not only stylistically awkward but analytically misleading. As the empirically grounded case studies in this book demonstrate, the creation of social identities always involves *both* categorization and self-understanding, *both* crafting and interpreting, *both* processes that are external and internal to the historical actors involved in them. We suggest that identity is in fact the nexus of categorization and self-understanding, and it is their very simultaneity that must be confronted by historians.[59] That is, identity comprises the relationship between the categories one is born into or placed into, such as Spaniard, Indian, mulatto, Otomí, slave, master craftsman, or tribute payer, and the lived reality of those categories: their meaning for an individual, the sense of groupness they may or may not create, the possibilities and limits they create for human agency, and so on. Researchers thus need a term such as identity that embraces the simultaneity at the heart of social difference, a term that captures the categorization (external to the individual or group or other unit of analysis) and lived experience (internal to the individual or group). The concept of identity reminds us to keep categorization and self-understanding in a holistic analysis, which is an essential methodological premise, since the two processes overlap and constitute one another, in both historical experience and the documents that recorded it. Placing identity at the center of the research agenda does not mean sidelining the analytic categories of gender, ethnicity, race, or class. Far from it, by structuring studies around the metaconcept of identity, we insist on the interrelatedness of these categories, a fact which has been noted in so many case studies of identity formation.

Now let us consider the application of these ideas to the colonial experience, and their implications for historical method. As we have noted, the study of identity is itself a hybrid endeavor at the level of analysis. On the one hand, the topic considers practices of categorization, things like census taking, proto-ethnography, legal codes, and other activities that imagined, identified, and distinguished colonial subjects. Collectively, we might call these social distillers, since they simplified human diversity into supposed elementary particles, into perceived or imagined essential characteristics.[60] All social distilling was carried out by historical actors who were themselves situated in a context of social relations and identifications, and we should be careful not to reify these techniques or disentangle them from the individuals who executed them. Practices of social distilling focus on an "external" world; they are public attempts to describe and order other human beings; they organize a social reality that is thought to exist "out there" in the "real world." As social constructivists have amply pointed out, of course, such practices help bring into existence the very reality that they purport to describe. The historical study of identity must take as a starting point social distilling practices, often linked to institutions of governance, which describe and craft the external social world.

But categorization represents only half of the equation. Identity also embraces self-understanding, that is, the affective meaning of social categories, the sense of groupness as experienced by an individual, the lived reality of sameness or difference. Despite the real-world consequences of external categorization on human relations, the discursive description of groups does not necessarily lead to the *creation* of actual groups or collective identities.[61] The experience of group membership, which by definition must always be mediated through an embodied self, is thus another side of identity, one that in contrast to the external elements of categorization considers the internal construction of difference. Here again, Brubaker and Cooper offer a compelling criticism of identity, pointing out how recent scholarship often concludes that "identities are constructed, fluid, and multiple."[62] Case study by additional case study, such insistence on the social construction of identity, they argue, drains the term of its meaning. "If identity is everywhere, it is nowhere."[63] This is a trenchant critique, since it unmasks a trend in recent scholarship to ascribe unwarranted agency to historical actors, thus overestimating their ability to create or modify social identities.

But identity, we offer, is a term and a concept that is best understood through practices, and this methodological premise provides a natural check on the proliferation of agency (and identities) referred to by Brubaker and Cooper. One of the most salutary developments from scholarship falling under the general rubric of "practice theory" is a renewed attention to the mutually constitutive relationship of structure and agency.[64] Summarizing the work of Anthony Giddens and others, William Sewell describes this "duality of structure" as the way that "historical agents' thoughts, motives, and intentions are constituted by the cultures and social institutions into which they are born, [and] how these cultures and institutions are reproduced by the structurally shaped and constrained actions of those agents, but also how, in certain circumstances, the agents can (or are forced to) improvise or innovate in structurally shaped ways that significantly reconfigure the very structures that constituted them."[65] For Sewell, a more robust theory of "duality" must take into account the way that mental structures ("schema") are materially practiced (forming "resources"). Resources, in other words, are embodied performances of schemas that form a sort of cultural text, from which mental structures/ schema are "read" and reproduced by historical actors.[66] Following from these insights, a fruitful method for analyzing the two sides of identity, we submit, is to focus on the interactions of colonial subjects around institutions at the moment when social categories are articulated, publicized, internalized, contested, and sometimes altered. Such an approach must examine not only the discourse surrounding these events—the "talk" of categorization and self-understanding—but also the contests over re-sources that usually accompanied such interaction. We might call these contact points, since colonial institutions created a space where ideas of social difference, of otherness and sameness, of us-them were realized and became tangible.[67] This method constitutes a new institutional history of sorts, revisiting the records of colonial institutions to examine the public meanings of social difference.[68]

Of course, contact point is only a metaphor for thinking about social interaction and a conceptual tool for gaining analytical purchase on the messiness of a distant past. By invoking this physical and temporal image we do not mean to imply the existence of distinct social identities prior to the moment of "contact," before the social interaction under investigation. To the contrary, it is the emergent meaning of social categories and identities that are the analytical quarry of this method. The goal is to focus on the processual nature of identity formation.[69] Bringing these moments and spaces into analytic focus helps to capture the lived experience of social categories and their historical contingency, without suggesting an unfettered agency on the part of subjects to negotiate or contest social categories. By placing the moment of institutional interaction and practice under scrutiny, the study of contact points highlights the social norms and rules, or, to use Sewell's terminology, the schema and resources that govern (and limit) agency. But because extant records of institutional interaction tend to record moments of extraordinary practice, they also reveal moments of creativity and agency, when individuals activated latent cultural schema, at once reproducing and potentially modifying the meaning of identities.[70] The case studies gathered here employ this analytic approach to varying degrees and attempt to integrate the different facets of identity into a holistic analysis. Collectively, these studies demonstrate a sophisticated and practical understanding of culture and its relationship to identity. Culture is no longer seen as an all-encompassing category, from which an individual's sense of self is derived.[71] Instead, by probing identity formation in contact points, these studies view culture as a tool kit that allows individuals to interpret the social world and act within it.[72] One potential benefit of the topic of identity, then, is that it offers a way to think about the relationships of colonial subjects in a way that moves beyond the well-worn paradigm of domination and resistance.

## Identities Examined

Having discussed the theoretical challenges and rewards the study of identity offers to students of early Latin America, we now conclude by previewing the volume's case studies, paying special attention to the ways that its contributors engage the concept of identity through the lens of colonial institutions. Although our authors cover a wide expanse of territory and span the length of the colonial era and even beyond, they share a common goal of exploring how imperial subjects fashioned various identities given underlying constraints, and how that fashioning helped shape in turn the "new worlds" they inhabited. Of course, the historical actors that constitute the subjects of the following nine chapters did not enjoy equal access to power and resources. Indeed, some occupied positions of little standing within their local community and exercised even less sway vis-à-vis the highest echelons of the imperial bureaucracy. Yet, taken together, their accumulative actions all contributed to an evolving and enduring imperial discourse on the meaning of difference. To repeat one of our initial points, then, the private and public aspects of identity are always deeply intertwined and inherently political, all the more so in a colonial environment buttressed by a presumed human gradient of relative inferiority and superiority. In such a setting, identity—that ascribed onto others and that embraced by oneself—could never be divorced entirely from issues of power for both imperial authorities and their subjects.

In the first chapter, Jeremy Mumford reconstructs the so-called Perpetuity Controversy in sixteenth-century Peru, a conflict that underscored the uncertain relationship between the Crown, indigenous (Wanka) lords, and their Spanish counterparts in the early colonial period. Spaniards recognized that indigenous lords possessed ancestral rights to aristocratic status that predated even Inca rule, yet many Spaniards hesitated to equate these "natural lords" of Peru with Old World aristocrats given their concurrent racial status as "Indians." Indeed, Mumford argues that these very assertions compelled some Spaniards to articulate in a much more explicit way what had been previously inchoate understandings of racial difference. Andean nobles, though, pushed for just such a conclusion by fostering a new hybrid identity that combined characteristics of both Spanish and Andean lordship. Ironically, kurakas protected their noble status much more successfully than the early conquistador elite, despite the kurakas' nominal position as vanquished, indigenous subjects. In essence, native lords, like the Spanish newcomers, benefited from the opportunities to reinvent oneself that the early New World offered to those daring and ambitious enough to seize them.

Turning to market relationships, Jane E. Mangan traces in chapter 2 the evolution of colonial racial hierarchies and categories that developed during the second half of the sixteenth century for the indigenous and mestiza women who dominated the urban trade of the great silver city of Potosí. As this introduction has demonstrated for imperial subjects more generally, these women were not passive objects who received their status and place in colonial society by benefit of Spanish fiat. Demarcated as much by gender, social class, and generational cohort, officials and other subjects tried to describe the countless indigenous women who plied their wares in the open-aired markets and stores of the burgeoning city. The author's careful reconstruction of these terms (for example, *indias gateras, regatonas*) highlights how indigenous and mestiza women subverted colonial assumptions of their gendered and racial deficiencies through their successful and assertive participation in the colonial economy.

David Tavárez also highlights the ambiguities of colonial racial terminology. Whereas Mangan's chapter shows how daily practice in the marketplace helped to generate new identities for an increasingly complex social environment, Tavárez reveals how even common racial categories like indio and mestizo failed to capture the complexities of plebeian experience for both colonial institutions and their subjects. Tavárez adapts the approach of the microhistorian to reconstruct the lives of three racially ambiguous individuals in seventeenth-century New Spain. Otherwise typical of the viceroyalty's mobile and culturally hybrid population, the three individuals eventually crossed paths with the Mexican Inquisition as a result of the bigamy and idolatry charges leveled against them. The Holy Office, often considered the most emblematic of the early-modern era's repressive institutions, was keenly interested in establishing the ethnic identities of the accused, since Indians had been removed from its jurisdiction in the last quarter of the sixteenth century. Yet inquisitors found it difficult to establish firm legal identities for individuals whose kinship and social networks belied easy definition. In all three cases the inquisitors came to accept the prisoners' claims to indigenous status despite the legal ramifications and the doubts they continued to harbor. While on the surface the outcomes may appear to be clear evidence of the colonial subalterns' ability to renegotiate or "pass" into a more favorable racial category as their interests and circumstances dictated, Tavárez cautions the reader from drawing such a hasty and facile conclusion. For one matter, such judgments are relatively rare in the historical record, but more importantly the highlighted cases demonstrate the extent to which both the prisoners and the inquisitors fell hostage to the bureaucratic logic of the institution itself.

Thus far, our chapters concern primarily institutions and imperial subjects in or near the core zones of colonial power. In contrast, Cynthia Radding's chapter on the borderland societies of northwestern New Spain and the lowland Charcas zone of the South American interior highlights the ways in which collective identities and histories could both change and persist over the *long durée* in areas removed from the imperial heartland. Although living in dissimilar regions in terms of ecology and cultural development, the inhabitants of both borderlands faced similar pressures emanating from a constellation of colonial arrangements and institutions dominated by the Spanish presidio complex, the Jesuit mission, forced labor regimes, migration, and commercial mining. As they did elsewhere, indigenous people responded through creative and adaptive forms of resistance and accommodation. The histories of Charcas and northwestern New Spain remind us once again of the fluidity of what Tavárez calls the "colonial lexicon of difference." As each society remained in flux due to migration, demographic collapse, and other disruptions of colonial rule, so did the meaning (and even the composition) of the ethnic categories that coalesced to describe the regions' inhabitants.

Mariana Dantas's chapter shifts our attention to the use of colonial racial categories in eighteenth-century Brazil. Focusing on the enslaved and free inhabitants of African origin and descent in the mining district of Minas Gerais, Dantas describes a regional economy heavily reliant upon black labor. Although they constituted the lowest echelons of local society, blacks enjoyed a modicum of mobility and agency as evidenced, for instance, in comparatively high manumission rates. Nevertheless, such conditions cannot belie the extent to which the legacy of slavery continued to cast a large shadow over the lives of the free-born and freed. Colonial institutions and prevailing social attitudes considered black individuals of poor esteem due to their base "quality" (*qualidade*), an essence informed by their lowly racial origins and connection to slavery. Tax policies and census reports, for instance, typically lumped free blacks and slaves into one category, while many Portuguese settlers considered them inappropriate spouses for their children. Still, Dantas demonstrates that the enslaved and free were not simply the passive receptacles of prevailing mores. As individuals and in groups, blacks carved their own spaces in colonial society, and in the process reworked and even transcended the racial categories imposed upon them. Significantly, one of the cumulative effects of rallying for their rights was the embracing of the racial labels used by religious sodalities. These became a core element of the members' personal identity as honorable, Christian vassals—in other words, black imperial subjects.

The possibility of black social mobility generated similar tensions in Spanish America, which Ann Twinam explores through the efforts of late-colonial blacks (*pardos* and *mulatos*) to secure a white identity from the king and his Council and Cámara of the Indies. Although the cases are numerically small, they offer a valuable glimpse into how royal bureaucrats, colonial elites, and at least some blacks understood the nature of whiteness and blackness. Once again we are confronted with the inadequacies of modern concepts and terms, such as "race" and "ethnicity." Paying careful attention to language and its subtle shifts over time, Twinam shows that the colonial discourse over whiteness drew from two principal sources: Iberian tradition and American innovation. In the end, race continued to hinge on intangible qualities tied to descent that only roughly mapped out onto modern conceptions of phenotype. Remarkably, all sides understood that a black subject *could* become white. Instead, they debated whether such a process *should* be allowed to occur. As Twinam points out in her concluding remarks, the legacy of this political impasse lingered long after colonial rule ended as the denizens of the new republics struggled to define the nature and limits of citizenship.

Whereas late-eighteenth-century imperial policy fueled antagonisms between Creoles and both peninsulares and castas in places like Caracas, Venezuela, Sergio Serulnikov's essay on the political landscape of La Plata (today Sucre, Bolivia) captures a moment where frictions with the metropole actually helped to bridge the gap between Creole patricians and nonwhite plebeians. How did this seemingly unlikely outcome come to pass? The principal grievances concerned the abolishment of the city's militias, the imposition of a royal garrison of "foreign" Spanish troops, and the impunity with which these outsiders preyed on the city's citizens. As Serulnikov shows, all the city's inhabitants shared these grievances, not just its leading citizens. That the city's diverse population, and its militia, had united to defeat a siege of tens of thousands of indigenous peasants during the maelstrom of the Túpac Amaru rebellion just a few years earlier only served to foster the growing sentiment that La Plata itself was a besieged colonial city set apart from a nefarious Indian and Spanish "other." Although class and ethnic divisions did not disappear, two riots in the 1780s compelled the city's Creole-dominated municipal council to support the unruly behavior of the urban plebeians against the king's own troops. He does not state this explicitly, but Serulnikov seems to share Twinam's debt to Brubaker and Cooper's concept of "situated subjectivity," although the situations the two authors describe are remarkably different in outcome. While the Venezuelan Creole elite mobilized to protect their own group's interest in opposition to unpopular royal policy and socially mobile blacks, the patricians of La Plata mobilized in support of the town's nonwhite populace, each group brought together by a common antagonism with the Crown and the peasantry. Although the outcome was essentially more inclusive in Bolivia than in Venezuela, the legacy of the growing antagonism between Hispanic urban dwellers and an indigenous hinterland endured all the same in the Andes for decades (indeed, centuries) after the end of colonial rule.

María Elena Díaz's chapter also analyzes the ways that imperial subjects fashioned "social identities" through a dialogue with the state and Church, a conversation channeled through their adaptation of the Iberian municipality and town council. The author excavates the striking history of the royal slaves of El Cobre, a community situated along the imperial frontier of eastern Cuba. Originally the laborers of a privately contracted copper mine, the slaves of El Cobre became property of the Crown in the 1670s and almost immediately began seeking ways to shape the meaning of this unusual status to their best advantage. Most critically, the slaves of the king secured pueblo status and some degree of self-governance in return for their obedience (and tacit promise not to flee bondage through any other means besides future manumission). The ensuing dialogue between the slaves and a range of sympathetic and hostile officials illustrates quite provocatively the multivalent nature of identity formation. In setting up her study of this process Díaz rightly argues that historians must move beyond familiar conceptualizations (such as race or caste) to explore how the individuals they study employed a much more expansive "repertoire of social categories and identifications available to old regime imperial subjects." Such a "total" approach to identity formation recognizes that an individual or group's identity constitutes a range of nodal points in which understandings of race, for instance, are informed and inflected by considerations of class and place of birth, among other factors. Similar to earlier chapters on free and enslaved blacks, the chapter emphasizes aspects of the *cobreros'* hybrid identity that elided their presumed lack of agency as slaves. In their petitions and recorded collective memory, the community placed great stock in their inside, "native" position within colonial society. They presented El Cobre as a Creole (rather than African) community of loyal vassals whose labor and military service profited and protected the imperial enterprise. It is perhaps not surprising that community members often mentioned parallels with Indian pueblos, institutions also defined by their locally controlled town councils and state labor drafts. Indeed, these similarities and the inhabitants' own efforts to emphasize their native-born identities eventually merged into a foundational myth that linked a community of free blacks to an indigenous collective identity that preceded Spanish rule on the island.

Karen Caplan's chapter concludes our case studies with an examination of how indigenous communities and the state governments of Oaxaca and Yucatán retained, modified, and challenged three centuries of colonial institutions and political culture in the decades immediately following Mexican independence. Drawing on Tristan Platt's notion of a "pact of reciprocity"—in which indigenous groups agreed to offer tribute, labor, and deference to the colonial state in return for a degree of local autonomy, particularly as it related to land—Caplan argues that indigenous groups in both states retained traditional expectations of state obligations and community responsibilities. Yet, by the mid-century mark, local political culture was also deeply informed by each state's experimentation with political liberalism and its championing of the universal rights of citizenship (and its own notion of municipal autonomy). In effect, indigenous groups expected that the governors and legislatures based in distant state capitals would continue to respect the "special" relationship they had long enjoyed with the Spanish Crown, particularly as it related to tax collection and local governing councils, while they simultaneously clamored for the same rights afforded to virtually all (read: male) citizens of the republic. But, as Caplan shows, the abolishment of juridically inscribed racial hierarchies hardly ended their political influence or simplified the complicated matter of governability at the local level. Overall, key demographic and economic differences between the two states meant that the ruling elite of Oaxaca were more apt to accept the modifications their state's indigenous groups brought to the liberal tradition than their counterparts in Yucatán. The inhabitants of both states, however, had to wrestle with the thorny question of what it meant to be a citizen and the extent to which that decidedly modern and presumably universal political identity included the myriad categories and self-understandings inherited from the colonial past.

No single answer emerged in Mexico, and even less so across all of Latin America. Indeed, the matter of identity, and how it maps over political, social, and economic inequality, remains one of the prominent "legacies" of the colonial era that continues to fascinate and preoccupy scholars of the region. The need to grapple with the concept and historical practices of identity, including all their theoretical and conceptual challenges, will likely remain with us for quite sometime. Thus, rather than an endpoint or culmination of what has come before, we envision this volume as a methodological inflection, deeply indebted to previous scholarship but offering a new approach to the study of the interactions that occurred among imperial subjects within the arena of colonial institutions. The essays in this collection demonstrate some of the fruits of this method, but they also suggest its potential for generating new questions and directions for future research. A tightly bounded inquiry on institutional contact points, for instance, might lend itself to the still-incipient effort to study colonial Latin America within the broader Atlantic world. Or, conversely, it offers the possibility of tracing the continuities (or discontinuities) of political independence through the changing praxis of Latin American subjects/citizens whose lives straddled these two eras. We also suggest that colonial identities might be productively traced as they rippled away from institutional contact points and into society. But whatever directions future studies take, it is our hope that this volume contributes to a collective enterprise that seeks to understand the constrained creativity exercised by imperial subjects when they interpreted, reproduced, and refashioned their worlds.

## Notes

The first epigraph quotation can be found in Gibson, ed., *The Spanish Tradition in America*, 135–36. The second epigraph is drawn from Felipe Guaman Poma de Ayala, *Nueva corónica y buen gobierno*, 869; cited in Powers, *Women in the Crucible of Conquest*, 69. The original passage can also be viewed online at http://www.kb.dk/permalink/2006/poma/868/en/text/?open=id2977584.

1. For this idea as it relates to the environmental impact of contact, see Melville, *A Plague of Sheep*, chap. 2.

2. For a suggestive critique of the view that interracial mixture was insignificant to early U.S. history and strongly discouraged, see Nash, "The Hidden History of Mestizo America."

3. This is not to suggest Iberians completely controlled and manipulated these exchanges. Indeed, recent scholarship on the northern borderlands, for example, suggests that early diplomatic relations were controlled by indigenous groups and through their own gendered understanding of power and interethnic relations; Barr, *Peace Came in the Form of a Woman*.

4. Martínez, "The Black Blood of New Spain," 485. On these strategies, see Carrasco, "Indian-Spanish Marriages in the First Century of the Colony"; Metcalf, *Go-Betweens and the Colonization of Brazil*, 85–86; Mannarelli, *Private Passions and Public Sins*, chap. 1. For an argument that colonialism eroded the status of indigenous women (and others) over time, see Powers, *Women in the Crucible of Conquest*. A valuable exploration of the intersection of race and gender in a broader Atlantic context can be found in the essays compiled in Jaffary, ed., *Gender, Race and Religion in the Colonization of the Americas*.

5. One expert of the period estimates that the ratio of Spanish men to women in early colonial Peru may have dropped from a high point of ten to one to as low as seven or eight to one from the high male mortality rates caused by the era's many military campaigns and civil wars; Lockhart, *Spanish Peru*, 169–71.

6. Vinson, "Estudiando las razas desde la periferia," 258–60; Schwartz, "Brazilian Ethnogenesis," 7–27.

7. The classic study of the Spanish preoccupation of vexatious outsiders interacting with ostensibly innocent or defenseless natives is Mörner, *La corona española y los foráneos en los pueblos de indios de América*. On the subject of racial intermixture, see by the same author, *Race Mixture in the History of Latin America*, and Harris, *Patterns of Race in the Americas*. The implications for social relations between indigenous and black subjects, an important but marginalized subject of inquiry, are explored in Restall, ed., *Beyond Black and Red*.

8. Adorno, *Guaman Poma*; Mannarelli, *Private Passions and Public Sins*, 157, n. 22; Ramírez, *The World Turned Upside Down*.

9. Cope, *The Limits of Racial Domination*. For a discussion of artistic representations of the sistema de castas, see Katzew, *Casta Painting*; Carrera, *Imagining Identity in New Spain*.

10. Representative works in this rich historiographical vein include O'Gorman, *La invención de América*; Pagden, *The Fall of Natural Man*; Keen, *The Aztec Image in Western Thought*; Mignolo, *The Darker Side of the Renaissance*; Cañizares-Esguerra, *How to Write the History of the New World*; Dupeyron, *Indios imaginarios e indios reales en los relatos de la conquista de México*; Restall, *Seven Myths of the Spanish Conquest*; Flint, *The Imaginative Landscape of Christopher Columbus*; de Asúa and French, *A New World of Animals*.

11. The most well-known manifestation involved the polemic between two of Spain's most prominent twentieth-century intellectuals, Américo Castro and Claudio Sánchez-Albornoz. For a critical synthesis of their respective approaches, see Manrique, *Vinieron los sarracenos*, 40–57. See also Nirenberg, *Communities of Violence*.

12. Williams, *Capitalism and Slavery*; Eltis, *The Rise of African Slavery in the Americas*. See also, Sweet, "The Iberian Origins of American Racist Thought."

13. An early and influential example was Harris, *Patterns of Race in the Americas*.

14. Wallerstein, "The Construction of Peoplehood," 382–83; see also Balibar and Wallerstein, *Race, Nation, Class*.

15. Stern, *Peru's Indian Peoples and the Challenge of Spanish Conquest*, 186–87. For his critique of Wallerstein's approach, and his effort to situate his work vis-à-vis previous scholarship on Latin America's alleged dependency, see Stern, "Feudalism, Capitalism, and the World-System in the Perspective of Latin America and the Caribbean."

16. For one matter, despite a shared emphasis on inherited, fixed, and "natural" differences of descent, limpieza de sangre focused much more on religious criteria (associated with the various impurities that condemned infidels, heretics, and false converts to eternal damnation) than do most variants of modern-day racist thought (anti-Semitism serving as an obvious exception).

17. Key studies of hybridity include García Canclini, *Hybrid Cultures* and *Consumers and Citizens*; Bhabha, *The Location of Culture*. For work on the recent surge in ethnic rights and identity movements in the region, see Postero and Zamosc, eds., *The Struggle for Indigenous Rights in Latin America*; Langer and Muñoz, eds., *Contemporary Indigenous*

*Movements in Latin America*; Pallares, *From Peasant Struggles to Indian Resistance*; Higgins, *Understanding the Chiapas Rebellion*; Hale, "Does Multiculturalism Menace?" While both globalization and contemporary ethnic rights movements have drawn significant attention in Latin America, and the focus of the region's scholars, until recently studies of colonial Latin American identities have had a decidedly North American provenance no doubt owing to the influence of U.S. political developments on that country's historical profession. For further discussion of the historical context that led to the growth of identity as an academic field of study, see Gleason, "Identifying Identity."

18. On these genealogies, see Wade, *Race and Ethnicity in Latin America*, 6–19; Morse, "The Multiverse of Latin American Identity, c. 1920–c.1970," 1–2.

19. Wade, *Race and Ethnicity in Latin America*, 37–39.

20. That is not to say that the idea of race is not also seen as historically and culturally constructed. Indeed, because it is, some scholars continue to rely on it for their analysis of the colonial past. We would argue, however, that its more recent manifestations can still obscure this constructionist interpretation. Moreover, unlike our preferred term of choice (identity), race is less accommodating to other dimensions of ascription (e.g., gender, class position, etc.). The formulation of a "social race" (see below) was one attempt to address this shortcoming, although it remains a somewhat clumsy formulation.

21. These forms of socialization include things like sumptuary norms, types of greeting, and ritualized deference, which Bourdieu has called the "arbitrary content of the culture" and is stored like memories in (and on) human bodies. Bourdieu, *Outline of a Theory of Practice*, 94.

22. Barth, Introduction to *Ethnic Groups and Boundaries*. On the term "nodal points," see Laclau and Mouffe, *Hegemony and Socialist Strategy*. For an example of its application, see the essay by Díaz in this volume.

23. One of the unintended consequences of initial efforts to focus greater attention on the history of non-European people and women was to obscure the fundamental point that ideas of race encompassed all groups, just as the concept of gender informed ideas of both masculinity and femininity.

24. Weinstein, "Buddy, Can You Spare a Paradigm?" 462. Admittedly, Weinstein refers specially to how the study of race has shifted in Brazilian studies, but again we would suggest that the point is made even more powerful by adopting the term *identity* when it concerns individual and group formation (rather than, say, official racial discourse).

25. Van Young, "The New Cultural History Comes to Old Mexico," 228. See also Van Young, "The Cuautla Lazarus."

26. Suggestive statements regarding early native views of Westerners include Lockhart, "Double Mistaken Identity"; Clendinnen, " 'Fierce and Unnatural Cruelty' "; and Wood, *Transcending Conquest*, especially chap. 2. See also various essays included in Schwartz, ed., *Implicit Understandings*; Andrien and Adorno, *Transatlantic Encounters*.

27. The concept is most commonly associated with the historian Magnus Mörner, although, in fact, he draws this idea from a study that predates his own; see Mörner, *Race Mixture in the History of Latin America*, 54; Mörner, "The History of Race Relations

in Latin America," 24. A contemporary of Mörner's similarly argued against the primacy of class by suggesting that social position was derived "from ethnic and cultural qualities recognized in law;" McAlister, "Social Structure and Social Change in New Spain," 363.

28. Mörner, *Race Mixture in the History of Latin America*, 61; see also, by the same author, "Economic Factors and Stratification in Colonial Spanish America with Special Regard to Elites."

29. Aguirre Beltrán, *La población negra de México*, 175–78, 273–74.

30. Mörner, "The History of Race Relations in Latin America," 21, 25–27.

31. Chance and Taylor, "Estate and Class in a Colonial City"; McCaa, Schwartz, and Grubessich, "Race and Class in Colonial Latin America"; Chance and Taylor, "Estate and Class: A Reply"; Seed, "The Social Dimensions of Race"; Seed and Rust, "Estate and Class in Colonial Oaxaca Revisited"; Anderson, "Race and Social Stratification." Similar questions emerged regarding colonial marriage endogamy and exogamy. See, among others, Seed, *To Love, Honor, and Obey in Colonial Mexico*; Cosamalón, *Indios detrás de la muralla*; Martinez-Alier, *Marriage, Class and Colour in Nineteenth-Century Cuba*.

32. Brading, *Miners and Merchants in Bourbon Mexico*, 254–59; Chance and Taylor, "Estate and Class in a Colonial City," 472–73. For a differing conclusion regarding creoles, see Seed, "The Social Dimensions of Race," 579; Lutz, *Santiago de Guatemala*, 156–57.

33. For a fairly recent attempt to address how the caste system operated in rural settings, see Jackson, *Race, Caste, and Status*.

34. Seed, "The Social Dimensions of Race," 574, 591; McCaa, "Calidad, Class, and Marriage in Colonial Mexico." In his study of colonial Antequera, Chance argued for a similar phenomenon, noting: "A man regarded his racial identity not so much as an indicator of group membership or even as a badge of self-definition within a static and rigid social system, but rather as one component of his personal identity that could be manipulated and often changed"; Chance, *Race and Class in Colonial Oaxaca*, 130–31.

35. Seed, "The Social Dimensions of Race," 601.

36. Cope, *The Limits of Racial Domination*.

37. On the former point, it has been argued that the introduction of the categories castizo and morisco responded to elite concerns by making it more difficult for individuals of partial indigenous and black descent from satisfying ever more stringent qualifications of descent for entering the criollo group; Chance, *Race and Class in Colonial Oaxaca*, 176; Chance and Taylor, "Estate and Class: A Reply," 428. On the latter point, see Carroll, *Blacks in Colonial Veracruz*.

38. Other historians had developed a similar vantage point. A rich historiography had developed, for instance, among those exploring the impact of colonial rule on indigenous societies and among African slaves and their descendants; see notes 45 and 46 below.

39. Boyer, "Negotiating *Calidad*," 64, 66; see also Cahill, "Colour by Numbers."

40. Kellogg, "Depicting *Mestizaje*"; Lewis, *Hall of Mirrors*; Silverblatt, *Modern Inquisitions*.

41. On this point, see Loveman, "Is 'Race' Essential?"

42. Wolf, "Perilous Ideas," 6.

43. Interest has grown recently, for example, in how colonial subalterns interacted with religious and secular authorities when faced with charges of witchcraft and similar religious crimes; see Few, *Women Who Lead Evil Lives*; Lewis, *Hall of Mirrors*; Silverblatt, *Moon, Sun and Witches*; Behar, "Sexual Witchcraft, Colonialism, and Women's Powers."

44. This is an immense body of scholarship that cannot possibly be traced in its entirety here. Significant Anglophone works not cited elsewhere in this essay include Gibson, *The Aztecs under Spanish Rule*; Lockhart, *The Nahuas after the Conquest*; Stern, *Peru's Indian Peoples and the Challenge of Spanish Conquest*; Spalding, *Huarochirí*; Farriss, *Maya Society under Colonial Rule*; Martin, *Rural Society in Colonial Morelos*. Scholarship on indigenous society in the Andes benefited immensely from the coupling of historical and anthropological perspectives, which resulted in innovative studies of how collective identity was expressed, reinforced, or rearticulated through circuits of exchange and migration patterns, two characteristics that shaped Andean social organization prior to the conquest. Emblematic of this effort is the collection of essays found in Larson and Harris with Tandeter, eds., *Ethnicity, Markets, and Migration in the Andes*; Wightman, *Indigenous Migration and Social Change*; Powers, *Andean Journeys*. Borderland studies likewise have been energized with a recent turn toward ecological perspectives for understanding the cultural transformations of indigenous groups and their interactions with dominant colonial institutions, particularly Catholic missions. See, for example, Radding, *Wandering Peoples* and *Landscapes of Power and Identity*; Deeds, *Defiance and Deference in Mexico's Colonial North*; Jackson and Langer, eds., *The New Latin American Mission History*. In some areas, most notably Mesoamerica, indigenous notables left a wealth of native-language sources that further allowed historians to excavate a group's own lexicon of difference and sameness. This vein of research is perhaps most commonly associated with James Lockhart and a cadre of former students and associates. For an assessment of these studies by two of its principal participants, see Lockhart, "A Vein of Ethnohistory," and Restall, "A History of the New Philology and the New Philology of History."

45. Scholars have long known that the linguistic and ethnic provenance of African slaves varied across time and space depending on the areas of Africa that supplied a given colony's demand for labor. Yet for many years U.S. scholarship on identity was marred by the belief that slavery had stripped blacks of any significant connection to their African roots. The debate between Melville Herskovitz and E. Franklin Frazier over the social structure of the African American family is indicative of this early problematic, with Frazier suggesting blacks were "nearly stripped of [their] social heritage" by the Middle Passage and slavery; Frazier, *The Negro Family in the United States*, 20. In his seminal essay on comparative black experience in the Americas, Frank Tannenbaum likewise contrasted the "stubborn, uncommunicative and isolated" ways of Native Americans vis-à-vis European acculturation with blacks in the United States, who he deemed "[had] become culturally a European, or, if you will, an American, a white man with a black

face;" Tannenbaum, *Slave and Citizen*, 41. Herskovitz led a bold charge against this so-called myth of the negro past, seeking to identify cultural "survivals" in living populations that could be traced back to African traditions, an approach that inspired students of Latin America, most famously Gonzalo Aguirre Beltrán; Herskovitz, *The Myth of the Negro Past* and *The New World Negro*; Herskovitz and Herskovitz, *Rebel Destiny*; Aguirre Beltrán, *La población negra de México* and *Cuijla*. An alternative model emerged by the 1970s, made in a succinct yet suggestive essay by Sidney Mintz and Richard Price, that while African traits can be discerned in African American culture, the experience of enslavement and the Middle Passage required a fundamental restructuring of the underlying matrix, which led to a fairly rapid development of a distinct "Creole" culture; Mintz and Price, *The Birth of African-American Culture*. More recently still, a younger generation of historians, often influenced by John Thornton's work, has posited that a significant degree of retention of African culture did occur over specific periods of the colonial era (and beyond); Thornton, *Africa and Africans in the Making of the Atlantic World*. Superior studies within this vein of research seek to demonstrate a correlation between recorded behavior and beliefs within certain ethnic slave groups and the corresponding supply area of Africa, as recorded in records of that time. See, for example, Sweet, *Recreating Africa*. Equally important, recent studies demonstrate how group distinctions changed as the black population itself evolved. Herman Bennett, for instance, links a shift in the importance of African and New World identities to the degree of racial mixture, phenotype, and legal status in the formation of community boundaries for the viceroyalty's increasingly Creole population; Bennett, "Lovers, Family and Friends." See also his *Africans in Colonial Mexico*.

46. Among many others, the work of the French ethnohistorian Serge Gruzinski provides fine examples. Of principal import: *The Conquest of Mexico*; *Images at War*; *L'Aigle et la sibylle*; *The Mestizo Mind*.

47. Sherry Ortner has recently called for anthropologists to pay more attention to the construction of subjectivity in their work. For Ortner, subjectivity or "the ensemble of modes of perception, affect, thought, desire, fear, and so forth that animate acting subjects" provides the key to understanding the origins of individual agency, even as they exist within a social structure that partially determines their actions. "Subjectivity and Cultural Critique," 31.

48. See especially his Introduction. For more recent work, see Barth, "Boundaries and Connections," and "Enduring and Emerging Issues in the Analysis of Ethnicity."

49. Jenkins, *Social Identity*, and *Foundations of Sociology*, chap. 4.

50. Cohen, *The Symbolic Construction of Community*. For relevant studies of Latin American communities, see, among others, Van Young, "Conflict and Solidarity in Indian Village Life"; Mallon, *Peasant and Nation*, especially chap. 3; Farriss, *Maya Society under Colonial Rule*.

51. Amit, "An Anthropology without Community?," 59–60.

52. Jenkins, *Social Identity*, 75–76.

53. Brubaker, Loveman, and Stamatov, "Ethnicity as Cognition."

54. Geertz, *The Interpretation of Cultures*, 5.

55. Cohen, *Self-Consciousness*, 119.

56. On the cognitive mediation of ethnicity, see Brubaker, Loveman and Stamatov, "Ethnicity as Cognition."

57. Brubaker and Cooper, "Beyond 'Identity,' " 18.

58. Brubaker and Cooper, "Beyond 'Identity.' " See also Bendle, "The Crisis of 'Identity' in High Modernity."

59. Brubaker and Cooper themselves gesture to the difficulty of separating the strands of identity when they refer "situated subjectivity," or "one's sense of who one is, of one's social location, and how (given the first two) one is prepared to act." "Beyond 'Identity,' " 17. In different venues, Jenkins and Cohen make compelling arguments for placing individual and collective identities in the same analytic field. See Jenkins, *Social Identity*, especially chap. 3, and Cohen, *Self-Consciousness*.

60. For a discussion of practices that make humans "legible" to governments, see Scott, *Seeing Like a State*.

61. Loveman, "Is 'Race' Essential?" 892; Brubaker and Cooper, "Beyond 'Identity,' " 27; Amit, "An Anthropology without Community?" 19–20.

62. Brubaker and Cooper, "Beyond 'Identity,' " 1.

63. Ibid.

64. This is a large body of scholarship, and one without clearly defined boundaries, but notable works include Bourdieu, *Outline of a Theory of Practice* and *The Logic of Practice*; Giddens, *Central Problems in Social Theory* and *The Constitution of Society*; Swidler, "Culture in Action"; Sewell, "A Theory of Structure." For an older review of the field, see Ortner, "Theory in Anthropology since the Sixties." For more recent interventions, see among others Biernacki, *The Fabrication of Labor*, and the essays collected in Schatzki, Cetina, and Savigny, eds., *The Practice Turn in Contemporary Theory*.

65. Sewell, "A Theory of Structure," 5.

66. Ibid., 13.

67. By focusing on specific, institutionalized encounters between colonial subjects, our notion of contact points differs from Mary Louise Pratt's well-known "contact zones" metaphor, which she uses to refer to the cultural frontiers of the colonial world, where "subjects previously separated by geographic and historical disjunctures [now met], and whose trajectories now intersect." *Imperial Eyes*, 7. Both of these terms, however, are attempts to capture the subjectivities and identities that are produced in colonial encounters.

68. This is a technique employed by the anthropologist Irene Silverblatt, whose recent work explores the tight linkage between colonial institutions and "race thinking." Examining the contact point of the Peruvian Inquisition, Silverbatt demonstrates how colonial identities were the product of subjects interacting with categories of social difference, categories whose backbones were the institutions and bureaucratic practices of the colonial state. Such interaction formed the "cultural dialectic of colonialism." *Modern Inquisitions*, 219. In a different institutional setting, see the innovative study on free-colored militias in New Spain by Vinson, *Bearing Arms for His Majesty*.

69. On this point, see Jenkins, *Social Identities*, 75–76.

70. By "extraordinary" we mean not just those records usually thought of as "limit cases" (e.g., Inquisition records, criminal litigation) but also things usually considered mundane (records of births, deaths, testaments), since these also recorded moments when the meaning of identities could be reproduced or modified.

71. Cohen, *Self-Consciousness*, 119.

72. This is an approach advocated by Swidler in "Culture in Action."

# Aristocracy on the Auction Block

*Race, Lords, and the Perpetuity Controversy*
*of Sixteenth-Century Peru*

Early in 1565, Don Antonio de Ribera rode into the valley of Jauja with a group of Spanish horsemen to confront the valley's indigenous lords. One of those lords, Don Felipe Guacrapaucar, had recently visited the royal court in Castile as a noble vassal of the king and had returned with a coat of arms and other signs of the king's favor. Ribera himself had made a similar visit to court not long before. The honorific "don" which the two men shared, an aristocratic marker jealously guarded within Hispanic society, seemed to place them in the same class.[1] However, on instructions from the colony's governor, Don Antonio confiscated Don Felipe's and the other lords' Spanish weapons and horses, implements of power which were also marks of noble identity within the Spanish idiom. Henceforth, as "Indians," they would no longer have the right to own or use them.[2]

This chapter examines the events that led to this confrontation in Jauja and those that followed it, an episode from the very beginning of race formation in Spanish Peru. In the 1530s, some four decades after Columbus's first landfall in the Caribbean, Spaniards invaded the Andes, overthrew the Inca empire, and established the Spanish Viceroyalty of Peru. They meant what they said when they called America a New World, new for both colonists and colonized: a Spaniard crossed the Atlantic precisely in order to become a new person, while indigenous people had no choice but to become different from whom they had been—they became "Indians." People of all backgrounds struggled to shape their own identities in this chaotic environment. But neither Spaniards nor Andeans knew just what the word "Indian" was going to mean.

Its meaning was important for both the landscape of identities and the institutions of power. Spanish officials exercised direct authority over Spanish colonists but governed indigenous Andeans through the already-existing power structure: the Andean lords whom they had found governing the provinces when they arrived. These lords—called *kurakakuna*, *kurakas*, or *caciques*, depending on the context—had ruled their people under the authority of the Inca kings, and expected to continue to do so under the authority of the Castilian king. For them, "Indian" was less significant than "lord" in defining who they were. The evolving relationship between these two kinds of identity would help shape colonial rule.[3]

Meanwhile, a class of Spaniards—the *encomenderos*—tried to define their own identities as lords in colonized Peru. In gratitude for their service to the king, especially military service during and after the conquest, the Crown had granted them *encomiendas* (trusts), a limited and temporary overlordship over specific Andean kurakas, which the encomenderos wanted to improve and extend.[4] They differed from the kurakas in background: most kurakas were born lords, but most of the early encomenderos came from far less exalted families within their own culture.[5] What raised them above the kurakas was the fact of conquest—one of the empirical realities that would, over time, make possible the imagined reality of "race."[6]

Two themes linking the chapters in this volume are race and identity. Both are familiar concepts, used and often misused by generations of historians to make sense of people and the past. Both are today the subject of epistemological debate, which is part of the motivation of this volume. Juxtaposing the identity of race with that of lordship shows how indeterminate both were at the dawn of the colonial era and brings to light the contingent series of events that helped define both.

Kurakas and encomenderos wanted the same thing: to rule the Andes on behalf of the Spanish king. To obtain what they wanted the two groups engaged in an extraordinary bidding war, known to historians as the *perpetuity controversy*, in which each tried to buy the status and privilege of aristocracy from the king.[7] He sent a commission to investigate the competing offers. But in the end he disappointed both sides. Instead of ruling through hereditary lords, whether Spanish or indigenous, the Crown created new officials whose power derived from appointed political office, not lordly status. It was in this context that the king's governor banned kurakas from owning arms and horses, markers of nobility, and sent the encomendero Don Antonio de Ribera to disarm his indigenous counterparts. While repudiating both groups' aspirations, the Crown further stigmatized the kurakas as racially barred from the status of Spanish nobility.

Yet this was not the end of the story. While the Crown stripped encomenderos of virtually all aristocratic power, it could not marginalize the kurakas: it needed their cooperation to control their indigenous subjects. Ironically, the conquered kurakas fared better than the conquering encomenderos in retaining their identity as lords. In spite of everything, the kurakas succeeded in converting themselves into a hybrid aristocracy within the Spanish empire.

### Encomenderos

The valley of Jauja, in central Peru, was home to the Wankas, one of the many different ethnic groups the Incas had ruled, whose labor and fertile lands made their kurakas and encomenderos rich. In the struggle between native and Spanish lords, Jauja produced a leader for each of the two camps: the encomendero Don Antonio de Ribera and the kuraka Don Gerónimo Guacrapaucar, Don Felipe's father. In the year 1554, the two men fought side by side against the enemies of their king. They fought to defeat a rebellion by certain encomenderos against royal attempts to limit the power of their class, the last of a series of civil wars which had roiled the viceroyalty since its founding. Other encomenderos, however, remained loyal to the king. Ribera was one of the loyalist captains, leading men on horse and foot against the rebel leader, Francisco Hernández Girón. As the wet summer gave way to fall and winter the two sides skirmished and maneuvered. The king's knights—for so they saw themselves, living out a medieval dream of glory at the ends of the earth—wore down the rebels month by month. At last a loyalist band including Guacrapaucar's Wanka fighters defeated Girón in Jauja.[8]

Don Antonio de Ribera had fought at the beginning but was not present for the victory. His fellow loyalist encomenderos had sent him as their representative to the Spanish court, to ask the king, ironically, for the same thing for which Girón had rebelled: more power for encomenderos.[9] They had originally had the right to Indian labor but were now limited (at least theoretically) to collecting tribute; the typical encomienda, furthermore, was limited to two lifetimes, those of the original recipient and his heir. On behalf of his peers, Ribera asked for two things. First, for *perpetuity:* the right to pass their titles to their descendants indefinitely; and second, for *jurisdiction:* the authority to appoint judges over their Indian subjects, as Spanish lords did. These two rights, together, would make the encomenderos' office tantamount to aristocracy.[10]

Encomenderos argued that enlarging their powers would be good for the viceroyalty, by giving its natural leaders a stake in peace.[11] The current situation was a vicious cycle in which Spaniards rebelled against the king, then switched sides at the last minute to help the king defeat the rebellion, receiving new or larger encomiendas as a reward. With no standing army except the encomenderos themselves, the Crown could not break the cycle. Don Antonio de Ribera was well qualified to discuss Peru's troubles: he himself had sided with the rebels in an earlier civil war, before proclaiming his loyalty and taking up arms against the king's enemies.[12]

More important than Ribera's arguments, however, was the offer that accompanied them: to purchase perpetuity and jurisdiction from the king. There was nothing corrupt about the proposed transaction. In the social thought of the era, it reflected the complementary roles of subject and king: the subject offered a *servicio*, or service (possibly in the form of money), and the king gave a *merced*, a gift or reward. Ribera caught the king's attention with an extravagant offer. In exchange for perpetuity and jurisdiction, the encomenderos of Peru would collectively pay the Crown 7.6 million pesos—twice the national debt of the chronically cash-strapped monarchy.[13] The offer came at an opportune time. Charles V, who was both king of Spain (1516–55) and Holy Roman Emperor in Germany, was worn down by failed wars with France and other European rivals. He was preparing to abdicate the Spanish throne, passing it to his son Philip II (1555–98) under the shadow of bankruptcy.

Were the encomenderos' hopes realistic? It seems incongruous to imagine them as seigneurial lords over Andean vassals, since historians have emphasized the limitations on an authority which was only temporary and included no rights over Indians' land or labor.[14] The encomendero, however, was much more a lord than this description implies. It is not just that he could demand labor and land from his subjects illegally (although he often could). More significantly, the status of Castile's territorial lords was close enough to his own to make the transition seem feasible.

Castilian lords, like colonial encomenderos, had little direct control over their subjects' lands and labor, compared to lords elsewhere in Europe. In underpopulated Castile, where true feudalism never evolved, land was less valuable to a lord than subjects were; he acquired the former as a means of getting the latter, going to great lengths to induce peasants to settle on his land. But once they were there he could neither force them to leave nor to stay against their will. Castilian peasants were subject to few of the demeaning forms of personal service common in other countries and lived in tight-knit, self-governing communities that controlled their lands in exchange for annual payments to the lord.[15] In their organization and autonomy they resembled Andean peasant communities, and Castilian lords' rent was structurally equivalent to encomenderos' tribute; the two forms of limited lordship were remarkably similar, although historians have downplayed the resemblance.[16] Besides collecting rent, Spanish lords' one form of authority was the right to judge crimes and disputes, which provided both fees and influence over their subjects; this was what the encomenderos sought in 1554.[17] Finally, with respect to encomiendas' early expiration date, encomenderos had an encouraging precedent. In the past, Castilian kings had granted most seigneurial titles for a single lifetime only, like encomiendas in the New World. But during the fifteenth century, they changed this system, rewarding their supporters with new titles that they could pass on to their descendants—what one historian has called "one of the most radical social revolutions of Castilian history."[18] In bargaining for perpetuity, the Peruvian encomenderos sought to recapitulate what the Castilian aristocracy had achieved not long before.

The institution of the New World encomienda seemed designed to encourage such hopes. Based on a Castilian feudal grant, it required the encomendero to serve the king in arms.[19] Frequent rebellions meant that encomenderos such as Ribera pulled on their chain mail regularly in the king's service (if not, as in the case of Girón and other rebels, against him). The life they led, along with the chivalric romances they read, confirmed their self-image as medieval knights.[20] To encourage settlement, the Crown had even offered to make common-born settlers *hidalgos*—minor nobles—and to raise those already noble up a rank.[21] The medieval frontier of the *reconquista* had offered such opportunities; why should the new frontier promise anything less?

The 1550s, in fact, were an unusually propitious moment for the encomenderos' hopes at the Spanish court. Although Charles V saw his hopes in Europe dashed by military defeats, it seemed still possible to rescue the situation—to redeem lives and treasure already sacrificed—with new cash. Both the abdicating emperor and his son Philip wanted to keep fighting. Philip immediately placed the Peruvian proposal at the top of his agenda. Following debate among his advisors about the dangers of alienating so much power, Philip decided to sell the encomenderos half of what they wanted: perpetuity, but not legal jurisdiction. He appointed a commission to go to Peru to negotiate a sale on these terms. But he ordered them to proceed cautiously and keep all options open: he had heard that the kurakas were considering a counteroffer.[22]

## Kurakas

In that same year, 1559—five years after Don Antonio de Ribera departed for Spain, and as the king was preparing to send commissioners to Peru—a group of kurakas met to formulate a response. The kurakas, representing seventeen encomiendas in the region of Lima, appointed two Spanish friars to represent them at the Spanish court, Bartolomé de las Casas and Domingo de Santo Tomás.[23] Speaking in the kurakas' name, the friars offered the king one hundred thousand pesos more than whatever the encomenderos might bid, and a minimum of two million pesos if the encomenderos could not muster a bid for what the king was prepared to sell (perpetuity without jurisdiction). In exchange, the king would not appoint new encomenderos when the current ones died off but (under his own overlordship) would restore "the old political order they had in the time of the Inca kings, because in this consists their entire conservation."[24]

Although the kurakas had served the Inca empire, as they did the Spanish, their authority was independent of it. The Andes were a patchwork of local ethnic groups with their own histories and customs, and most had lived under Inca rule for less than a century before the Spanish arrived. The Incas depended on the local lords for the same reason the Spanish did later: to control their subjects and deliver tribute and labor. With the Spanish conquest the kurakas exchanged one empire for another, and the difference, at least initially, may not have seemed very great to them.[25]

Each encomendero received tribute from one or more kurakas. As overlord, the encomendero depended on the kuraka for his power, but the kuraka did not depend on the encomendero for his own. The historian Karen Spalding called kurakas the "cutting edge" of colonialism, since their local knowledge and authority made Spanish rule possible. This cutting edge could be a double-edged sword for the conquerors: the kurakas' knowledge of both worlds could also help them thwart the Spanish.[26] Many colonists despised and feared the kurakas, but the viceroyalty could not function without them.[27]

The kurakas' identity was therefore enigmatic. They were subject to abuse from even low-ranking Spaniards. Yet colonists accepted them as the Andeans' "natural lords" (señores naturales)—in the words of a kurakas' petition in 1581, "like the dukes and counts and marquises in Spain." Militarily, politically, and economically, almost any encomendero was superior to almost any kuraka, yet kurakas had the greater right to be called "lords."[28]

If anyone understood the ambiguous position of the conquered kuraka, it was Don Felipe's father Don Gerónimo Guacrapaucar, lord of Lurin-guanca, a community neighboring Ribera's encomienda in the valley of Jauja. Don Gerónimo came to power before the Spanish conquest and died some time after 1565, in one lifetime witnessing a whole era of transformation.[29] But to understand what the Spanish conquest meant to Guacrapaucar, we have to go further back, to the Inca conquest of Jauja some seventy-five years before. Before the Incas came, the Wankas' world was a hard one. They lived in small chiefdoms perpetually at war; we can still see the remains of their walled towns, dense with small round houses high up on the mountain peaks. The Wankas lived in the peaks, a punishing climb from their fields in the thin air at 3800 meters, for protection; the chiefdoms were perpetually at war. Incas described the Wankas as savage warriors who stretched their enemies' skins for their battle drums.[30] From the bones in the graves beneath their houses, we know that their nutrition was poor, their lives short. Even their leaders were humble. Colonial Wankas said that their ancestors' chiefs were simply those fiercest in battle, to whom others looked for protection. Archaeology shows that elite households were a bit larger than others, with better tools, but not by much: the leaders did not live very differently from their subjects in that rough-hewn world.[31]

Inca conquest brought the Wankas both costs and rewards. It brought new labor demands and the burden of foreign rule, but also a peace which allowed them to move down from the peaks and spread out in the valleys.[32] The Incas retained some of the preexisting leaders as kurakas to rule on their behalf, as they did throughout their empire, while bringing the kurakas' sons home to educate in Cuzco, the Inca capital. They modified Wanka customs they disapproved of, for instance pressing them to substitute deer skulls for dog skulls as musical instruments.[33] Excavating elite Wanka households, archaeologists map a slow spread of Inca architecture and implements, evidence that kurakas were embracing Inca culture.[34]

The relationship between Inca kings and kurakas drew on an Andean discourse of reciprocity, unequal but complementary, between ruler and ruled. At the local level, when commoners labored on a kuraka's field, he reciprocated with a feast; its value was less than their labor, but its abundance and spectacle made up the difference. The Inca kings established a similar relationship, providing feasts and participatory rituals, an appearance of empire-sized "generosity," in exchange for their subjects' labor as mediated by the kurakas. In the formation of the Inca empire, the kurakas surrendered their preexisting authority to the king who then "generously" returned it to them, under Inca overlordship.[35] This resembled the encomenderos' relationship to the Castilian king. In their own eyes, the encomenderos had conquered Peru for their king (or reconquered it from rebels), surrendering to him the lordship they had won with their own strength; it was his part of the bargain to give it back to them in the form of an encomienda. The Castilian economy of servicio and merced resembled an Andean pattern, making it all the less surprising that the kurakas adapted so easily to Spanish rule.

The kurakas, after all, had a model for what it meant to be a conquered lord. Don Gerónimo's grandfather, perhaps, had made the transition: collective defeat, personal advancement, and the seductive embrace of a powerful outside culture. So it was natural for the grandson to expect a similar outcome from Spanish conquest. He gave up the name Apu Manco Guacrapaucar and was baptized Don Gerónimo. The lord of Luringuanca sent his sons (including the young Don Felipe) to school with Spanish friars and raised them to serve their faraway Castilian king. He built a Christian church where he would one day be buried.[36]

A kuraka's most immediate relationship, though, was with his encomendero, not his king. The historian Steve Stern described the alliances that grew up between encomenderos and kurakas as each learned how to benefit from the other. The contact point between Andean labor and Spanish capital and connections generated wealth; encomenderos and kurakas together controlled that point, and both had opportunities to get rich. Some kurakas established lucrative businesses, for instance growing coca and selling it in the mines of Potosí (as Jane E. Mangan discusses in her chapter). But as Stern pointed out, these alliances did not last indefinitely. Spanish demands steadily increased, while kurakas' ability to meet them declined.[37]

One difference between the Inca conquest and the Spanish one was that the Incas brought peace but the Spanish brought wars that never seemed to end. During his long reign, Don Gerónimo watched his people die around him: he had fifty to sixty thousand subjects when he came to power, but a census soon after his death showed only a third of that number.[38] Some died from Spanish diseases, some fled Spanish demands, and others perished in Spanish wars, both the encomendero rebellions and a slow-burning war against Inca princes who had taken refuge on the upper Amazonian forest refusing to submit to the Spanish.[39] These losses were the heavy price of Don Gerónimo's loyalty to Spain.

The Wankas had embraced the Spanish cause from the beginning. Don Gerónimo recalled that he was among the first to pay homage to Francisco Pizarro, giving the conqueror food, clothing, gold and silver, and Wanka men and women to serve him in future battles; over seven hundred of this group never came home. They were not the last. Every time the king's captains marched between the mountains and the coast they marched through Jauja and conscripted Wanka servants and fighters for their battles. The capture of the rebel Girón in Jauja was only the most recent. "In the encounter," Guacrapaucar reported laconically to the king, "some Indians died."[40] Having begun his career as an Inca and Wanka lord, Don Gerónimo might now be described as a Spanish and Wanka lord. And when a Spanish lord performed a servicio for his king, sacrificing lives and treasure, he expected a reciprocal merced. Should not Don Gerónimo receive honor from his king, rather than being sold into a perpetual encomienda?

This was the position of Peru's kurakas who gathered in Lima in 1559 (and in other regional assemblies throughout the country that soon followed their example, with the support and advice of Spanish friars), calling the bluff of a colonial class that needed them to control the masses but was not willing to concede them aristocratic power. They claimed a political role, not as conquered subjects but as natural lords freely acknowledging an overarching emperor. And they offered to pay for it, with insouciant self-confidence: "They had learned that the King was . . . constrained by necessity, and many of them were rich and powerful, and they wanted to give some *servicio* of money in order to supply his necessity."[41]

But could the kurakas afford to pay the millions of pesos they offered? They had just endured two decades of avaricious encomenderos, war, and disease. Many Spaniards doubted the kurakas' promises—and, for that manner, the encomenderos' as well. Yet neither offer was entirely implausible. In the past, Peru had created extravagant fortunes for the luckiest encomenderos, and Pizarro's companions had won legendary wealth from the Incas' gold. Some said that far more Inca gold remained hidden in places known only to the kurakas. The king, in any case, was willing to hope that both sides could back up their promises. He sent the kurakas' representative fray Domingo de Santo Tomás to Peru with the commissioners, encouraging him to keep negotiating on the kurakas' behalf.[42]

In 1562 the friar traveled through the southern Andes with two Inca princes, convening a series of assemblies to canvas the kurakas' views. The kurakas of Jauja took an active role in these assemblies, in the Lima meeting of 1559 and in a larger one in the village of Mama in 1562. At that assembly over a third of the attendees (the largest single contingent) were under the authority of three Jauja kurakas. Don Gerónimo Guacrapaucar sent one of his sons, Don Carlos, to represent him.[43]

But he sent his son Don Felipe to plead his merits directly at the royal court in Spain. Like any Spanish lord, he submitted a record of his past servicios and asked for royal mercedes. The courtiers had likely never encountered anyone like Don Felipe—a kuraka's son educated by Franciscan friars, who had helped capture the last Spanish rebel in Peru—and he must have made an impression. From the autumn of 1563 to the following spring, accompanying the king on his travels from one Spanish city to another, Felipe received from him more than ten different grants and privileges. They included a royal pension, a prohibition against Spanish cattle ranching in Jauja, a coat of arms, and the title of paramount lord of Jauja. Young Don Felipe more than satisfied his father's hopes.[44]

The encomenderos' negotiations in Lima, meanwhile, had gone poorly. They wanted both perpetuity and jurisdiction, but the commissioners were only authorized to sell them perpetuity. And even if the commissioners could have given them everything they asked for, the encomenderos were now willing to pay far less than what Ribera had at first proposed.[45] Many doubted that either encomenderos or kurakas could afford to pay what they claimed.[46]

Frustrated at the lack of a deal, King Philip ordered the commissioners home; together with the viceroy they drafted their final report.[47] They had come to Peru determined to sell perpetuity to the encomenderos, but they now believed that only a few could afford it. They proposed a compromise: selling a third of the encomiendas to their encomenderos in perpetuity, selling a third to their kurakas under royal jurisdiction, and keeping a third to give to new candidates on a temporary basis, as before.[48] Whatever weight the commissioners' suggestions might have had, however, vanished when they were unexpectedly caught in a corrupt influence-peddling scheme.[49] The project of selling perpetuity to encomenderos, which had seemed to promise great things, had wound down to a discouraging stalemate.

The new governor whom Philip appointed, Lope de Castro, had scarcely taken office in 1565 when he received disturbing news: a secret plot to rebel had come to light among the Indians of Jauja. The planned uprising was to encompass the whole of the Andes, in concert with the unconquered Inca princes of the upper Amazon.[50] Royal officials uncovered a large hidden cache of Spanish-style pikes—seemingly damning evidence. Don Gerónimo and the other Wankas denied the plot, saying they had made the pikes for a planned Spanish expedition to the Chilean frontier. Castro dismissed this alibi, though he was all the more shocked by the plot since (as he reported to the king), "The Indians of this valley are those who have served your Majesty better than any others."[51]

Was the conspiracy real or imaginary? Historians have tended to believe that the Wankas were indeed turning against their ruthless European overlords.[52] But along with Spanish pikes, the Jauja kurakas had adopted relationships and commitments that made switching sides difficult. It is unlikely, for instance, that they would have allied with the Inca princes after years of fighting against them on the Spanish side; Don Felipe's new coat of arms, in fact, featured three severed Inca heads, representing his family's military service for the Crown. This service had included manufacturing pikes for the war against Girón,[53] and there is little reason to doubt that these new pikes were for the same purpose. The kurakas' service to the king was the basis for their ambitions: just like the encomenderos, they traded in the economy of servicio and *merced*, a natural extension of the Inca-era politics of reciprocity.

But the colony's embattled and insecure state, which might have made a shipment of pikes a welcome gift for Castro, made them all the more menacing in the circumstances in which they were found. Fixed in the ground and pointing up at an angle, pikes could stop charging horses, which were the Spaniards' most important military advantage over Andeans. Andean acculturation was beginning to reduce that advantage. And Jauja was a center of Spanish acculturation. Many Wankas learned artisanal trades in Spanish workshops, which made the mass production of pikes possible in the first place; it was the Indian servant of a Spanish carpenter who first reported the alleged plot.[54] Wanka Hispanicization had assisted the loyalist defeat of Girón, but now it seemed to threaten the colonial state.

This acculturation prompted Castro to ban native Andeans from riding horses or using Spanish arms—skills he knew many had learned all too well.[55] The image of a kuraka on horseback was a disturbing one for Spaniards.[56] Juan de Matienzo, an influential colonial official, expressed alarm that some Indians could ride and shoot better than many Spaniards, made excellent gunpowder, and even excelled in the *juego de cañas*, a polo-like Spanish game played on horseback. To reconcile this with the deficiencies he perceived in them, he asserted, "The Indians of the kingdom are so skillful (*hábiles*) that there is nothing they are taught which they do not learn very well, as long as it is not something which requires prudence. . . . If this [prudence] were not lacking, they would not be among those who Aristotle says were born slaves by nature (*de naturaleza siervos*)."[57]

Aristotle's statement in the *Politics* that some people are destined by nature to be slaves had recently come into fashion among some Spanish intellectuals. The medieval worldview had rationalized inequality on the basis of legal status (noble, commoner, slave), not race. But in the 1530s a well-known scholar in the Spanish court had invoked Aristotle's idea to explain what he saw as Native Americans' inherent inferiority, and it became one strand of a nascent ideology of race.[58] In the context of Andean kurakas, the allusion was significant. No one denied that kurakas were natural lords, but if they were also natural slaves, their lordship must be of a peculiar, racialized kind. This was not the lordship for which the kurakas had attempted to bid.

Castro responded firmly to the apparent treason of the Wankas: ordering the arrest of Guacrapaucar's son Don Carlos, he deputized the encomenderos of Jauja to disarm their own subject kurakas. The encomendero Ribera, riding with thirty Spanish horsemen to take command of the valley from its native lords, might have reflected that he had won at last.[59]

### Aristocracy Denied

If Ribera thought so, he was mistaken. Even while Governor Castro was sending encomenderos to crack down on kurakas, he was laying plans for a new class of royal officials who would finally end both sides' hopes of seigneurial rule. The Indians' thwarted rebellion served as justification for appointing new, unprecedentedly powerful rural governors, called *corregidores de indios*. A corregidor's jurisdiction was large, typically the territory of four or five encomiendas. The new officials promised a level of centralized royal control over the countryside well in advance of that exercised in Spain itself.[60]

Among the first corregidores Castro appointed in 1565 was Juan de Larréinaga, to rule the valley of Jauja. Larréinaga was inferior to Ribera in social background, connections, and wealth.[61] Castro may have selected him precisely because he thought he would be easy to control. Yet in appointing him corregidor, Castro gave him nominal powers that dwarfed either Ribera's or Guacrapaucar's. According to his instructions, he was to resettle native Andeans in centralized villages, police them closely, impose a new tax, and carry out a general census.[62] The new towns would govern themselves through Spanish municipal institutions, with indigenous *alcaldes* (judges or mayors) and *cabildos* (town councils), to be selected from the Andean commoners, not the kurakas. By creating a population of visible, governable Andean subjects and by delegating local authority to commoners, the new system would help the Crown to rule directly, rather than through lords.

In Jauja, the new corregidor began his work with vigor. Within weeks of his appointment, Larréinaga had chosen sites for a new town in each of the valley's three encomiendas, to which the whole population would later be moved. Each site had streets laid out in a grid surrounding a plaza, church, whipping post (*picota*), and jail. In the town he founded for Don Gerónimo's people he himself marked out the plaza with a cord. He appointed alcaldes. The new forms of authority, it seemed, had already begun to extend royal control directly into the Andean countryside.[63]

Yet just six months later he was gone from his job, disconsolately seeking new opportunities in Lima. A Spanish priest appealed to Castro on his behalf: "For all that he has worked in this province and the great beginning he has given to what your Lordship assigned him, he should be compensated for a life which his unhappy fortune has made far from what it should be."[64]

While the precise nature of Larréinaga's unhappy fortune in unclear, his "great beginning" as corregidor was not all that it appeared: he failed to tame the power of the kurakas. In fact, instead of appointing a commoner as alcalde for Guacrapaucar's community, he appointed Guacrapaucar himself. This appointment overturned the purpose of the reform, but it was probably necessary for Larréinaga to establish himself at all. Even encomenderos such as Ribera, with greater personal resources and connections than Larréinaga had, did not try to deal with Andean peasants except through their kurakas. Although his son Don Carlos languished in prison on an accusation of rebellion, Don Gerónimo Guacrapaucar's power remained unchallenged.

Throughout the valley of Jauja, kurakas and their relatives became the alcaldes and cabildo members, treating the new offices not as threats but as vehicles for their own ambitions to Spanish-style lordship. This is not surprising; in Spain itself, nobles and oligarchies tended to control the once-popular institutions of municipal self-government. Members of one cabildo near Jauja appealed to the king to grant them "the privileges and preeminances which such officials [town councilors] have" in Castile, including holding their office in perpetuity and being ranked as gentlemen (*cavalleros*).[65]

Castro's attempt to neutralize the kurakas was his one major failure. In the long term, the rest of his reforms succeeded.[66] The corregidores took hold, Andeans moved to centralized towns (*reducciones*), and the encomenderos lost all hope of seigneurial power. Viceroys continued to distribute encomiendas, but they were little more than royal pensions. The kurakas, too, failed to get what they hoped for. Far from becoming noble *cavalleros* (literally horsemen, knights), they remained prohibited from owning horses and swords, the symbols of Spanish lordship. But the kurakas remained the lords of their Andean subjects.

It was this that most distinguished Peru from other colonies. While this chapter has focused on Peru, similar struggles took place elsewhere. In New Spain, too, encomenderos pushed for perpetuity and Spanish governors flattered but resisted their hopes, ultimately establishing Spanish corregidores and indigenous cabildos. Throughout the Spanish colonies, Indian society remained largely autonomous, organized partly by indigenous norms and partly by Spanish municipal institutions, answering to royal officials who tapped it for tribute and labor. This separation underlay the idea of "two republics," one of Spaniards and one of Indians. While always more theoretical than real, the separation remained until the nineteenth century, when the founders of Latin American independence tried to abolish it in favor of a single universal citizenship. Their efforts succeeded only in part, as Karen Caplan's chapter in this volume shows. In some places the institutions of the "republic of Indians" survive and have even become stronger in the twenty-first century.[67]

But within this general picture, Peru stood out for the success of the native lords. Elsewhere, commoners serving in municipal cabildos became the primary agents of Indian self-government.[68] In Peru the kurakas continued to govern as lords. Royal officials tried to control them by appointing their successors as they died but found that without popular legitimacy kurakas had little effective power, so they preserved hereditary succession.[69] Kurakas kept their central position in Peruvian society until the late colonial period, when a period of upheaval and rebellion (discussed in Sergio Serulnikov's chapter) prompted a major reorganization of the "republic of Indians" in the Andes.[70]

The later history of Jauja illustrates the kurakas' persistence. Spanish governors targeted the Guacrapaucars in the years after the discovery of the pikes. In the 1570s, viceroy Don Francisco de Toledo publicly burned the Jauja kurakas' royal documents and privileges, probably including Don Felipe's coat of arms.[71] But Don Felipe had allies in the Church and the Lima high court, who protected him from Toledo's attempts to neutralize or banish him.[72] Shortly afterward, he was assisting the corregidor as an "educated Indian [*indio ladino*] who [had] been in Spain" and in time became governor of the encomienda's Indians.[73] A man claiming descent from the family went to the Spanish court in the 1660s to ask the king to create an order of nobility for the kurakas.[74] Another descendant of a sixteenth-century Jauja kuraka, holding power in 1755, confronted Spanish attempts to take his people's land.[75] The kurakas survived as lords, controlling Andean subjects and mediating their contact with the Spanish world, yet at the same time limited by the racial restrictions that Castro, in the 1560s, helped create.

## Conclusion

"Identity" is an ambiguous word. It combines as least three elements: that of being assigned to a category, that of being part of a group, and that of having a specific understanding of oneself.[76] "Race," for instance, is sometimes an external act of naming, sometimes a community of shared experience, sometimes an internal sense of self, and often a combination of these, but it is not necessarily any one of them in a given situation. The native-born people of the Americas had many identities—based on age, sex, ethnicity, property, status—but it was colonialism that stamped on them the label "Indian." This identity was never fixed or impermeable, and at first it was a mere name whose meaning remained undetermined.

Scholarship on Andean kurakas has treated their traditionalism as a matter of identity and their acculturation as a matter of opportunism.[77] But our common observation of status competition shows that in times of change, people attain or retain status by being alert to styles and values emanating from new centers of power and internalizing them. Responding to subtle cues, even unconsciously, we adopt new styles of dress, speech, and self-carriage, new likes and dislikes—to a degree, new identities. Lords (male and female) are typically traditionalists, claiming a status legitimized by antiquity. But within a changing power structure, lords can be flexible and creative in redefining their identities.

Sixteenth-century kurakas—at least some kurakas, in the region of the central Andes—reinvented themselves in hybrid terms. They retained some of the practices and mentalities of pre-Hispanic lordship, even in some cases leading secret non-Christian religious rites, but they also collaborated actively and creatively with the colonial regime.[78] Internalizing and manipulating the Spanish concept of *señor natural* (natural lord), they hoped to become the dukes and counts of Peru.[79]

In tracking their bid for advancement, this chapter has focused as much on institutions as on identities, because lords' and would-be lords' identities were bound up with the institutions of the evolving state. Historians once thought that early modern European monarchies were locked in struggle with an entrenched aristocracy, but most now agree that kings negotiated various, sometimes contradictory alliances with lords and other social groups, offering them a stake in state institutions.[80] Perry Anderson observed kings allying with the aristocracy against the commoners, while Helen Nader observed them allying with local towns against certain lords.[81] As the dominant figures in this multipolar politics, kings encouraged competing factions to bid for royal favor—as the encomenderos and kurakas did in the mid-sixteenth century.

Throughout the expanding Iberian empires, some local leaders tied their fortunes to those empires, inserting themselves into the competition for royal favor. Such leaders might or might not owe their position to the Christian king but certainly counted on him for future advancement. It was natural for them to adopt new styles of thought and self-presentation, even while retaining their own traditions. In sixteenth-century Morocco, the Berber leader Yahya-u-Ta'fuft forged a close military alliance with the Portuguese; he kept his own Muslim religion, but his letters to the king called on the vocabulary of Iberian noble honor, servicio, and merced. Portuguese nobles in the colony intensely resented his competition and repeatedly accused him of treachery. But the king refused to take sides, infuriating the Portuguese lords by inviting Yahya to court and consistently showing him favor and gratitude.[82]

The Berber's career resembled that of Andean nobles such as the Guacrapaucars. But while Yahya's Portuguese rivals could invoke his religion against him, Spaniards such as Ribera could not find any obvious leverage against indigenous nobles who expressed a fervent Christianity, had served the king with blood and silver, and seemed to be as innately capable as any Spaniard. Recall that the official Matienzo asserted that in spite of appearances, Andeans were radically deficient: they lacked "prudence." "If this were not lacking," he continued (as quoted above), "they would not be among those who Aristotle says were born slaves by nature."[83] The phrasing suggests a process of reasoning: Andeans, particularly kurakas, appear to be gifted, yet it cannot be that they are equal to Spaniards. What, then, are they missing? It is prudence, or good judgment, a quality often defined as necessary for noble honor. It was, in part, kurakas' pretensions to Castilian lordship that spurred colonial Spaniards to articulate ideas of Indian race.[84]

## Notes

I thank Matthew O'Hara and Andrew Fisher for their work as editors, and the following colleagues (among others) for advice and criticism: Donato Amado, Silvia Arrom, David Garrett, Karene Grad, Anna Guillemin, Renzo Honores, Martin Kenner, Yuen-Gen Liang, Jane Mangan, Kenneth Mills, David Mumford, José de la Puente, Stuart Schwartz, and Daniel Stolzenberg.

1. Among Castilians at this time, the honorific "don" was restricted to those associated with the aristocracy (*señores de vasallos*) and denied to lesser nobles (*hidalgos*): Lockhart, *Spanish Peru, 1532–1560* [1968], chap. 2. In this chapter I distinguish between nobility, a privileged legal status implying freedom from taxes and other burdens of the common people, and lordship or aristocracy, the power of rule over subjects. A lord was always a noble, but a noble was only rarely a lord.

2. Lic. Castro to king, March 6, 1565, in Levillier, ed., *Gobernantes del Perú*, 3: 59–60.

3. Cleaton, "Caciques into Indios"; Góngora, *El estado en el derecho indiano*, 198–221.

4. The two most important studies of the early Peruvian encomienda are Puente Brunke, *Encomienda y encomenderos en el Perú*, and Trelles Aréstegui, *Lucas Martínez Vegazo*, especially chap. 7.

5. Lockhart, *Spanish Peru, 1532–1560* [1968], 44–45.

6. O'Toole, "Inventing Difference." See also Fields, "Whiteness, Racism, and Identity."

7. Historical accounts of the perpetuity controversy include Abercrombie, "La perpetuidad traducida"; Assadourian, "Los señores étnicos y los corregidores de indios en la conformación del Estado colonial"; Goldwert, "La lucha por la perpetuidad de las encomiendas en el Perú virreinal"; Pereña Vicente, "La pretensión a la perpetuidad de las encomiendas del Perú."

8. Fernández de Palencia, *Primera y segunda parte de la historia del Peru*, part 2, book 2, chaps. 28–58.

9. The proposal had been made before, at the urging of Mexican encomenderos in earlier decades, but had never gone beyond idle discussion.

10. Abercrombie, "La perpetuidad traducida," 92; Moxó, *Feudalismo, señorío, y nobleza en la Castilla medieval*, 164.

11. Mercado de Peñalosa to king, Lima, February 25, 1558, in Levillier, ed., *Gobernantes del Perú, cartas y papeles, siglo XVI*, 1:198–201.

12. Mendiburu, *Diccionario histórico-biográfico del Perú*, 378–79.

13. Goldwert, "La lucha por la perpetuidad de las encomiendas en el Perú virreinal, 1550–1600," 351. In 1553–54, Castile's debt had risen from 3.1 to 4.3 million ducats (Rodríguez-Salgado, *The Changing Face of Empire*, 4–5). If Ribera meant his offer in *pesos ensayados de tributo*, as is likely, it amounted to 8.6 million ducats. (The two coins at this

time were worth 425 and 375 maravedises: Luengo Múñoz, "Sumaria noción de las monedas de Castilla e Indias en el siglo XVI." 363–66.)

14. Góngora, *El estado en el derecho indiano*, 181–85; Lockhart, "Encomienda and Hacienda"; Morse, "Claims of Political Tradition," 99–100; Zavala, *La encomienda indiana*.

15. Izquierdo Martín, *El rostro de la comunidad*.

16. But see Romano, "Entre encomienda castellana y encomienda indiana."

17. Suárez Fernández, *Nobleza y monarquía*, 21; Nader, *Liberty in Absolutist Spain*, 46–47; Guilarte, *El régimen señorial en el siglo XVI*, 110–35.

18. Nader, *The Mendoza Family in the Spanish Renaissance, 1350–1550*, 108.

19. Solórzano, *Política indiana*, book 3, chap. 25.

20. Leonard, *Books of the Brave*; Rodríguez Prampolini, *Amadises de América*.

21. Schwartz, "New World Nobility," 26, citing Konetzke, *Colección de documentos para la historia de la formación social de hispanoamérica, 1493–1810*, 1:126–27. Schwartz shows, however, that the Crown did not follow through on such promises.

22. Instruction to commissioners, Brussels, March 15, 1559, in Zabálburu and Rayon, eds., *Nueva colección de documentos inéditos para la historia de España y sus Indias*, 6:191–93.

23. Power of attorney, Lima, July 19, 1559, in Hanke, "Un festón de documentos lascasianos."

24. Las Casas and Santo Tomás, Memorial, ca. 1560, in Las Casas, *Obras escogidas de fray Bartolomé de las Casas*, 5:467.

25. *Kuraka* was the most common of several different Andean words for a native lord. Spaniards, however, were more likely to use the word *cacique*, which they borrowed from Caribbean languages and used all over the Americas. Within the large literature on kurakas, see especially Cahill, "The Long Conquest"; Díaz Rementería, *El cacique en el virreinato del Perú*; Guevara Gil, "Los caciques y el señorío natural en los Andes coloniales (Perú, siglo XVI)"; Pease, *Curacas, reciprocidad y riqueza*; Ramírez, *To Feed and Be Fed*.

26. Spalding, *Huarochirí*, chap. 7.

27. Santillán, "Relación del origen descendencia política y gobierno de los Incas"; Bandera, "Relación general," 178.

28. Espinoza Soriano, ed., "El memorial de Charcas," 132; Chamberlain, "The Concept of the 'Señor Natural' as Revealed by Castilian Law and Administrative Documents."

29. Espinoza Soriano, ed., "Los huancas aliados de la conquista," 218.

30. Garcilaso, *Royal Commentaries of the Incas and General History of Peru*, 1:335.

31. Earle, *How Chiefs Come to Power*, 54, 61; Información, Jauja, November 20, 1570, in Levillier, *Don Francisco de Toledo, supremo organizador del Perú*, 2:14–37, see 18. The Upper Mantaro Archaeological Research Project has reconstructed Wanka prehistory: see D'Altroy, "Transitions in Power"; Hastorf et al., "Settlement Archaeology in the Jauja Region of Peru"; Hastorf, "One Path to the Heights"; and Earle, *How Chiefs Come to Power*.

32. D'Altroy, "Transitions in Power."

33. Garcilaso, *Royal Commentaries of the Incas and General History of Peru*, 1:334–36.

34. D'Altroy, "Transitions in Power."

35. Murra, *The Economic Organization of the Inka State*, chap. 5.

36. Espinoza Soriano, "Los huancas, aliados de la conquista"; Murra, "Litigation over the Rights of 'Natural Lords' in Early Colonial Courts in the Andes"; Pease, *Curacas, reciprocidad y riqueza*, 154–58.

37. Stern, *Peru's Indian Peoples and the Challenge of Spanish Conquest*, chap. 2. See Spalding, "Social Climbers."

38. Vega, "La descripción que se hizo en la provincia de Xauxa"; Lurinhuanca had 12,000 tributaries (i.e., households) under the last Inca king and 3,500 in 1572; I am assuming four to five members in an average household.

39. Assadourian, "La gran vejación y destruición de la tierra."

40. Espinoza Soriano, ed., "Los huancas, aliados de la conquista," 226.

41. Francisco Hernandez testimony regarding offer made by Cuzco kurakas, 1561, Archivo General de Indias, Seville (hereafter, AGI), Justicia 434, N 2, R 1, pieza 2, f. 6v.

42. Philip to viceroy and commissioners, Toledo, February 7, 1561, in Jiménez de la Espada, ed., *Relaciones geográficas de Indias*, 1:40–41.

43. Power of attorney, Mama, January 21, 1562, AGI Indiferente General 1530, ff. 615–43.

44. Espinoza Soriano, ed., "Los huancas, aliados de la conquista," 180–84; Murra, "Litigation over the Rights of 'Natural Lords,'" 55–56.

45. Goldwert, "La lucha," 214.

46. Undated parecer, in Zabálburu, ed., *Nueva colección de documentos inéditos para la historia de España y sus Indias*, 6:270–74.

47. King to commissioners, Madrid, February 13, 1562, in *Colección de documentos inéditos*, first series, 18:25–27.

48. Conde de Nieva to king, Lima, May 4, 1562, in Levillier, ed., *Gobernantes del Perú, cartas y papeles, siglo XVI*, 1:395–472.

49. Zabálburu, ed., *Nueva colección*, 6:136–65.

50. Felipe de Segovia Balderrábano de Briceño to Lope de Castro, received December 5, 1564, in Odriozola, ed., *Documentos históricos del Peru en las épocas del coloniaje despues de la conquista y de la independencia hasta la presente*, 3:6–8.

51. Castro to king, Lima, March 6, 1565, in Levillier, ed., *Gobernantes del Perú, cartas y papeles, siglo XVI*, 3:54–69, see 59.

52. Wachtel, *The Vision of the Vanquished*, 179.

53. Probanza of Don Gerónimo Guacrapaucar, printed in Espinoza Soriano, ed., "Los huacas, aliados de la conquista," 225.

54. Odriozola, ed., *Documentos históricos*, 3:6–8.

55. Castro to king, Lima, April 30, 1566, AGI Lima 121, loose file, f. 5.

56. Spalding, *Huarochirí*, 213.

57. Matienzo, *Gobierno del Perú*, 69.

58. Ginés de Sepúlveda, discussed in Pagden, *The Fall of Natural Man*, 109–18.

59. See Levillier, ed., *Gobernantes del Perú, cartas y papeles, siglo XVI*, 3:59–60.

60. Lohmann Villena, *El corregidor de indio en el Perú bajo los Austrias*.

61. Mendiburu, *Diccionario histórico-biográfico*, 9:338.

62. Instruction for Juan de Larreinaga, corregidor of Jauja, Lima, June 27, 1565, Biblioteca Nacional de España, Madrid, MS 3043, ff. 1–5.

63. Cabildo de Jauja, parcialidad Ananguancas, to king, Jatunjauja, January 3, 1566, AGI Lima 121, loose file, ff. 45r-48r; Espinoza Soriano, "Reducciones, pueblos, y ciudades."

64. Fray López de la Fuente to Castro, Jauja, January 14, 1566, AGI Lima 121, loose file, f. 51.

65. Cabildo of Chongos to king, January 8,1566 [misdated 1565], AGI Lima 121, loose file, ff. 57–58.

66. Viceroy Francisco de Toledo further institutionalized Castro's reforms in the 1570s.

67. Maybury-Lewis, ed., *The Politics of Ethnicity*.

68. Haskett, *Indigenous Rulers*, 60–85; Menegus Bornemann, "El gobierno de los indios en la Nueva España, siglo XVI."

69. Spalding, *Huarochirí*, 219–22.

70. O'Phelan, *Kurakas sin sucesiones*; Garrett, *Shadows of Empire*.

71. Toledo to king, March 12, 1571, Biblioteca Nacional de España, MS 3044, N 4, f. 44v.

72. Toledo to king, in Levillier, ed., *Gobernantes*, 3:374 (February 8, 1570) and 5:64 (March 20, 1573).

73. Vega, "La descripción que se hizo en la provincia de Xauxa [1582], " 166; Espinoza Soriano, "Los huancas, aliados de la conquista," 406.

74. He may, however, have been an imposter: see Puente Luna, "What's in a Name?"

75. O'Phelan, *Rebellions and Revolts in Eighteenth Century Peru and Upper Peru*, 127.

76. Brubaker and Cooper, "Beyond 'Identity,' " 14–21.

77. "identity": Ramírez, *To Feed and Be Fed*; "opportunism": Spalding, "Kurakas and Commerce."

78. On continuity in kurakas' religious role, see Ramírez, *To Feed and Be Fed*, 115–54. On continuity in the symbols of rule, see Martínez Cereceda, *Autoridades en los Andes*.

79. Guevara Gil, "Los caciques y el señorío natural en los Andes coloniales (Perú, siglo XVI)," 145.

80. Zmora, *Monarchy, Aristocracy, and the State in Europe, 1300–1800*, chap. 4.

81. Anderson, *Lineages of the Absolutist State*; Nader, *Liberty in Absolutist Spain*.

82. Racine, "Service and Honor in Sixteenth-Century Portuguese North Africa."

83. Matienzo, *Gobierno del Perú*, 69.

84. Rodríguez Salgado, "Christians, Civilised, and Spanish."

# A Market of Identities

*Women, Trade, and Ethnic Labels in Colonial Potosí*

In 1550 Spaniard Pedro Cieza de León described the *gato* or main market plaza of Potosí: "In one part of it went a row of baskets of coca, that was the best wealth in these parts; in another, piles of shawls and luxurious shirts, thin and thick; in another part there were mountains of maize and of dried potatoes [*chuño*]."[1] Cieza de León also observed in great detail the city's people. Potosí, he commented, attracted "large groups of *yanaconas*" and "the most beautiful *indias* of Cuzco and all the kingdom."[2] As the abundance of silver turned Potosí into a boomtown, indigenous inhabitants were at the heart of the creation of urban colonial culture. Despite their common category devised by Spanish rulers, "Indians" were in no way a monolithic group. Cieza's observations about types of people reveal how Spaniards grappled with differentiation among Indians while holding onto a racialized notion of how Indian and Spaniard differed. But if Spaniards tried to figure out how to label Potosí's residents, so too did indigenous peoples. Preconquest identities and colonial developments converged to influence the social hierarchies in these cities. The Indian types Cieza observed are objects in his writing; yet in the history of the city they emerge as actors in the very market that captured his attention. Indeed, instead of purely passive constructions such as those Cieza de León offered, indigenous people's actions in the urban markets of colonial Peru shaped new ethnic identities.

This chapter uses labeling of women in early Potosí markets to explore the creation of colonial identities. The expansion of markets and trade in Potosí prompted extraordinary social differentiation for indigenous peoples. To be sure, the role of indigenous women in trade was larger than that of indigenous men. In the space of a few decades, Cieza's indias from Cuzco claimed a distinct economic role: the sale of coca from Cuzco. Not only did officials, customers, and merchants recognize the women by the products they sold but they gained a reputation for their aggressive manner of trade, their profits, and their dress. The labels that identified women marketers reveal a Spanish need to categorize so as to control subjects both indigenous and female. Yet it would be shortsighted to consider these identities as solely colonial constructions. The labels serve as a window onto change in market women's activities.

The period between 1545 and the early 1600s saw subtle but important shifts in women's roles in Potosí's market and the identities shaped and reinforced therein. This chapter explores three such urban colonial identities that merged gender and urban trade with ethnicity. First is a discussion of the broad category of *indias gateras*, indigenous market women, with attention to subgroups like *pallas*, indigenous noblewomen. Next, the pernicious *regatones*, indigenous hucksters, serve to highlight how different types of marketing tactics emerged in response to given social and economic factors. Finally, the *mestizas en habito de india*, literally, mestiza women in Indian habit, reveal a sector of urban women whose Spanish bloodlines and indigenous lifestyle counter traditional thinking about trends toward Hispanicization. In each instance these female figures, non-Spanish all of them, played integral roles in the urban economy. These women came to represent a decidedly non-Spanish urban female type with economic know-how and strong will.[3] The tenacity of the characterization suggests that while indigenous women's aggressive economic activities led to business success, they clashed with expectations of appropriate female and indigenous roles. Thus emerged colonial market identities based on Indianness, gender, and economy. If markets were, as I argue elsewhere, an Indian domain, female vendors constructed an identity based on roles within urban trade and expressed this identity through customs, language, and dress.[4]

Indigenous market women are ubiquitous in the Andes even today, but this chapter treats the first historical period to give birth to the role of women in the market economy and the labels associated with that era. The opening section of the chapter deals with concepts of ethnicity in the sixteenth-century Andes. Next, the discussion moves from concepts to historical context with a discussion of Potosí's early history and emergence of its markets. The heart of the chapter explores labels used frequently in the colonial era to indicate a female identity linked both to indigenous heritage and market activities. The female traders of Potosí serve as fodder to clarify how social and economic factors in the sixteenth-century Andes combined to link the ethnic identities of first indigenous and then mestiza woman with occupations in trade. As women's specialization in markets increased, their power as economic actors was palpable. Labels to differentiate among female traders helped merchants, officials, and customers understand the hierarchies of urban economy. These labels also helped to control specifically female economic activities. Ultimately the labels used to identify these women stand as evidence of a new ethnic identity among indigenous peoples—one rooted in the urban colonial experience.

*Race and Ethnicity in a Changing Landscape*

In colonial Spanish America, new identities were in the making as Spaniards, Indians, and Africans began to produce children and families in the 1500s. Constructions of identities changed as Spaniards acted to control the demographic realities of miscegenation that threatened basic tenets of colonial rule. People distinguished their kind from others through a variety of factors including skin color, physical features, place of origin, language, dress, religion, and occupation. As the Spanish extended their rule in the Americas, *race* as defined by skin color, physical features, parental identity, and lineage became increasingly important in defining one's place in society. Much of what historians use to discuss racial identity exists because Spanish officials, notaries, scribes, priests, and observers chose racial terms to identify people in official documents that we can read today. As we will see, however, these labels suggest not only Spanish efforts at control but also native Andeans' shifting circumstances.[5]

Spanish officials in colonial Peru attempted to organize people into groups of Spaniards, Indians, and Africans and to discourage social and sexual mixing of those populations. Spaniards used race to exercise control over economic issues. Tribute categories, for instance, had a racial basis. Moreover, acculturation to the dominant power in society, a process known now as Hispanicization, had a powerful draw. The reality of colonial life in sixteenth-century Peru, however, was infinitely more complex than this trio of racial groups. In particular, additional labels of identity emerged to deal with individuals of mixed race, mestizos being a

prime example. Moreover, cultural distinctions within those three dominant racial groups prove that individuals did not always think of themselves in the terms Spaniards used to describe them.

Many people, both Spaniard and Indian, used ethnicity to distinguish
themselves from others of their biological race. Spaniards on the Iberian
peninsula had long used religion and culture to differentiate themselves
from Jews and Muslims. Native Andeans did the same in preconquest
Peru to highlight identities of different native groups such as the Inca
royalty, the Lupaca of Lake Titicaca, or the "uncivilized" lowland Chi-
riguana.[6] But the practice of ethnic distinction changed when the two
worlds met in the colonial Andes.

New ethnic identities for urban indigenous people emerged in this era.
Remarkably, some of the most common identities had a gendered component. When someone used the word *gatera*, for instance, it connoted an Indian woman who worked in urban markets. Thus, sixteenth-century labels
for native Andeans came from occupation as much as ethnic identity. A
language of the urban economy emerged because words, phrases, and
labels of identity developed a currency in the discourse of the colonial market. If an observer or a customer in the market spoke of an *india palla*, or
Inca noblewoman in the Quechua, as opposed to an *india gatera*, the label
implied more detail about the relationship of that woman to the colonial
economy. These terms, respectively, suggested elite or nonelite status—a
"beautiful india from Cuzco" was not so similar to a rural indigenous
vendor from Chayanta. Each term connoted a specific identity in the urban
economy in Potosí: what women sold, where they sold, the size of their
trade ventures, their profits, and, relative to profits, the style and quality of
their dress. As urban markets grew and became more complex, market
women were no longer all of one stripe. In due course, new labels emerged
through which to classify marketers and their activities.

*Markets and Exchange in Potosí*

With the discovery of silver as the draw, Spaniards founded the Villa
Imperial de Potosí in 1545 in the high mountainous plateau of the Andes
nearly fourteen thousand feet above sea level. No city existed previously
on the isolated site. Yet in the sixteenth century the Spanish Crown sent
thousands of Indians to mine the silver. These men, called *mitayos*, often
arrived in the company of family members. African slaves soon followed

to work in refineries or Spanish homes. Within decades of its 1545 founding, Potosí boasted over one hundred thousand inhabitants. City residents purchased food and clothes, and the marketplace grew as did the number of women with significant roles in trade.

Between the discovery of silver in 1545 and the early 1550s, Potosí's most important market, the *gato*, or *kjato* in Quechua, had already become an institution.[7] Native Andean items dominated the market. Coca leaves, which helped the body adjust to high altitude and suppressed appetites for workers, were the most often traded item in early Potosí markets. So valuable it was, coca functioned as a type of currency; salaries and debts were often paid in baskets of coca.[8] Trade also boomed in maize, chuño, oca, quinoa, and *ají* (dried peppers).[9] In the second largest market, known as the *plaza del carbon*, women sold hens, eggs, lard, and charcoal.[10] Smaller markets throughout town sold flour, barley, firewood, ore, llama dung (for fuel), wax, and even the corn beer start-up known in Quechua as *muk'u*.[11] All types of merchandise imaginable were for sale, many at inflated prices.[12]

Among the more remarkable qualities of Potosí's great market was the participation of indigenous vendors: "the trade was so great that only among Indians, not involving Christians, 25 and 30,000 pesos de oro . . . were traded in the time that the miners were prosperous."[13] Silver drove commerce in the early days of the gato—typically traded as unrefined ore after being removed from the mines. Thus this "time that the miners were prosperous" served as the platform for indigenous women to move into profitable positions.

In the first days of the gato, these women worked hand in hand with the leaders of their ethnic communities, known as *kurakas*, who supplied Potosí with many of its marketable commodities. Kurakas made trade agreements with European merchants and then drew on Andean modes of production to supply them with goods.[14] Given Potosí's booming market, some Spanish encomenderos developed arrangements for native communities, known as *ayllus*, to put mandatory tribute payments to good use in the gato. Don Alonso de Montemayor received tribute from a group of Sakaka Indians in the Audiencia of Charcas. In the years immediately following the civil wars in Peru, Montemayor set tribute amounts in a host of items that found a ready market in Potosí.[15] For instance, the Sakaka provided maize, chuño, llamas, and cloth, all items sold in Potosí.

Instead of handing these goods to Montemayor, the ayllu members trucked the products to Potosí where they delivered them to an agent of Montemayor. This tribute arrangement reveals one pattern by which ayllu members entered Potosí's urban economy.[16] Theirs was a swift and direct encounter with the changing economic structures of the Andes.

Ayllu members who traveled to Potosí noticed in quick order that the city provided opportunities to earn money from endeavors related to mining and to markets which they could use to pay tribute. Indeed, Spanish observers noted the keen indigenous interest in trade. For one early Spanish visitor to Potosí, the priest Cristobal Díaz de los Santos, Potosí offered "such great benefits for the said indios and yanaconas as in this said Villa because together they bring things to the market in this Villa [and] from everything they make money."[17]

In the colonial era, male Andeans supplied bulk goods through ayllu structures, while native Andean women worked in the marketplaces. In the earliest years of Potosí's markets, indigenous women may well not have acted as individual entrepreneurs but traded goods at the behest of kurakas and in support of their ayllu community. The integration of male and female labor into this community effort is representative of a gender parallelism scholars find elsewhere in the pre-Hispanic Americas.[18] This framework is indicative of preconquest trade whereby ayllu members traded, in collective fashion, for items produced in ecological zones outside their own. The noted anthropologist John Murra argued that instead of markets, these so-called vertical archipelagos moved goods around the upper Andes (Bolivia).[19] In 1550, traditional modes supplied the goods to Potosí's markets, yet colonization and urbanization increased the size and tempo of these market exchanges. Instead of engaging in occasional trade with those from other ayllus, women moved to cities to play a more permanent role in exchanges with Indians and Spaniards alike. For women, these circumstances marked important changes from preconquest patterns and paved the way for even more changes by the end of the sixteenth century.

Kurakas were not the only men who used indigenous women to sell for them. The women also worked for Spanish men and served as a bridge between the few Spanish merchants and thousands of indigenous customers, products, and suppliers. The relationship could prove lucrative as "many Spaniards became rich in this mining town of Potosí with having only two or three *indias* with whom they dealt in these markets."[20] Indigenous women's familiarity with the cultural landscape endowed them with an element of power within an overall structure where Spanish men dominated. The female marketers, however, recognized their unique value in the increasingly entrenched customs of trade in the *gato de las indias*.

The historical context of incipient colonialism and the silver boom, in other words, made it possible for indigenous women to have a unique place in Potosí's economy. At the time when silver production was high (the 1550s and then the 1580s through 1600), the women profited. While women often participated in the market in the 1550s in support of their ayllus, over time this changed as men and women set up trade ventures as individual urban residents. If no longer ayllu Indians, who were these marketplace actors? They formed part of an urban indigenous culture in the process of creating colonial economic practices and cementing city-based relationships. These urban lives-in-the-making prompted new colonial labels for identification.

The impetus to create new labels came from within and without. The size and volume of urban trade in Potosí forced Spaniards to categorize women in the city's markets. Yet a parallel trend in identity formation occurred from within those market sites. Indigenous market women contested Spanish regulations. Some mestiza traders embraced indigenous-style dress and indigenous language to counter Spanish definitions of Indianness. The decades between 1550 and 1600 witnessed the creation of a new identity at once urban, female, indigenous, and entrepreneurial.

## Market Women and Ethnicity

Ethnicity did not automatically determine the role of anyone in these sixteenth-century urban Andean markets. Yet it would be remiss to ignore the significance of ethnicity in these economic settings, foremost the predominant role of indigenous women. Merchant women in Potosí were a key factor for native Andeans to meet colonial economic demands and for Spaniards to conduct business. Over time, women assumed more individual roles. Indias gateras were not simply indigenous women who worked in markets but had emerged as a new cohort.

How was it that one's daily activities were indicative of ethnicity? On the Iberian peninsula during the sixteenth century, women in markets in

Seville might be "Spanish" or Muslim, but indigenous women held the market spots in Potosí and most highland Andean cities.[21] The name of the market, the gato de las indias, or indigenous women's market, reveals an institutionalization of women's roles in this early marketplace economy.[22] By the 1550s, the date for the first evidence of marketplace exchanges in Potosí, the women vendors were described as "indias."

Market selling as the domain of Indian women resulted from three major factors in sixteenth-century Andean life. First, as mentioned above, indigenous women had access to foodstuffs through kin. Second, these women had the privilege to sell items produced by their ayllus without paying the *alcabala*, or sales tax, to the Spanish Crown. Specifically, Spanish officials did not tax Andeans selling native products, like local textiles, coca, chuño, charqui, and maize in an effort to offer native peoples a chance to earn tribute money.[23] Third, the demographics of the region of Peru and of the city of Potosí reveal another reason for the predominance of indigenous women in these economic roles. Few Spanish women lived in Potosí until the 1570s. Thus, from 1545 to 1570, Potosí's population was overwhelmingly indigenous. From its inception, the urban market was a space where indigenous women dominated economic exchanges. In contrast to the infrequent nature of preconquest trade, women's concentration in one urban area on a daily basis formed a concrete group based on gender, ethnic identity, and economic roles.

By the 1570s, one finds increasing evidence that indigenous women acted as individuals in the markets, seeking individual profit as opposed to acting on behalf of an ayllu. Catalina Palla was one such trader. The surname of Palla suggests that this woman was likely among the cast of Cieza de León's "beautiful indias." Pallas had ties to the former Inca nobility centered in the Cuzco region. To Cieza de León the pallas were attractive because of physical characteristics linked to women from that region. Others in Potosí would recognize the economic characteristics of palla identity: namely, a link to the coca trade. Given the value of coca, these female merchants enjoyed good profits from which they crafted an identity through dress, style, jewelry, and other elements of material culture. Catalina Palla's will confirms that she did trade in coca and basic foodstuffs to a mainly indigenous clientele. [24] Further, her will suggests she traded not for any native Andean community but on her own, or her family's, accord.

In addition to those indigenous women who sold on their own, numerous Spaniards continued to hire *Indian* women to help them, but with one critical difference from the 1550s: they did not make arrangements through an ayllu. By the 1570s, Spaniards like Francisco de Salazar de Mejía made contracts directly with indigenous men and women rather than their kurakas. Salazar de Mejía hired the indigenous couple Juan Ynaso and Juana Viscama for the period of one year.[25] While Ynaso agreed to serve Salazar as needed, the agreement specified that Juana would sell coca, clothing, and other goods given to her by Salazar. As we have seen, the forms of market trade changed from the 1550s to the 1570s, but indigenous women remained *the* face of market trading throughout the period.

*Regatones: Aggressive Marketing*

By the 1580s, trends in Potosí's economy and society shifted, and along with those shifts, the practices of indigenous market women (indias del gato) changed. The silver industry slowed, and when it regained speed, more Spaniards were poised to reap profit. When fewer indigenous residents of the city profited from the silver industry, this cast negative results on the earnings of market women. Likewise, the demographics of the city shifted in the years between 1570 and 1600. First, a generation of mestizas came of age and entered urban society as a distinct social group. Second, Spanish women began to arrive and gradually increase their presence in the urban economy around the early 1600s. As a result of these economic changes, some indigenous market women initiated more aggressive practices. These tactics had the potential to give the women higher profits but ultimately made the women common targets for market policies by Spanish officials. The bold merchandizing techniques earned these women a reputation *and* a new label: *regatones*.

Regatones were not limited to Potosí; in Potosí, and perhaps most highland Andean cities, indigenous women constituted this category.[26] Regatones functioned as go-betweens who bought items from vendors on the outskirts of town and then resold those items within the city limits, often at inflated prices. The town council complained, for instance, that the women bought partridges for eight or nine reales only to charge two pesos (sixteen reales) to customers in city markets. These regatones, who were not unique but rather in "great quantity," proved to be a thorn in the side of council attempts to control supply and pricing.[27] Town council regulations specifically targeted urban regatones to fix prices of staple goods.[28] The regatones' ethnic identity reflects the dominance of indigenous control within city marketplaces as well as their ability to operate on the margins of the city, a zone that formed the spatial link to the indigenous countryside.

The regatones had a relatively easy time obtaining goods from male merchants from outside the region who ignored the prices fixed by the town council. Peru's viceroy don Fernando de Torres y Portugal denounced the merchants or "powerful persons" who brought food and sustenance goods from regions bordering Potosí like Cochabamba, Tomina, and Mizque and then sold them to regatones.[29] The comments of Torres y Portugal highlight a critical element of gender that underlies the construction of urban economic categories. Out-of-town suppliers, who ultimately profited from exchanges with regatones, were often men. Yet local policy, as articulated by the cabildo, focused on the small-scale operations in the city and targeted the women vendors as problematic. When men (relatives or bosses) controlled indigenous women vendors, their activities prompted less regulation. When the women began to act on their own, the nature of non-Spanish female actors in the urban economy prompted strong responses about their efforts to turn healthy profits.

These women also earned the ire of some merchants. One Spanish representative for a wealthy indigenous merchant, Don Diego Chambillas, expressed his frustration to his master over negotiations with market women in Potosí. The women, he complained, had gone into business for themselves and were "bold *regatonas*."[30] The Spanish dealer implied that the women did not work for their kuraka and ayllu nor did they report to a Spaniard. Thus, not only did regatonas acquire a reputation for charging excessive prices to consumers but some apparently drove a hard bargain with the merchants who supplied them.

Regatonas are the most hidden of the market categories because of their illicit trading practices. Since these vendors ran the risk of being punished by the town officials, they appear as a renegade group of marketers from the pages of town council records. Yet when viewed from the perspective of the female vendor herself, the economic practice of regatonas reveals something more routine. The resale of goods was an organic marketplace practice. A young Potosina named Madalena Taquima reported that she helped her aunt buy and resell goods in the public plaza.

This anecdotal report, buried in an inheritance case, suggests the common nature of this practice.[31] With the growth of Potosí's urban economy, the competition for products and prices escalated. Regatones stepped in to mediate rural suppliers and city customers.

Finally, the emergence of the regatona label emphasizes the development of new roles within the urban economy. Gateras were a powerful "India" presence in the markets, but by and large they followed the rules—they were contained. The regatona, however, was Indian, female, and problematic. The differentiation between the gatera and the regatona emerged precisely at the point at which indigenous women faced challenges to the relative economic prosperity they enjoyed in Potosí's markets. One might wonder if the regatona was simply a gatera breaking rules. However, the economic context in which the regatona emerged suggests a category of indigenous vendor who was distinct in terms of experience in the urban context and class position. Given her high degree of comfort with urban economic practices and regulation as well as confident engagement of out-of-town merchants, the regatona likely represented a second-generation urban indigenous woman rather than a new arrival. Yet by this era some women ran their own stores and businesses, and the regatonas did not have this status in the upper echelon of women traders. The regatona label highlights Potosí's officials' concern with regulating female trading practices. Yet this new category also emerged as a result of class and generational hierarchies among market women.

### Mestizas en Habito de India: *Spanish Blood, Indigenous Identity*

Another label that was, like regatona, at once ethnic and gender based, emerged as the population of mestizos grew in late-sixteenth- and early-seventeenth-century Andes. By that point, certain women came to be known as *mestiza en habitos de india*, or mestizas in Indian habit.[32] Spanish officials were conscious of the link between their identity and the colonial economy because indigenous women enjoyed exemption from the royal alcabala. As mentioned above, this exemption was given exclusively to men and women of indigenous descent who sold *productos de la tierra*. The easy assumption is that mestizas dressed like Indians to escape paying taxes. In Potosí, though, the women who appear in historical record as mestizas en habito de indias left clues about their dress, their language, their place of residence—even their diet. And all these clues suggest they did not "dress up" for their job but that indigenous culture was part of their lived identity. These women's situations vis-à-vis the economy and society in sixteenth-century Potosí illustrate how markets created new attention to mestiza women who self-defined as indigenous.

The late-sixteenth-century urban mestizas who dressed according to their indigenous roots did not fit neatly into Spanish racial hierarchies. Spaniards in official positions in Quito were vexed by this practice of mestizas retaining the *acsu*, or traditional dress.[33] They were equally vexed with indigenous men who wore Spanish dress to pass as mestizos. Why were women with Spanish blood content to walk around looking like indias while men were eager to pass themselves off as Spanish? The relationship between ethnic identity and tribute obligations created the gendered response to dress and identity. Whereas indigenous men might avoid tribute by looking like a Spaniard, women had no such pressure. In fact, since indigenous peoples paid no taxes on the sale of numerous native food products, women who worked in the marketplace might benefit from donning Indian dress.

Spanish officials defined mestizas as females who had one Spanish and one indigenous parent. Typically, Spanish men fathered children with indigenous mothers. Scholars have shown that mestizos of the first generation were incorporated into Spanish society, if elite, or left to their indigenous mothers, if nonelite.[34] Concern about the fate of young men and women of mixed Spanish and Indian heritage was no small matter. In their very ancestry, mestizos posed a problem for Spanish rule in the Americas, since the Crown used race to divide peoples for reasons of economy, law, and society. In an example of how Spanish fathers hoped to solve this "problem," conquistadors founded the Santa Clara convent in Cuzco to house and educate their mestiza daughters.[35]

Spanish concern over mixed-race girls grew as the sixteenth century progressed. Historians argue that Spanish colonial society approached mestizos as a problematic social category, especially by the early seventeenth century. When Iberian-born women began arriving in Peru, mestiza daughters lost status in the Spanish ranks of colonial society, and their chances of marrying Spanish men decreased.[36] Mestizo identity became increasingly synonymous with illegitimacy as well as other negative characteristics that defined mixed-race society (that is, non-Indians and non-Spaniards). Occupation, and its attendant economic status, served as the markers of identity.[37] Citing examples from the late seventeenth century, Stuart Schwartz and Frank Salomon argue that "up to a point, mestizo was as mestizo did. Dress, association, custom, and appearance could make the difference."[38] They emphasize the practice of males to act Spanish, and not Indian, by wearing Hispanic clothes and taking urban artisanal occupations. The sparing use of the label "mestiza en habito de indias" in documents from Potosí during the late 1500s and the early 1600s reflects a group of women with Spanish blood who chose not to acculturate toward Spanish society but to define themselves and their roles in the urban economy by wearing indigenous clothing. This makes us rethink whether "mestiza was as mestiza did," assuming, as historians have typically done, that a mestiza is a women with Indian blood who acculturates up the social scale to Spanish. This label indicates that when cultural markers were not sufficient, colonial society tried to separate mixed-race women from indigenous or Spanish women through the use of a label.

The lack of Spanish cultural habits was precisely what required the designation of "habito de indias." This "Indian habit" included various elements of native culture such as language, food, occupation, or even place of residence. The defining characteristic, however, was clothing. Fray Diego de Ocaña described the dress of indigenous women in a *cofradía* in Potosí in the early seventeenth century. The women were "dressed in very fine silk patterned with velvet, and underneath the *azú* [acsu] a skirt better than the Spaniards. The '*liquidas*' [llicllas]—which are what they wear over their shoulders like shawls—of velvet and damask; and the *ñañaca*, which is the clothing that they wear over the head, of the same; the *chumbes*, which are what cinches the waist, are of their wool of many colors."[39] The costume of these women had changed in the colonial era because of the availability of new textiles, like the damask and silk mentioned by Ocaña. It was, however, a markedly Indian dress.

How was it that mestiza women came to privilege these clothes and eat foods like maize and chuño or belong to indigenous cofradías? Plenty of daughters of Spaniards and Indians grew up in households of their mothers and maternal relatives, speaking Quechua and practicing cultural traits that, while colonial, bore the heavy stamp of indigenous tradition.[40] Thus many women of mestizo ancestry in late-sixteenth-century Potosí went about in habito de indias yet they were not labeled as such. Why was this label used if numerous mestizas were "vestidas de indias"? Further, no category existed for mestiza women who lived in Spanish dress. This was, apparently, considered a more normal occurrence—even though in some colonial cities like Potosí more mestizas probably lived in indigenous dress. This new category might have been useful for legal concerns related to inheritance and the legacy of a Spanish father. More generally, however, it appears to be an identity associated with differentiation in women's socioeconomic status as attained through trade.

The label reveals bureaucratic concern for fixing race and for determining who had Spanish blood and who did not. It also lays bare the impossibility of such a task. Where these women fit in colonial society could be confounding—especially for outside observers. Fray Diego confuses our understanding of mestiza identity when he comments, from his visit to Potosí, that the pallas are "*indias* of better faces because they are daughters of Spaniard and *India*." Ocaña's definition clearly suggests that pallas were mestizas. Further, by putting together his descriptions of women's dress with this definition of palla, he indicates these women were mestizas en habito de india. Yet the pallas or well-off women he saw in Potosí were typically understood to be of indigenous heritage. Further, in wills of 1570s the word "palla" continued to indicate someone with two indigenous parents, though not necessarily a noble.[41] Ocaña's mistake thus reminds us that ethnic identity was not obvious to observers, nor was it static during the period in question.

The clothing and sexual partners of these women may have been misleading to outside observers. Ocaña watched the pallas with their elegant and sumptuous manner of dress, their signs of elevated economic status, and their Spanish partners and misread these social and cultural cues as evidence of Spanish blood. During the republican period in the Andes, the ability of indigenous women to achieve higher economic status brought with it connotations about their use of sexual relationships to earn higher status and special clothes. Laura Gotkowitz contends that to nineteenth-century society, "The chola was an india in disguise, an india underneath the clothes one or many men procured for her."[42] Did Ocaña make similar assumptions in 1600? Did he assume a "mestiza is as mestiza does" because these women embodied an urban Indian identity that appeared distinct from rural ayllu Indians?

For women who earned the label "mestiza en habito de indias" in a legal document, the label held less meaning in their daily lives where cultural cues suggest they lived in an indigenous, if urban and colonial, fashion. The historical record of Juana Payco, a mestiza en habito de indias, provides a detailed case study. Born in sixteenth-century Potosí, Payco was a property owner in the city center. She lived down the street from the bustling San Agustín inn in the vicinity of the gato. Payco joined the cofradía of Nuestra Señora de la Soledad, a religious sodality based in the convent of Our Lady of Mercy, and spent three years, from 1624 to 1627, as the prioress of the cofradía. Her leading role in the cofradía mimicked a strong role in the urban economy. Not only did she own her home but she furnished the house in excess of the average trappings and left savings of 520 pesos in her will.[43] Payco was a model of urban women's ability to achieve material reward and leadership in the colonial era.

Despite having one Spanish parent, she lived in a culturally indigenous manner. Her possessions reveal that material culture operated as an important marker of ethnicity. In her home she had stores of corn and chuño. What she wore (and did not wear) had an impact on how society viewed her. At the time of her death, Payco had in her possession thirteen acsus, thirteen llicllas, eleven ñañacas, five chumbes, and five topos. In contrast to this stockpile of indigenous clothing, she had two Spanish skirts and three shirts.[44] Because Payco represented herself to others through indigenous dress, she suggested to outside observers that her primary location within colonial Potosí society was with the indigenous population. Interestingly, some of her clothing reflected the colonial mutations of indigenous dress which Ocaña had noted. One chumbe, for instance, was made of purple silk. The majority of Payco's llicllas and acsus, however, were made either of avasca (common) or cumbe (finely woven) wool, both typical Andean cloths noted in Quechua categories.

Finally, Payco's niche in the urban economy fits with the typical roles of indigenous women traders in Potosí. Several practices hint at a business selling clothing, a common practice. Payco's will reveals a warehousing of clothing and skeins of wool, from which she might have made or ordered special pieces of clothing. Moreover, she engaged in the practice of selling and lending in exchange for pawn items.[45] Juana Payco's choice to live in the habit of an indigenous woman, when she could have represented herself as a mestiza in Spanish clothes, was a strategic choice that allowed her to access important economic and social elements of Potosí's urban society.

*Conclusion*

Potosí was home to a vibrant urban economy in the sixteenth and seventeenth centuries. Spanish desires to exploit silver claims in the Cerro Rico fueled this market, but ultimately it served as an economic hub for men and women of Spanish, indigenous, African, and mestizo backgrounds. Of particular interest in the city's markets and stores are the indigenous and mestiza women who became predominant as agents for kurakas or Spanish storeowners, and later as individual vendors. These women's marketplace roles gave rise to new ethnic identities for Indians.

Given women's fundamental presence in the petty economy in the Andes today, the example of Potosí's female marketers helps us to explore how women came to hold these positions and how these activities of selling became linked to particular ethnic categories. Indigenous women were the first vendors of food, alcohol, coca, and textiles in Potosí. Spaniards learned quickly that they needed to work with these women as consumers *and* as entreprenuers. It was no coincidence that Spanish merchants who sought to do business in Potosí worked with indias.

Yet in this urban economy no single india experience existed. The labels from within the colonial marketplace reveal the distinct indigenous female experiences within the city and highlight the different degrees of Spanish concern over their economic activities. These labels also expose how the construction of identity was linked explicitly to gender. That these labels dealt not only with indigenous but also *female* subjects suggests how women experienced colonial change in distinct fashion. Women who moved away from the control of male relatives might experience a degree of economic, social, or cultural autonomy. This did not go unnoticed by Spanish officials who regulated indigenous women in the urban economy to a far greater degree than they ever regulated men of any background or Spanish women.[46]

Gradually these indias came to be known by new labels—labels that were constructs of Spaniards but prompted by the changing roles for women in the colonial economy. Spanish chroniclers and officials created a negative characterization of these market women. Rather than allow Spanish men to dominate, these women took aggressive tactics to earn profits. Because their practices often evolved despite town council regulations, they received more complaints at council meetings for violations of price regulations for everyday foods than did Spanish wholesale merchants who tried to get around taxation. These women used their positions to earn profits and created sites and practices in urban economy that resisted Spaniards. Their dress, always indigenous but tailored with European textiles as money allowed, identified them easily to Spaniards. Yet this dress and attendant cultural practices were critical to the women themselves as markers of a successful new urban identity for Indian women.

Herein I have argued that we should not take for granted terms like the "indias del gato" but rather explore the development of such labels as indicative of historical events and change in the sixteenth-century colonial Andean world. The labels signify how colonial ethnic identity incorporated occupation and economic status and, for women, the type of clothing they wore. As women created lives in new cities like Potosí their economic activities affected products and practices of urban trade; their social and sexual relationships with Indians or Spaniards gave rise to a generation of men and women with new identities of colonial Andeans, mestizos and "intra-indigenous mestizos," to borrow a phrase from Stuart Schwartz and Frank Salomon.[47] Markets and positions in the urban economy served as places for the creation and reinforcement of said categories. The actions of women marketers prompted Spaniards to label them carefully, yet markets and the exchanges and profits therein led indigenous women to form new ethnic categories. However many goods passed through the gato in colonial Potosí, the city's urban economy was equally significant as a marketplace of identities.

## Notes

1. Arzáns Orsúa y Vela, *Historia de la villa imperial de Potosí*, 149, citing Pedro Cieza de León. Translation mine.

2. Yanaconas were a special class among Andean peoples who drew their distinct identity from their position of serving the Inca king directly. By 1550, many yanacona worked for Spanish masters. The quote is from Arzáns, *Historia de la villa imperial de Potosí*, 149, citing Cieza de León.

3. Such characterizations are similar to those of *chola* marketwomen who dominated the cultural and economic landscape of the Andes in the late nineteenth and early twentieth centuries. Gotkowitz, "Trading Insults," 93.

4. For general characterizations of women's roles in urban economy I draw on my book *Trading Roles*.

5. The determination of racial and ethnic identity in colonial society was a subjective process in which phenotype, language, dress, and social networks all played roles. Moreover, numerous examples in Potosí's notary and judicial records show that identity was rarely fixed. For discussions of both of these issues for other cities and regions of Spanish America, see Kuznesof, "Ethnic and Gender Influences on 'Spanish' Creole Society in Colonial Spanish America"; Cahill, "Colour by Numbers"; Cope, *The Limits of Racial Domination*, and Seed, "The Social Dimensions of Race." For a general discussion of mestizaje in the colonies, see Mörner, *Race Mixture in the History of Latin America*.

6. Cahill, "Colour by Numbers."

7. For a description of early Potosí, see Escobari de Querejazu, "Conformación urbana y étnica en las ciudades de La Paz y Potosí durante la colonia."

8. On the role of indigenous women profiting from Cuzco-grown coca in this market, see Numhauser, *Mujeres indias y señores de la coca*.

9. Arzáns, *Historia de la villa imperial de Potosí*, 149, citing Cieza de León.

10. "Descripción de la villa y minas de Potosí," 373. On these market plazas, see also Arzáns, *Historia de la villa imperial*, 148–49.

11. Fray Reginaldo de Lizarraga, *Descripción breve de toda la tierra del Perú*, 89, 91.

12. Larson, *Colonialism and Agrarian Transformation in Bolivia, Cochabamba, 1550–1900*, 46.

13. Arzáns, *Historia de la villa imperial de Potosí*, 149.

14. On kurakas, see Murra, "Aymara Lords and their European Agents at Potosí," and Spalding, "Social Climbers."

15. Platt, " 'Without Deceit or Lies,' " 225–65.

16. Ibid., 236, 240.

17. "Sobre que los yndios que biben en esta villa para el beneficio y labor de las minas biben sanos," September 18, 1565, Archivo General de Indias (hereafter AGI) Charcas 32, f. 26v, extant folio 3v. On the same point, see Bakewell, *Miners of the Red Mountain*," 44; on Chucuito, 57.

18. Kellogg, "The Woman's Room."

19. Murra, "El control vertical de un máximo de pisos ecológicos en la economía de las sociedades andinas." On long-distance traders and pre-Hispanic markets in the northern Andes, see Ramírez, "Exchange and Markets in the Sixteenth Century," 140–42, and Salomon, *Native Lords of Quito in the Age of the Incas*, 97. Salomon draws on the work of Roswith Hartmann. See Hartmann, "Mercados y ferias prehispánicos en el area andina."

20. Arzáns, *Historia de la villa imperial de Potosí*, 149.

21. On market women in Seville, see Perry, *Gender and Disorder in Early Modern Seville*, 16–20.

22. Town council records and wills routinely referred to marketeers using the feminine, such as *yndias gateras*, *yndias fruteras*, or *yndias vendedoras de pan*. On street vendors elsewhere in Latin America, see Karasch, "Suppliers, Sellers, Servants and Slaves."

23. On the issue of nonpayment of alcabalas by indigenous traders, see the extensive analysis by Gauderman, *Women's Lives in Colonial Quito*, 92–116. See also Minchom, *The People of Quito*, 62–63, and "La economia subterranea y el mercado urbano," 175–86.

24. Will of Catalina Palla, India, September 3, 1572, Archivo Historico de Potosi—Casa Nacional de la Moneda, Escrituras Notariales (hereafter AHP-CNM.EN) 4, Martín de Barrientos, cuaderno #6, f. 31v. The collas were divided into urco (west) and uma (east). See also the example of the indigenous merchant Magdalena Guairo in carta de poder, Pedro Ochoa, AHP-CNM.EN 12, f. 242.

25. "*Asiento* Juan Ynaso y Juana Viscama su muger asentaron a servir a Francisco de Salazar de Mejía," December 17, 1577, AHP-CNM.EN 8, Luis de la Torre, f. 1469v.

26. See, for example, discussion of regatones in Guatemala in Lutz, *Santiago de Guatemala, 1541–1773*, 142, 148, 149. The term "regatones" is not gender specific, though in Potosí some documents use the feminine "regatonas."

27. Council report on *regatonas*, January 21, 1615, Archivo Nacional de Bolivia, Cabildo de Potosí, Libro de Actas (hereafter ANB.CPLA), vol. 14, f. 75. "Regatonas" translates to the English as "regrater" or "hawker," period terms for street vendors.

28. Town council records highlight concerns over the sale of fruits and vegetables, eggs, poultry and meat, bread, candles, and chicha. Among many examples, see Meeting on street sales of poultry and fish, May 17, 1594, ANB.CPLA, vol. 7, f. 285v; Excess and disorder by barley vendors, July 23, 1614, ANB.CPLA, vol. 14, f. 9; High prices blamed on regatonas of barley and yerba, January 21, 1615, ANB.CPLA, vol. 14, f. 75.

29. Viceroy don Fernando de Torres y Portugal conde del Villar to Captain Juan Ortiz de Zárate justicia mayor y visitador del Cerro, November 22, 1586, ANB.CPLA vol. 5, f. 309. On long-distance supply and high prices, see Wolff, *Regierung und Verwaltung der kolonialspanischen Städte in Hochperu*, 65–67.

30. Murra, "Aymara Lords and their European Agents at Potosí," 236.

31. Memoria contained in lawsuit between the convent of San Agustín and the convent of the Company of Jesus over the ownership of the goods left by the soltera Juana Payco, also called the Lunareja, mestiza en abitos de india, 1631–33, ANB.EC, document 1633.4, f. 36–36v.

32. See Ares Queija, "Mestizos en hábito de indios."

33. Minchom, *The People of Quito*, 63.

34. Powers, *Women in the Crucible of Conquest*, 77–78; 81.

35. Burns, "Gender and the Politics of Mestizaje."

36. Powers, *Women in the Crucible of Conquest*, 85–88, 89.

37. Schwartz and Salomon, "New Peoples and New Kinds of People," 482–83.

38. Ibid., 491.

39. Ocaña, *Un viaje fascinante*, 200.

40. Powers, *Women in the Crucible of Conquest*, 83

41. Will of Catalina Palla, India, September 3, 1572, "hija de Chuypollo mi madre y de Gualpa Coro mi padre," AHP-CNM.EN 4, Martín de Barrientos, cuaderno no. 6, f. 31v.

42. Gotkowitz, "Trading Insults," 102.

43. Petition of Pedro de Teves Talavera to retrieve bedspread and blouse, ANB.EC, document 1633.4, f. 67v.

44. The skirts (*faldellines*) are clearly female clothing; the shirts are identified only as *camissas*, so while they are likely women's shirts it is impossible to know for certain. ANB.EC, document 1633.4, f. 3v.

45. Petition of Pedro de Teves Talavera to retrieve bedspread and blouse, ANB.EC, document 1633.4, f. 67v. See also "Petition of Catalina Cussi to retrieve an acsu and lliclla" on f. 112 of same document.

46. See Mangan, *Trading Roles*, discussion of regulations in chaps. 2 and 3.

47. Schwartz and Salomon, "New Peoples and New Kinds of People," 463.

# Legally Indian

*Inquisitorial Readings of Indigenous Identity in New Spain*

In Spanish America, the colonial lexicon of what may be designated, using contemporary terms, as "race" or "ethnicity" was both ambivalent and highly diversified.[1] Both the primordial categories in colonial classification systems—*español*, *indio*, and *negro*—and the ensemble of identities resulting from mixed descent involving any of these categories were referred to as *castas* or "castes," a highly pliable word. As labels, "castas" indicated membership in collective identities based on terms that denoted biological descent—*sangre* (blood) and *origen* (origin)—reinforced by a particular *crianza* (upbringing) and rooted in one or more *lenguajes* (languages or dialects) and geographical localities with particular characteristics linked to *tierra* (land) and *clima* (climate). A broader reading of an individual's casta, which could index both putative ethnic category and perceived socioeconomic status, was indicated by terms like *naturaleza* or *calidad*. Even the more recurrent labels—such as *criollo*, *mestizo*, *castizo*, *mulato*, *lobo*, or *pardo*—defined by the three basic categories listed above refer to a number of traits whose capacity to define a category varied widely, according to the eye of the beholder and the context of the identification.[2] The constant deployment of these casta terms in institutional discourses, a subset of the broader definition of social hierarchies through descent that Irene Silverblatt has called "race thinking,"[3] could be designated as "casta identification."

Casta labels, thus, were based on a variety of early-modern discourses about nature, society, and language and referred to social identities that were negotiable under certain circumstances. When these labels were assigned to colonial subjects at baptism in parishes where this practice was common, they could be modified by design, customary practice, or accident. As shown by Patricia Seed's and R. Douglas Cope's quantitative studies, urban plebeians completed with relative ease transitions from one category recorded at birth to a different one recorded on marriage, census, or burial records. Furthermore, Ann Twinam has discussed legal mechanisms that allowed individuals of illegitimate birth or low ethnic status to claim membership in more socially advantageous categories.[4] In fact, upon noting the shifts triggered by marriage and social relations, Cope astutely noted that "a person's race might be described as a short-hand summation of his social network."[5]

This chapter will highlight the difficulties that colonial institutions faced in terms of their discursive and procedural practices when confronted by a protean landscape of social arrangements and cultural practices. Through an engagement with three case studies—a man with a disappearing hometown, a man with no known parents, and a woman whose casta self-adscription was refuted by local officials—I will discuss inquisitorial adjudications of casta identity for jurisdictional purposes and note the relation between individual economic and social survival strategies and public casta identification. I will also show how institutional casta identification seized on discrete traits that may be regarded as stereotypical—such as complexion, hair, linguistic competence, clothing items, or shoes—but yielded to a pragmatic consideration of these traits within a contextualized interpretation of both identity claims and socio-cultural practices. Moreover, the extent to which contingency played a role in casta identifications will be highlighted here: in these cases, plebeian self-identification seemed to hinge on who was doing the asking, and why.

Although casta identification was undoubtedly a highly pragmatic process that relied on beliefs and practices that may not be directly reflected by the historical record, I wish to underline three identification processes that remain accessible to us. The first—visual and contextual readings of ethnic identity—was certainly the currency of the realm, as it was the most widespread process, involving both well-formed and contingent subjectivities. Such readings were as anecdotal as a quick reading of someone's face, skin color, and clothing in a crowded street,[6] but they could inform substantial decisions, such as a parish priest's visual corroboration of the casta label claimed during baptism, marriage, or death.

A second one—institutional readings and adjudications of ethnic identity, particularly within legal proceedings—is perhaps the best understood process, and it lends itself to comparative analyses that employ quantitative tools: such institutional adjudications have produced records that suggest a permeability between categories—Indian and mestizo, or African and mulatto—and indicate trends in endogamy that vary by ethnic group.[7] The third one—individual strategies that sought to embrace or elude a particular casta identification—was perhaps the most complex, unyielding, and unpredictable of these three phenomena.[8] This chapter contains a heuristic account of how these three processes intersected each other in seventeenth-century central Mexico. It should be noted that these processes should not be confused with the empirical correlates of identity they deployed: in other words, these discourses sought to uphold or contest a legal construction of identity that was quite separate from any local or contextual ways of determining colonial identities.

## Bigamy and Plebeian Life Trajectories: Francisco Rojas and Francisco Hernández

The two cases this section addresses have been mentioned or summarized by two other scholars,[9] but they have never been the subject of a substantial comparison. Since these cases are quite similar structurally and involve the imprisonment of the defendants—as well as inquiries into their identity—during the same period in 1610, a comparative glance at these proceedings will shed light on both procedural issues and the social meanings of the default casta category these defendants occupied and then contested. In both cases, these individuals traversed the permeable line between Indian and mestizo—canonically defined as the descendant of a Spaniard and an Indian. As was the case with many bigamists in New Spain, the status of these two defendants as migrants was a factor in their establishment of bigamous relations; as Richard Boyer has observed, their life paths displayed the disparities "between society's labels and life."[10] The trajectories of Francisco Rojas and Francisco Hernández reflect marriage calculations made at different life stages; while Rojas deserted his first wife in his early twenties after a five-year cohabitation and married a socially prominent native woman, Hernández wedded his second wife twenty years after his first marriage, as he approached the age of forty, and only after a seemingly plausible notification of his first wife's death. On the other hand, these two cases present one crucial similarity: they exemplify the various itinerant possibilities that may have followed after a young man with weak family links left his town of origin to seek a means of subsistence elsewhere. These divergences and similarities can be better understood through a comparative glance at the lives of Rojas and Hernández.

According to his own testimony, Francisco Rojas was born circa 1582 in the *sujeto* of Guayangáreo, located near Pátzcuaro in the province of Michoacán, left his hometown around age thirteen, and claimed to be twenty-eight years old when he was interrogated by the inquisitors in February 1610. Hernández's first wife, an indigenous woman called María Mónica who was born in San Juan Teotihuacan, testified having met Rojas when he was reputed to be an itinerant mestizo. She married him at the Mines of Xichú in 1597; at this time, this region—located about seventeen leagues to the northeast of the city of Querétaro—was a multi-ethnic enclave where newly established mining camps had begun to attract an influx of Spanish, Otomis, Nahuas, and people of various castas.[11] The newlyweds lived together in three different locations within a five-year span, before entering the service of Luis de Soto Cabeçón, *encomendero* of Tezcatepec, a town located a few leagues west of Tula.[12] María Mónica's brief account of her married life with Rojas summarizes in a deceivingly flat and unemotional tone the uncertainty that plagued a young, uprooted plebeian couple: "After [their] marriage took place, they lived for two years in the said mines of Xichú, living in public as husband and wife . . . and then they moved as a couple to the mines of Pachuca, where they lived for one year, and then they came to live at a sujeto of this town of Tezcatepec, and they remained there for a few days, and then they moved into the estate of Luis de Soto Cabeçón. Having borne to the said Francisco Rojas a daughter called Juana—who is still alive and is eight years old now—he [Rojas] ran away and deserted them, and she had no tidings about him until she was told he lived near Tulancingo and had married an Indian noblewoman [*yndia principala*] there."[13] Family ties appear to have been a weak element in the life of Rojas and his first wife; thirteen years after her marriage to Rojas, María Mónica did not know whether her own parents—who served as witnesses at her wedding— were alive or dead. On the other hand, Rojas's marriage witnesses were the Spanish man in whose household the couple worked as servants and another fellow servant, rather than family members. Even after five years of marriage, Rojas's first wife believed he had been born south of Mexico City in Coyoacán, rather than in Michoacán.

After leaving his first wife to fend for herself with a newborn child circa 1602, Rojas surfaced eighteen leagues east of his former residence at Tezcatepec in Xaltepec, a town near the district head town of Tulancingo, where he married Doña Clara Xocoiotl in 1604. Undoubtedly, Doña Clara could be regarded as a more desirable marriage partner than Rojas's first wife from a social and economic standpoint; her father had been the *alcalde* (one of two indigenous mayors in the local town council) of Xaltepec, and the use of the honorific "Don" and "Doña" by members of her family suggests they were still regarded as leading citizens in the Tulancingo region. Rojas's in-laws did not appear to dwell on his origin or ethnicity; his mother-in-law believed him to be a mestizo from Coyoacán and voiced no complaints about him. It is only through the testimony of a resident of Tulancingo, who identified Rojas as a previously married man after hearing rumors about his first wife at the household of the encomendero who employed her, that Rojas's new life as the husband of a socially prominent Indian woman was thwarted by an inquisitorial inquiry six years after his second wedding.[14]

Unlike Rojas, Francisco Hernández did not derive social dividends from his second marriage. Hernández declared himself to be "under age forty" in 1610, which would place his birth in the early 1570s. According to his own testimony and that of his first master, he began serving Baltazar Hernández, a native of the island of Terceira in the Azores, at the tender age of ten in Tecamachalco, a town a dozen leagues to the southwest of Puebla. Since Baltazar Hernández was an *escudero* (equerry) in the service of Rodrigo de Vivero the Younger—the son of Tecamachalco's second encomendero [15]—in the 1580s he and Francisco followed Vivero from Tecamachalco to his two separate appointments as *alcalde mayor*— one in Cholula, and the second one in Pátzcuaro. In fact, Baltazar was regarded as an adoptive father of sorts by Francisco, who began to use his master's last name as his own and who later would identify himself as the son of a "Portuguese man" when an employer inquired about his family. It was in Pátzcuaro that Francisco Hernández, circa 1588, married a Phurépecha woman known both as Matachi and as Magdalena, who was a servant of the wife of Spanish merchant Juan Gómez de Tagli.[16] At some point under the employ of Gómez, Hernández's public identity was given a permanent mark: for reasons not addressed in his trial records, a man scarred the left side of his face with a knife during a fight. No account exists of his activities in the last decade of the sixteenth century. Around 1603, he surfaced without his first wife at an *obraje* (workshop) in the city of Puebla, where he worked as a wool carder to the entire satisfaction of Lope de Carrera, the enterprise's owner.[17]

It is hard to ascertain whether Hernández simply deserted his first wife, as Rojas clearly did; for a number of years, Hernández repeatedly begged Carrera "for the love of God" to allow him to bring his wife from Michoacán, or to send someone to bring her. Nevertheless, given the distance, the decision to bring her was postponed, and Carrera eventually heard tidings about her death in May 1608 from a "mestizo" who identified himself as Hernández's brother. Only three months later, Hernández claimed that his wife had been dead for about a year and married an Indian woman called María Isabel. As in Rojas's case, hearsay would reveal evidence of Hernández's first union. Only two months after Hernández's second marriage, a Spaniard reported to the Holy Office that his first wife was still among the living, and an inquiry into the matter began. In what can only be seen as a coincidence, the Holy Office soon learned that Hernández's first wife had indeed passed away—not in 1607 or 1608, but at a hospital in Pátzcuaro on a December day in 1609.[18]

*Casta Identification and Institutional Readings*

Judging from the legal inquiries that preceded the arrest of Rojas and Hernández by the Inquisition, a visual and contextual consensus coalesced in terms of their public casta identification: both were identified as mestizos, either without qualifications or with the addition of the hedge "It is said he is mestizo." The only notable exception in this pattern is the registry itself of Hernández's second marriage, which identifies him unambiguously as an "Indian from Tecamachalco." In spite of this record —which may reflect Hernández's self-adscription of casta identity—his own employer identified him as a "mestizo" on the basis of his "appearance, and since he is so fluent in Castilian." Nevertheless, in February 1610, first Rojas and then Hernández were able to redirect the tide of bigamy accusations that had been collected against them by claiming, as soon as they were ushered in to be questioned by the inquisitors, that they were Indians rather than mestizos, and that their newly reaffirmed casta identity prevented them from falling under the redoubtable jurisdiction of the Holy Office.

Rojas's and Hernández's expedient claims rested on a relatively recent change in jurisdiction. Between the 1520s and 1571, the investigation of crimes against the Christian faith committed by members of any casta, including Indians, fell under inquisitorial jurisdiction, which was represented in New Spain by either an appointed inquisitorial judge called "apostolic inquisitor" or a specially appointed commissioner. In several cases, members of the regular orders in isolated regions exercised faculties very similar to those of an inquisitor, claiming the precedent of a papal bull issued in 1522 that granted them episcopal faculties if they resided beyond a two-day journey from the nearest bishop's seat. After the formal establishment of separate inquisitorial tribunals in Mexico City and Lima in 1571, the investigation of faith crimes by Indians—which included bigamy, failure to pay tithes, idolatry, and superstition, among other common transgressions—was transferred from the inquisitorial to the episcopal jurisdiction, which presided over ecclesiastical tribunals whose staffing and structure varied from one diocese to another.[19] To complicate matters, civil judges claimed jurisdiction over natives accused of sorcery and idolatry both before and after 1571, and in certain dioceses such as Oaxaca bishops allowed alcaldes mayores to assist them by staging civil trials against idolaters.[20]

Therefore, Rojas's and Hernández's claims forced the inquisitors to begin a set of inquiries whose objective no longer was to establish whether bigamy had been committed but to adjudicate the defendants' casta identification. In order to determine the truthfulness of the defendants' claims, the inquisitors sent instructions to their agents located in the defendants' towns of origin, so that testimony from neighbors and relatives with knowledge of their genealogy and casta identification could be entered into the legal record. The preponderance of documentary proof—in baptismal, marriage, or burial records—complemented by testimony offered by the defendants' neighbors and acquaintances served as the most common inquisitorial strategy to adjudicate the ethnic identity of defendants.[21]

However, as it occurred in both Rojas's and Hernández's cases, this strategy faltered when the visual and contextual criteria for calling someone a mestizo was corroborated neither by parish records nor by the testimony of casta identification witnesses. Thus, when Rojas declared himself a son of "Juan Martín and his wife Catalina, both *yndios naturales* (Indians born or raised in) the Phurépecha town of Guayangáreo in Michoacán,[22] he offered several details to assist in the corroboration of this claim: he mentioned the name of two town residents who, if found, may corroborate his claim, and identified a Spaniard named Márquez as the man who raised him after his parents died, leaving him an orphan at an early age. Rojas's contention was met with great skepticism by Don Diego de Orduña, Holy Office commissary in Valladolid, who noted that most of the residents of a town he calls Guayangáreo in his correspondence—which used to have about sixty households—are now dead, and that not one current resident, or even the Franciscans at a nearby convent, had heard about the two residents or the Spaniard substitute father cited by Rojas, which forced Orduña to conclude that "it is impossible for me to inquire into anything." [23] In spite of Orduña's assertion, an episcopal report from Valladolid indicates that by 1619 twenty household heads resided in a locality by the name of Guayangáreo, which suggests either a confusion about the locality's name or its sudden repopulation during the second decade of the seventeenth century.[24]

In any case, Orduña's testimony left the inquisitors in possession of few adjudication elements. The original certificate of Rojas's first marriage—a copy of which was submitted by a priest at the Mines of Xichú—listed him as a "native of Coyoacán" without specifying ethnicity, suggesting a default adscription as "Indian"; however, there is a clear contradiction between this claim and Rojas's later claim of being a native of Guayangáreo.[25] The two witnesses who had more detailed knowledge of Rojas's provenance—his first wife and the mother of his second wife—regarded him, puzzlingly, as a "native of Coyoacán" who may or may not have been a mestizo. On the other hand, any attempts to investigate Rojas's statements about his parents seemed futile, since no one alive was able to corroborate or disprove his claims in Guayangáreo. Notably, the inquisitors cut this Gordian knot with a pragmatic decision that combined both a relinquishment of their jurisdiction and a de facto finding of bigamy; only four months after beginning their inquiries, Rojas was released from custody "for being an Indian" and admonished not to return to his second wife, lest he be punished with excommunication and two hundred lashes.

Hernández's case also features several systematic but futile attempts to find witnesses who may have had a memory about the early years of an uprooted plebeian. In February 1610, Hernández claimed during his first interrogation that he was the son of Gaspar del Castillo, a prominent indigenous resident of Tecamachalco, gave precise details about the location of Castillo's house and about his neighbors, and suggested the names of some witnesses that could confirm his statements. The first of these witnesses remembered Castillo but did not know whether he was Hernández's father. The second witness—a former African slave called Juan de Murcia—confirmed some key points of Hernández's story, such as his service under Vivero's Portuguese equerry, and lent a rather subjective tone to the proceedings by recalling an earlier encounter with Hernández at the prison in Puebla, where he recognized his boyhood acquaintance in spite of the knife scar that now marred his face. Murcia could not attest to the identity of Hernández's father: although he confirmed that the defendant had told him twenty-three years earlier that Castillo was his father, he never witnessed them behaving as father and son in public. Furthermore, a publicly acknowledged son of Castillo—the Tecamachalco native nobleman Don Felipe del Castillo—denied any knowledge of Hernández and repeatedly refuted Hernández's claims of having being sired by his own father.

The inquisitors' last resort turned out to be the only parental figure Hernández had ever had: his former master, the Portuguese Baltazar Hernández. Baltazar, who was sixty-four years old in 1610 and a resident of Cuauhtitlan—a town located about five miles to the north of Mexico City—confirmed having taken Hernández into his service as a young boy and bestowed his own last name upon him. Moreover, he directly acknowledged the futility of establishing the genealogy of an itinerant, uprooted plebeian in colonial Mexico. When asked if he knew of any person who could have any information about the identity of Hernández's parents, Baltazar answered that no one could possibly have an answer for such a question, for even he, who had been Francisco's master and surrogate father from a very early age, did not know the answer, and "he believes it rather difficult that some one else may, since this affair belongs in the distant past."[26] Therefore, although witnesses corroborated the main points in Hernández's account about his early years—and while he could not be publicly regarded as a legitimate son of the man he identified as his father, according to the witnesses who came forward—the inquisitors failed to produce any strong oral or documentary evidence to confirm or disprove Hernández's genealogical claims. The inquisitors resolved this procedural cul-de-sac in a manner similar to their handling of Rojas's impasse: four and a half months after Hernández's first interrogation, they freed him after instructing him not to return to his second wife, upon pain of two hundred lashes.

### Private Indian, Public Mulatta: The Case of Nicolasa Juana

A third case features quite a different dynamic of public casta identification: the attempts by Nicolasa Juana, a woman married to an Indian man, to be regarded as Indian against the testimony of the local officials in her hometown. As in the previous two cases, the adjudication process was triggered by suspicions of a crime against the faith—in this case, idolatry. The driving force behind Nicolasa Juana's trial was Diego Xaimes Ricardo Villavicencio, author of the most widely circulated idolatry extirpation manual printed in New Spain—*Luz y methodo de confesar idolatras* (Guide and Method for Confessing Idolaters), printed in 1692.[27] Villavicencio was a curate and ecclesiastical judge fluent in Mazatec and Chocho who made idolatry extirpation a priority in the two parishes he occupied— Teotitlán del Camino, a Mazatec-speaking parish in the diocese of Oaxaca in the 1670s and 1680s, and Santa Cruz Tlacotepec, a Chocho-speaking parish in the diocese of Tlaxcala, sixteen leagues to the southeast of Puebla, starting in 1688.[28]

In August 1688, as he investigated the ritual activities of Diego Hernández, an elder Chocho ritual specialist, Villavicencio learned that one of Hernández's main clients was Nicolasa Juana, a woman publicly identified as a mulatta, about thirty-nine years old, who had married Juan Mateo, a Chocho Indian, and had borne him two children, Pedro Hernández and Pascuala María. In order to prevent Nicolasa from fleeing, Villavicencio had her incarcerated in the Tlacotepec jail in September 1688. A special commission against idolatry that the bishop of Tlaxcala granted Villavicencio allowed him to try natives, but he had no jurisdiction over a nonindigenous woman reputed to be a mulatta, since the Holy Office had not given him a permanent inquisitorial commission. Therefore, his report on Nicolasa Juana's activities to the Holy Office agents in Puebla yielded a commission to investigate the ceremonies that Hernández performed on Nicolasa's behalf. This procedural solution was repeated in 1689, when Villavicencio began investigating the ritual practices of a couple identified as mestizo; in order to preserve inquisitorial jurisdiction, Villavicencio was granted a commission to record his interrogation of these suspects.[29] According to a native specialist, Nicolasa and this mestizo couple were actively engaged in unorthodox ritual practices. They possessed their own effigies and ritual implements and some basic notions of Chochon-Popoloca ritual practices. What they lacked was specialized knowledge of ritual practices and appropriate incantations, which were provided them by a series of local specialists they hired at various times.

In December 1688, Villavicencio rendered explicit his visual and contextual identification of Nicolasa's casta to the Holy Office by noting that she was "a white mulata with curly hair, because she is the daughter of a dark-skinned mulata and a Spaniard, and for her manner of dress she has flannel petticoats and a native blouse [huipil], sometimes silken, sometimes woolen. She wears shoes, and her natural and common language is not Spanish, but Chocho, as she was brought up among Indians with her mother, from which she contracted the vice of drunkenness, to which she often succumbs, as Indians do, and from them she has also received the crime of [idolatry]."[30] However, four months after having been imprisoned by Villavicencio, the illiterate Nicolasa had an unnamed scribe draft a petition in which she disputed the judge's identification by insisting on two points: first, she asserted she was a "legitimate and natural Indian on all parentage lines," gave the names of her parents—Lucas Hernández, deceased, and Gerónima María—and grandparents—Sisilia María and Joseph Juan; second, she asked to be placed under detention by payment of a bail (depósito) at a local residence, since her public reputation as a married woman was imperiled by continuous imprisonment. As a result, the Holy Office in Puebla instructed Villavicencio to record the testimony of local residents regarding Nicolasa's "casta and naturaleza."

It was at this point that three influential men in Tlacotepec with facility in both Chocho and Spanish—principal and cacique Don Bernabé de Luna, principal Nicolás Bautista, and Villavicencio's very own court interpreter, Don Luis Cortés de las Nieves—stepped forward to deny that Nicolasa could be regarded in public as an Indian in the town of Tlacotepec. The first point in their argument echoed Villavicencio's visual identification—the interpreter confirmed that Nicolasa wore "flannel petticoats, a scarlet blouse, and shoes, and it cannot be denied she is a mulata, since she has very wavy hair, and is light-skinned."[31] Second, Luna revealed that some residents of Tlacotepec obtained an order to banish Gerónima, Nicolasa's mother, from the town, as she was a troublesome mulatta, and since crown regulations forbade non-Indians to live in *pueblos de indios*—in fact, Gerónima was forced to move to nearby Tehuacan. Third, all witnesses noted that Nicolasa's father was regarded as a mestizo, and that as such he was allowed to bear a sword, a dagger, and an arquebus.[32] Fourth, the interpreter noted that Nicolasa was addressed and recognized publicly as a mulatta in Tlacotepec. The striking similarities among these three testimonies, which were all recorded on the same day, suggests that these officials shared the intention of calling into question Nicolasa's claim. Enmity or resentment toward Nicolasa and her family appear as distinct possibilities: her own mother was forced into exile by some residents of Tlacotepec, one of her maternal uncles was later murdered in Tehuacan under unspecified circumstances, and the *fiscal mayor* of Tlacotepec—an official who supervised the participation of local residents in Christian observances—took a leading role in confirming Nicolasa's engagement in Chocho ritual practices.

Regardless of her parents' casta identification, Nicolasa seems to have built strong family ties with some of the indigenous residents of Tlacotepec. There is some evidence that, on occasion, residents of an indigenous community could shift between an indigenous and a mestizo public identity as a response to expedient concerns.[33] However, it should be noted that, despite the expediency of her claims, Nicolasa's life was firmly rooted in a domestic indigenous household. In 1667, she married a widower—Juan Matheo, a Chocho Indian—becoming stepmother to at least one of his sons and bearing him at least two more children. In passing, it should be noted that her casta identification was not entered into her marriage certificate—only her age and marital status were recorded.[34] Even ritual practices seemed to belong within Nicolasa's family sphere: the ritual specialist whom Nicolasa had hired was in fact her husband's brother-in-law; her own eight-year-old daughter served as an assistant; and Nicolasa used two cult effigies she had inherited from her own mother, a woman regarded by the town as a mulatta. Given that her first and only language was Chocho, even Villavicencio's visual reckoning of

Nicolasa's ethnicity contrasted with her deep social and cultural integration within an indigenous extended family in Tlacotepec.

In the end, if Nicolasa's ethnic identity was indeed a summation of her social network, the testimony about this network painted a fragmented portrait. On the one hand, Nicolasa's familial sphere seemed congruent with that of a Chocho Indian, while public perceptions—even if driven by enmity—were based on commonly accepted visual criteria, and on strong counterclaims regarding the casta identification of Nicolasa's parents. Faced with this quandary, the inquisitors issued an eminently pragmatic decision": "[The defendants'] crianza, lenguaje, and other items relating to the calidad and lenguaje they had and do have are solely and purely those of Indians; we refer to Nicolasa, wife of Mateo, Indian, and their two sons. Since they possess little fluency in Spanish [bozalidad] and employ exclusively the Chocho Indian language, it seems that the Holy Office is not capable of holding a trial against them, even if in some regard they may have blood that is not of an Indian; in consequence, [the inquisitors] did and do declare that the inquiry into the crimes of idolatry for which testimony exists, along with their punishment and censure, must belong to the ordinary ecclesiastical judge of Indians in the bishopric of Puebla."[35] This decision, it should be noted, did not hinge on linguistic expediency.[36] While the inquisitors ruled that, "in some regard," a primeval form of classification by descent based on sangre (blood) could have been used to adjudicate Nicolasa's identity, their words drew a clear distinction between sangre and three other terms that indexed social and cultural traits— crianza (upbringing), calidad (social condition), and lenguaje (language). This legal decision, in fact, introduces a turn toward a more relativistic form of ethnic classification whose implications are discussed below.

### Conclusions: Indigenous Identity and Subjecthood

What made a colonial subject an Indian, from a legal standpoint? Why would a colonial subject insist on being regarded as an Indian? These three cases suggest that one potential answer is that the adjudication of one's identity as an Indian always implied what could be termed "double subjecthood"—the acknowledgment that an Indian was both a colonial subject and a member of a rigidly defined legal construct; thus, an Indian was twice a person and twice a legal entity. This may be seen as a more precise formulation of Fredrik Barth's well-known assertion that, among subaltern populations, ethnic identity should be seen as an "imperative," or necessary condition; in other words, institutional practices emphasized the ethnicity of subaltern colonial subjects as a primary marker of identity, rather than class, gender, or occupation.[37] It is no mystery that Rojas, Hernández, and Nicolasa of Tlacotepec wanted to avoid being tried by the Holy Office;[38] nevertheless, it is plausible that had none of them been accused of a crime against the faith, they would not have had any reason to make a public or legal pronouncement that clarified their casta identification in their towns of residence. In any case, all three defendants successfully moved from one form of subjecthood to a more restrictive and peculiar one: that of having their casta identification adjudicated by the Holy Office, which regarded them as Indians.

Although one may use "ethnic passing" or "racial variability" to describe the colonial cases discussed here, it is difficult to argue that a single mimetic gesture captures the ethnic and social identity of these three colonial subjects. During most of their adult lives, all three of them inhabited a public casta identification that was seldom defined as a discrete category. Moreover, both Rojas and Hernández, as plebeian migrants with uncertain parentage and places of origin, inhabited a social world in which constant interactions between Indians and non-Indians meant that daily survival was not directly tied to one's public casta identification. If this was a species of "passing," then one must clearly separate this process in a colonial context from contemporary instances of ethnic "passing," in which individuals perceive their responses to external casta identification as a direct expression of inner subjectivities and pursue systematically a particular form of ethnic identification.[39] This is not to suggest that the defendants in these cases lacked subjectivities—they possessed them in the form of memories about their birthplace, families, and parental figures—but, in the absence of an inquisitorial inquiry, these subjects' naturaleza and calidad were more closely linked to patterns of marriage and socialization.

Rojas and Hernández possessed an unverifiable familial and social context of origin; their claims to public casta identification rested solely on their own recollections, which proved extremely difficult to corroborate or disprove. This is why we still lack—as the inquisitors did—a decisive empirical purchase on the identity of these two subjects: we truly cannot—and should not—adjudicate in our thoughts whether these two enigmatic men were mestizos who successfully passed as Indians, or Indians who unwittingly passed as mestizos. For Rojas and Hernández, the label "mestizo" did not designate a concrete ethnic category but an externally driven shorthand for a highly pliable category: that of the migrant plebeian whose lineage and place of origin consisted of a few fleeting personal remembrances. On the other hand, Nicolasa's case suggests a higher degree of intentionality: as a resident of Tlacotepec with kinship ties to a traditional ritual specialist, she appeared willing to engage in clandestine ritual practices that were tied to the Chocho ritual calendar and to Chocho life cycle observances. Although reports about her physical appearance suggest that she may have had a parent or grandparent who would not have easily passed as an Indian outside their place of residence, her private, familial claims to identity trumped her public casta identification by influential members of her community.

Some contemporary cases that result from the conflict in legal competences between autonomous indigenous municipalities and constitutional law in Latin American nation-states bear a strong resemblance to the colonial dynamic of indigenous double subjecthood. For example, in 1996, the indigenous political activist Francisco Gembuel—a former president of the Indigenous Regional Council of Cauca (CRIC)—was convicted of being an accomplice in the murder of the mayor of Jambaló, a Nasa village in southwestern Colombia, and sentenced to receive sixty lashes. Gembuel appealed to a lower court, which found that his constitutional rights had been violated. However, Colombia's Constitutional Court, citing Gembuel's residence and political career, decreed that he was "a person with all the status and qualities of a [Nasa] Indian, and in consequence . . . the former should accept and obey" the jurisdiction of Jambaló's authorities, which had issued a sentence based on *usos y costumbres* (usage and customs) guaranteed to indigenous municipalities by the Colombian constitution of 1991. Although this adjudication of ethnic identity has an inclusive rather than exclusive jurisdictional effect, its motivation and dynamics mirror the three cases discussed here: in adjudicating the indigenous component of a Colombian citizen's split personhood, Colombia's constitutional court was in fact mimicking the procedural steps of Mexico's Holy Office.[40]

It may be striking for contemporary observers to regard the Mexican

Inquisition as an institution with the capacity to limit its own jurisdictional procedures in a way that almost appears to be self-reflective. However, a necessary corrective to this initial impression must emphasize two points that contextualize the apparent flexibility of the Mexican inquisitors within their own bureaucratic practices. First, it bears noting that the number of cases in New Spain during which inquisitorial adjudications of casta become a central procedural issue is quite limited—about a dozen or less known cases in my reckoning.[41] This fact suggests that challenging one's legal casta identification was a strategy that was neither pursued successfully by a large number of defendants nor questioned by inquisitors as a common maneuver to escape from prosecution.

Second, in all of these three cases, both inquisitors and their commissioners scrupulously followed established procedures for collecting testimony about a subject's public identity and were in full control of both the evidence and the conceptual assertions that rendered it coherent as a legal construct. As noted by Henry Kamen, the men behind inquisitorial procedures were a group of elite bureaucrats who excelled at following established procedure and collecting testimony—including the screams of those subjected to juridical torture.[42] Such exercises took social constructions of identity and transformed them into legal assertions in the courtroom through the application of bureaucratic procedure. In turn, inquisitors were the most powerful members in a group of colonial subjects subdued by the logic of procedure and were hostages to it. This is why the adjudication of Rojas's, Hernández's, and Nicolasa's public identity as indigenous is not a direct institutional acknowledgment of their ability to define themselves but a logical corollary to bureaucratic thinking. Since their arguments could not be contradicted by testimony procedurally determined to be credible, they gained salience by default and were subject to further juridical review, as hinted by the inquisitors' admonition to the two bigamists to relinquish their second marriages and return to the monogamous model, on pain of becoming once again a prosecutorial target.

Thus, these cases suggest that the Holy Office was prepared to issue—on a case-by-case basis—a de facto recognition that, as a result of the intermarriage of Indians with castas in both pueblos de indios and urban or work settings, their offspring were quickly acculturated into the predominant social and linguistic norms of their community of residence.[43]

In such cases, the institutional understanding of sangre—an early modern notion of biological descent expressed through the language of kinship—was modified by the contextual use of lenguaje and calidad and allowed to reflect a default reading proposed by the colonial subject under scrutiny. This is not to say that the Inquisition employed a full-fledged sociocultural definition of identity *avant la lettre*. As Irene Silverblatt has argued, the Holy Office embraced the momentous task of passing judgment on "the nature of human personhood" through a set of practices that were highly rationalized and bureaucratized, perhaps to an extent that may call to mind the workings of modern institutions.[44] In the three cases discussed here, the traits that colonial subjects frequently used as yardsticks for determining ethnic identity in the fluid social world of central Mexican cities, mining camps, and obrajes gave way to what amounted to a tentative institutional recognition of the complex nature of colonial identities. In these three fleeting moments, both institutions and colonial subjects converged in their acknowledgment of the complex social and cultural practices that were both concealed and rendered manageable by the discourse of casta identities.

## Notes

1. In this chapter, instead of "race"—a term with a checkered history in terms of its rhetorical use and the popular assumptions it awakens—the term "ethnicity" will be employed to refer to contemporary notions of differentiation based on descent criteria, and "caste" will be used to refer to colonial categories that may coincide with—but also differ from—contemporary notions of ethnic identity. This is not to say that ethnicity itself is an impartial designation; its use here simply highlights a distinction between colonial and contemporary lexicons of difference. For a poignant critique of race as an analytical category, see Loveman, "Is 'Race' Essential?"

2. For four influential summaries, see Aguirre Beltrán, *La población negra de México*; García Martínez, *Los pueblos de la Sierra de Puebla*; Israel, *Race, Class and Politics in Colonial Mexico*; Mörner, *La corona española y los foráneos en los pueblos de indios de América*.

3. Irene Silverblatt's innovative reading of inquisitorial practices in colonial Peru (*Modern Inquisitions*, 17–18) uses the term "race thinking" to denote "any mode of construing and engaging social hierarchies through the lens of descent." Given the broad scope of this definition, casta identification would refer to a more circumscribed set of practices that resulted in the public adjudication of casta identity to a colonial subject.

4. See Cope, *The Limits of Racial Domination*; Seed, "Social Dimensions of Race"; Seed and Rust, "Estate and Class in Colonial Oaxaca"; Twinam, *Public Lives, Private Secrets*; and chapter 7 in this volume.

5. Cope, *The Limits of Racial Domination*, 83.

6. Hasty contextual readings could carry immediate legal consequences. For example, a woman who denounced herself in 1713 for using the services of Micaela, a healer from Toluca, described her after one meeting as having the "face and appearance of a Spanish woman, since she is white" and contrasted this swift visual reading with the fact that Micaela wears "Indian dress" (Archivo General de la Nación (hereafter AGN) Inquisición 753, 624r—627v). Henceforth, the inquisitors refer to Micaela—whom they did not necessarily arrest or investigate—as a woman "said to be Spaniard, who wears Indian dress."

7. Cope, *The Limits of Racial Domination*, 82–83.

8. Beyond the inquisitorial context analyzed in this essay, self-identification strategies varied considerably. See Althouse, "Contested Mestizos, Alleged Mulattos," for a recent study that examines self-identification dynamics employed in early-eighteenth-century Pátzcuaro in western Mexico by men suspected of being mulatto who claimed to be mestizo in order to embrace a more desirable public identity.

9. Richard Greenleaf cites Rojas's case in his bibliographical essay "The Mexican Inquisition and the Indians." Cope cites Francisco Hernández's case to illustrate his observation that those plebeians without strong links to their parents often received second names only after marriage or through association with their masters; Cope, *The Limits of Racial Domination*, 59.

10. Boyer, *Lives of the Bigamists*, 55, 156.

11. Gerhard, *A Guide to the Historical Geography of New Spain*, 233. For a broad discussion of settlements and sociopolitical dynamics in Xichú de Indios, see Lara Cisneros, *El cristianismo en el espejo indígena*, 61–92.

12. The original Tezcatepec *encomienda* had been granted to Francisco de Estrada, who managed to transfer it in the 1540s to Cristóbal Cabeçón—see Gerhard, *A Guide to the Historical Geography of New Spain*, 297. Luis de Soto Cabeçón was in all likelihood Cristóbal's son.

13. AGN Inquisición 287, no. 8, pp. 42–43. Some of the AGN Inquisición cases cited in this essay do not have numbered folios, so the author has provided page numbers, counting from the title page forward.

14. Ibid., pp. 11–12.

15. The Tecamachalco encomienda was originally granted by Cortés to his secretary, Alonso Valiente; in the early 1560s Melchora Pellicel Aberrucia, Valiente's widow, married Rodrigo de Vivero the Elder; see Gerhard, *A Guide to the Historical Geography of New Spain*, 278.

16. In fact, Tagli's wife asserts in 1610 that Francisco "stole said Indian woman from me, taking her to Tzipimeo, where he married her" (AGN Inquisición 287, no. 7, p. 81). Gaspar Tzitziqui and Cristina López, "Indians from the Cheuén barrio," served as the couples' godparents.

17. AGN Inquisición 287, no. 7, p. 108. In New Spain, obrajes were labor-intensive workshops specializing in a particular product that were usually administered by Span-

ish or creole owners. Itinerant laborers could receive a salary by working at an obraje, and the labor of convicts sentenced to work at an obraje could be sold to the highest bidder.

18. Ibid., p. 79.

19. This bull was known as *Exponi nobis* in Latin and *Omnímoda* in Spanish. For synoptic discussions of these procedural issues, see Greenleaf, "The Inquisition and the Indians of New Spain," *The Mexican Inquisition of the Sixteenth Century, Inquisición y sociedad en el México colonial*, "Historiography of the Mexican Inquisition"; Moreno de los Arcos, "New Spain's Inquisition for Indians from the Sixteenth to the Nineteenth Century"; Viqueira, "Una fuente olvidada."

20. See Tavárez, "La idolatría letrada," "Idolatry as an Ontological Question."

21. That was the procedure followed in the cases that Cope notes in his work—Francisco Cano Moctezuma, Bernabé de la Cruz, Felipe García or Pérez, and Micaela Francisca; see Cope, *The Limits of Racial Domination*, 53–55. In respective order, these cases are found in AGN Inquisición 680, no. 34; 677, no. 4; 667, no. 2; and 667, no. 3.

22. AGN Inquisición 287, no. 8, p. 72.

23. Ibid., p. 76.

24. Uayangareo or Guayangareo probably existed as a settlement before the arrival of the Spanish, and Viceroy Mendoza promoted the establishment of a Spanish township and a barrio populated by Nahuatl-speaking settlers near the original Guayangáreo in 1541. In 1601, 1,000 natives were ordered to settle in the area as part of a *congregación* order. A *barrio* called "Guayangáreo el viejo" existed by 1580; by 1619, an episcopal report states the twenty families in Guayangareo received sacraments from seculars. See Paredes Martínez, "Grupos étnicos y conflictividad social en Guayangareo-Valladolid, al inicio de la época colonial." For the 1619 report, see Lemoine, *Valladolid-Morelia 450 años*.

25. AGN Inquisición 287, no. 8, p. 70. Could "Coyoacán" be an erroneous rendering of "Guayangareo"? This is only a weak conjecture; however, the notary did manage to enter Rojas's first wife's name and place of birth incorrectly—she became known as "Mónica Juana, native of San Juan Teguacan," rather than María Mónica from San Juan Teoti-huacan.

26. AGN Inquisición 287, no. 7, p. 134.

27. This work was printed in Puebla in 1692 at the workshop of Diego Fernández de León. Villavicencio dedicates the book to Isidro Sariñana, bishop of Oaxaca, who devoted a large amount of resources to the extirpation of idolatries in Oaxaca and who built the first prison for idolaters in Oaxaca City in 1688–92. See Tavárez, "The Passion According to the Wooden Drum."

28. It should be noted that, while colonial records and Villavicencio's legal proceedings designate the language of this parish as "Chocho," they were probably referring to a seventeenth-century variant of a language that contemporary linguists now designate as "Popoloca," in contrast to other closely related language variants now known as "Chocho" or "Chocholteco" (Michael Swanton, personal communication, 2006). In 1674, as *juez eclesiástico de idolatrías* under Bishop Tomás de Monterroso, Villavicencio confis-

cated several idols in San Francisco de la Sierra and forwarded them to the bishop (AGN Bienes Nacionales 1076, no. 10). It was during this period that Villavicencio acquired a good knowledge of Popoloca language variants—a skill that he would put to use during his interrogation of Chocho and Mazatec native specialists. By 1688, Villavicencio had been named *beneficiado* and ecclesiastic judge of Santa Cruz Tlacotepec, a Chocho-speaking parish about sixteen leagues to the southeast of Puebla.

29. Villavicencio received a commission against native idolaters from the provisor of Indians of the bishopric of Tlaxcala in July 1688 (AGN Inquisición 674, no. 26).

30. AGN Inquisición 669, no. 10, 481r–v.

31. Ibid., 499v.

32. Ibid., 498r.

33. For instance, in her discussion of AGN Civil 270, no. 1, Laura Lewis notes that the residents of an indigenous community near Mexico City conducted a public feud with the Rosas family, regarded as mestizo, in the early 1680s. The sons of Lorenzo Rosas, who had married a native noblewoman and inherited her land, could claim indigenous identity but shifted to being regarded as mestizos during their conflict against local residents, whom they accused of being idolaters. See Lewis, *Hall of Mirrors*, 86–88.

34. AGN Civil 270, no. 1, 508r–508v.

35. Ibid., 511v; my emphasis.

36. Using a Chocho interpreter in an inquisitorial court was not an impossibility, given that Indian testimony with or without interpreters in inquisitorial cases was not unusual, and that Villavicencio already had designated a Tlacotepec resident as his Chocho interpreter. However, after 1571, indicting an individual known to be indigenous as a defendant in an inquisitorial trial would have been a violation of the bishop's jurisdiction over natives.

37. See Barth, Introduction to *Ethnic Groups and Boundaries*.

38. One could even conjecture that Rojas had an opportunity to give some strategic suggestions to Hernández before the latter was questioned; after all, Rojas was interrogated on February 5, and Hernández arrived in prison on February 12 and was questioned three days later.

39. For a discussion of subjectivity in ethnic and linguistic passing in the United States, see Bucholtz, "From Mulatta to Mestiza."

40. Rappaport and Gow, "The Indigenous Public Voice."

41. This tentative figure includes the cases discussed by Cope in *The Limits*, Althouse in "Contested Mestizos," and the three cases in this article.

42. Kamen, *The Spanish Inquisition*, 144; Silverblatt, *Modern Inquisitions*, 59.

43. For a detailed discussion of an unusual case of casta acculturation within the legal framework of pueblos de indios, see García Martínez, *Los pueblos de la Sierra de Puebla*, 106–8.

44. Silverblatt, *Modern Inquisitions*, 218.

# The Many Faces of Colonialism in Two Iberoamerican Borderlands

## Northern New Spain and the Eastern Lowlands of Charcas

Ethnicity, gender, and identity are three central concepts that express the many faces of colonialism in the Americas. "Faces" refers only metaphorically to phenotypes; its meaning embraces the fiscal and legal categories established by colonial institutions as well as the social networks that developed among colonial subjects. This chapter compares two frontier regions of the interior provinces of North and South America that bore striking contrasts in their environments and landscapes but equally marked historical similarities in the institutions that tied them to the Spanish Crown for over two centuries. I refer to northwestern New Spain, including portions of Nueva Vizcaya, Sonora, and Sinaloa, and the lowlands of Charcas extending eastward from the Andean escarpment through Chiquitos to the Paraguayan basin. Both regions constituted complex ecological, cultural, and political borderlands in which political allegiances and territories were contested in different ways through numerous historical cycles of conquest, migration, and survival. Institutions that brought together diverse peoples in these contested grounds included missions, mining centers, commercial circuits, military garrisons and presidios as well as the bureaucratic networks of audiencias, local magistrates, and viceregal ordinances.

Why compare these two regions that appear to be so distant, and different, one from the other? Their histories woven together illustrate significant contrasts in natural environments and preconquest cultural formations, yet when viewed comparatively they point to the nuanced meanings of historically derived ethnic identities. The interior riverine networks of South America contained multiple environmental biomes ranging from Amazonian rainforest to the savannas of the Chiquitano Precambrian Shield and the semi-arid Chaco Boreal. At the same time these varied landscapes were formed as overlapping borderlands among a dense and changing variety of peoples and settlements. Their incorporation into the Spanish American imperial realm came gradually through the institutions of *encomienda* and religious missions under the aegis of the Society of Jesus (Jesuit Order), linked economically to the great mining center of Potosí in the Andean highlands. Northwestern New Spain developed in the foothills and cordilleras that rose from the Desert of Sonora in a series of valleys and mountain ranges extending eastward to the Sierra Madre Occidental. Here, as in eastern Charcas, Jesuit missions established the formative institution for the native communities that reconstituted themselves as frontier settlements in the changing environmental and social landscapes of colonial New Spain. Encomienda— forced tribute payment or labor services by Indian communities to Spaniards—had a much shorter history in northwestern Mexico than in eastern Charcas. The development of mining camps and *reales*, centers for the processing of metallic ores, created labor demands satisfied through *repartimiento*—rotated labor drafts—and wage labor. The mining industry in Sonora and Nueva Vizcaya brought a significant Hispanic and mixed Afro-mestizo population to northwestern New Spain, in contrast with eastern Charcas, where the vast majority of the people constituted indigenous nations and bands throughout the colonial period.

We find layered meanings of "borderlands" in the different communities that emerged, fragmented, and consolidated through unequal power relations in these interior frontiers on the boundaries of Spanish America. The birth of new ethnic identities, explained by anthropologists and historians through the process of *ethnogenesis*, refers not only to the mixtures of Indians, Europeans, and Africans that produced many subgroups in the colonial imagination but also to the stratification and realignment of different indigenous communities and lineages through the crucible of colonialism. Historical persistence of different peoples over time—if not always in the same place—balances the notion of ethnogenesis, which implies the creation of new identities and allegiances.[1]

Thus, the "faces of colonialism" emerge historically from complex processes of population decline and recovery, migration and changing settlement patterns, political affiliations, and cultural identity. The present comparative study of two borderlands along the imperial frontiers of Spain in North and South America illustrates the evolving and changing qualities of borderlands peoples and spaces in ways that emphasize one of the central arguments of this volume, namely, that race and ethnicity do not constitute fixed categories or absolute values but develop as "markers of difference" by diverse historical actors in different times and places.

## Borderlands Stories and Cultural Survival

The following stories whose fabric is woven from the historical archives for Sonora and Chiquitos assert individual and collective claims to community identity and royal protection within the institutional framework of the Spanish American colonies. The first concerns land rights for three villages of Pima commoners in central Sonora, and the second relates one family's struggle for freedom from forced labor in Santa Cruz de la Sierra, in the eastern lowlands of Charcas.

In 1716, Pima *alcaldes*, council officers from the mission of Cumuripa in the middle Yaqui valley, petitioned Thomás de Esquivel, the Spanish magistrate (*teniente de justicia mayor*) at the Real de San Miguel Arcángel in the name of the *común* of indigenous villagers to restore to them the lands of Buena Vista that Captain Antonio Ancheta had violently wrested from them and converted into a ranch for raising horses and cattle. Following Ancheta's death, leaving Buena Vista "despoblado," the Pimas secured approval from Esquivel and the audiencia of Guadalajara to reclaim the site for their own use, "so that we may found a pueblo there for the good of our souls and the protection of our lands."[2] Pima council officers bolstered their petition with personal testimonies by their elders —in their own language, through interpreters—to substantiate both the longevity of their occupation of the land and the cruelty of Ancheta's seizure of their cropland and village site. Teniente Esquivel validated the Pimas' use of the land through his first-hand inspection of their planted and irrigated fields.

Alcalde Diego Camorlinga—the principal author of this striking document—composed a history of occupancy, dispersion, and resettlement in Buena Vista and the nearby villages of Oviachic and Xecatacari, based on the memory of six living witnesses he brought before the Spanish magistrate. Their arguments rested on effective occupation of the land and the

Indians' status as Christians desirous of living in a settled pueblo. Their petition was supported by a census showing seventy-six Christian households and eleven households of non-Christian adults (*gentiles*) with baptized children. Heading the list of Christian families were four *cabildo* (village council) officers: Diego Camorlinga, *alcalde*, married with five children; Lázaro, *alguacil*, married with one child; Sebastián, *topil*, married, with four children; and Baltasar, *topil*, married, with one child.

All the witnesses spoke in the Pima tongue, but their identity rested not so much on a particular ethnic origin as on their status as *el común y naturales de Xecatacari*, meaning they were commoners with a shared stake in a particular territory. The común had material, political, and religious significance in the cultural production of community under the conditions created by colonialism. In this case, the común was linked to arable land, to the founding of a pueblo, and to the Indians' ties to Catholicism. The gendered presentation of the Pimas' community census, naming only the male heads of household, assuming the presence of unnamed wives, and enumerating the children, may well reflect their familiarity with Spanish legal and social customs and with colonial conventions for taking censuses of households. What stood out as important for the indigenous petitioners was their status as Christian commoners and their proven ties to the land. Ethnicity and identity blend in this instance as markers of religious and social status: Christian and gentile, village commoners led by their cabildo, and their bonds to the locality of Xecatacari.

Our story from eastern Charcas illustrates a different context for ethnic status, one in which rival claims to land were not the principal motive of conflict between Indians and Spaniards. In the interior tropical lowlands of Chiquitos and throughout the Paraguayan basin, the encomienda of forced labor and outright enslavement of captives continued to be common practices well into the eighteenth century. Encomienda enjoyed legal protection in this Spanish Portuguese borderland, where Spanish settlers and their descendants argued forcefully that in these poor provinces Indian labor was their only source of wealth and social prestige.

The prolonged legal struggle between two Chiquitos brothers, Eugenio and Jacinto Masavi, and Don Lorenzo de la Roca illustrates in dramatic terms what was at stake in the contested claims to freedom and privilege that surrounded the institution of encomienda in Santa Cruz at the mid-eighteenth century.[3] Both parties claimed the principle of paternal lineage and the relationship of vassalage that formally bound them to the Crown: Roca, in his pretension to exercise his "feudal right" to keep an allotment of Indians in his household, and the Masavi brothers, in their determination to gain freedom for themselves and the rest of their family. The Masavis claimed their status as "in the service of his Majesty, may God keep him, and now tributaries . . . like all those of our nation."[4] Don Lorenzo demanded recognition of his hereditary right to the "second life" of the encomienda granted to his father, Don Joseph de la Roca, in 1703, in recognition of his military services.

The Masavi family history, covering three generations, illustrated well-established patterns of migration between their villages and the Spanish settlements of Santa Cruz. Eugenio and Jacinto, together with the witnesses whose testimony they solicited to support their case, identified them only as "of the Chiquitos nation," without specifying a particular ethnicity or place of origin. The Masavis' grandfather, Gregorio, had left his pueblo and arrived in San Lorenzo during the 1690s, in search of a master whom he could serve. He first settled in the household of one Alonso Pardo but later moved to the house of Joseph de la Roca, where he married Lucía Choe, a Chiquitos woman who lived and worked in the Roca encomienda. The Masavi-Choe couple, with their children and grandchildren, had remained in the Roca household until the death of Don Joseph in 1742. Their situation worsened when Don Lorenzo assumed control of his father's encomienda. Eugenio and Jacinto argued that Lorenzo's harsh treatment, in violation of the terms and conditions of an encomienda grant, forced them to seek their freedom. Advised, perhaps, by the Protector of Indians, a royal official appointed for the Province of Santa Cruz, they accused Lorenzo de la Roca of physical punishment (beatings) and sexual abuse of several women (of different generations) in their family, and of neglecting his duties to supply them with food, clothing, and religious instruction.[5]

The centerpiece of the Masavis' legal petition concerned the illegality of Don Lorenzo's claim to the encomienda. They insisted that their grandfather had migrated to San Lorenzo of his own free will and that they, as his descendants, should enjoy the same liberty. Eugenio and Jacinto argued further that they could not be held in bondage for, as befitted the Chiquitos nation, they were free from the conditions of servitude reserved for war captives and ransomed prisoners. "For the *chiquitos* were not to be brought in at the point of war . . . since the time that raiding expeditions ran [through the province] they themselves delivered the *piezas* that the residents of this city needed. It is laughable to look at the nominal list of the *encomienda* granted to Don Joseph de la Roca, deceased not so long ago, when we consider how much time has passed since those wars took place."[6] The identity that the Masavi brothers established for their family lineage in order to defend their liberty was entwined with the history of violence that had enslaved so many lowland Indian peoples. The cabildo of San Lorenzo and the governor of Santa Cruz denied the Indians' petition; they imprisoned Jacinto and punished the Masavi family by forcing them to work in the restoration of the Convent of the Mercedarians in San Lorenzo. Jacinto managed to escape his confinement and traveled to La Plata in order to present his case in person before the audiencia. Acting on its authority as an appellate court, the audiencia issued three provisions, from March 1751 to August 1752, ordering the cabildo of San Lorenzo to free the Masavi family from Roca's household.[7]

This case illustrates the elasticity of ethnic identities in Santa Cruz. From the Masavis' story we may infer that a significant population of Indians lived outside the Jesuit missions of Chiquitos and sought a livelihood in the Spanish sphere of colonial society. Their social status, whether free, enslaved, *encomendados*, or resident in the missions, determined their ethnic identity to a significant degree. Furthermore, we can detect a network of communication among Indians, clergy, and colonial officials through which the Masavi brothers gained knowledge of the law and access to sponsors or protectors who helped them along the way—including Jacinto's trek of over 120 miles, rising over 7,500 feet, from Santa Cruz to La Plata, the seat of the audiencia of Charcas.

### Anthropologists and Historians in the Borderlands

What questions may we ask of these historical actors to bring their particular stories into a broader narrative of change and endurance over time and space? In defense of their claims to communal land, in Sonora, and to freedom from the rigors of encomienda, in Chiquitos, Diego Camorlinga and Gregorio Masavi assumed colonial identities as Christian Indians and subjects of the king. Do we see this as ethnogenesis or as persistence? The

Pimas of Xecatacari persisted—or returned—to the land from which they had been temporarily expelled by force so—they said—to found a pueblo and to serve God and the king. Alcalde Camorlinga presented his petition as the senior officer of the cabildo, a colonial institution. He spoke in the name of the común, a concept that gained currency among all Sonoran villagers and that may well have developed as a cultural value under colonialism. The villagers of Xecatacari, as portrayed in these early-eighteenth-century documents, seemed to be uniformly indigenous and Pima-speaking; yet the identities they claimed in order to reclaim their land were built largely out of colonial categories of Catholic religious spirituality and loyalty to the king.

The Masavi family's fear of being held as captives or slaves is mirrored by the anthropologist Isabelle Combès's comprehensive study of the "Guaraní of Izozo," in the semi-arid Chaco south of Chiquitos, straddling an ecological and cultural borderland between present-day Bolivia and Paraguay. Combès has shown convincingly that the very people of Izozo who claim to be Guaraní and argue emphatically that they were never enslaved are historically the Chané who fled from the Guaranís' slaving expeditions and later assumed the linguistic and ethnic identity of their captors. Combés's work advances our thinking about ethnicity, building on the foundations established by José María García Recio, Juan Carlos Garavaglia, Rossana Barragán, Ana María Presta, James Saeger, Barbara Ganson, and Erick Langer—among others—on the complex and overlapping social and ethnic identities carved out for Chanés, Chiriguanos, and Guaranís through repeated colonial encounters over more than three centuries in the eastern margins of the Chiquitos lowlands known as the Pantanal and the greater Paraguayan basin.[8] Documentary evidence drawn from the earliest *entradas* by encomenderos, adelantados, and missionaries, corroborated further by archaeological studies along the eastern rim of the Andean-Amazonian ecological divide, offers suggestive descriptions of trading and raiding networks among a fragmented mosaic of bands and tribes into which Spaniards would stumble and later learn to exploit for a wide range of productive and reproductive services.[9] The Masavis' testimony of the mid-eighteenth century historicizes through the biography of one extended family both the generational practices of warfare that perpetuated conditions of captivity and servitude and the indigenous people's fear of enslavement.

Comparable processes of ethnogenesis as were described for the Paraguayan basin may be traced in northern New Spain, where gendered terminology evolved to express ethnic identity in the context of warfare, captivity, and enslavement. Chantal Cramaussel has argued that the Indian tribal names recorded in seventeenth-century Nueva Vizcaya emerged, in at least some cases, from the distribution of encomiendas among Spanish claimants, who "named" them in order to claim power over their labor.[10] In northwestern Mexico were the *nijoras*, captives from Yuman, Athapaskan, and other tribes living beyond the bounds of the missions—typically women, children, or adolescents—traded for different kinds of goods and distributed as a servant class among Spanish and some elite Indian households and the missions. Although nijoras were never a "tribe" or ethnic nation, the name persisted in colonial records as an ethnic label.[11]

Captives across northern New Spain were known by different ethnic designations and filled multiple roles as enslaved persons and as surrogate kinsmen and women to rebuild lineages and households ravaged by wars, diseases, and raiding. The *genízaros* of mixed ethnic origins—labeled variously Comanches, Navajos, or Apaches—in New Mexico filled complex roles as enslaved laborers, militias in defense against the Plains nomads, and a mestizo caste of ambivalent identity between "Hispanic" and "Indian." Their histories hold charged meanings for the political economy of colonial provinces in these complex borderlands, in the spatial interstices between nomadic and sedentary peoples, for gendered and ethnic boundaries, and for the cultural discourses that developed around honor, family, and sexuality.[12] The territorial significance of raiding and captive labor under the guise of encomienda set apart northeastern New Spain—Coahuila, Nuevo León, Nuevo Santander, and Texas—where Spanish hegemony was fiercely contested by native confederations and ethnic identities were fragmented and reformed under the pressures of intermittent warfare and dislocation.[13]

Internal ethnic borderlands developed along different lines in the areas of mixed settlements created by colonial missions, mining centers, and ranching economies of Nueva Vizcaya and the northwestern provinces of Sinaloa, Sonora, and Pimería Alta.[14] Indigenous identities were distinguished by degrees of sedentarism, labor regimes of repartimiento and free, contractual labor, and by the communities created within the institutional boundaries of the colonial missions. Diego Camorlinga and the cabildo officers of Xecatacari asserted the ethnic boundaries of their común against the history of violence they had endured at the hands of armed Spanish cattlemen who had invaded their land. Furthermore, ethnic distinctions and amalgamations were complicated by the presence of numerically significant populations among African descendants—*negros* and *mulattos*, *coyotes* and *lobos*, both enslaved and free—who mingled with Indians, Spaniards, and mestizos in the missions, *reales de minas* and commercial towns that formed networks of trade along the roads and trails for moving goods, silver, and persons through the colonial economy.

Susan Deeds's analysis of the Jesuit mission provinces of Topia, Tepehuana, and portions of the Tarahumara, in the heart of Nueva Vizcaya, shows that by the mid-eighteenth century these missions located within proximity of mines and the major wagon trails (*camino real*) no longer constituted a *república de indios*. Their mixed demographic profiles reflected decades of Indian population decline through repeated epidemics, labor drafts, and flight from the mission compounds, parallel to the rise of Spanish and mixed-race populations in haciendas, towns, and reales de minas. The hybrid ethnic composition of the missions was compounded by the impoverishment of their communal economy, as measured in arable land, harvested crops, and livestock. Missionaries, bishops, and magistrates (alcaldes mayores) warned viceregal authorities that Indians and *vecinos* alike barely survived at subsistence level, as mission pueblos lost productive capacity and markets. The Jesuit Order conceded the altered status of the Topia and Tepehuan/Tarahumara Baja missions when, in 1745, the leader of the order in Mexico proposed secularizing these missions, thus freeing missionaries for new conversions among the gentiles of Pimería Alta and California.[15]

In the highland regions of northwestern Mexico, where missions and Spanish settlements existed in close proximity and depended on the same sources of labor, mission communities survived with core populations and viable economies to a greater extent than in Topia and Tepehuana. Through my work on Sonora and Sinaloa I have found that putatively indigenous pueblos were ethnically mixed, with notable evidence of Indian migrations to the mines and Spanish towns and increasing numbers of settlers and squatters establishing themselves in the missions. The missions absorbed non-Indian populations with somewhat greater success than in Nueva Vizcaya because the pueblos retained a communal land base until the end of the eighteenth century and supported active village councils (cabildos) for internal governance and representation to colonial authorities. In both provinces, but especially in Sonora, Indian men gained leverage with Spanish military commanders through military service as paid auxiliaries in the presidios. Their strategic importance for frontier defense, against the Apachean *bárbaros*, translated into limited but visible degrees of status and mobility.[16]

Parish censuses enumerated by household for three Sonoran parishes at the turn of the nineteenth century—Oposura, Tepache, and Ónavas— show a continuum of ethnic blending, from a predominantly indigenous population in Ónavas to Hispanic and mestizo majorities in Tepache and Oposura. Oposura, the largest and most complex of the three parishes, included two pueblos, three privately owned haciendas, and three ranching settlements. Significantly, in the language of the census compilers, "Indian" signified *indios del pueblo* while "mestizo" was rendered as *indios laboríos y otras castas*. Only the two pueblos of Oposura and Cumpas mustered a substantial number of households who counted among the indios del pueblo, albeit a minority (29 percent); in the haciendas and ranches, Spanish and mixed populations—including the indios laboríos— constituted their entire roster of households. The ethnic distinctions implied in these terms of caste suggest class differences of locality and social status more than racial categories. "Laboring Indians," the indios laboríos in the parish of Oposura, typically constituted relatively young households that supplied the haciendas and ranches with labor in return for payment in kind and land for subsistence farming. Their migration away from the core mission pueblos and their status as free laborers outside the mission común distinguished them from the indios del pueblo and associated them with the ambivalent, mixed group of castas.[17]

Gender intersected with class and ethnicity in these Hispanized provinces in ways that were both predictable and intriguing. Gendered divisions of labor were blurred when women from the poor strata of Indians and vecinos worked in the fields and tended small family holdings of livestock as well as weaving cloth, preparing food, and tending to the sick.[18] Forced labor drafts to mines and haciendas often took whole families away from the pueblos—as the missionaries were quick to lament— bringing indigenous men, women, and children into the cultural maelstrom of mestizaje. If, indeed, patriarchal prescriptions of male authority defined the norms of social behavior in the missions and Spanish settlements, as we observed in the formal petition of the Xecatacari Pimas, gendered and ethnic discourses of separation and hierarchy bowed before the exigencies of survival. Flight from enslavement, the rigors of repartimiento, or an oppressive mission regime brought men and women of mixed Indian, mestizo, and mulatto castes into varied circumstances of coexistence and intimacy, at times fleeting and at others of longer duration. Denunciations of witchcraft and sorcery, encountered with surprising frequency in the ecclesiastical and secular court documents, attest to the criminalization of heterodox spiritual practices of intercession and healing and to social avenues of mobility that transgressed conventional boundaries of ethnic and gendered roles.[19] Contemporaries seemed to associate the skills of witchcraft and its presumed ties to demonic power with Indians, yet it is telling that incidences of witchcraft occurred in the interstices of society where Indians and non-Indians mingled in varying degrees of intimacy.

Mestizaje carried a different connotation in the borderlands of Chiquitos, on the eastern edge of Charcas. The imperial boundary with Portuguese Mato Grosso opened the Chiquitanía to occasional blacks and mulattoes who fled the bonds of slavery or worked as muleteers and guards for both Spanish and Portuguese travelers and officials. Jesuit missionaries and—after 1768—diocesan priests accompanied by lay administrators, the provincial governor and his small staff, and scattered presidial garrisons established a Hispanic presence in the mission pueblos. Nevertheless, the number of permanent non-Indian settlers in the Province of Chiquitos remained small during the entire colonial period and contemporaries understood mixed populations as the interethnic blending of different indigenous bands known as *parcialidades*. Periodic censuses for the Chiquitos missions rarely included the categories of Spanish, mestizo or casta. Nineteenth-century developments with increasing numbers of non-Indian settlers, herders, and squatters in the Chiquitos pueblos and rising labor demands in the city of Santa Cruz de la Sierra produced a more complex provincial society but one that centered on indigenous labor in the pueblos and through peonage on the sugar cane and cattle *estancias*.

## Conclusions

The pervasive, enduring, and violent legacies of conquest and colonial regimes in the Americas have conditioned our perceptions of the ethnic subject for both the remote and recent past and in contemporary observations. Cultural and social differences nearly always derived from or translated into stark inequalities of entitlement and privilege, reified by the very terms of colonialism: *indio, natural, pieza de rescate, bárbaro* or *negro*, which connoted enslavement, servitude, or tributary status.[20] Colonial regimes over five centuries in the Caribbean and American continents produced a myriad of outcomes with many different ethnic, gendered, and social configurations. Furthermore, the particular ethnic identities espoused for indigenous authenticity and, thus, to stake a claim to recognition by the colonial hierarchy or—after the Spanish American independence movements—the national state more often than not are artifacts of the historical conditions of colonialism. Here we may cite the equestrian tribes and confederations of the South American pampas or the North American Great Plains,[21] the Mesoamerican and Andean lordships, in which rival *caciques* and *kurakas* vied bitterly for power as different lineages merged or replaced one another,[22] and the transculturated religious practices through which colonial Indian peoples sacrificed to ancient gods even as they venerated Catholic saints. Historians, anthropologists, and ethnohistorians have all contributed to the conceptualization of movement, mobility, and unstable ethnic identities that has guided a voluminous and rich literature into the historically contextualized ethnicity of Iberoamerica, in both the "core" regions and borderlands of Spanish and Portuguese frontiers in the circum-Caribbean and along the riverine networks of South America and the northern deserts of New Spain.

As we consider the roads that lead to further research we will do well to rethink the meaning of "ethnogenesis" in the light of demographic change. Ethnic labels that are repeated so often in the historical record and in ethnographic literature are but one way of expressing in shorthand the demographic profiles that emerge from population movements in time and space. Their appearance in different historical moments reflects processes of biological decline and recovery, geographical displacements, the abandonment of some settlements and the creation of new communities. Different peoples may persist even as the configuration of their communities is altered—from large pueblos to small rancherías—or their material culture adapts to new crops or tools, and their ceremonial life and cosmologies adopt new symbolic meanings. Over time, the same people may appear in different ethnic garments. As historians, anthropologists, art historians, and archaeologists learn to cross the boundaries of our disciplines, we may sharpen our lenses to capture the complexities of hues and textures that are woven into those garments and hear with greater clarity the many voices that arise from colonized peoples and their descendants.

## Notes

1. Ramenofsky, Church, and Kulisheck, "Investigating Differential Persistence of Pueblo Populations."

2. "Los pimas de Xecatacari y Obiachi a Thomas de Esquivel, teniente de justicia mayor del Real de San Miguel Arcángel y su jurisdicción en la Provincia de Sonora," Biblioteca Pública del Estado de Jalisco, Archivo de la Real Audiencia de Guadalajara, *Ramo Civil*, 27-9-359, 1916, 15 ff. The document is published in Radding, *Entre el desierto y la sierra*, 139–53.

3. The term "Chiquitos" came into use under Spanish colonialism during the seventeenth and eighteenth centuries, as a collective ethnic designation for numerous tribal and linguistic groups in the lowlands between the Guapay and Paraguayan river basins. The province became known as Chiquitos and, more expansively since the early twentieth century, as "la gran Chiquitanía." During the entire colonial period and until well into the nineteenth century, the separate tribal names encompassed in the Chiquitos "ethnicity" endured as meaningful identities with perceptible differences in speech. See Radding, *Landscapes of Power and Identity*, 124, 132, 136–43; Tomichá, *La primera evangelización en las reducciones de Chiquitos*, 154–97.

4. Archivo y Biblioteca Nacionales de Bolivia (hereafter ABNB), *Ramo Mojos y Chiquitos* (legal petition by residents of Chiquitos), Ch. 23, 1751–53, 7, fs. 28–29: "Eugenio y Jacinto Masavi, naturales del Pueblo de Chiquitos, por nosotros y en nombre de todos nuestros descendientes [por] . . . ser todos los de nuestra nación libres dados por soldados de su Magestad, que Ds Guarde, y agora tributarios, ocurrimos a la justificación de V.S. para que mediante justicia se sirva . . . darnos por tributarios para aumento delos haberes reales así como todos los de nuestra nación."

5. Cutter, *Protector de indios in Colonial New Mexico, 1659–1821*.

6. ABNB, *Ramo Mojos y Chiquitos*, Ch. 23, 7, f. 23. "Pues para los chiquitos no se ofreció . . . ser traidos a punta de guerra . . . desde el tiempo que corrieron rescates en que atraían de ellos mismos las piezas que querían los moradores de esta ciudad. Con una cosa ridícula como véase el padrón de encomienda de Dn Joseph de la Roca, difunto él poco tiempo que ha, a lo mucho a que pasaron esas guerras." On the *protector de indios*, see García Recio, *Análisis de una sociedad de frontera*, 255–56.

7. This case is analyzed further in Radding, "Voces chiquitanas"; Tomichá Charupá, "La encomienda en Santa Cruz de la Sierra (1751–1753)."

8. García Recio, *Análisis de una sociedad de frontera*; Langer, "Missions and the Frontier Economy"; Combès, *Ethno-Historias del Isoso*; Saeger, *The Chaco Mission Frontier*; Ganson, *The Guaraní under Spanish Rule in the Río de la Plata*; Barragán, "*¿Indios de arco y flecha?*"; Presta, *Espacio, etnias, frontera*.

9. Nordenskiöld, *Exploraciones y aventuras en Sudamérica*; Núñez Cabeza de Vaca, *Comentarios de Alvar Núñez Cabeza de Vaca*; Lucas Caballero, *Relación de las costumbres y religión de los indios manasicas*.

10. Cramaussel, "De como los españoles clasificaban a los indios" and *Poblar la frontera*.

11. Dobyns et al., "What Were Nixoras?"; Montané Martí, "De *nijoras* y 'españoles a medias.'"

12. Gutiérrez, *When Jesus Came, the Corn Mothers Went Away*, 149–202; Brooks, *Captives and Cousins*; Lamadrid, *Hermanitos Comanchitos*.

13. Sheridan, *Anónimos y desterrados*; Barr, *Peace Came in the Form of a Woman*.

14. Deeds, *Defiance and Deference in Mexico's Colonial North* and "Double Jeopardy"; Radding, *Wandering Peoples*; Cuello, "Racialized Hierarchies of Power in Colonial Mexican Society."

15. Deeds, *Defiance and Deference*, 142–71.

16. Radding, *Wandering Peoples*, 256–63; *Landscapes of Power and Identity*, 168–76.

17. Radding, *Landscapes of Power and Identity*, 147–58.

18. P. Marcelo de León to bishop San Ignacio, 1749, Archivo de la Catedral de Durango, Varios, 1749, cited in Deeds, *Defiance and Deference*, 160.

19. Deeds, "Subverting the Social Order"; Lewis, *Halls of Mirrors*, 167–72. Both authors analyze in different ways the intriguing case of Antonia de Soto, a mulatta slave who disguised herself as a man, first to escape her bondage and then to acquire the skills and power of men in a male-dominated world of *vaqueros* and muleteers. Archivo General de la Nación (Mexico), *Ramo Inquisición*, vol. 252, exp. 48, f. 500–520, 1691.

20. Weber, *Bárbaros*.

21. Jones, "Comparative Raiding Economies."

22. Spores, *Mixtec Kings and their People*; Terraciano, *The Mixtecs of Colonial Oaxaca*; Spalding, *Huarochirí*; Powers, *Andean Journeys*.

# Humble Slaves and Loyal Vassals

*Free Africans and Their Descendants in Eighteenth-Century*
*Minas Gerais, Brazil*

In 1755 the *crioulo*, *preto*, and *mestiço* men and women of the towns
of Sabará, Vila Rica, Serro Frio, São José, and São João, in the captaincy of
Minas Gerais, Brazil, petitioned the king of Portugal through the Overseas
Council to appoint a public defender who would represent them in legal
suits against whites.[1] They claimed that since the beginning of settlement
in the mining district their participation in commerce and their dealings
with *todo genero de pessoas brancas* (all sorts of white people) was *publico e*
*notório* (public and notorious). Yet, because of their inability to read or
write and their ignorance of the law, they often suffered abuses at the
hands of white persons whenever a commercial, property, or personal
dispute arose between them, resulting in great harm to their property,
honor, and household. Listed among their complaints were the frequency
with which they were subjected to disadvantageous terms in commercial
and other contracts, unjust arrests for debt, and their inability to protect
their wives and daughters from sexual abuses perpetrated by their white
creditors. In order to remedy the state of helplessness in which they found
themselves, the petitioners requested that the king appoint one of the
many men of African descent in Minas Gerais who were well versed in
Portuguese law to serve as their public defender.[2]

Though evidence from this period suggests that this request was never
granted, the document deserves our attention for the questions it raises
about identity and practices of social and racial differentiation in colonial
Brazil. In their interaction with the Overseas Council and the king the
petitioners employed several categories of self-identification to present

their appeal. They introduced themselves as His Majesty's loyal vassals. They referenced their African origin and African or mixed ancestry, calling themselves, as did most colonial authorities, pretos, crioulos, and mestiços. Finally, they referred to themselves as townsmen with a traditional role in Mineiro economy, and as property holders, heads of households, and persons of honor who were entitled to defend these markers of social distinction. Persons of African origin and descent in Minas Gerais were part of an environment ordered by institutions that sought to make sense of and, to some extent, control their presence by placing them within specific social, economic, political, and racial categories. This practice of differentiation could, and often did, translate into discrimination with harsh implications, as the petition suggests, for the socioeconomic well-being of this group. Yet the petition also shows that persons of African origin and descent had their own ideas about the categories they fit into and how these defined their place in that society and their relationship to each other, to white people, and, ultimately, to the king. By resorting to different categories of social and racial identification, these men and women reveal the several layers of identity they embraced to better understand and negotiate the impact discriminating colonial practices had on their daily lives.

In this sense, the petition from the crioulo, preto, and mestiço men and women of Minas Gerais speaks to recent debates in the study of race, ethnicity, and identity in colonial Latin America. The presence of a racially, ethnically, and socially diverse population in that region has always been acknowledged by scholars of the colonial period. More recently, however, studies have sought to gain a better understanding of the process by which notions of categories of individuals and collective identity have taken shape and the impact they had on the lives of those who were subjected to or embraced them. This approach has led historians to realize that even though racial, ethnic, and social categories were strongly ingrained in colonial Latin American culture and society, they did not always translate into daily practices or attitudes in predictable ways.[3] Colonial authorities, institutions, and social groups could, and often did, bend their notions of these different categories and the constraints they imposed on individuals to accommodate local circumstances. Thus, despite the general limitations imposed on the rights and privileges of persons of African and native descent in colonial Latin America, regional or local political, military, and economic needs allowed individuals to take on certain roles and enjoy the social benefits they afforded that may have otherwise been beyond their reach. Individual members of colonial Latin American societies, on the other hand, could, and occasionally did, embrace or reject a particular ethnic, racial, and social identity at different moments in their lives to secure a more desirable status or position in society. The confluence of these institutional, social, and individual practices produced an environment that was once portrayed as being fairly flexible regarding racial and social practices, especially when compared to colonial British North America.[4] What the aforementioned petition and other colonial documents suggest, however, is that this flexibility, if in fact present, did not necessarily reside in this society's general attitudes toward race and social status. Instead, it was a function of the social maneuverability that colonial Latin America's use of complex, multilayered categories to identify and order its members afforded individuals and groups of people.

This chapter approaches the issue of race and identity in colonial Latin America through an examination of the use of racial and social categories in colonial Minas Gerais, Brazil, and the efforts free persons of African origin and descent made to negotiate the meaning and impact that practices of differentiation and discrimination had on their lives. The region of Minas Gerais stands out in the context of eighteenth-century Brazil because of its large African and slave population, as well as the very particular social environment that gold mining and urbanization helped to create. As the historiography on Minas Gerais has commonly pointed out, the relatively fluid social order that particular setting produced, when compared to other regions of Brazil, resulted in a higher rate of manumission among slaves and more opportunities for the rise of new wealth.[5] There remains a need, however, to better understand how that fluidity impacted, if at all, the interactions that persons of African origin and descent had with other members of Mineiro society, as well as their individual and collective identity. The analysis of colonial documents such as parish records and petitions shows that while persons of African origin and descent interjected contemporary notions of social and racial categories, reinforcing them in the process, they also explored a range of possible individual and collective identities to secure their interests when interacting with different colonial groups and institutions.

Early Mineiro society was a product of the mining industry. The discovery of gold in the backlands of southeastern Brazil in the late seventeenth century initiated a process of settlement quite unlike what had occurred in other regions of the colony. In the captaincies of Pernambuco, Bahia, and São Vicente, all of which held a prominent economic role in colonial Brazil at one point or another, settlement and subsequent population growth occurred at a slow pace, often following significant private and metropolitan investment in local development.[6] Minas Gerais, on the other hand, witnessed a spontaneous settlement process as a great number of people migrated to the region attracted by its rich deposits of gold.

As the general population of Minas Gerais grew so did its slave population. Because the size of land grants in mining zones was determined by the size of the grantee's workforce, the influx of potential mining entrepreneurs led to a growing demand for workers.[7] The lack of a numerous and sedentary native population from which, following the example of Spanish America, workers could be drafted, and the impossibility of hiring workers for wages in an environment with more promising economic opportunities, led to a heavy reliance on the labor of enslaved Africans. Though relying initially on the internal slave trade with neighboring captaincies, Minas Gerais quickly became a major importer of African slaves. During the early eighteenth century these forced migrants crossed the Atlantic in ever greater numbers destined to the ports of Salvador and Rio de Janeiro and from there to the mining sites in the interior of the colony.[8]

The continuous importation of African slaves into Minas Gerais led to an astonishing growth of the captaincy's slave population during the first half of the eighteenth century. According to a 1729 tax list, there were 52,348 slaves in Minas Gerais that year, a striking figure when compared to the 45,482 slaves in the captaincy of Bahia in 1724.[9] In less than half a century, Minas Gerais had managed to form a slave population more numerous than that of Bahia, a settlement almost two hundred years old and the leading producer of sugar in Brazil. By 1735, the year in which the *capitação*, a per capita tax on slaves, began to be employed, the number of taxable slaves had risen to 93,541.[10] It is important to keep in mind, however, that because slave children and older or incapacitated slaves were not counted as taxable the actual numbers of slaves in Minas Gerais was potentially higher. The numbers that are available, though, show an average annual population increase of 6,000 individuals in the six years between each tax record. Census records for the second half of the eighteenth century point to the continuous growth of the Mineiro slave population: 126,603 individuals in 1767 and 188,781 slaves by the beginning of the nineteenth century.[11] The labor demands of gold mining and other regional industries thus ensured that Minas Gerais concentrated one of the largest slave populations of colonial Brazil.

The strong presence of slaves in colonial Minas Gerais contributed, moreover, to the formation of a fairly diverse regional population. Because of their various places of origin and ancestral descent, African- and Brazilian-born slaves formed a complex demographic group that quickly became differentiated on the basis of their ethnic and physical differences. A tax assessment record from 1742, listing recently arrived slaves in the Comarca do Rio das Velhas (one of the four judicial districts of the captaincy), shows, for instance, slave traders and owners' use of *nações* (nations) to distinguish the place of origin of African slaves.[12] Imported from Central or West Africa, these slaves were registered as Angola, Benguela, Congo, Cabo Verde, Courana, Fon, Mina, and Nagô. Historians today have used colonial references to nações to reconstruct the ethnicities of African slaves and better understand the various cultural identities they may have brought to the Americas.[13] African nações, however, were not the only category of identification employed at the time to make sense of slaves' cultural and physical diversity. Among Brazilian-born slaves, those of solely African descent were often identified as crioulo while those partially of white, or even Indian, descent were referred to as pardo, mestiço, mulato, or cabra.

Slaves also contributed to shaping a diverse population through their involvement in a variety of economic activities. As gold mining started to develop in Minas Gerais the region became increasingly attractive to persons seeking opportunities for enrichment as merchants, tradesmen, and other professionals. The very nature of gold mining strongly encouraged economic diversification among early settlers. Because it was extremely labor intensive, those engaged in this activity, whether free people or slaves, had little opportunity to provide for their subsistence. On the other hand, mining generated ready and abundant currency, namely, gold in the form of dust and nuggets, that facilitated commercial exchange. The many entrepreneurs who flocked to the region in the early eighteenth century quickly adopted the local practice of purchasing and employing slave labor. As part, and in some cases the majority, of the nonmining labor-force slaves contributed to local economic diversification. In the process they also helped to shape a socially, economically, and professionally diverse Mineiro population.[14]

Finally, the presence of a numerous slave population in Minas Gerais led to the formation and gradual rise of a *forro* (freed) population of African origin and descent. The economic opportunities the mining economy offered entrepreneurial slaves, along with the formation of a group of slaves born of often illicit unions between white men and slave women and the practice some slave owners adopted of rewarding productivity with financial compensation, produced the conditions that allowed some slaves to negotiate their freedom through manumission.[15] Throughout the eighteenth century free migrants as well as local free-born individuals of African origin and descent joined the population of forros to form a free population of crioulos, pretos, and mestiços that eventually outnumbered both slaves and free whites. In the case of the Comarca do Rio das Velhas, the free population of African origin and descent rose from 12,062 individuals in 1776 to 31,307 in 1810. More importantly, this group, which in 1776 represented 31 percent of the entire population of the Comarca do Rio das Velhas, comprised the majority, or 51 percent, of the local population by the beginning of the nineteenth century.[16] Population diversity in colonial Minas Gerais was thus not limited to cultural and physical differences between enslaved and free persons but was also a marked characteristic of the captaincy's free population in general.

The gradual and later rapid growth of a free population of African origin and descent in Minas Gerais raised local concerns and questions about their place and role in colonial society. Early records of the capitação reveal one way in which the colonial administration, for instance, viewed the local forro population. A per capita tax on able-bodied slaves, the capitação was employed to collect the Crown's share of the gold extracted in the captaincy through the taxation of the mining labor force. Records of the capitação show, however, that slaves were not the only ones taxed through this system: in 1735, the first year the capitação was collected, 1,420 forros were also taxed.[17] As far as the administration was concerned, freed slaves, though they recognizably enjoyed a different legal status from that of slave, were thought to participate in the same type of labor as slaves and thus were taxed accordingly. Census records from the 1770s offer another insight into the colonial administration's understanding of the place forros and free persons of African origin and descent in general occupied in colonial society. Two population maps sent to the Overseas Council, one for the Comarca do Rio das Velhas in 1772 and the other for Minas Gerais in 1776, use sex and age to differentiate between classes of people. Furthermore, within each class they distinguish three *qualidades* (qualities) of persons: white, pardo, and preto.[18] Yet while these documents provide the number of pardo women aged fourteen to forty years old, or of preto men aged seven to fifteen years old living in the comarca and the captaincy, no distinction is made between those who are slaves and those who are free. Produced possibly with the intent of informing the Crown of the size of the economically active colonial population, or the number of adult men capable of serving in local militias (which in fact was organized in regiments by quality), these documents, like the records of the capitação, indicate officials' willingness to group free persons of African origin and descent with slaves.

Indeed, free preto, crioulo, and pardo individuals in colonial Minas Gerais often lived in the shadow of slavery. Forros, in particular, had a hard time distancing themselves from that association. Persons who had been slaves and then became free were thus described in commercial records, in marriage certificates, in the baptismal records of their children, and finally in their wills and inventories. To use an expression from that period, these documents made it "public and notorious" that these individuals shared a slave past. Their association with slavery, whether because of their legal status as forros or their potential descent from former slaves, often had constraining implications for free persons of African origin and descent. In different petitions to the Overseas Council, the *câmaras* (municipal councils) of colonial Mineiro towns repeatedly expressed their concern over the growth of the free population of African origin and its threat to the white inhabitants of the captaincy. In a petition to the king requesting that persons of African origin and descent not be allowed to serve as militia officers, the câmara of the town of São João del Rei argued that the hated forro and freed-born pretos and pardos held for whites was as extensive as that of slaves. Moreover, it was only their poverty and dependency on whites that allowed for peace in the colony.[19] The councilmen were concerned that if these individuals were allowed a position of authority they would certainly use their power against the white population. Similar views of a strong divide between white people and free peoples of different quality ultimately resulted in the passing of acts that aimed to set strict limitations on preto and pardo freedom.[20] Through regulation of the dress, personal ornaments, and weapons they were able to display in public, or in the civil and military positions in which they were allowed to serve, free persons of African origin and descent were consistently discriminated as separate, different, and inferior to whites.

Petitioning the Crown for favors remained, however, a strategy for social assertion that, though not always successful, remained available to all persons who could claim to be subjects of the king. Thus, when in 1749 the Crown passed a law prohibiting the use of swords or daggers to "apprentices of a mechanical trade, lackeys, porters, sailors, pilots, negroes, and others of equal or inferior condition," the pardo men of the *confraria* (brotherhood) of Saint Joseph in the town of Vila Rica requested that they be excluded from the prohibition. In their justification for why the law should not apply to them, the petitioners appealed to a wide set of markers of their social distinction, choosing to engage the Crown on the basis of not race but political, professional, economic, and social status. Thus, they argued, they should be excluded because the law made no direct mention of them; because they were legitimate vassals of His Majesty and nationals of the country who lived with rectitude; because some of them were masters of trade, with authority over several apprentices and journeymen, while others were masters of the liberal arts: musicians, grammar tutors, surgeons, and physicians. They also argued that some were the sons of noblemen and were recognized as such; that in their commercial and other dealings with others they often behaved as white men; and, more importantly, that they were esteemed according to personal merit and possessions.[21] The Overseas Council recommended that the petition be granted so the brothers could, on procession days, present themselves in public ornamented not only with the typical cloak of the brotherhood but also with their swords and daggers.

The significance of this petition and of the council's concession to the pardo brothers must not be overlooked. Pardos, like mulattoes, mestiços, or cabras, though further distanced from slavery than pretos or crioulos because of their partial white ancestry, often still carried the physical and, for those who were forros, legal markers of that connection. Consequently, town councils and other colonial institutions were not always as willing to treat them with "esteem," a reality that was particularly evident when the issue was civil or military service in positions of authority or legal and commercial privileges and rights over whites. The colonial environment created by Portuguese laws and social practices, however, afforded these men and women the means to interact with those institutions not as the descendants of slaves or of Africans but as persons of legitimate birth, honor and rectitude, distinguished professions, and wealth. By employing the same markers of social distinction that were often the basis of white privilege, pardos, and occasionally even pretos, were sometimes able to circumvent their "inferior condition." While trying to make sense of an increasingly diverse free population and control its impact on the rights and privileges of white colonists, colonial Mineiro society enforced a general rhetoric and practice of social distinction and superiority that was based on a wide array of categories of identification. Ironically, that same rhetoric and practice provided free persons of African origin and descent with alternative markers of social identity they could employ to negotiate their place and privileges in Mineiro society.

## Marriage Practices, Qualidade, *and Race*

Individual strategies to better navigate the social environment of racial and social categories produced in colonial Minas Gerais are perhaps most evident in documents related to marriage practices. Marriage dispensation files, in particular, offer a unique view into couples' motivations and reasoning for marriage and the role individual identity and public perception of identity played in that process. According to ecclesiastical laws enforced in colonial Minas Gerais, couples wishing to marry had to obtain a marriage dispensation. The purpose of this procedure was to ensure that there were no legal impediments to the union. In other words, the prospective bride and groom had to prove that they were willing participants, were not already married, had not taken religious vows, and were not closely related. In cases where an impediment existed, couples could appeal. Incest, which according to the Church constituted a sexual relationship between relatives within the fourth degree of consanguinity, was the most common impediment appealed.[22] Because petitions for dispensation had to justify a union that would have otherwise been condemned by the Church, petitioners often revealed a great amount of personal information, such as illicit sexual liaisons, financial hardship, or social and racial concerns regarding the potential union.[23] Consequently, marriage dispensation files provide an important insight into individual attitudes toward race and social status.

The process of marriage dispensation initiated by Manuel Dias de Sá and Maria Francisca de Sá in 1756, for instance, illustrates the influence racial and social concerns could have on marital choices. Manuel, a native of Portugal, and Maria Francisca, the daughter of a Portuguese man and a parda forra, were first cousins. According to his statement, Manuel had falsely promised marriage to his cousin in order to convince her to have sexual relations with him. Maria Francisca, on the other hand, declared she did not take his promises seriously because she knew them to be closely related. Having consensually started a sexual relationship outside of wedlock, the couple faced a serious problem when Maria Francisca became pregnant. Arguing that under these circumstances Maria Francisca stood to lose her honor and potentially her chances of contracting a good marriage (if one at all), Manuel stated his desire to marry his cousin and requested dispensation of the impediment of incest. But according to the couple's petition, as well as testimonies from different witnesses, it was not just Maria Francisca's honor that was at stake. They all expressed the concern that, because it was "public and notorious in the parish that the petitioner was pregnant," "if she did not marry [Manuel Dias de Sá] it would not be easy for her to find another white man."[24] Maria Francisca found herself in a delicate situation. The daughter of a Portuguese man and a pardo woman, she was probably able to pass as white, as suggested by the petition's omission of a description of her color or race. Marriage to a white man would further reinforce that identity.[25] Pregnancy and an illegitimate child, however, both evidence of her illicit sexual activities, could make her an undesirable marriage partner and significantly compromise her chances of improving her social status through marriage. Under these circumstances, Maria Francisca, and potentially her family too, found breaking the taboo of incest to be the lesser of two evils.

If racial considerations could influence individuals' decision to get married, they also shaped peoples' ideas of what marriage arrangements were undesirable. The process of marriage dispensation of Francisco Alvares de Magalhães and Francisca Ferreira Guimarães illustrates how notions of race and social status could create added challenges to marriage. According to his statement, Francisco had promised Francisca to marry her and "under that promise took her honor and virginity." Yet, despite having conceived a child together and being denounced to the ecclesiastical authorities for living in concubinage, Francisco had not fulfilled his promise of marriage. He explained that his mother "would not agree to the said arrangement because [Francisca Ferreira Guimarães] was a mulata."[26] Francisca was in fact the illegitimate daughter of José Ferreira Guimarães, a white man, and Arcangela Ribeiro, a preta forra woman. Their petition for marriage dispensation also revealed the couple was related within the fourth degree of consanguinity: their fathers were second cousins, making them third cousins. Because the couple was ultimately granted dispensation from that impediment, it seems family objections and not consanguinity had been the main reason preventing their marriage. What is not clear from the document is what changed in their circumstances that encouraged them to seek the authorization to marry when they did. It is possible that Francisco and Francisca, who were twenty-eight and thirty-two years old respectively when they filed for a marriage dispensation, had initiated their relationship before he was twenty-five years old and legally old enough to marry without parental consent. It is also possible that Francisco's mother had changed her mind about the union or that she had died. While we may never know the answer to that question, the document remains an important indication of how ideas about race and social position affected people's attitudes toward each other in that society.

Francisco's mother's concern over his marriage to a woman of mixed descent was not an isolated case of racial discrimination. Shaped by Iberian cultural and social practices, colonial Mineiro society inherited from the Old World the idea of quality (*qualidade*). In Portugal the definition of one's quality was usually based on family background, distinguishing persons of noble birth from commoners, farmers from artisans or merchants, Catholics from converts. In a society heavily marked by ethnic difference, however, skin color, and ultimately racial categories, inevitably became yet other markers of an individual's quality. Yet, because quality was so closely associated to certain social privileges and practices, publicly displaying them, whether legitimately or not, could have the reverse effect of defining, rather than reflecting, one's quality. The owner-ship of slaves by persons of African origin and descent, some of whom may have been slaves themselves, though seemingly contradictory, is a good example of this social behavior. Because owning slaves allowed these individuals to avoid the types of labor usually associated with slav-ery, it marked more publicly their transition from property to property holder, improving the general perception of their quality.[27] Similarly, the practice of emulating the dressing habits of members of the elite, seeking government offices, adopting titles and demanding deferential treatment, or joining the military ranks illustrate different individual strategies to gain public recognition of the social status, or quality, to which one aspired.[28] Marriage and the creation of personal associations between individuals and families was yet another form of public display of one's family origins or claims of quality.[29] Choosing an adequate spouse, one that would improve the status of the newly formed family, or at least not jeopardize it, was therefore one among many possible strategies Mineiros employed to secure a desirable social status.

Eighteenth-century marriage records from the parish of Sabará illus-trate the potential marriage had to influence public perception of an individual's quality. Maria Alves dos Santos, for instance, is referred to in the inventory of Francisco Alves dos Santos, a Portuguese man, as his wife and as a preta forra. When in 1762, twelve years after her first husband's death, she remarried Antônio da Silva Lessa, another Portuguese man, the marriage record simply referred to her as the widow of Francisco Alves dos Santos, her status as such replacing any reference to her color or legal status as a freed person. Moreover, when three years later Maria's son, Vicente Alves dos Santos, got married, his marriage record made no mention of his or his mother's African and slave origins. Marriage to two white, Portuguese men provided Maria, and by extension her son Vicente, with the means to avoid being publicly identified on the basis of racial category.[30] Marriage records of the descendants of Luiza Rodrigues da Cruz, a preta forra and the wife of Domingos Rodrigues da Cruz, a white man, tell a similar story. At the time of Luiza's death, the couple had nine living children, including three daughters who were all married to Por-tuguese men. The marriage record of Luzia, Luiza's oldest daughter, stated

TABLE 1 *Endogamy in the eighteenth-century town of Sabará, Minas Gerais, shown by racial categories of spouses*

|  | Husbands: | | | | | Total |
|---|---|---|---|---|---|---|
|  | White | African | Crioulo | Pardo | Unspecified |  |
| Wives: | | | | | | |
| African | 4 | 26 | 1 | — | — | 31 |
| Crioula | 2 | 13 | 33 | 8 | 2 | 58 |
| Parda | 7 | — | 1 | 25 | 1 | 34 |
| Unspecified | — | 2 | — | 2 | 5 | 9 |
| Total | 13 | 41 | 35 | 35 | 8 | 132 |

Note: The table is based on the description of 132 married couples found in marriage and baptismal records from 1750 to 1800. I have included only couples whose racial description was available for both partners or whose racial description I was able to determine from other notary records. Unspecified husbands and wives are persons of African descent whose records did not indicate whether they were of mixed or solely African descent. Sources: Paróquia de Sabará, Livros de Assentos de Casamento, 1758–1800, Arquivo da Cúria Metropolitana de Belo Horizonte. Paróquia de Sabará, Batizados, Livro 6, vols. 1 and 2, 1750–1800, Cúria Metropolitana de Belo Horizonte.

that the bride was a parda forra while the groom was originally from the town of Porto, in Portugal. Born before her parents' marriage, when her mother and, consequently, she were still slaves, Luzia was unable to escape the public recording of her former slave status, illegitimate birth, and African descent. However, when her daughter Maria Josefa Freire married thirty-one years later, the marriage record made no mention of the bride or Luzia being pardas. Married to a Portuguese man for three decades, Luzia was by then more likely to be recognized publicly as sharing her husband's quality than that of her preto forro mother.[31]

Parish records in general, however, suggest that marriages between persons perceived to be of different quality were in fact not that common. While some cases suggest persons in eighteenth-century Sabará sought to establish formal unions with a partner who could be considered of superior quality, most individuals seemed to have pursued unions with those who were of an equal quality. Among a sample of 132 couples found in marriage and baptismal records in which at least one of the spouses was of African origin or descent, eighty four (nearly two-thirds) comprised persons with the same racial description. These records also reveal that the frequency with which endogamous marriages occurred varied from one group to the next, some groups counting more marriages between persons of the same quality than others.

As illustrated in table 1, African women, for instance, rarely married non-African men. On the other hand, when marrying non-Africans, they were more likely to marry white men than men of African descent (crioulo or pardo). African men, on the other hand, could not restrict their marital choices to African women, who, because of the demographic nature of the Atlantic slave trade, were less numerous than crioulo or pardo women. Similar to Africans, pardos appear to have married within their own racial category more often than not. Seventy-one percent of the pardo men and 73 percent of the pardo women in the sample espoused partners who fit the same description as themselves. Finally, crioulo men show the greatest consistency in choice of spouse: 94 percent of the crioulo men who appear in the records married crioulo women. Because pardo women seemed to have favored unions with men of the same racial group or of a more privileged racial group, namely, whites, while African women appear to have favored unions with men who shared their cultural and ethnic background, this particular group may have been more restricted in their choice of spouse than any other.

The evidence provided by this sample of married couples suggests that marriage in colonial Minas Gerais was heavily endogamous. Studies of other regions of colonial Brazil indicate a similar trend.[32] Because the demographic composition of population in Sabará reveals a strong gender unbalance, adult men being nearly twice as numerous as adult women, and a marked predominance of pardo women, it seems marriages between these women and persons of different quality should have been more common. The fact that they were not confirms that members of this Mineiro society chose a spouse not necessarily based on available candidates but among those to which they wished to associate themselves.

Still, marriage was hardly the only form of stable relationship members of that colonial population could establish. As scholars have pointed out, the bureaucracy involved in obtaining a marriage license could be both time consuming and expensive. As a result, some couples opted to live in concubinage instead. Though not legally recognized or sanctioned by the Church, these unions could nevertheless be long-lasting.[33] Moreover, because natural children, that is, children born out of wedlock, enjoyed the same inheritance rights as legitimate children, the practice of concubinage did not necessarily jeopardize their access to family property.[34] In an environment heavily marked by notions of quality and practices of social differentiation based on ideas of race, concubinage offered men and women an opportunity to pursue an intimate relationship with someone perceived to be a socially inferior partner without compromising their own social status through marriage. For some women of African origin and descent, becoming the concubines of white men may have been a means, albeit usually a more exploitative one, of gaining access to the social and material advantages their lovers enjoyed and of securing a better social and racial status, or quality, for their children.[35] The processes of marriage dispensation that opened this section are suggestive of that very behavior. Both reveal women of African descent who procured an intimate relationship with white men and eventually bore their children. In these two particular cases the relationship evolved to marriage. Several others, however, did not.

As records of marriage dispensation suggest, individuals and families often had their own notions of what constituted a desirable marriage based on ideas of what racial categories made for suitable spouses. The racial description of married couples available in parish records indicates, moreover, that individuals more often than not established formalized unions with persons perceived to be their social and racial equals. The discussion of marriage practices in colonial Minas Gerais thus reveals that persons of African origin and descent in that society were aware of existing racial categories and the social hierarchy they created. More importantly, their individual choices and attitudes when establishing personal relationships suggest how they employed these categories to negotiate their identity and place within that racial and social environment.

## Preto *and* Pardo *Brothers*

Colonial notions about race and social status influenced behavior and social strategies in Minas Gerais not only at an individual level but also a collective one. The common employment of racial and social categories and their discriminatory implications helped to promote a sense of collective identity within certain groups as well as collective effort to negotiate the meaning of that identity. Perhaps the best sources available for examining collective response to racial and social categorization in colonial Minas Gerais are the documents of lay brotherhoods. Widespread in Portugal and other parts of Europe since the Middle Ages, lay brotherhoods were confraternities that sought to promote involvement in religious life and, by offering support to the needy and to the sick as well as overseeing funerary arrangements, to provide members with communal assistance both in life and in death. In the context of Portuguese colonial expansion, lay brotherhoods were further viewed as useful tools for the spread of Christianity, consequently their establishment in the colonies was encouraged by both the Church and the Crown. In Brazil missionaries and secular priests were initially responsible for their foundation, but by the late colonial period most brotherhoods were founded by laymen and women. Like several religious orders, lay brotherhoods were selective in their membership and were often organized along socioeconomic divides. Believing in their obligation to convert Africans and their descendants and the need to better integrate them into Portuguese society and culture, but not willing to allow them membership in their own brotherhoods, white religious and government authorities, as well as slave owners, encouraged slaves to form separate brotherhoods. Initially, these confraternities were opened to all persons; with time, however, they became more selective, reflecting the development of new ethnic and racial divisions in Brazilian colonial society.[36]

Most brotherhoods were devoted to a specific patron saint, and in the case of those founded by Africans and their descendants the most common devotions were to Saint Benedict, Saint Gonçalo, Saint Efigênia, Our Lady of Mercy, and, above all, Our Lady of the Rosary. The worship of Our Lady of the Rosary was first introduced in Brazil in 1552 by Jesuit missionaries concerned with the catechization of slaves in the captaincy of Pernambuco. Popular in Portugal and Catholic Europe because of the belief in the power of the rosary to invoke the mercy and assistance of the Virgin Mary, the devotion also spread with great force among slaves and their descendants in Brazil.[37] Studies of lay brotherhoods in Minas Gerais also point to the popularity of this particular devotion in that captaincy, especially among slaves and free persons of African origin and descent.[38] Suggestive of the racial and ethnic divisions that would mark these religious associations, the brotherhoods of Our Lady of the Rosary were usually identified as being preto men. Similarly, one finds in Minas Gerais, as well as in other parts of Brazil, crioulo brotherhoods of Our Lady of Mercy and pardo brotherhoods of Saint Gonçalo.

Different studies have examined documents describing the composition and general activities of preto, crioulo, and pardo brotherhoods in

Brazil to discuss their role in shaping and reinforcing collective racial or ethnic identity.[39] Papers documenting the history of these brotherhoods' interactions with the Crown and other colonial institutions, mainly in the form of applications for approval and petitions, reveal, moreover, how these confraternities shaped a collective understanding and negotiation of the role and place of persons of African origin and descent in that society. Through their brotherhoods, pretos, crioulos, and pardos, whether slave, forro, or free-born, sought to shape how they, as a group, related to their environment, to different sources of authority, to other racial or ethnic groups, and ultimately to each other.

In 1798 the brotherhood of Our Lady of Mercy and Saint Benedict of the Villa do Príncipe, a major township in the north of the captaincy of Minas Gerais, petitioned the Crown through its Overseas Council for the approval of their *compromisso* (statute). The petitioners argued that since its creation the brotherhood had "offered well-known proof of its extraordinary feats to the benefit of the Church and inspired Christian and devout sentiments in the hearts of brothers and other peoples." They further boasted a membership of 266 men and women, comprising whites, crioulos and pardos—with a predominance, however, of crioulo and pardo men—and the acquisition of twenty licensed graves. Finally, the petitioners declared the brotherhood did not "waste a single opportunity to fulfill its obligations as determined in the compromisso, attending to the sick by providing for their needs in life and accompanying them after death."[40] In pointing out the many accomplishments of the brotherhood of Our Lady of Mercy and Saint Benedict of the Villa do Príncipe, the petition reveals what this and similar confraternities viewed to be their role in their respective environments and communities. While they understood their main purpose and obligation was to provide for the needs of their brothers and ensure that theirs would be a good death, with the expected funeral procession and burial in consecrated ground, they also sought to provide religious instruction and spiritual aid to a wider community of nonbrothers.

Interacting with a social environment that far exceeded the limits of their community of brothers was not rare among colonial brotherhoods. The preto brothers of Our Lady of the Rosary of Vila Rica, for instance, built a new street leading to the town's main church on the occasion of the procession of the Most Holy Sacrament. The municipal council had promised the brotherhood property concessions along the new street in exchange for their work. Ownership of town lots would have allowed the brotherhood to generate through rents the income it required to support itself. Consequently, when the council failed to fulfill their promise the confraternity promptly petitioned the king for assistance in the matter. The Crown representative who reported on the situation advised the king to support the cause of the brotherhood, commenting that "being miserable preto men . . . [and] having completed such a huge and considerable work for the benefit of the city and the public," it would have been unfair to deny them what they had been promised.[41] It was not uncommon for the crown or local governments to provide brotherhoods with certain privileges, whether the right to collect tithes or urban property, that could ensure their financial well-being. Through the assistance they provided to the needy, their efforts to build churches, and other works, brotherhoods fulfilled an important role in colonial society, often relieving the Crown and local governments of some of their obligations toward subjects and townspeople.[42] Through the construction of a new street in Vila Rica, the brotherhood of Our Lady of the Rosary was doing its part to secure a role for itself in the life of the town. By demanding that the terms of their agreement with the municipal council be fulfilled, the "miserable" preto men of the town ensured, furthermore, public recognition of that role and the benefits that came with it.

The crown's concession to the demands of the preto brothers in Vila Rica illustrates one way in which participation in lay brotherhoods empowered persons of African origin and descent. As different authors have suggested, religious associations were often attractive to minorities faced with an oppressive social order because they offered an institutional structure around which individuals could congregate to voice and protect their interests.[43] Indeed, living in a society that otherwise tried to limit their freedoms, confraternities potentially afforded this group a legitimate space of conviviality, participation in local religious and public events, and the means to demand of religious and government authorities the same rights and privileges enjoyed by white brotherhoods.

Still, preto, crioulo, and pardo brotherhoods often faced different attempts by outsiders, whether parish priests, government officials, or local whites—including the owners of some of the enslaved brothers—to control their activities. In an effort to secure as much autonomy as they could afford, they repeatedly requested that the crown grant their chaplains more religious authority and allow them to build their own churches. In fact, several brotherhoods in colonial Minas Gerais kept an altar to their patron saint in the church of another brotherhood. An arrangement that heavily compromised their autonomy, sharing the space of a church was nonetheless a necessity for some brotherhoods of lesser means. Thus the aspiration to build their own church where, according to the petition of the preto brotherhood of Saint Elisbão and Our Lady of the Rosary, they "could carry out their functions with all liberty . . . and worship the Virgin with the appropriate reverence" was fairly widespread.[44] The free and enslaved preto men of Our Lady of the Rosary in the hamlet of Ibituruna, for example, complained of having to worship "in a strange church [where] they were always forced to wait and often interrupted, either by fear of or respect for the white men, the majority of whom are the owners of those captive brothers." Having their own church would therefore "[suspend] all the obstacles that offend that incorporation's devotion."[45]

Similar petitions by other brotherhoods reveal the strong effort of preto but also crioulo and pardo brothers to separate physically their space of conviviality from that of whites. That separation was pursued further in their compromissos, which limited or excluded whites, and in some cases other groups of African origin or descent, from holding administrative positions in the brotherhood or from becoming members altogether.[46] These practices point to a strong awareness of existing or desired boundaries between these groups of peoples. As suggested above, the creation of lay brotherhoods of persons of African origin and descent was often encouraged in Minas Gerais, and Brazil in general, as a means of enforcing among that group acceptable religious and cultural behavior, as well as a particular social order. Yet if these brotherhoods contributed to strengthening the religious, cultural, and social practices of that society, they also reinforced the racial practices that marked colonial Minas Gerais. Lay brothers of African origin and descent ultimately forged out of the divide they experienced and gradually embraced an understanding of themselves as distinguishable racial groups.

The corporate nature of religious brotherhoods provided, moreover, a fertile ground on which individuals of African origin and descent could develop a sense of common needs, interests, and, ultimately, cultural identity. Thus, in the context of the daily lives of brotherhoods and their members, the categories of racial differentiation often employed to distinguish persons of African origin and descent in that society could be internalized as parameters of a collective identity. In fact, creating collective identity was crucial to the development of a sense of collective responsibility that could justify and support the existence of brotherhoods.[47] It was that sense of collective responsibility that led, for instance, the preto brotherhood of Our Lady of the Rosary in Campanha da Princesa to include in their compromisso a requirement that members review the care their ill brothers received from owners. The implication that the brotherhood could reserve the right to interfere with a slave owner's treatment of a slave was not well received. The Crown representative who examined the brotherhood's petition for the approval of the compromisso considered it inappropriate and arrogant, arguing furthermore that it could cause great tension and disorder. The approval of the compromisso was thus conditioned on revisions.[48] From the perspective of the brotherhood, what the Crown deemed arrogant was simply their attempt to fulfill their responsibility to look after their members' interests. What is more, collective responsibility in this case transcended social and legal divides between brothers to rest instead on their common preto identity and membership in the same confraternity.

In 1786 the pardo brotherhood of São Gonçalo García in São João del Rei petitioned the queen for the power to force unwilling slaveowners to sell the freedom of their slaves when offered a just amount. They justified their request by stating that "because freedom was a natural right, it was not reasonable that several of their brothers, being able and wanting to offer a just amount for themselves, were kept in captivity by their respective owners who refused payment under the pretext that no one can be forced to sell anything." They argued further that it was a general rule of law that "if a matter of public utility, anyone could be forced to sell their property." They claimed their case fit that rule because through the manumission of their brothers the Crown would "acquire new useful vassals to the state, new farmers for the land, new settlers for the back lands, new explorers of gold, new masters in all sorts of trades, and that it would ultimately be an act of public good towards so many miserable men and women who could be living in freedom."[49] Though the request was not granted, having been deemed potentially too subversive to the local social order, it revealed the brotherhood's view of its role as a mediator between different sources or structures of power in that society and their members. Through this and other requests the preto, crioulo, and pardo brotherhoods in Minas Gerais attempted to translate the often discriminating racial and ethnic categories imposed on their members into a common ground on which to build a collective effort to negotiate and better define their place in Mineiro society.

## Conclusion

When, in 1788, the preto brotherhood of Our Lady of the Rosary in the parish of Santo Antônio do Rio das Velhas was threatened with the annulment of a previously granted authorization to build their own church, they petitioned the queen of Portugal for help. They declared that they had started the construction work in 1773 and had completed the main chapel and other parts of the building, which they used for their functions and festivities in honor of the Virgin. They further appealed to the queen's mercy by reminding her of all the work and resources they had invested in the construction. Finally, they declared that "being the petitioners preto men they were, for that reason, worthy of the support of Her Majesty." The brotherhood's appeal had the desired effect, resulting in an order by the Overseas Council to remove the annulment and approve the church.[50] Yet if brotherhoods petitioning the Crown for the authorization to establish and maintain a separate church were commonplace in colonial Minas Gerais, the appeal to the queen's potential sentiment of responsibility toward preto men is noteworthy.

In this chapter I have explored how different social and racial categories were employed by Mineiro colonial society to make sense of, order, and control its population. As these categories gained meaning for individuals, becoming more closely associated with ideas of social status and quality, they influenced how people interacted and the interpersonal relationships they pursued. At an individual level the employment of these categories could be experienced as rather artificial attempts at identifying people by an ascribed social or racial identity. Moreover, because this practice was based heavily on public perceptions, some individuals pursued any opportunity they had to associate themselves with social or racial categories that could prove more beneficial to them, for example through marriage. Yet these categories of identification were also experienced at a collective level, as illustrated in the papers of lay brotherhoods.

Developed on a model of membership that was organized along socioeconomic or racial divides, preto, crioulo, and pardo brotherhoods helped to reinforce such distinctions. More importantly, as their members developed a sense of their shared interests and experiences, they embraced notions of social and racial distinction as the parameters of their collective identity and their corporate responsibility toward one another.

It was through their collective identity that the preto brotherhood of Our Lady of the Rosary in the parish of Santo Antônio do Rio das Velhas chose to interact with the queen when seeking permission to keep their church. By identifying themselves as a group who, because of their racial identity, deserved the queen's attention and favors, they sought to establish a particular relationship to the Portuguese monarch, one that would better protect their interests. Persons of African origin and descent in colonial Minas Gerais were continuously negotiating the terms under which they integrated into their social environment. In their efforts to secure the position they desired, and the opportunities and privileges it offered, they appealed to different elements of their individual or collective identity: birth, family origins, social and economic conditions, religious devotions, roles within a community or town, economic activities, and the like. In that context, race became one more marker of identity they chose at times to ignore and at others to embrace.

## Notes

1. The term *preto* (black) was commonly used to identify Africans of unknown ethnic origin. *Crioulo* referred to persons solely of African descent born in Brazil. Persons of mixed ancestry were commonly identified as *mestiço* or, in a reference to the lighter color of their skin, *pardo* (gray or brown).

2. "Requerimento dos humildes escravos e leais vassalos, os homens crioulos, pretos, e mestiços machos e femeas, moradores nas Minas do ouro," October 14, 1755, *Coleção do Arquivo Histórico Ultramarino*, doc. (68) 66, Arquivo Público Mineiro (hereafter cited as APM).

3. This subject is addressed throughout the present volume. See also Stavig, *The World of Túpac Amaru*; Twinam, *Public Lives, Private Secrets*; Dean, *Inka Bodies and the Body of Christ*; Vinson, *Bearing Arms for His Majesty*; Bennett, *Africans in Colonial Mexico*.

4. Freyre, *The Masters and the Slaves*; Tannenbaum, *Slave and Citizen*; Elkins, *Slavery*; Davis, *The Problem of Slavery in Western Culture*; Klein, *Slavery in the Americas*; Degler, *Neither Black nor White*.

5. Luna, *Minas Gerais*; Figueiredo, *O avesso da memória*; Paiva, *Escravos e libertos*; Bergad, *Slavery and the Demographic and Economic History of Minas Gerais*; Higgins "Licentious

*Liberty" in a Brazilian Gold-Mining Region*; Paiva, *Escravidão e universo cultural na colônial*; Furtado, *Chica da Silva e o contratador dos diamantes*.

6. Initial settlement in Brazil was encouraged through a system of land grants called *capitanias donatárias*. These grants were distributed among a few men deemed worthy of the king's favors either for their military or administrative importance in the organization of the Portuguese empire. For a history of the early colonization of Brazil, see Boxer, *The Portuguese Seaborne Empire*; Holanda, *História da civilização brasileira*; Johnson, "Portuguese Settlement, 1500–1580."

7. Grantees were entitled to request 2 *braças* (each braça equivalent to 2.20 meters) for every worker employed, but no more than 30 braças. Antonil, *Cultura e opulência do Brazil por suas drogas e minas*, 215–16.

8. Zemella, *O abastecimento*, 97–114; Florentino, *Em costas negras*, 37–44; Fragoso, *Homens de grossa aventura*, 155–61. For a general discussion of the slave population in Minas Gerais, see Bergad, *Slavery and Economic History of Minas Gerais, Brazil*.

9. Barbosa, *Dicionário da terra e da gente de Minas*, 85; Schwartz, *Sugar Plantations in the Formation of Brazilian Society*, 75–97.

10. According to Iberian law, the Crown had claim to one-fifth of all minerals and other riches extracted from the imperial territories. The Portuguese Crown employed two tax systems to collect the royal fifth: the *capitação*, which consisted of a per capita tax on all working slaves; and, after 1750, the direct collection of the royal fifth in official smelting houses responsible for processing all gold extracted in the captaincy. Barbosa, *Dicionário da terra e da gente de Minas*, 160–61; "Regimento da Capitação," July 19, 1735, in Figueiredo, ed., *Códice costa matoso*, 381–409.

11. Mapa geral de fogos, Filhos, Filhas, Escravos, Pardos, Forros e Pretos, 1767, *Coleção Arquivo Histórico Ultramarino*, doc. (93) 58, APM; População da Província de Minas Gerais, 1776–1821, *Coleção Arquivo da Casa dos Contos*, pl. 30099, APM.

12. "Matrícula de escravos adventícios e fugitivos," 1742, Câmara Municipal de Sabará, códice 14, APM.

13. For further discussion of the ethnic composition of the Brazilian slave population, see Ramos, "Community, Control, and Acculturation"; Soares, *Devotos da cor*; Sweet, *Recreating Africa*.

14. For studies that reveal the economic diversification of Minas Gerais, see Costa, *Minas colonial*; Furtado, *Homens de negócio*; Chaves, *Perfeitos negociantes*.

15. For a case study of manumission in Minas Gerais, see Higgins, "*Licentious Liberty*," 145–74.

16. "Mapa de população de 1776 das freguesias da Comarca do Rio da Velhas," 1776, *Coleção Arquivo Histórico Ultramarino*, doc. (112) 11, APM; "Recenseamento da população de alguns termos da antiga capitania depois província de Minas Gerais," 1810, *Arquivo Casa dos Contos*, pl. 21115, APM.

17. Figueiredo, ed., *Códice costa matoso*, 407–11.

18. "Relação abreviada das Pessoas existentes nas Freguezias da Comarca do Sabará," 1772, *Coleção Arquivo Histórico Ultramarino*, doc. (104) 61, APM; Mapa dos Habitantes

actuates da Capitania de Minas Geraes, 1776, *Coleção Arquivo Histórico Ultramarino*, doc. (110) 59, APM.

19. "Representação dos oficiais da Camara de Vila de Sao Joao Del Rei," July 30, 1774, *Coleção Arquivo Histórico Ultramarino*, doc. (107) 27, APM.

20. Russell-Wood, *Slavery and Freedom in Colonial Brazil*, 67–82.

21. "Requerimento dos homens pardos da Confraria de Sao Jose de Vila Rica das Minas," March 6, 1758, *Coleção Arquivo Histórico Ultramarino*, doc. (73) 20, APM.

22. The Church also defined as incestuous sexual relations between spiritual relatives— that is, persons connected through godparentage—within the fourth degree of consanguinity. Almeida, *O gosto do pecado*, 80–85.

23. For a general discussion of marriage in colonial Brazil, see Ramos, "Marriage and the Family in Colonial Vila Rica."; Silva, *Sistema de casamento no Brasil colonial*; Nazzari, *Disappearance of the Dowry*; Metcalf, *Family and Frontier in Colonial Brazil*; Figueiredo, *Barrocas famílias*. For specific studies using marriage dispensations, see Silva, *História da família no Brazil colonial*, 171–206; Faria, *A colônia em movimento*, 140–62; Goldschmidt, *Casamentos mistos*.

24. Manuel Dias de Sá and Maria Francisca de Sá, November 23, 1756, Sabará, matrimonial dispensation, Arquivo do Arcebispado de Mariana.

25. Marriages between women of mixed descent and Portuguese men as a strategy to "whiten" the family lineage and improve the women's social status were not uncommon in Minas Gerais and have been observed in other regions of the colony as well. See Nazzari, *Disappearance of the Dowry*, 28–34; Metcalf, *Family and Frontier in Colonial Brazil*, 87–119; and Lewkowicz, "As mulheres mineiras e o casamento."

26. Francisco Alvares de Magalhães and Francisca Ferreira Guimarães, July 16, 1770, Sabará, matrimonial dispensation, Arquivo do Arcebispado de Mariana. The term *mulato/a* refers to an individual of mixed Portuguese and African descent. Though commonly used to describe slaves of mixed origin, the term *pardo* was more often used to refer to free people of mixed descent.

27. In the Mineiro town of Sabará, 86 percent of the forro individuals whose property was inventoried after their death owned slaves. See Dantas, "Inheritance Practices among Individuals of African Origin and Descent in 18th-Century Minas Gerais, Brazil." For a more lengthy study of forros' ownership of slaves, see Luna, *Minas Gerais*.

28. Paiva, *Escravidão e universo cultural na colônia*; Bicalho, *A cidade e oimpério*, 322–336; Twinam, *Public Lives, Private Secrets*; Vinson, *Bearing Arms for His Majesty*.

29. For a longer discussion of the role of quality in marriage practices, see McCaa, "Calidade, Clase, and Marriage in Colonial Mexico."

30. "Inventário de Francisco Alves dos Santos," February 29, 1750, Cartório do Segundo Ofício, doc. (13) 5, Museu do Ouro de Sabará/Arquivo Casa Borba Gato (henceforth, MOS/ACBG); Assento de Casamento, November 27, 1762, Paróquia de Sabará, 1758–1800, Arquivo da Cúria Metropolitana de Belo Horizonte (henceforth ACMBH); Assento de Casamento, May 5, 1765, Paróquia de Sabará, 1758–1800, ACMBH.

31. "Inventário de Luiza Rodrigues da Cruz," February 1, 1779, Cartório do Segundo Ofício, doc. (48) 6, mos/acbg; Assento de Casamento, July 31, 1759, Paróquia de Sabará, 1758–1800, acmbh; Assento de Casamento, February 10, 1790, Paróquia de Sabará, 1758–1800, acmbh.

32. See Nazarri, *Disappearance of the Dowry*; Faria, *A colônia em movimento*, 140–62; Soares, "Mina, Angola e Guiné."

33. Figueiredo, *Barrocas famílias*; Silva, *História da família no Brazil colonial*.

34. Lewin, "Natural and Spurious Children in Brazilian Inheritance Law from Colony to Empire."

35. Nazarri, "Concubinage in Colonial Brazil."

36. Russell-Wood, *Fidalgos and Philantropists*; Mulvey, "Slave Confraternities in Brazil"; Russell-Wood, *Slavery and Freedom in Colonial Brazil*, 128–60; Borges, *Escravos e libertos*.

37. Souza, "Viagens do rosário entre a Velha Cristandade e o Além-Mar." In her study of slave brotherhoods in Brazil, Patricia Mulvey, working with a sample of 165 brotherhoods, found that nearly half of them were dedicated to Our Lady of the Rosary. Mulvey, "Slave Confraternities in Brazil."

38. Caio Boschi was able to identify sixty-two brotherhoods of Our Lady of the Rosary in Minas Gerais; Marcos Magalhãs de Aguiar, in his study of Mineiro brotherhoods, identified eighty-two. See Boschi, *Os leigos e o poder*; Aguiar, "A evolução da vida associativa em minas colonial e a sociabilidade confrarial negra."

39. Scarano, *Devoção e escravidão*; Kiddy, "Ethnicity and Racial Identity in the Brotherhoods of the Rosary of Minas Gerais"; Soares, *Devotos da cor*.

40. "Requerimento dos irmãos da Irmandade de Nossa Senhora das Mercês e São Benedito da Vila do Principe," September 24, 1798, *Coleção Arquivo História Ultramarino*, doc. (145) 48, apm.

41. "Consulta do Conselho sobre requerimento dos oficiais da Irmandade de Nossa Senhora do Rosário dos Homens Pretos de Vila Rica," January 21, 1769, *Coleção Arquivo História Ultramarino*, doc. (94) 6, apm.

42. Boschi, *Os leigos e o poder*, 71–79; Russell-Wood, *Slavery and Freedom in Colonial Brazil*, 144.

43. Boschi, *Os leigos e o poder*, 29–31; Herzog, "Private Organizations as Global Networks in Early Modern Spain and Spanish America."

44. "Requerimento do juiz e mais irmãos pretos da Irmandade de São Elesbão e Senhora do Rosário," June 20, 1803, *Coleção Arquivo História Ultramarino*, doc. (167) 10, apm.

45. "Requerimento dos homens pretos, libertos e escravos," June 26, 1805, *Coleção Arquivo História Ultramarino*, doc. (176) 43, apm.

46. Borges, *Escravos e libertos*, 79–89; Soares, *Devotos da cor*, 199–213.

47. Herzog, "Private Organizations," 126.

48. "Consulta do Conselho Ultramarino sobre o requerimento da Irmandade de Nossa Senhora do Rosário da Vila da Campanha da Princesa," September 12, 1805, *Coleção Arquivo História Ultramarino*, doc. (177) 41, apm.

49. "Representação da corporação da Irmandade de São Gonçalo García," August 22, 1786, *Coleção Arquivo Histório Ultramarino*, doc. (125) 20, APM.

50. "Requerimento dos irmãos da Irmandade de Nossa Senhora do Rosario dos Pretos da freguesia de Santo Antônio do Rio das Velhas," December 22, 1788, *Coleção Arquivo Histório Ultramarino*, doc. (130) 59, APM.

# Purchasing Whiteness

*Conversations on the Essence of Pardo-ness and*
*Mulatto-ness at the End of Empire*

In 1783 Bernardo Ramírez, a pardo from Guatemala, appealed to the Council of the Indies to make him white.[1] There were many unique aspects to his request, but the most extraordinary proved to be the comment of the royal official who reviewed it. He noted that the favor Ramírez asked was "repugnant or at least excessive" because it was "evident" that he "can neither disguise nor dismiss his infected quality [*cualidad*] even if he tries."[2] His statement proved provocative because of its rarity. During the closing decades of the eighteenth century the Council of the Indies received a significant if small (twenty-six) number of petitions from mulattoes and pardos to be considered white.[3] Such requests generated a substantial documentation, given that petitioners wrote about their lives and their service to the Crown, provided letters of recommendation from local elites, had applications investigated or commented on by officials in America, and then reviewed by the lawyers (*fiscales*) as well as members of the Council and Cámara of the Indies. Years of correspondence might pass between a first application, a decision, and final correspondence. Yet in all this flood of paper, this was the sole instance where any of the hundreds of people involved in the process ever questioned whether a pardo or mulatto might be able to become white. Even though royal officials might reject such requests or local elites might vigorously protest whitenings, no one but this official ever challenged the fundamental proposition that pardo-ness and mulatto-ness existed as transformable categories or that whiteness was a possible goal.

What is going on here? Such a resounding absence reminds that sometimes historical silence can be more revealing than historical sound. This chapter revisits exchanges over whitening that took place between pardos, mulattoes, viceregal and imperial officials, and local elites during the closing decades of the colony. Their letters, depositions, reviews, and protests provide rare insight into multiple constructions inherent in conceptualizations of identity. Correspondence from pardos and mulattoes not only reveals their self-identity but also what Frederick Cooper and Rogers Brubaker describe as "situated subjectivity"—"one's sense of who one is, of one's social location and of how (given the first two) one is prepared to act." As pardos and mulattoes sought whiteness, they revealed how they viewed themselves in relationship to the Spanish state, to whites, and to other pardos.[4] Yet other elements of identification are external "categorizations"—how outsiders, whether the Spanish state or local elites, constructed and revised similar or alternative pardo and mulatto identifiers. Such analysis resonates with one of the overarching objectives of this collection: to probe those liminal "contact points" between institutions and subjects "when social categories are articulated, publicized, internalized, contested, and sometimes altered."[5]

The important "institution" in this instance is the Council and Cámara of the Indies. Some members of the Council served on the Cámara subcouncil, which was the group that made decisions concerning grants of royal favor, or *gracias*. It was to this Cámara that Bernardo Ramírez directed his letters and proofs of royal service. He requested a *gracias al sacar*, a royal decree that literally gave him "permission to take" himself away from his state of pardo-ness. When he petitioned in 1783, there was no specific legislation concerning gracias al sacar and whitening. However, twelve years later when the Crown issued a new price list (*arancel*) for the gracias al sacar petitions in the Americas, it included—for the first time—the option for the purchase of whiteness. There is strong evidence that those petitions that predated 1795 had provided the precedent for royal officials to include whitening in the new list.[6] Not only did applications subsequently increase but so did protests from the Venezuelan establishment, who felt so threatened that they issued an *Obedesco pero no cumplo* (I obey but I won't comply)—that rare rejection of Spanish state policy—and temporarily banned publication of the whitening clauses.[7] Their remonstrations eventually convinced the Cámara to table and not rule on applications received after 1803 until it developed a coherent policy concerning whitening. Cámara officials proved reluctant to resolve this thorny and contentious issue and petitioners languished with their cases undecided until independence.

Even though the whitening gracias al sacar had a short history (1760–1808), it promoted rare conversations among mulattoes and pardos, royal officials, and elites concerning whitening. Understanding this dialogue from the perspective of these participants necessitates fine attention to detail. There are portions where the documentation is formulaic; other times the voices and vocabularies of those involved emerge clearly. Although pardos and mulattoes sent letters with personal details of their lives, their representatives, or *apoderados*, likely drafted part of all of their petitions. When local elites testified in favor of whitening it was through the traditional process where they responded to a series of set questions posed to benefit the petitioner. Sometimes they simply parroted the wording of the question back as an affirmative; other times their responses proved more spontaneous and revealing. When the *fiscal* on the Cámara reviewed whitening applications, sometimes he repeated phrases used in the original petition; other times he employed his own vocabulary. Similarly, when the Venezuelan establishment—the city council, the bishop, university and state officials—protested gracias al sacar whitenings, they both repeated official discourse and added their own language. Given such filters, it is imperative to note who is using a certain vocabulary, when it is shared, when it is not, and when it changes.

Attempts to comprehend how the historical actors in the whitening process viewed pardo-ness and mulatto-ness also demands a ruthless ridding of preconceived stereotypes—particularly more contemporary concepts such as race—in exploring how late-eighteenth-century participants self-identified or were categorized by others. Most parties generally seemed in agreement that those pardos and mulattoes who applied for whitening descended from some ancestors who were themselves pardo or mulatto and somewhere down the generations there had been mixing with whites as well. Yet it is equally clear that neither race nor ethnicity adequately captures pardo or mulatto self-identification or their categorization by others.

Rather, the gracias al sacar whitenings reveal a different vocabulary suggesting a development along parallel tracks. First were Hispanic traditions mutually shared by all the parties providing a language that both grounded external "categorizations" of pardo-ness and mulatto-ness as well as shaped pardo and mulatto self-image throughout the gracias al sacar years. Second were changing variants arising from the Americas. By the late 1780s, the Venezuelan establishment introduced negative "categorizations" of pardos and mulattoes as they sought rationales to justify their permanent inferiority. Both spontaneously and in response, pardo and mulatto applicants introduced new modes of self-identification, including the variables of color and of appearance. Their "situated subjectivity" altered as they distanced themselves from others of their caste as part of a larger strategy to become white. Understanding the traditional ways that Spaniards customarily defined attributes such as pardo-ness and mulatto-ness proves an essential first step to appreciate these changes and colonial variations.

## Historic Spanish Traditions

Historic Spanish traditions provided a shared vocabulary for royal officials, pardos and mulattoes, and local elites to discuss the essence of pardo-ness and mulatto-ness—their presence, transmission, absence, and alterability. Spaniards had not invented language for that purpose; rather it derived from customary ways that Spaniards constructed other positive or negative attributes including nobility, Jewishness, or illegitimacy. These identifications were "external" given that Spanish traditions and law imposed them on pardos and mulattoes. Yet as Brubaker and Cooper point out, such "categorizations" not only set parameters as to "how one is regarded and treated by others" but also can be fundamental to self-identification, the "shaping one's own understanding of oneself."[8] There existed a conceptual plane where all parties shared a language not only to explain how pardo-ness and mulatto-ness came into being (*naturaleza*) but how they might be passed on (*naturaleza, limpieza*), what it meant (*limpieza, cualidad*), and if it might be altered (*defecto*). Sometimes pardos and mulattoes, royal officials, and others used these words alone, other times they combined variants of this vocabulary. Understanding language from the perspective of those involved provides insight into the interplay between those outside categorizations defining pardo identification and pardo acceptance or rejection of those constructions. It also explains why—except for one fiscal—there seemed to be a mutual understanding that pardo-ness and mulatto-ness were not permanent conditions but might be changed.

How did pardo-ness come into being? Havana petitioner Manuel Baez de Llereno expressed his understanding of the process in 1773 when he asked the Cámara to "dispense all defect, stain, or imperfection" due to his "*naturaleza*."[9] In 1786, Joseph Luis Paz from Panama also explained that his problem originated because he was "of *naturaleza, quinteron*" (one-fifth pardo).[10] Early expressions of naturaleza appear in the *Siete Partidas*, the law of medieval Spain. The *Partidas* defined naturaleza as closely linked to nature: "Nature is a virtue that makes all things be in that state that God has ordered."[11] "Naturaleza" the *Partidas* explained, "is something like nature, and that helps it to be and *to keep all that descends from it*" (my emphasis). "Nature" was what "was," while "*naturaleza*" governed the transmission of that essence from both the father and mother. This distinction was key, because there were other characteristics such as nobility (*nobleza*) where only paternal inheritance counted—for example, if a father was a noble and the mother was plebeian, any off-spring still inherited the paternal trait.[12] In contrast, in transmission through naturaleza, if only one parent had a flaw such as illegitimacy, Jewishness, or pardo/mulatto-ness, the condition of that parent was sufficient to pass the imperfect naturaleza to all descendants.

The Spanish construct of *limpieza de sangre* was closely related to the concept of naturaleza. When Joseph Francisco Baez, a brother of Manuel, applied to the Cámara in 1759, he asked for a "decree . . . which dispenses from now on the point of *limpieza*."[13] With this simple word Joseph Francisco referenced a fundamental external "categorization"—the Spanish state's definition of the condition and the consequences for those who did or did not possess "clean blood." Crystallizing in the formative era of the late fifteenth century, the purity of blood edicts were originally instrumental in the forging of early Spanish nationhood, as they encouraged Spaniards to identify each other through shared discrimination against the despised "other." In the peninsula, the primary targeted other proved to be the non-Catholic, be it the Jew, Moor, heretic, or *converso* (converted Jew).[14] More than three hundred years later, Spaniards still identified themselves in reference to the presence or absence of limpieza. Andrés Manuel de Seide of Santiago forwarded a typical peninsular version when he petitioned the Cámara of Castile for legitimation in 1760, the year of the first whitening petition. He proclaimed that his parents "were Old Christians, free of all bad race [*raza*] of Jews, Moors, Heretics, Sects recently converted to Our Catholic Religion, penitents of the Holy Tribunal of the Inquisition . . . nor did they suffer any other defect or infection that would have deprived them nor deprive their descendants of honor and the holding of honorable offices in the republic."[15]

In the colonies, definition of the non-Catholic other became complicated with the addition of pardo and mulatto to the limpieza definition, although it remains unclear precisely what precipitated the change or when it occurred. María Elena Martínez has traced a seventeenth-century discourse in which legalists, the Inquisition, royal officials, and colonists debated the limpieza of Indians as well as Africans.[16] She concludes that religious origin remained a fundamental definer of who did or who did not possess limpieza through the seventeenth century. Two historically inaccurate interpretations surfaced to rationalize such distinctions. The first posited that Indians had—when given the opportunity—fully accepted Catholicism and therefore met limpieza standards. In contrast, Africans—according to this equally dubious historical rendering—had not embraced Catholicism when it was offered to them in the Old World, had been forcibly converted en route to the Americas, and therefore did not conform to the cleanliness guidelines.

Another possible origin of the colonial limpieza version might derive from discrimination against the Moor. While Iberian prejudice was originally driven by religious differences (Islam vs. Christianity), the association of Moors with darker phenotype may have rationalized the extension of limpieza de sangre discrimination to blacks, mulattoes, and the castas. While the temporal and conceptual origins of the colonial limpieza definition remain murky, by the eighteenth century, Spanish American Creoles typically defined those with limpieza de sangre as having "always been known, held, and commonly reputed to be white persons, Old Christians of the nobility, clean of all bad blood and without any mixture of commoner, Jew, Moor, *Mulatto* or converso in any degree, no matter how remote."[17]

In the Americas, the limpieza ordinances created a category of Spaniards and white creoles with full civil rights and privileges alongside inferior categories of others. Official discrimination against pardos and mulattoes because they lacked "clean blood" was severe, equal to a "civil death." Both imperial and colonial laws forbade that they hold political office, practice prestigious professions (public notary, law, surgery, pharmacy, smelter), or enjoy equal social status with whites.[18] Military orders, the military, religious congregations, and universities issued similar discriminatory ordinances restricting pardo and mulatto military service and forbidding profession to the priesthood or attendance or graduation from university.[19] Similar to the underlying dynamics of transmission associated with naturaleza, so too with limpieza: the negative characteristic of one parent proved sufficient to prejudice the clean blood of succeeding generations.

Not all pardos fully accepted such categorizations, either the revised American definition or the accompanying discriminations. Even though the Habanero Joseph Francisco Baez conceded that his father had "pardo" ancestors, in his 1760 application he also declared that "they were offspring of sons of white Spanish men and held as Old Christians."[20] In 1808, the Mexican pardo Manuel Caballero Carranza also asserted his limpieza, turning the tables on the colonial clean blood definitions. His request for whitening quoted the traditional Spanish version of limpieza that did not refer to pardos and mulattoes. He stated that his family were "neither descended from Moors, Jews, nor from those newly converted to the guild [gremio] of our Catholic faith, and from Old Christians."[21]

More substantively, throughout the colonial centuries and throughout the empire, upwardly mobile pardos and mulattoes strategized to bypass the limpieza de sangre restrictions.[22] Even though the pardos and mulattoes who petitioned for whitening acknowledged that they were subject to the discriminations imposed by the colonial limpieza restriction—indeed this was why they were applying—this cohort had proven quite successful in evading them. Many had already "passed" informally to enjoy privileges reserved for whites, such as graduation from university, the acquisition of skills to practice as notaries or surgeons, or—for pardo females—the opportunity to marry white males. When pardos and mulattoes eventually sought a whitening gracias al sacar, it was to receive an official mandate to practice forbidden professions, to send children to university, or to enjoy the totality of white perquisites for themselves and succeeding generations.

Another more common vocabulary shared by pardos, mulattoes, royal officials, and local elites surrounded definitions of *calidad* or *cualidad*, which translated as "quality," "state," or "condition." Calidad/cualidad served as a shorthand expression for the effects of naturaleza and limpieza and, as were these characteristics, it was inherited from both parents. Such assumptions underlay a request in 1786 when the Cámara asked local officials in Panama to check "the calidad of the birth status [*natales*]" of a petitioner. They received in reply a detailed description of "the calidad of his birth [*nacimiento*]."[23] In the case of pardos and mulattoes, the term *calidad* usually carried with it adjectives describing inferiority. For example, when the governor of Cuba responded to a petition by the pardo Juan de la Mena asking that his son enter the University of Havana, the official noted Mena's "humble calidad."[24] When the secretary of the university reported on the incident that led to Mena's petition, he remembered that when "the boy called Mena" attempted to register for classes he had turned him away because university rules required that he produce information on his "calidad and limpieza." Since the secretary could see that "the said Mena is mulatto" he counseled him not to apply given "the notorious defect of his calidad."

Reference to calidad also appeared in the wording of the 1795 gracias a sacar fee schedule, for the two relevant clauses dispensed "the calidad of pardo" and the "calidad of quinteron."[25] After that date petitioners employed the vocabulary of calidad more often, as they commonly quoted the gracias al sacar wording to request Cámara dispensation. The Valenzuela brothers in 1796 explained that they sought whitening because their "ancestors had been reputed to be of the calidad of pardos."[26] In 1803, Jose de Barbua wrote of the "calidad of pardo that he has due to his birth" asking they "dispense said calidad of pardo ordering he be held and reputed and esteemed as a white person."[27] When Venezuelan Francisco de la Cruz Marquez petitioned for whiteness in 1806 he assured royal officials that neither "himself, his wife, nor family" would "abuse" the situation if they were given "someday the cualidad that now is lacking."[28] Royal officials also used the calidad reference, although the comments of the Viceroy of Santa Fe foreshadowed future problems. Although he supported the whitening of a law student, Joseph Ponciano de Ayarza, he worried of the "inconveniences it might cause to open the door for everyone of equal calidad."[29]

Not only did parties describing the essence of pardo and mulatto-ness share mutual vocabulary as to how it originated (faults in naturaleza) how it was transmitted (by naturaleza and/or limpieza), what prejudices it entailed (limpieza), and what inferior condition (calidad/cualidad) it produced—they also shared assumptions concerning its alterability. Inherent in this dialogue was the understanding that the monarch and his representatives had, over the centuries, erased other "defects" in naturaleza, limpieza or calidad. As one Spanish historian put it: "The king counts more than blood."[30] In Spain, in rare instances monarchs had even dispensed the "defect" and "infection" of those with Jewish ancestry. In 1604, Phillip III had ordered that descendants of famous converso Pablo de Santa María be granted limpieza, in spite of their ancestry. The royal decree ordered that this former rabbi's descendants might be eligible for "all the honors, offices, benefices and patronage" that would go to "gentlemen, nobles, [and] Old Christians free of taint."[31]

More common erasures occurred in the case of illegitimate birth. From 1475 to 1800 more than five thousand Spaniards applied to the Cámara of Castile to remove this "defect."[32] In the eighteenth century, several hundred illegitimates from the colonies sought similar decrees from the Cámara of the Indies.[33] The idea that the redress of legitimation and whitening shared a common dynamic became even more explicit when both appeared as purchasable favors in the 1795 American gracias al sacar list. Centuries of tradition whereby the Crown relieved defects in naturaleza, limpieza and calidad rationalized a similar process: just as someone of Jewish background might be transformed into an Old Christian or an illegitimate into a legitimate, pardos and mulattoes might become white. This was so, even though defects such as Jewishness, heresy, or illegitimacy tended to be invisible while pardo-ness or mulatto-ness often was not. Just as any other inherited imperfection, it had a customary remedy.

As pardos and mulattoes applied for whitening and royal officials reviewed their cases, they did so within this historic context of mutability. Petitioners never questioned the promise that pardo-ness or mulatto-ness—what one pardo characterized as "these essential American defects" —might be corrected just as any other.[34] In 1773, Manual Joseph de Baeza appealed that the Cámara dispense "the defect of limpieza."[35] Reapplying in 1786, he asked them to "remove the defect that he suffers."[36] Joseph Maria Cowley applied for relief in 1797 from the "defect of being descended from pardos through the maternal line" so he could obtain "employments that whites hold."[37] In 1808 Manuel Caballero Calderón of Mexico explained that because of the marriage of his great grandfather "he finds himself with the almost extinguished defect of the calidad de pardo."[38]

Cámara officials responded to petitions in similar language referencing the release from "defect" which they conceptualized as an absence to be filled by royal favor. One official in the Cámara of the Indies put it best: "It is certain that the king, generously or by just motives can take a vassal from obscurity graciously placing him in a distinguished sphere."[39] Thus in response to Joseph Francisco Baez's request to be a surgeon, the fiscal suggested that he should be "free of the defect of limpieza de sangre that he suffers."[40] Although his brother Manuel Francisco Baez applied twice for whitening and never received it, the reviewing official gave him a positive recommendation, judging that his "merits" seemed sufficient "to dispense him of the defect that he suffers in his birth of the cualidad of being a descendant of pardos."[41] Other officials responded with similar language. In 1767 and 1786 they suggested that the Cámara reprieve Juan Evaristo de Jesus Borbua and Luis Joseph Paz "of the defect of quinteron" that they suffered.[42] In 1806 officials debated Juan Martin de Aristimuno's request to "dispense the calidad of pardo" in his wife and children.[43]

When local elites testified in favor of pardo and mulatto whitening, they used a similar language of defect and remedy of defect. A Maracaibo witness, Tomás Fernández, explained that Petronila Peralta, the pardo wife of Don Joseph Briceno, was just as "other families . . . with the same defect of mulattoes and other mixtures . . . admitted to the communication with the most decent."[44] Another noted that her situation resembled others "who are held as clean [limpias] [though they] were formerly associated with equal defect." When the Bogotano Don Pedro Groot supported the whitening of the law student Joseph Ponciano de Ayarza, he confirmed his acceptance in Bogotano society, noting that any deficit "raised by his birth" was offset by his "operation, mode and address."[45] These, he concluded, "made up very well [for] all defect that might be noted." Bogotá city council member Dr. Don Joseph Rey also saw in Joseph Ponciano the "qualities that have made him worthy (in spite of his calidad) to the greatest attentions merited in this place." The gracias al sacar whitening documents reveal that petitioners and imperial and local elites engaged in a mainstream conversation about the essence of pardo-ness and mulatto-ness that revolved around constructs of naturaleza, limpieza, calidad and remedy of defect. As time passed, a distinctive American vocabulary eventually entered into the whitening dialogue as well.

## American Variants

A turning point in the language of whitening occurred even before the official appearance of the 1795 gracias al sacar fee schedule that dispensed the "defects" of pardo and quinteron. In 1788, two pardo families from Caracas began collecting information to apply for whitening. The first, Diego Mexias Bejarano, requested whitening so his son might attend the University of Caracas, become a priest, and assume a chaplaincy (*capellanía*) left by his uncle. The second, Juan Gabriel de Landaeta, sought general whitening for himself and his descendants.[46] Their activities roused the ire of the Venezuelan establishment as the city council, the university, and the bishop mobilized and sent multiple reports to the Council and Cámara of the Indies protesting these applications. Even after the Cámara whitened these two petitioners, Venezuelan elites thwarted their social mobility for years. When the Crown issued the 1795 gracias al sacar with the whitening clauses, the Caracas city council responded even more vehemently with an *Obedezco pero no cumplo* and refused to publicize the relevant clauses.[47] The resulting exchanges between imperial officials, pardos and mulattoes, and the Venezuelan establishment as they attempted to solve this impasse both replicated traditional vocabularies and introduced alternative conceptualizations of pardo-ness and mulatto-ness.

In the end, the Crown forced the cabildo to publish the whitening clauses. Even though the Venezuelan elites complied reluctantly and worked actively to subvert the ordinances, they still acknowledged the legitimacy of the process. They never questioned that whitening was a valid and achievable option. The city council of Caracas accepted that if a pardo received such a dispensation, "he would be eligible for all the functions that the laws of the kingdom [currently] forbid him and for all those that have been up until now proper for a 'clean' [limpio] white man in these Indies." The result would be that a "pardo from the inferior class . . . would be held as an individual who is white."[48] They added they considered such a possibility to be "terrifying." University officials also vehemently opposed the whitening option but never challenged its ultimate outcome. They understood that once the king dispensed calidad that pardos "will not only be preferred among their class but also seen and attended by the whites."[49] The Venezuelan establishment never questioned traditional Hispanic processes where the king might erase defects in naturaleza, limpieza and calidad.

While the Caracas city council employed traditional language accepting the mutability of pardo-ness and mulatto-ness, they also categorized pardos and mulattoes in harsh and negative terms, emphasizing their inferior status. City council members charged that pardos were "ambitious for honors and to equal themselves with the whites in spite of that inferior class in which the Author of their naturaleza has placed them."[50] The cabildo pointed out that "pardos or mulattoes are seen here with full disdain and are held and reputed to be in the class of despicable people, both because of their origin and because of the taxes that Your Royal laws impose on them and also by the honors of which that they themselves are deprived." Pardos had but the "little education that their parents can give them as much because of their poverty as because of the baseness in which they live. They generally practice the mechanical arts given the lack of public schools to teach them." Local officials complained that "the mulattoes or pardos of this province . . . live with the greatest ease and liberty in their small houses taking [those] hours of work that seems [necessary] to them to earn the bread for the day without wanting to apply themselves to other jobs." The cabildo concluded that it "didn't want to participate in public ceremonies" with "people who in our houses one would not give a seat or our arm in the streets."

Beyond these explicit and implicit references to the traditional vocabulary of naturaleza or limpieza, the Venezuelan establishment attempted to add another "categorization" to identify pardos and mulattoes. They charged that they should be permanently branded because they "descended precisely from slaves, [and] from illegitimate offspring, because those that are called mulattoes or pardos are those that trace their origin to the union of white [males] with black [females]."[51] An even more pointed characterization linking pardos and mulattoes with slaves originated from officials of the University of Caracas who pointed out the "note of slavery" that has "engraved" in pardo "hearts an indelible public opinion of the lowness of their origin and of their conduct."[52] Even after the Crown whitened Diego Mexias Bejarano's son, university officials justified their refusal to permit him to matriculate and study for the priesthood. They noted that "even though Mexias and his sons have arrived at the condition of being free, they descend precisely from black *bozales* [recently arrived slaves] from Africa" and so they carried with them the "despicable note" of those linked to slavery. The Bishop of Caracas provided a similar verdict: "There are no mulattoes eligible for the sanctuary."

Royal officials considered but rejected the argument that slavery constituted any intrinsic and permanent identifier of the inferior origin of pardos and mulattoes.[53] In the case of Diego Mexias Bejarano, a Cámara official noted that he "comes from free pardos and with the considerable circumstance that [neither] he, his parents nor his grandparents are neophytes or those first ancestors of the condition [of] blacks and slaves taken from the barbarity of the country of their birth and converted to our Holy Faith."[54] He pointed out that the son Mexias Bejarano wanted to whiten was "of the fourth generation" and came from the "legitimate marriage of his parents and grandparents on both sides and from families, even if pardos, free and of distinction." Imperial officials refused to accept that the "American defect" differed from any other as to mutability.

What was the response of pardo and mulatto petitioners to the protests against the whitening clauses? There was a change in their "situated subjectivity" both relative to whites and to other pardos or mulattoes. Petitioners gradually adopted a new vocabulary that mentioned color and their whitish appearance as markers of identity. Equally notable is that imperial officials as well as local elites mostly rejected the concept of "color" as an acceptable categorization. In relationship to peers, petitioners moved from pride in pardo achievements and hope for future whitenings to a strategy that distanced themselves from the pardo community. Such conclusions resonate with Anne Stoler and Frederick Cooper's comment that the "contingencies and contradictions of colonial rule" do not always lie in "grand oppositions" but in "new and renewed discourses and by subtle shifts in ideological ground."[55]

Since the word "color" carries reverberations of more contemporary variants of race and racism, it is imperative to trace when it appears, who used it, and the context. The earliest documentation for gracias al sacar— the six cases from 1760 to 1788—contain three mentions of the word "color." The first appears in 1760, when Joseph Francisco Baez y Llereno of Havana applied to be whitened to practice as a surgeon. Although his letter did not refer to his own color, his request reminded royal officials that even though his father had been "of the color pardo" he also had served the king.[56] It took four more petitions and twenty-three more years before the word "color" ever appeared again. In 1783, Bernardo Ramírez commented (inaccurately) that "neither his parents nor grandparents were of the color and name of negros and pardos."[57] Three years passed before the next petition and the next reference. When a local Panamanian official provided information on the background of Luis Josef de Paz to practice as a notary, he commented that the applicant's uncle was also a notary, although he had found it necessary to receive a dispensation "being of the color pardo."[58] From 1760 to 1786, when petitioners, royal officials, and local elites described the process of whitening, they employed the language of naturaleza, limpieza, calidad and defect. The only three references to "color" did not even describe the petitioners but rather their relatives.

It is likely no accident that color begins to appear in whitening documentation when a cluster of petitions originated from Venezuela and when that local establishment campaigned to put an end to whitening. Grammar matters here: while pardos and mulattoes in earlier decades tended to use color as an adjective describing a hue, they now began to use it as a noun describing a condition. The early communications of Diego Mexias Bejarano to the Cámara illustrate this subtle transition from one vocabulary to another. In 1796 he used traditional language admitting his "disgrace of being a pardo or of inferior calidad."[59] Even after the Crown whitened Diego and his son, they continued to struggle for acceptance. By 1803 he was still pressing university officials to accept his son "as the other scholars without insulting, berating or offending" him. However, he now characterized his son's problem as "the accidental difference of his color."[60]

Unlike Diego Mexias Bejarano, Juan Gabriel de Landaeta evidenced self-identity as a person of color in his first petition; in 1788 he challenged the Caracas elite, asserting that "in his entire ascendance one does not find slavery, illegitimacy or other vice that might serve as impediment for his offspring to mix in marriage with white citizens."[61] When he spoke of his self-image, it was that of a worthy person discriminated against due to color. He asked that "his sons, grandsons, and the rest of the family of the petitioner not be impeded by the difference of color to be able to . . .

contract marriage with whites, to enter and profess in whatever approved religion and wear clerical habits, to continue studies, to ascend to the sacred orders." When protests arose in Caracas concerning his successful petition, he wrote of his "distress" because even his "good circumstances" and the "merits of his ancestors" could not overcome the "vulgar preoccupation that prevails against persons of color" that deprives them of "the decorous establishment of which they are worthy."

After the 1790s, petitioners began to identify themselves as people of color. Either explicitly or implicitly, these references occurred in a context where pardos and mulattoes complained that their status as persons of color meant that they suffered discrimination in spite of their individual merit. In 1796 the Valenzuela brothers from Antioquia, Colombia, noted that they sought the gracias al sacar "so that from now on" they might obtain "some of the positions that are barred them due to the laws" given that they were "of the color pardo."[62] In 1806, when Venezuelan Francisco de la Cruz Marquez discovered that the Cámara had tabled his petition, he complained of the "misfortunes occasioned by his color."[63] He had hoped that his sons might be "excluded from the general rule of a wise politic that distinguishes vassals of various colors." That same year Juan Martin de Aristimuno paid similar lip service to colonial hierarchy affirming the "general rule" that there is "difference between vassals of various colors."[64] However, when he found his petition stalled, he complained that "now he and his sons and perhaps his grandsons would have to renounce the hope that today animated them of being able to serve the state as his white compatriots." He feared that his family would be "pushed aside with those citizens most disgraced by public opinion to bear that irremediable obscurity of his color." [65]

It is intriguing that references to color originated from the discriminated rather than the discriminators. Neither imperial officials nor local elites innovated the vocabulary of color as part of any altered consciousness to justify further discrimination. Rather, both groups rejected color as a signifier. For example, in 1800, officials of the Council of the Indies had to decide whether to collect tribute from pardos and mulattoes who had been *expósitos* (abandoned children) in the wake of a royal decree in 1794 that gave them the official benefit of the doubt as to their caste status. The fiscal who reviewed the case used customary guidelines and suggested "that tribute from Indians, blacks and mulattoes was original and unique to the Americas and it ought to be governed by the particular laws of imposition, not judging by colors and appearances but by naturalezas."[66] He concluded that color was too unpredictable given that "the signs of color, skin, and physiognomy are very fallible and always leave a doubt if the expósito was of the calidad [to pay] tribute." Eventually the Council of the Indies decided that they would permit local officials to rely on local custom for the assessment of taxation.

The Venezuelan establishment also rejected color as an identifier. Even though the city council of Caracas sent pages of protests to the Council of the Indies protesting the whitening option and disparaging pardos and mulattoes, they only referred to "color" one time. This sole reference concerned the pardo militia. Elites were upset that when a pardo officer with "a little of color in his face" wore his "dragoon uniform and sword," he might receive "mistaken deference that raised his thoughts to other higher objectives."[67] When university officials protested the whitening clause, their only use of the word was to deny its influence. While admitting that they looked with "horror" on the "incorporation of pardos in their guild" they added that this was not due to "the difference of color that accidentally distinguishes those born in a country more distant from the equator and beneath a more benign zone."[68] They felt they had "more elevated reasons" and "urgent motives" to "prohibit forever that the pardos profane and introduce their impure hands in the sanctuary of literature." For all their vociferous protests against whitening, local elites never directly introduced color as a factor in the whitening equation.

Whether pardo self-identification as persons of color originated as a defensive response to protests of whites, whether it was largely confined to Venezuela, or whether it spread to the wider pardo community necessitates research beyond the gracias al sacar documentation. What is clear is that pardo petitioners did not stop there, for they also began to introduce physical appearance as a variable in whitening applications. Here the goal was not self-identification of pardos as people discriminated due to color but the opposite—to emphasize that they looked white. For some families, this may have been the result of generations of planning. Petitioners often submitted genealogies that resembled casta paintings as they documented alliance after alliance with lighter pardos or with whites that moved them ever closer over the generations toward whiteness.[69]

In early applications, such mentions of appearance seemed spontaneous. For example, in 1760 one witness commented that "even though it is certain that the parents of the applicant are pardos, they don't look it."[70] Later, however, some interrogatories seemed to prompt witnesses to comment on the hue of the petitioner. Testifying in favor of Petronila Peralta, the parda wife of Don Joseph Briceno, in 1794, Diego de Gallegos noted that "she has never been subject to servitude [presumably slavery] nor does her aspect manifest it."[71] Since another witness commented that Petronila "was given the note of mulata even though her aspect does not manifest it," the similarity of wording suggests that both responses proceeded from a question that emphasized that point. Juan de la Cruz went even further concerning Petronila's "note of mulata" and status, adding that "it is evident that she never was a slave nor does her appearance indicate it for she appears as a white person."

Similar references to appearance surfaced in later gracias al sacar applications. The local royal treasurer of the city of Antioquia noted that the Valenzuela brothers "were held here as of the calidad pardo" even though "one would not consider them so given their absolutely white color."[72] A witness in favor of Manuel Caballero Calderón of Mexico praised his "good birth."[73] It may be that petitioners who looked white deliberately encouraged such comments to improve their chance for a favorable verdict. While rare occasions occurred where witnesses made patent that petitioners did not look white, such negative comments had not been solicited. For example, when discussing the whitening of Joseph Ponciano de Ayarza, the director of studies at San Bartolomé in Bogotá cited royal decrees that officially discriminated against "mulattoes" and then added his observation that such "calidad" was "notorious in this candidate."[74]

By the 1790s, not only petitioners but also witnesses and royal officials were making comments on appearance and color. When Juan Manuel de Cagigal testified in favor of Francisco de la Cruz Marquez in 1806 he wrote of his "irreprehensible conduct" and praised "the Christian and politic education with which he has raised his children, which distinguishes him from those of his color."[75] When the Cámara reviewed the case of Joseph Maria Cowley, who was in Madrid and may have applied personally in 1797, the fiscal commented that "nothing appears . . . of his calidad nor of the origin of pardo which one supposes [was] in his maternal ancestor."[76] In 1800 when Don Nicolas Francisco Yanes applied to whiten his parda wife María Nicolasa Garces, he also asked permission to purchase the title of "don," another favor sold in the gracias al sacar. In response, the fiscal noted that the use of "don" "has come to be distinctive to white Spaniards in contrast to the different castes of vassals of color."[77]

Even though petitioners increasingly referred to themselves as persons of color this did not mean that their "situated subjectivity" included any identification with their local pardo and mulatto communities. This was a marked contrast from earlier applications where pardos identified with and exhibited a lively awareness of others who were upwardly mobile. Such shared consciousness was particularly evident—as Ben Vinson has noted—among pardo militia officers.[78] For example, in 1760 the Cuban Antonio Flores, commander of a pardo infantry battalion, applied so that his son Joseph Ignacio might attend the University of Havana to study medicine. The registrar rejected the boy, noting that the ordinances "did not admit . . . mestizos, zambos or mulattoes."[79] When Flores asked for an exemption for his son, he demonstrated knowledge of others in his situation. He remarked that being "pardo" was not a sufficient reason to refuse his son's admission "for repeated times in the convent and in other schools of that city" there had been students "of the same calidad." His knowledge of pardo mobility extended beyond Havana, for he added that "it is alleged that the son of a Colonel of Pardos of Mexico, another from Puebla de los Ángeles and another of the Commandant of pardos of Cuba have been raised to greater honors and nobility such as the dignity of the priesthood." Nor, as would occur in later applications, did Flores distance himself from the local community. He noted that "in Havana it is not only the nobility and the whites who are professors of letters, but also the pardos . . . are learned men." He concluded that "not only the whites and nobles aspire to and love letters but also the pardos seek wisdom." He saw this as a positive development that added "a special timbre to the city."

Another example of early pardo "situated subjectivity" was that petitioners identified not only with peers who were equally mobile but with the rest of the community that was not. Some suggested that their mobility should serve as inspiration for other pardos to emulate. The Guatemalan Bernardo Ramírez asked to be whitened not only for himself but "for the stimulus of the class of pardos and others."[80] Diego Mexias Bejarano also saw his upward mobility as setting a model for pardos and mulattoes. He reminded the king and Cámara: "since a considerable part of the population of Caracas is composed of pardos, who are deprived of all hope of leaving their state, it would consequently take from them the most powerful motive that would oblige them to be useful and to occupy themselves for the benefit of the public good and utility of themselves."[81] The Pardo Guild of Caracas seemed to agree, for they exclaimed that "if the pardos remain separated from the whites without hope of mixing with them or of arriving at the enjoyment of the same honors, what induce- ment or incentive would be powerful enough for them to offer them- selves and embrace their interests and defend them as their own?"[82]

By the late 1780s, the "situated subjectivity" of pardo petitioners had changed. Applicants were more likely to originate from Venezuela, where discrimination against the pardo and mulatto community was fierce. In response, petitioners took pains to separate themselves from fellow par- dos, to seek only their own whitening, and to reject any possibility of general uplift. In 1788 Juan Gabriel de Landaeta was just as critical of pardos as were the Venezuelan elites. He charged that "usually they are born of adultery and other illicit and punishable couplings that makes them slanderous and unable [to hold offices] accompanying these defects by bad upbringing, vices, and worse customs." He railed against the "vul- gar" who failed to differentiate "the one from the other, they make all of color unworthy of society and of participation in public honors."[83]

After the Cámara tabled applications in 1803, with the rationale of developing a general policy concerning whitening, frustrated petitioners awaiting resolution of their cases sought to distance themselves even further from the pardo community. In 1806 Francisco de la Cruz Marquez asked that the "general policy . . . not influence the issuance of the favor that this petitioner seeks."[84] He reminded the Cámara that "there is a great difference between the petitioner and the rest of the pardos of other colors who have not served the public." The representative of Juan Martin Aristimuno feared that if his client had to wait for the "policy . . . he, his sons and even his grandsons would have to renounce the hope that they have of being useful to the state as their white compatriots." Therefore, he asked that he "separate out the cited instance of this petitioner from the general policy."[85]

Much had changed since pardos began to receive official grants of whitening in the 1760s. The mutual vocabulary and shared understand- ings of the origins, effects, and mutability of naturaleza, limpieza, calidad, and defect that bound imperial officials, pardos and mulattoes, and local elites together remained intact. Even during the colonial twilight no one involved in the process ever questioned that whitening could occur.

Rather, the issue became: should it occur?[86] Faced with increasing uncertainty that the Cámara would approve whitening petitions, pardos and mulattoes introduced a contrapuntal discourse that reflected altered identifications and changed stratagems. They began emphasizing their closeness to whiteness through references to their appearance. They more openly separated themselves from identifying with local pardo and mulatto communities or envisioning any upward mobility but their own. When pardos and mulattoes introduced the identifier of color, it was not in solidarity with their peers but to define their self-awareness of a discriminatory condition that they desperately sought to escape.

While the concept of "race" did not openly figure either as a rationale for discrimination or as a vehicle for pardo and mulatto self-identification, intimations of its appearance began to emerge. Imperial and local elites had to face the contradiction between their acceptance of a traditional discourse that permitted alteration of "defect" and their insistence that pardos and mulattoes suffer permanent discrimination. Deprived of official pathways to eliminate the prejudice against them, upwardly mobile pardos and mulattoes continued their quest for individual whiteness. Yet through their continued identification with the white hierarchy, they collaborated in the creation of a despised other, deprived of the potential for uplift and perpetually destined for discrimination. This divergence between the theory of relief of "defect" and its practical execution created dissonances and discontinuities foreshadowing later, more explicit racial constructions.

The era of gracias al sacar whitenings ended with royal officials at an impasse, local elites enraged, and pardo petitioners aggravated. Even when the Cámara approved a purchase of whiteness, there was no guarantee that status would change. The frustration of Diego Mexias Bejarano of Caracas emerged unmistakably as he found local elites thwarting his mobility. He exclaimed that "whether he was by fate a mulatto, whether black, his actions had showed that he has received a soul that makes him esteemed as a white. Why then should he be impeded to enter into a class that he has merited and that your majesty has granted?"[87] The very fact that he could even ask such a question underscores the importance of understanding the dialogue between royal officials, pardos and mulattoes, and colonial elites concerning the essence of pardo-ness and mulatto-ness. Yet as Napoleon's armies invaded the Spanish peninsula and the empire crumbled, these colonial vocabularies would yield to altered and equally tense dialogues concerning whether pardos and mulattoes would—or would not—participate as citizens of the newly independent republics.

## Notes

1. *Pardo* usually means "dark skinned" although the term can be used interchangeably with "mulatto." Some pardos and mulattoes, such as those applying for whitening, tended to be products of generations of mixing, and some appeared very light or even white.

2. Archivo General de Indias (Seville, Spain, henceforth AGI), Guatemala 411, n. 8, 1783. While the whitening *gracias al sacar* option has long fascinated historians, little has been published on it because it was impossible to locate the petitions. Breaking an AGI archival code permitted not only systematic collection of the gracias al sacar requests for legitimation that formed the basis of Twinam, *Public Lives, Private Secrets*, 346–47, but also location of the petitions for nobility, *mayorazgos* (entail), *naturaleza* (becoming Spanish), and whitening. A systematic analysis of the whitening petitions will appear in *Erasing the American "Defect": The Purchase of Whiteness in Colonial Spanish America* (forthcoming, Stanford University Press). Earlier references to whitening include King, "The Case of José Ponciano de Ayarza," who published partial documents from one case; Rodulfo Cortés, *El regimen de "las gracias al sacar" en Venezuela durante el periodo hispánico*, who printed selections of cases, again not complete and mostly from Venezuela. Konetzke, *Colección de documentos para la historia de la formación social de hispanoamérica, 1493–1810*, reproduces parts from other cases. Also see Mörner, *Race Mixture in the History of Latin America*, who used Konetzke for analysis and is most quoted on whitening. McKinley, *Pre-Revolutionary Caracas*, 115–19, discusses the whitening gracias al sacar, which he (wrongly) sees as a revenue-enhancing measure. He underestimates local tensions due to caste mobility, intermarriage with whites, and the challenge posed by the pardo militias. When printed versions (which usually do not include the full document) are available in Konetzke or Rodulfo Cortes I will cite them the first time I cite the archival version. All translations of archival documents are my own.

3. Of the twenty-six total applications, twelve came from Venezuela, six from Cuba, five from Panama, and one each from Mexico, Guatemala, and Santa Fe. Chronologically, cases came earliest from Cuba and latest from Venezuela.

4. Brubaker and Cooper, "Beyond 'Identity,'" 17. Brubaker and Cooper argue strongly against the use of "identity" given its acultural, ahistoric, and nonprocessual dynamic. While I take their point and borrow gratefully from their many excellent points, I find "identity" still useful although I try to take into account their pertinent caveats. Also see the discussion of this issue in the introduction to this volume.

5. See the introduction to this volume.

6. See Twinam, "The Etiology of Racial Passing."

7. There were five petitions in the 1760s, one in the 1770s, two in the 1780s, nine in the 1790s, and nine in the 1800s, ending with Napoleon's invasion in 1808.

8. Brubaker and Cooper, "Beyond 'Identity,'" 18.

9. AGI, Santo Domingo 1463, n. 8, 1776.

10. AGI, Panama 286, n. 4, 1786.

11. *Las Siete Partidas del sabio rey D. Alfonso el nono*, Partida IV, Título XXIII, Ley I.

12. Ibid., 343, index entry "*nobleza.*" For analysis of how colonists manipulated the difference between naturaleza and nobleza see Twinam, "Playing the 'Gender Card.'" Aubert, "The Blood of France," par. 33, suggests similar ideas about male and female transmission for seventeenth-century France.

13. AGI, Santo Domingo 1455, n. 10, 1760.

14. For a classic monograph on limpieza, see Sicroff, *Los estatuos de limpieza de sangre*.

15. Archivo Histórico Nacional (Madrid, Spain), Consejos Suprimidos, Legajo 4539, n. 128, 1760. Notice that raza does not translate easily as "race" given that heretics and those sentenced by Inquisition had defective raza as well.

16. See Martínez, "Religion, Purity, and 'Race,'" and "The Black Blood of New Spain." Aubert, "The Blood of France," par. 29, suggests that seventeenth-century French conceptualizations of clean blood were also "cultural rather than racial, with a special emphasis on religious differences."

17. AGI, Santo Domingo 1474, n. 11, 1789 contains a traditional American rendering. My emphasis.

18. Sicroff, *Los estatuos de limpieza de sangre*, 293.

19. Ibid., 119–20.

20. AGI, Santo Domingo 1455, n. 10, 1760.

21. AGI, Mexico 1909, unnumbered file, 1808.

22. Twinam, "The Etiology of Racial Passing," traces trends in pardo mobility including informal whitening through "passing."

23. AGI, Panama 286, n. 4, 1786. The petitioner was Luis Joseph de Paz.

24. AGI, Santo Domingo 1357, unnumbered file, 1764. (Konetzke, *Colección de documentos para la historia de la formación social de hispanoamérica, 1493–1810*, vol. 3–1, doc. 191.)

25. A reprint appears in Rodulfo Cortés, *El regimen de "las gracias al sacar" en Venezuela durante el periodo hispánico*, vol. 2, doc. 7.

26. AGI, Santa Fe 721, n. 12, 1796. Similar requests can be found in AGI, Caracas 378, n. 47, 1800 and AGI, Caracas 4, unnumbered file, 1802. (Rodulfo Cortés, *El regimen de "las gracias al sacar" en Venezuela durante el periodo hispánico*, vol. 2, doc. 23.) AGI, Santo Domingo 1457, n. 7, 1763. (Konetzke, *Colección de documentos para la historia de la formación social de hispanoamérica, 1493–1810*, vol. 3–1, doc. 189.)

27. AGI, Panama 293, n. 3, 1803.

28. AGI, Caracas 395, n. 5, 1806. (Rodulfo Cortés, *El regimen de "las gracias al sacar" en Venezuela durante el periodo hispánico*, vol. 2, doc. 32.)

29. AGI, Panama 293, n. 2, 1803. The story of the Ayarza's quest for whitening is in Twinam, "Pedro de Ayarza."

30. Maravall, *Poder, honor, y élites en el siglo XVII*, quoting Vélez de Guevara, 84.

31. Sicroff, *Los estatuos de limpieza de sangre*, 218.

32. I am presently reading these cases for a monograph on sexuality and illegitimacy in the Hispanic Atlantic world.

33. See Twinam, *Public Lives, Private Secrets.*

34. AGI, Santo Domingo 1357, unnumbered file, 1764. (Konetzke, *Colección de documentos para la historia de la formación social de hispanoamérica, 1493–1810*, vol. 3–1, doc. 191.) This comment came in a letter Juan Cruz de la Mena sent in 1761.

35. AGI, Santo Domingo 1463, n. 8, 1773. AGI, Santo Domingo 1455, n. 10, 1760 contains a similar request from his brother. Also see AGI, Panama 286, n. 4, 1786.

36. AGI, Santo Domingo 1471, n. 2, 1787. For similar uses of "defect," see AGI, Santo Domingo 1457, n. 7, 1763. (Konetzke, *Colección de documentos para la historia de la formación social de hispanoamérica, 1493–1810*, vol. 3–1, doc. 189); AGI, Panama 286, n. 4, 1786; AGI, Caracas 4, unnumbered file, 1786. (Rodulfo Cortés, vol. 2, doc. 15.)

37. AGI, Santo Domingo 1493, n. 56, 1797.

38. AGI, Mexico 1909, unnumbered file, 1808.

39. AGI, Guatemala 411, unnumbered file, 1783. (Konetzke, *Colección de documentos para la historia de la formación social de hispanoamérica, 1493–1810*, vol. 3–2, doc. 272.)

40. AGI, Santo Domingo 1471, n. 2, 1787.

41. Ibid.

42. AGI, Panama 276, n. 3, 1767; AGI, Panama 286, no. 4, 1786. See another example in AGI, Santa Fe 721, n. 12, 1796.

43. AGI, Caracas 395, unnumbered file, 1806. (Rodulfo Cortés, *El regimen de "las gracias al sacar" en Venezuela durante el periodo hispánico*, vol. 2, doc. 29.)

44. AGI, Caracas 334, n. 61, 1794.

45. AGI, Panama 293, n. 2, 1803.

46. The Diego Mexias Bejarano case is AGI, Caracas 4, unnumbered file, 1796. The case of Juan Gabriel de Landaeta appears in Rodulfo Cortés, *El regimen de "las gracias al sacar" en Venezuela durante el periodo hispánico*, vol. 2, docs. 10 and 26.

47. Rodulfo Cortés, *El regimen de "las gracias al sacar" en Venezuela durante el periodo hispánico*, vol. 2, doc. 11.

48. The pertinent local city council documents are collected in ibid.

49. Ibid., vol. 2, doc. 25.

50. Ibid., vol. 2, doc. 11.

51. Ibid., vol 2, doc. 5.

52. Ibid., vol. 2, doc. 25.

53. Helg, *Liberty and Equality in Caribbean Colombia*, 92, 93, quotes a document from 1806 in which royal officials do suggest that there was a "stain of slavery." However, even though she links this clause with gracias al sacar whitenings in 1795, it appears in a later document written in 1806. It is likely that imperial officials were sending mixed and

contradictory messages about how slavery related to pardo-ness and mulatto-ness depending on the timing and context of the observation.

54. Cortés, *El regimen* vol. 2, doc. 5.

55. Stoler and Cooper, "Between Metropole and Colony,"18.

56. AGI, Santo Domingo 1455, n. 10, 1760.

57. AGI, Guatemala 411, n. 8, 1783.

58. AGI, Panama 286, n. 4, 1786.

59. Rodulfo Cortés, *El regimen de "las gracias al sacar" en Venezuela durante el periodo hispánico*, vol. 2, doc. 5.

60. Ibid., doc. 25.

61. Ibid. doc. 10.

62. AGI, Santa Fe 721, n. 12, 1796.

63. AGI, Caracas 395, n. 5, 1806.

64. AGI, Caracas 395, unnumbered file, 1806. Rodulfo Cortés, *El regimen de "las gracias al sacar" en Venezuela durante el periodo hispánico*, vol. 2, doc. 29, prints a selection.

65. Ibid, doc. 16. Such self-awareness of color also emerged in a petition that the Free Pardo Guild of Caracas sent to the Council of the Indies concerning the whitening option in 1797. They hoped that whitening would free "the dependence that the people of color actually have from the Europeans and whites." They wondered why the city council of Caracas would suffer any "inconveniences" if free pardos were permitted "the dispensation of color."

66. Konetzke, *Colección de documentos para la historia de la formación social de hispanoamérica, 1493–1810*, vol. 3-2, doc. 358. Also see Helg, *Liberty and Equality in Caribbean Colombia*, 93.

67. Rodulfo Cortés, *El regimen de "las gracias al sacar" en Venezuela durante el periodo hispánico*, vol. 2, doc. 11.

68. Ibid., doc. 25.

69. See Twinam, "Padres blancos, madres pardas," for details on the movement toward whiteness in the families of petitioners. On the casta paintings, see Katzew, *Casta Painting*, and Carrera, *Imagining Identity in New Spain*.

70. AGI, Santo Domingo 1455, n. 10, 1760.

71. AGI, Caracas 334, n. 61, 1794.

72. AGI, Santa Fe 721, n. 12, 1796.

73. AGI, Mexico 1909, unnumbered file, 1808.

74. AGI, Panama 293, n. 2, 1803.

75. AGI, Caracas 395, n. 5, 1806.

76. AGI, Santo Domingo 1493, n. 56, 1797.

77. AGI, Caracas 378, n. 47, 1800.

78. Vinson, *Bearing Arms for His Majesty*, mentions this case as an example of a unique cohort of pardos and mulattoes who were using militia service to further "social whitening." 85, 86. He rightfully differentiates the attitude of this special group to the masses serving in the pardo militias who had a less positive identification with peers.

79. AGI, Santo Domingo 1455, n. 5, 1760. Also see Konetzke, *Colección de documentos para la historia de la formación social de hispanoamérica, 1493–1810*, vol. 3–1, doc. 177.

80. AGI, Guatemala 411, unnumbered file, 1783.

81. Rodulfo Cortés, *El regimen de "las gracias al sacar" en Venezuela durante el periodo hispánico*, vol. 2, doc. 5.

82. Ibid., doc. 16.

83. Ibid., doc. 10.

84. AGI, Caracas 395, n. 5, 1806.

85. AGI, Caracas 395, unnumbered file, 1806.

86. See Twinam, "The Etiology of Racial Passing."

87. Cortés, *El regimen* vol. 2, doc. 5.

# Patricians and Plebeians in Late Colonial Charcas

*Identity, Representation, and Colonialism*

The demise of Spanish rule in Latin America in the early nineteenth century was linked, among other factors, to the consolidation of a Creole identity and the rise of novel modes of political representation. The former stemmed from the growing resentment of colonial domination and its agents and direct beneficiaries, the peninsular Spaniards, from whom the American elites had barely distinguished themselves during the previous centuries. This Creole consciousness or "nationalism" led to a gradual relaxation, although by no means suppression, of the old caste system owing to ideological changes (a trend toward greater social homogeneity), political imperatives (Creoles' need for support in their struggle against the metropolis), and sheer demography (a large part of the American elites was by then ethnically mestizo, mixed-blood). The advent of new representative practices, in turn, can be seen as a response to the sweeping powers that the Bourbon monarchy had been claiming with considerable success since the mid-eighteenth century. The increasingly defiant initiatives of the *cabildos*—an ancient body of municipal self-government—were a prominent expression of resistance to the infringement upon the perceived rights and privileges of local communities.

## Society and Politics in Charcas

This chapter explores these topics for the Upper Peruvian city of La Plata (present-day Sucre), the seat of the *audiencia* (high court) of Charcas in the late eighteenth century. In the years following the great indigenous uprisings of 1780–81, La Plata, also known as Charcas or Chuquisaca, witnessed a series of traumatic events that displayed forms of collective identity and political representation that called into question both traditional urban social hierarchies and the ideological tenets of late Spanish colonialism. Two popular riots, several *cabildos abiertos* (public meetings of city residents, including the members of the artisan guilds and shopkeepers), numerous collective petitions of patricians and plebeians, and virulent disputes within the ranks of the ruling elites were some of the consequences of this climate of political turmoil and, I will contend, of social changes with profound and long-lasting reverberations.[1]

Although these tensions have long and tangled historical roots, the particular circumstances that brought them to the fore can be discerned with some precision. They begin with the distinctive impact in this region of the mass indigenous insurrections that shook the Andean world, from Cuzco to La Paz and Charcas, generically known as the Túpac Amaru rebellion. Unlike other areas of the Upper and Lower Peru, in La Plata the fight against the insurgent forces rested on the local population, particularly during the unprecedented siege of the city by thousands of peasants from several neighboring provinces in February 1781. While a combination of rural militias and regular armies from Lima, Tucumán, or Buenos Aires defeated Andean rebels in other regions, here the weight of the war fell upon the urban militias composed of the patriciate and the castas. Detachments from the Río de la Plata only arrived in the region once the central focus of insurgency, led by the Katari brothers in the province of Chayanta, had already been quashed. But while the local residents bore the burden of the war, they would not enjoy the fruits of victory for long. In the ensuing months, the Crown established permanent garrisons of Spanish soldiers in the main Andean cities. Perceived as politically unreliable and economically costly, the militias of La Plata were eventually disbanded.[2] These measures of social control, as it is well known, formed part of a larger program of imperial reforms. Beginning in the mid-eighteenth century, the Bourbon crown tried to regain full command over its overseas possessions by, among other endeavors, maximizing colonial revenues, excluding American elites from high office, and undermining the autonomy of the social corporations and political communities that comprised the realm. The ensuing clash between the new absolutist policies and the emboldened urban population had explosive consequences. From the outset, mutual hostility and violence imbued the interaction of the foreign soldiers with the city residents, patricians and plebeians alike. Ultimately, the antagonisms gave rise to vigorous public debates about the premises of Spanish colonial power.

To understand the origins of this process of politicization, two contextual factors need to be highlighted. First, though it was a relatively small city (18,000 inhabitants by the end of the century) with limited economic development, La Plata hosted the main colonial institutions in the southern Andes: the audiencia, the university, and the archbishopric. Hence it served as the regional political center and the cradle of the intellectual and administrative elites. It is estimated that six hundred students—one hundred from Charcas and five hundred from other areas—and seventy lawyers resided in the city at this time.[3] In addition to the Universidad de San Francisco Xavier, the oldest institution of higher education in the Andean region, in 1776 the Academia Carolina opened its doors. This law school attracted Creole young men from throughout the viceroyalties of Río de la Plata and Peru. At the school, many future leaders of the independence movements encountered new ideas of the Enlightenment. Within the urban world, the academy served, according to the historian Clément Thibaud, as "a crucible of *democratic sociabilities* partially freed from the hierarchical and corporate values of a society of orders ("sociedad de órdenes" in the original)."[4] More significantly still, the lawyers and men of letters did not conform to a closed group. The very social composition of the university student body suggests the connection between the *letrados* and the society at large: as an audiencia minister complained at the time, the blood purity required to attend law school was not observed, since it had become common practice to admit "individuals who, due to their lowly and vile birth, could better be employed in activities suitable to their humble qualities and circumstances."[5] In his pioneering study of late colonial Charcas, the nineteenth-century Bolivian historian Gabriel René Moreno had already observed that distinguished Creoles, especially university students, "fraternized with mestizos"; these social relations "explain why *cholos* (mestizos) from Charcas, unlike *cholos* elsewhere, engaged at that time in discussions about public affairs without knowing how to read or write."[6] The joint mobilization of all La Plata dwellers to defend the city from the Indians, as well as the inherent democratizing effect of the militarization of the civilian population under such extreme circumstances, must have intensified those ties. As elsewhere in Spanish America, the militias mirrored existing social hierarchies. Two cavalry units comprised lawyers and men of letters, as did two infantry units of artisans and traders. But the place of these units in public ceremony, an unequivocal sign of social status in this society, is highly revealing: after claiming the right to occupy sites of privilege as individuals of personal nobility, the cavalry companies agreed to attend public events intermingled with the plebeian infantry.[7] Then, as we will see, when in 1785 the viceroy disbanded the last standing mestizo company, the patriciate strongly supported popular protests against the measure.

Second, these years witnessed the dislocation of traditional structures of authority. Since the foundation of La Plata in the sixteenth century, the ministers of the royal audiencia sat on the summit of the social order.[8] Yet, in the early 1780s, the court experienced a sudden loss of power and prestige. Its disastrous policies in the face of growing indigenous unrest, one of the prime triggers of the general insurrection, prompted the viceroy of the newly created viceroyalty of the Río de la Plata, Juan José de Vértiz (1778–83), to bestow all authority for Indian affairs on an outsider, Ignacio Flores, a Quito-born military man. Flores was first appointed commander of arms, then audiencia president, and, in 1782, first intendant of Charcas. The disruption provoked by the presence in the city of a magistrate of a higher rank than the audiencia was compounded by fierce disputes between Flores and the audiencia judges (all of them Spaniards) around key political issues of the time such as the right of a Creole to hold high office or his lenient treatment of former Andean rebels as well as the Creole groups who had headed the *tupamarista* uprising in neighboring Oruro.[9] These sharp ideological battles at the apex of government reached their climax when the intendant lent his full support to La Plata residents in their open clashes with the audiencia ministers, the Spanish garrison, and viceroy Marqués de Loreto (1783–89).

This chapter focuses on three aspects of the emergence of a Creole consciousness associated with collective challenges of patricians and plebeians to the existing order. The first part examines the responses of urban society to the establishment of a permanent military garrison. It delves into the sense of moral outrage and political discontent resulting from Spanish soldiers' violation of accepted rules of social behavior—most prominently their insults to the masculine honor of the local population—and from the perceived transgression of the city's rights and privileges. The most spectacular displays of disaffection—two popular riots that broke out in September 1782 and July 1785—are explored in the following section. The chapter concludes with an analysis of the predicament of the ayuntamiento of La Plata as a representative body of the urban population in open opposition to the main institutions of colonial rule. I will argue that the city patriciate and plebeians, who had forged bonds of cooperation during the dramatic years of the Túpac Amaru insurrection, began to regard themselves as a distinct political community vis-à-vis two other entities: the groups associated with the policies of the colonial state, a state increasingly seen as an agent of metropolitan interests, and the native peoples, whose radical alterity, their condition as "savages," had become indelibly imprinted in the memory of the nonindigenous population since the pan-Andean upheaval of the 1780s. Whereas the origins of Creole nationalism have been mostly approached from the perspective of the history of ideas, this chapter looks at this phenomenon through the study of political practices and collective actions. In brief, it inquires about the intersection, at a particular historical juncture, of issues of identity, representation, and awareness of colonial subordination.

*The Army and the City Residents: The Politicization of Honor*

Social hierarchies in colonial Latin American cities were shaped by a fundamental distinction between *gente decente*, the honorable people of Spanish descent eligible to town council offices, and the plebe, manual workers and petty traders identified as mestizos, mulattoes, cholos, and other castes. Racial categories, needless to say, were determined holistically rather than genetically or according to strict phenotypical traits. The diverse social composition of the student body at the Universidad de Charcas mentioned earlier is in itself a vivid reminder that by the late eighteenth century few Creoles were white.[10] Nonetheless, that dichotomous image of society must have been particularly significant in an administrative center as Charcas. Scholarship has shown that the historical capitals of viceroyalties and audiencias served as the template for the ideal baroque colonial city, an urban community based on the adoption of aristocratic codes of behavior and social dualism that mimicked the courtly lifestyle of their Iberian counterparts.[11] It is crucial to note that one of the organizing features of the *hidalgo* society of the Indies was that the patrician elite, as a matter of principle, encompassed both peninsular Spaniards and Creoles. The Habsburg conception of the overseas possessions as kingdoms rather than colonies, the diverse social backgrounds of the European immigrants, their tendency to assimilate themselves into local society, as well as the economic success of many American families and their ability to attain the highest posts in the imperial administration, all meant that until the mid-eighteenth century both groups tended to enjoy a similar status. For most of the colonial era, in fact, the word *español* referred to both Europeans and Creoles.

An unmistakable symptom of crisis is when social classifications no longer express actual relationships among human groups, when symbolic representations and social practices start diverging. The cartography of collective identities no longer matches the social topography. This is what happened in La Plata during the period under study as a fault line within the ranks of the urban elites began to develop between the *vecindario* (city dwellers) and *peninsulares* (categories that did not necessarily denote a place of birth). By the same token, patricians and plebeians developed a growing sense of shared interests and values. To be sure, the erosion of the old binary model of social stratification involved long-term economic, demographic, and cultural dynamics whose analysis exceeds the aims of this essay.[12] The point I want to make, nonetheless, is that this was not the natural outcome of gradual, cumulative, or structural processes. At least in late colonial Charcas, the undermining of the traditional urban order resulted from a historical conjuncture, and it was triggered by a particular event: the Crown's decision to establish, for the first time since the sixteenth century, a permanent garrison of Spanish soldiers a few yards away from the Plaza Mayor. Contemporary accounts indicate that the conduct of the troops recently arrived from Buenos Aires (belonging to the regiment of Saboya, known as the *Blanquillos*) insulted the honor of city residents from all classes and castes. As is well known, honor in Spanish America held two meanings: social precedence or purity of blood (*la nobleza*) and merit or virtuous conduct (*la honra*).[13] Historians have demonstrated that subaltern groups participated in this culture of honor. But a social hierarchy based on birth and lineage presupposed an uneven distribution of personal virtue based on honorable behavior since, to borrow Steve J. Stern's words, "social precedence, group-derived superiority in relations with others, usually implied enhanced virtue, a superior individual and familiar ability to sustain appearances of worthy masculinity and femininity."[14] External trappings of honor and wealth, as well as the ability to deal with challenges to their personal reputation through the court system instead of direct violence, distinguished the elites from the lower classes.[15]

The conflictive interaction between civilians and foreign soldiers led to a drastic redistribution of these forms of symbolic capital or, as it were, to a relative democratization of honor. In something as vital as the moral norms regulating social interaction, the divide between Creoles and peninsulars seemed greater than the divide between patricians and plebeians, at least the upper echelons of the latter. Hence the redefining of social identities became inextricably tied to a collective awareness of the subordination of the local community to metropolitan designs. This hastened the crisis of the city's self-representation as a *hidalgo*, courtly society, ideally split between Hispanic and non-Hispanic sectors. Without losing their distinct group identities, La Plata residents began to regard themselves as members of the same polity, which was defined in opposition to peninsular policies and those who implemented, advocated, and benefited from them. In short, they saw themselves as part of a full-fledged colonial society.

The grievances against the regular forces provide important clues for understanding the moral and ideological foundations of these bonds. To begin with, it is important to notice that these complaints were collected and recorded in 1782 in the course of an inquiry ordered by the ayuntamiento of La Plata, the main representative institution of the urban aristocracy. The most frequent cause of outrage was undoubtedly the soldiers' sexual behavior. A vecino summed up well this widespread feeling of indignation when he said that "no married woman was safe" from the troops.[16] As Patricia Seed has pointed out, a fundamental aspect of the honor system was for men to monopolize the sexuality of women belonging to their own social group. "This control," she argues, "created a basic social and sexual privilege for Spanish men by simultaneously granting them access to women of other racial groups and reserving exclusive access to women of their own group for themselves."[17] Command over the sexual behavior of women was central to notions of social status and male honorability. It could be said, as in the case of nineteenth-century England, that "men proved their public probity by the private virtues of the wives and daughters."[18] The direct effect of Bourbon absolutism was the establishment in the heart of the city of a permanent garrison oblivious to entrenched rules of patriarchal authority fixing the individuals' public reputation and their place in the hierarchy of privileges. Soldiers' advances on the wives, sisters, and daughters of patricians and plebeians alike (in addition to other acts of violence) thus posed a double dilemma: they called into question whether Europeans of low social status held preeminence over noble Creoles; and they placed the vindication of the masculine reputation of elites and castes on the same ground. Hence the assaults on the local population's claims to honor, in both of its meanings, nobility and virtue, stirred public debates on the premises of the existing social order.

Let us review some of the testimonies gathered by the ayuntamiento in 1782. One of the witnesses said, for instance, that the people "were shocked and oppressed by the violence that [the soldiers] commit at every step . . . because, by force of arms, they violate the homes of the honorable [hombres honrados] as well as the poor, taking away their women and committing other excesses."[19] A soldier named Manuel Lozada had first carried on an illicit friendship and later a sexual relationship "in a public store" with the wife of Casimiro Torricos.[20] Another Blanquillo "stole" Don Ignacio Valdivieso's wife and, more insulting still, "took her, sword in hand, from his house in his very presence."[21] Although Don Valdivieso complained to army Commander Christobal López "about his violated honor and credit," nothing was done to discipline this outrageous behavior. Because of the humiliation, his wife withdrew to a city convent for several days.[22] The son of a Don Lorenzo caught his spouse with a Blanquillo two or three times in his own home, "for which reason they lived apart for some time."[23] Another soldier carried on an "illicit friendship" with the sister of a master weaver named Blas González. After a heated argument between the brothers, the Blanquillo decided to take matters in his own hands. Ignoring the patriarchal authority of the head of the household, he forced his way into González's house and, not finding him there, beat his wife and allegedly threatened to set the store on fire. The artisans came out of the shop to defend their master and threw stones at the soldier. Then, late that night, several soldiers attacked the workshop to avenge their comrade. The Blanquillos had not only the force of arms but also the power to make a personal quarrel appear as a seditious act. The next morning, a military patrol headed by Commander López and the city's general prosecutor (procurador general) visited the workshop, alleging that the artisans had started a riot. It soon became apparent that nothing of the sort had happened, but the attack on the master weaver and his family went unpunished.[24] The popular revolt of September 1785 would vividly expose the intimate link between questions of gender and power nurtured by the conflictive coexistence of foreign soldiers and local residents. The only building stoned by the crowd during the riot, besides the garrison, was a beverage store belonging to a mestizo woman who had married one of the Saboya soldiers.[25]

The challenge to the manly honor of city residents was not restricted to assaults on the virtue of their wives and sisters. Other acts of violence also stained their public reputation. A patrician named Domingo Revollo was beaten and stabbed by soldiers in a store. The aggression not only remained unpunished: when Revollo reported the attack, he was arrested at the garrison.[26] Something similar happened to a mestizo who was badly wounded in a fight with a Blanquillo and then locked up at the army quarters. Other abuses of power were mentioned. People complained that the soldiers had no qualms about engaging in these acts of violence in broad daylight and in the presence of patricians. City residents were unable to repair injuries to their honor by themselves because the Blanquillos, as the witnesses repeatedly bemoaned, used to leave the barracks with their sabers. Until then, bearing arms was a privilege reserved to the urban elites, the militias, and town council officials. Hence the officers' failure to discipline the troops, if not their open complicity, was especially outrageous. "They are used to doing all these things," a testimony reads, "because their superiors have never bothered to correct them in the least; because of this, and the lack of punishment, they have been prone to commit any infamies they want."[27] The monopoly of force and legal protection enjoyed by the Spanish soldiers and the varied social rank of their civilian victims meant that issues usually confined to the realm of private relations appeared intrinsically tied to public policy. The personal became political in every sense of the word.

It is worth noting, finally, that the transgression of basic rules of social behavior also affected the Indian women and men who supplied the urban market with meat, firewood, charcoal, and other essential goods. An indignant resident recounted, "That the extortions and mistreatments of the *Regatonas* [retail merchants] are public and notorious, because [the soldiers] not only take the goods they sell by violent means, but when buying meat and snatching it away they have even cut their hands and beaten them. And since they are so daring, many people acquainted with the Blanquillos have snatched away foodstuffs from the Indians' fields to sell them here."[28] Native traders were also taken to the garrison by force for cleaning jobs and to serve the troops "under the title of service to the King."[29] Although this behavior had provoked some food shortages, the councilmen could do nothing about it. Recall that the two prime functions of cabildo officials were to secure the public order and to ensure a sufficient stock of basic foodstuffs.

The murder of three La Plata residents by Spanish soldiers buttressed popular perceptions of the troops as an occupation army governed by rules of behavior and legal privileges of their own. The first case occurred in 1781 when a young Creole died during a brawl with a Blanquillo in a *pulpería* [store] in the San Juan neighborhood. Much to the vecinos' surprise, the crime went unpunished as the soldier was immediately sent on to La Paz to fight the indigenous rebellion led by Túpac Katari. This incident had no apparent consequences. But when two additional murders occurred in 1782 and 1785, La Plata witnessed the first two mass riots since the foundation of the city two and a half centuries earlier.

### The Riots

On the night of September 18, 1782, during a brawl in a pulpería, a Spanish soldier named Josef Peti mortally wounded a young patrician, Don Juan Antonio León, by a saber blow to the neck.[30] La Plata residents and civil authorities, wary of what had happened the previous year in a similar incident, were this time determined not to let the crime go unpunished. The *alcalde de segundo voto* (town council magistrate), Francisco Xavier de Cañas, followed by a large crowd, immediately went to the garrison and demanded that Peti be handed over to him. The soldier then fled and sought sanctuary at the church of the Convento de Santa Teresa. As many people, allegedly plebeians, began to gather in front of the convent, a patrol had to be rushed there to rescue him. When Peti and his comrades left the convent, the crowd headed by alcalde Cañas followed them at a distance of fifty yards. Shouts and threats were exchanged. At some point, claiming that they had been stoned, the soldiers turned around and fired at the crowd. The shots continued even after Cañas, who was forced to run for his life, repeatedly asked them to stop. Cañas also denied that the people had thrown stones at the soldiers. In the end, at least three townspeople received bullet wounds. It is very significant that, while the people were naturally incensed by the shots, their spirits flared up *"even more when they saw that the soldiers, disregarding the alcalde's orders that the accused be sent to jail, decided on their own to take him to the garrison."*[31]

As soon as the soldiers stepped inside the garrison, around seven in the evening, a multitude began to convene in the Plaza Mayor. In short order, the people began to stone furiously the garrison doors. They demanded that Peti be transferred to the municipal prison so that he was tried in a regular court. The people shouted that the garrison "was not jail."[32] The barrage of stones continued for many hours. While this was going on, a crowd of rioters went to a construction site where the city's master pipes were being laid. There they freed several Creole soldiers who had been sentenced by Commander Cristóbal López to forced labor simply for having been caught outside the garrison at night. Later, thirty to forty young men, followed by some adults, amid much shouting, erected a gallows on the Plaza Mayor. They wanted to show the soldiers what was awaiting their comrade: "they said they wanted to hang the Blanquillo."[33] Eventually, to forestall worse evils, Commander López gave in to the pressure and handed Peti over to civil authorities. It is telling that it was soldiers from Charcas, headed by the commander himself and the alcalde, who transferred Peti from the garrison to the prison of the ayuntamiento.[34] More humiliating still, Peti had to walk through the crowd when crossing the plaza. Shouts, whistles, jeers, and stones followed him all the way to the municipal jail.[35]

The popular revolt brought to light two crucial phenomena: the complicity of urban aristocracy with the city's castas and the stark rejection of the Spanish soldiers' behavior and legal privileges. Although a judicial investigation later conducted by the cabildo maintained that only the "rabble" had taken part in the acts of violence, there is no doubt that large numbers of patricians and plebeians were present at the plaza. The councilmen and the gente decente walked among the crowd without being attacked. As noted above, the city residents, regardless of their social status, had recently fought the indigenous rebels together and had to cope together with public assaults on their male reputation. On the night of the riot, for example, "some *Gualaychos* [youngsters] were heard saying . . . if only we were not so shy and compliant to authority . . . [the Blanquillos] disrespect the noble vecinos and look at them with no respect, nor do they treat the plebeians with any kindness, for they have insulted and mal-treated the former."[36] Although it seems that the patricians did try to assuage the crowd, it is also evident that the two main ideological motifs of the uprising—the discourse of honor and the discourse of rights—appealed equally to both groups. Consider the following exchange between alcalde Cañas and the people, as told by a personal witness of the armed clash with the soldiers who escorted Peti from the convent to the garrison, *"Mister Alcalde, does your Highness see how the Blanquillos have injured this man? Because we like and respect your Highness we will do nothing to these thieves. The said Alcalde lovingly replied using the following words: My children, do not make any disturbances, you saw how I spent all afternoon working to have the accused handed over. I will punish him so that you are satisfied, you know well that I hold you in high esteem, and you also saw that I went with you to the Punilla* [the scene of the main battle with the indige-nous forces], *risking my life, and so, my children, in the name of God, control yourselves, give others no reason to talk about you."*[37]

It is worth mentioning that even the council authorities consented to the release of the Creole soldiers from forced labor in the master pipes. The rioters had told an alcalde in the Plaza Mayor "that he should feel sympathy for some young men who were in jail . . . that all or most of them were Creoles . . . *that only the Blanquillos were not punished and all their excesses were forgiven.* The Alcalde answered that he would impart justice."[38] Effectively, as soon as the Creole soldiers were liberated, they were conducted to the plaza and handed over to the alcalde so that it was the city magistrate, rather than Commander López, who decided what to do with them.[39]

The assault on the Spanish garrison, due to its levels of violence and conspicuous success, exacerbated rather than appeased the climate of political contention. The antagonisms would surface again three years later in a popular uprising of even greater proportions.[40] While the trigger of the riot of 1785 was the same—the murder of a resident by a soldier—resentment against the foreign troops was this time bolstered by the disbanding of the last militia company still in existence after the Túpac Amaru revolution. The standing unit was composed of mestizos under the command of a Creole officer. Its dissolution was made to coincide with the arrival in Charcas of a company of grenadiers of the second battalion of the Extremadura regiment that replaced the Saboya troops. Issued by Viceroy Marqués de Loreto, the measure had a simple rationale: "It is a settled matter that there must only be Spanish troops."[41] As may be expected, the vecindario perceived the news as an affront and an utter disregard for their services to the king. The disbanding of the militia deprived its members of a means of subsistence, their monthly salary, as well as a symbol of social prestige.[42] As a lieutenant of the Extremadura regiment recalled, they felt animosity as soon as they set foot in La Plata: "The same night that his unit arrived in the city, he was surrounded by cholos who would not let him pass when he tried to go from the Plaza to his lodgings, launching insults and whistling at him. In addition, the day before the night of the riot, he had heard that with even the slightest motive, "the reformed [disarmed] cholos would rise up and make them leave."[43]

The disturbances began on the night of July 21, 1785, when one of the recently arrived soldiers killed a young man with a saber in a quarrel. In the ensuing brawl, he injured two or three cholos and could only save his life because a patrol came to his rescue. The next day, numerous groups of plebeians, using their "calling drums," converged in the Plaza Mayor and pummeled the garrison with stones.[44] The soldiers fired back using rifles and cannons.[45] As had happened three years prior, "the crowd argued that the people were being killed like dogs, that the soldiers gravely insulted them, and that their crimes went unpunished since they kept on committing murders." The authorities tried to calm the people down by promising that the judges would see to it that justice was done, but "nothing sufficed, for the crowd in the Plaza kept growing."[46] The people eventually dispersed once the intendant of Charcas, Ignacio Flores, arrived at the plaza on horseback and, after heated discussion with the rioters, gave his word that the new crime would not go unpunished. He also handed out large sums of money.

Throughout the night, several patrician units patrolled the city on horseback in order to forestall further incidents. In the morning, however, the city woke up to new disturbances. Five soldiers who had gone to the Plaza to buy food for breakfast attacked a group of cholos with their sabers after an angry exchange of shouts and provocations. At least one of the cholos would later die from his wounds. A few minutes passed before a large crowd gathered once more in the Plaza Mayor and neighboring streets. Someone even began to toll the cathedral's bells in order to summon the people. About twenty soldiers went out to the street and fired on the crowd, killing one or two people and injuring many others. Despite the efforts of civil and ecclesiastical authorities, who marched in the streets carrying an image of the Holy Cross, the violence could not be contained. It was said that in their rage the mob disrespected the magistrates "insulting them with insolent words and expressions."[47] The battle reached its climax when a large number of people occupied the ayuntamiento building and set common felons free. Making much noise, the felons went into the streets armed with sabers, sticks, and knives. Not by chance the rioters had bemoaned "that they were repeatedly insulted without the delinquent [soldiers] being disciplined, whereas the cholos could not get away with anything."[48] More ominous still, those who stormed the cabildo tried to take weapons from the armory. Seeing that the situation was getting out of control, a group of soldiers crossed the Plaza Mayor discharging their rifles, evacuated the town council building by force, and installed an infantry cannon at its doors. After the soldiers fired cannonballs and their rifles, the crowd finally dispersed. Yet this did not prevent the people from gathering at various intersections and small plazas. One group broke the master pipes, thus cutting off the city's water supply. Another group went to the hospital where the soldiers wounded in the quarrels were being treated. A patrol had to be rushed to the hospital to avoid attacks; the injured soldiers were then taken back to the garrison.

There is no doubt that, unlike the occurrences three years before, the main driving force behind the new uprising was the rivalry between the regular Spanish army and the disbanded popular militias. The commander of the Extremadura battalion, Gregorio de la Cuesta, stated,"The gist of their demands was that the detained grenadier be handed over to them *and that the rest leave the city, because they had once been able to keep the city safe and would continue doing so.*"[49] Town council officials said that the plebeians complained that disrespect from Spanish soldiers and the disbanding of the militias "was the reward we obtained for serving the King in the campaigns [against the rebels]."[50] In fact, in the course of the riot, the people might have decided to take matters in their own hands: it was said that those involved in the assault on the ayuntamiento armory in order to take weapons were the veterans of the recently suppressed company.[51]

That the widespread repudiation of the foreign soldiers expressed an awareness, vague as it might be, of the emerging colonial dynamic is suggested by the fact that some of the Spanish-born residents seem to have been (or feared to be) the targets of popular violence. This anti-peninsular sentiment, despite the assertions of some of their victims, by no means encompassed all the Europeans but only those identified as supporters of the current imperial policies. Actually, several prominent Spaniards openly sided with the vecinos. Terms such as *chapetones* or *peninsulares*, not unlike the labels *criollos* or *mestizos*, were social constructs meant in this case to denote a political affiliation rather than a place of birth.[52] Still it is highly telling that the local population's foes were labeled in this way and, certainly, that some peninsulars, unlike municipal authorities and patricians in general, were indeed attacked by the rioters. For instance, a native of Santander, Gavino de Quevedo, said that on the night of July 22 many people were screaming that "all the chapetones would die that night."[53] The *teniente asesor* of the intendancy, Francisco Cano de la Puerta, also from Santander, reported that earlier that day his servant had heard "a group of cholos saying, in Quechua, that they will rise up that night and that it was necessary to hit all the chapetones on the head because they had killed a *paisano* (a Charcas native)." Cano added that this very night "a large crowd insulted him, and some were saying: [go after] that rascal who is a chapetón."[54]

The measures taken in the aftermath of the pitched battles underscore the open complicity of the patrician elites with the rioters. Just like three years before, when the soldier Josef Peti had to be handed over to the councilmen and placed in the municipal prison, this time Intendant Flores, with the full support of the cabildo officials and the resigned acquiescence of the audiencia ministers, decided to give in to the demands of the rioters and immediately restored the mestizo militia.[55] The rationale of this resolution underscores the ideological underpinnings of the conflict. It was asserted that the militia ought to be rearmed because its disbanding "had given rise to the feelings that the *Naturales* [Charcas natives] had developed that they had been deprived from this honor and from an occupation from which many of them drew their livelihood."[56]

Although the explicit goal of Viceroy Marqués de Loreto's order had been "to prevent the paisanos from being armed,"[57] he was told, not without irony, that the decision to rearm the militia would dissuade those paisanos "from the wrong notion they seemed to have that the new [Spanish] troops had been dispatched because of distrust and contempt toward them."[58]

### Representing the City's "Body Politics"

The core of the conflict between the city residents and the Spanish authorities was somehow prefigured in a statement made by Minister of the Indies José de Gálvez a few years before the riots. In 1779, reflecting on the sheer impossibility of protecting the Spanish empire with the regular army alone, the powerful Bourbon official called attention to the need for a colonial consensus. The fate of the Crown overseas possessions rested to a large extent on its American subjects' conviction that "the defense of the king's rights was linked to that of their own properties, the security of their families, their homeland, and their happiness."[59] Just one year would pass before the crucial participation of La Plata patrician and plebeian militias in the war against the great indigenous insurrection proved Gálvez right. But subsequently it was the same Crown that established a permanent Spanish garrison, disarmed the standing mestizo militia, and condoned foreign soldiers' recurring public challenges to the nobility and manly honor of Charcas residents. These actions made it impossible for the subjects of Charcas to identify their security and happiness with the preservation of the king's rights. In his essay on "the rebellion of the *barrios*" of 1765 in Quito, an insurrection prompted by changes in the royal liquor monopoly and sales tax, Anthony McFarlane writes that the movement was "a rebellion of a community rather than a class."[60] While this clearly applies to our case, I would offer that, because of its particular trigger and extraordinary historical circumstances, at the heart of the La Plata disturbances was not so much the community's prerogatives vis-à-vis the government but rather the community's sense of self. Unlike previous urban protests in Arequipa, Quito, La Paz, and Cochabamba, the disturbances did not revolve around matters of economic policy (fiscal reorganization) or even state power (no taxation without consultation) but rather basic issues of social and political identity. By problematizing the "link" existing between "the defense of the king's rights" and the advancement of his subjects' "security" and "happiness," the riots raised a fundamental question: was the city in essence a hidalgo society primarily structured along Hispanic and non-Hispanic sectors, or was it a colonial society divided into peninsulars and vecinos?

It is no wonder, therefore, that the ayuntamiento emerged as the main vehicle for representing widespread political dissatisfaction. Popular assaults on the Spanish garrison meant that politics, literally and figuratively, moved from state institutions to the public plaza. But, as everybody knew at the time, street violence, for all its noise and fury, was not the sole or even the most significant dimension of the conflict. Plebeian politics was inextricably intertwined with high politics, the kind that took place in the houses of the honorable and the halls of the town council.

The prominent role of the cabildo, a legacy of medieval Castilian traditions, as well as the resort to time-honored contractual notions of monarchical legitimacy (the theory of "historical constitutionalism"), does not mean the movement was a mere return to the past, an expression of "the nostalgia for the ancient representative institutions," or a quest for safe heaven in "the old liberties."[61] Political contention, whether in the guise of street violence or formal representative practices, was something more, or something other, than a conservative reaction to absolutist modernity. As is well known, since the late sixteenth century onward, when the spirit of broad participation in the Spanish American town councils came into conflict with the financial needs of the Crown, the cabildo had turned into a mere agency of municipal administration monopolized by a small group of patrician families in a symbiotic relationship with the royal bureaucracy.[62] During these years, on the contrary, the institution became an organ of political representation in overt opposition to the upper tiers of colonial government. Those it claimed to represent comprised, very tangibly and actively, patricians and plebeians. Needless to say, the inclusion of artisans and shopkeepers into the sphere of elite politics occurred de facto, without any formal institutional changes, and it did not mean egalitarianism. It points nonetheless to a growing sense of common identity, to a sense of belonging to a same political entity. And, as Octavio Paz wrote in an essay on colonial Mexico, "As it defines itself, every society defines other societies. That definition almost always takes the form of a condemnation."[63] The double condemnation of the otherness of the vast majority of the indigenous population prompted by the Túpac Amaru revolution and the coloniality of the structures of government prompted by the Bourbon reforms was the birthmark of Creole political consciousness.

The ayuntamiento of La Plata functioned as the institutional expression of the riots. In 1782, it became the vecinos' voice against the army. Hours after the September 18 clashes, the councilmen called for the convening of a cabildo abierto, an institution strongly linked to traditional ideas of corporate representation and municipal self-government.[64] In justifying the convocation, it was asserted, in obvious reference to the Saboya soldiers, that "there exist very justified fears that a few *evil foreigners*, moved by a well-known and malicious envy, through their influence and suggestions, pretend to agitate this city in order to stain the loyalty and nobility it has earned throughout history."[65] Although the regular army had just been stormed by unruly crowds, the municipal officials urged the audiencia to order Commander Cristóbal López "to forbid the soldiers from leaving the garrison with weapons, and to make them stay indoors after curfew." On September 21, the day the cabildo abierto met, "all the *vecinos principales*, both Creoles and Europeans" entered first into the main hall and, once they had taken their seats, a large number of plebeians followed suit, including "all the inferior persons and artisans of the capital, guild by guild, each made up of a master, minor officials, apprentices, and other dependents." The alcalde de primer voto opened the meeting by reminding everyone of the rights acquired by "this noble and brave Republic" as a result of old and recent services to the Spanish monarchs, especially its support to the regal army during the sixteenth-century civil wars and its decisive contribution to the defeat of the Túpac Amaru insurgents. Then he warned the "incautious" and "uninformed" craftsmen, apprentices, and dependents that they should not let that reputation be stained by "thoughtlessly promoting unrest that might produce dire consequences." It was a rhetorical warning, however. According to the meeting's minutes, the plebeians answered: "That the people who had shown up that night to create disturbances were only inconsiderate boys who, shouting and whistling, demanded justice, so that the Blanquillo soldier Josef Peti be punished as he deserved for the crime he had committed . . . this disturbance had started because they were used to seeing this city's judges meting out severe punishment even to minor criminals, and because, being young and not acquainted with royal military laws, it seemed to them that the garrison was not a suitable prison for someone accused of such a great crime, and they only asked that the soldier be sent to this Court's Public Prison."[66] The general assembly of city residents decided that these discharges were fair and truthful. Consequently, the artisans and shopkeepers were formally thanked and commanded to maintain their loyal and "proper conduct."

Over the following weeks, taking advantage of the weakness of the audiencia and the support of both Intendant of Charcas Ignacio Flores and Viceroy Juan José de Vértiz, the cabildo undertook a judicial inquiry into the events. This initiative went beyond the normal sphere of action for ayuntamientos, especially in seats of audiencias, which only heard minor legal cases. The investigation was entrusted to a prominent figure, a Creole lawyer named Juan José Segovia. He was the senior *relator* [court reporter] of the audiencia, commander of lawyers' militia during the indigenous uprising, and vice-rector of the Universidad de San Francisco Xavier. Ignacio Flores's close ally, the intendant chose him as his de facto assessor in place of the Cantabrian Francisco Cano, the official assessor appointed by the Ministry of the Indies. Ethnically mestizo or perhaps mulatto, Segovia served during these turbulent years as the main spokesman for the vecinos and the cabildo. He could be seen as a modern political figure in the sense that his leadership did not derive from his place in the colonial administration but rather from his personal reputation and public image.[67] Segovia took a great number of testimonies that described in excruciating detail the serious offenses and violence committed with impunity by the foreign soldiers against patricians, plebeians, their wives and sisters. Little was said about the perpetrators of the attacks on the garrison. As the newly arrived fiscal of the audiencia, Domingo Arnaiz de las Revillas, remarked with consternation, the official inquiry into the popular disturbances had directly targeted soldiers,' not rioters,' behavior. He went on to suggest that the reason was that many Creoles had been involved in the movement and, then, in its cover-up.[68] Whatever the truth might be, Segovia's investigation concluded that only young boys (gualaychos) and outside agitators provoked the incidents, that is to say, people not liable or impossible to find. No one was held responsible for the serious acts of sedition.[69]

In the aftermath of the events of July 1785, the association of patricians and plebeians, as well as the predicament of cabildo that was a vehicle for the political representation of both, would become even more apparent. In addition to the extraordinary decision to restore the mestizo militia the same day of the assault on the garrison and the storming of the ayuntamiento, a cabildo abierto was summoned. As three years earlier, the councilmen lamented the breakdown of order but justified the motives of discontent, blamed the Spanish soldiers for the unrest, and demanded full jurisdiction on the investigation of the incidents. This time, however, La Plata residents, the ayuntamiento, and the intendant of Charcas would meet a much more formidable opposition in the new viceroy of Río de la Plata, Marqués de Loreto, the audiencia, the teniente asesor of the intendancy, Francisco Cano, and the officers of the Extremadura regiment. They made a concerted effort to put an end to the politicization of the city and to reestablish crown officials' authority.[70] The viceroy commanded the immediate disbanding of the restored militia and, as to strengthen the standing of the regular army in the city, had another Spanish unit stationed in Potosí transferred to La Plata without previous warnings to either the councilmen or the intendant.[71] But even before receiving this order, Flores himself felt it necessary to disarm the mestizo company, "knowing of the disapproving, distrustful, and mischievousness comments against the patrician unit surreptitiously made by the very ministers [of the audiencia] who had agreed to its restoration . . . [and knowing that] good services can never be expected from mistrusted troops and from neglected and disrespected officers."[72] Not surprisingly, Loreto instructed the audiencia to take over the judicial inquiry into the events, leaving out this time both the cabildo and the intendant.[73] A stream of lengthy reports from royal officials in Charcas, accusing the city patriciate of complicity in the disturbances, began to flood the Buenos Aires and Madrid courts. They even asked Loreto to travel to La Plata to take charge of the matter personally. No viceroy had visited the city since the civil wars of the sixteenth century. It was argued that otherwise the true instigators and accomplices of the rebellion would not be found, once again.[74]

The vecinos publicly defied this conception of government. In an official communication to Loreto, signed by all the councilmen, the Spanish authorities' reports were held as "light and defamatory."[75] Juan José Segovia claimed that those who accused him and other Creoles of seditiousness "are themselves guilty of sedition, because with their intrigues, machinations, and pretences, they are the moths of the republics, they destroy the towns and they disturb the peace by spreading discord."[76] "The entire city," he warned the viceroy, "is submerged into the utmost confusion."[77] Ignacio Flores praised the mestizos for quietly accepting the order to return the weapons they had just gotten back, and the honorable for having done their best to keep the order. Acting as the spokesman for the vecinos, he told Loreto that both groups "became very upset when they saw that without consultation and in a mysterious way the unit that guarded Potosí arrived [in La Plata], for they believe that *Your Highness has no trust in their loyalty or has not taken note of their valuable services."*[78] Discrimination against Creoles and castes could yield only dire consequences. In a paradoxical echo of the statement of José de Gálvez quoted above, the first intendant of Charcas asked the viceroy: "Who can say that an army of sick men would serve your Majesty well, or that the republic will prosper with vassals that, unmoved by honor and trust, need to be paid in cash for the slightest hardships and minor acts of intimidation?"[79]

When the ayuntamiento received but a brief communication from Viceroy Loreto, stating that he was confident that the vecindario "would try to *erase the stain* that the recent occurrence could leave on its well-known loyalty," the exchange turned into open political confrontation.[80] On October 6, once Loreto's letter was received, an extraordinary petition was submitted to the audiencia. By virtue of a written authorization signed by one hundred and eighty-two patricians (*vecinos de honor*), a long document was elevated in the name of a putative collective entity: the vecindario. After recalling that it had been they "who, on their own, first destroyed and defeated [the Indian insurrection] on the hills of the Punilla," the vecinos explicitly blamed the Spanish soldiers for the recent disturbances. They also considered Loreto directly responsible for the distress that engulfed the "city's body politics" because, unlike his predecessor Juan José de Vértiz, he had decided to take sides with their enemies.[81] They called the request that Loreto traveled to La Plata to restore order "a reckless scheme . . . that notoriously affronts the conduct of some honorable vecinos." The journey was not advisable, unless it were to promote agriculture and other means of economic progress; but "his valuable presence is in no way necessary to contain disturbances, rebellions, and riots, because there are none. And if any were to happen, God forbid, the vecinos from Chuquisaca have exceeding resolve and loyalty to take care of them."[82]

The following day, a new cabildo abierto was convened, which was attended, once again, by "the noblest elements of the city and, not far away, the artisans and manual workmen."[83] With the pretext to comply with a viceregal decree to divide the city into four quarters and to elect *alcaldes de barrio* in charge of them, a public display of opposition to the main colonial powers–the army, the audiencia, the viceroy, and other crown officials—took place.[84] The election of the first of the alcaldes was in itself an open act of defiance, since Juan José Segovia, the alleged ringleader of the upheaval, was chosen. In any event, the appointment of alcaldes de barrio was only an excuse to deal with far more pressing matters. After three other municipal officials were elected, the discussion turned to the main agenda item: the repudiation of Loreto's letter. The clause concerning his purported confidence that the city would "erase the stain" caused by the riots was read aloud three times to leave no doubts about its ominous implications. Juan José Segovia opened the debate by remarking that the letter proved that Loreto "was not satisfied with the loyalty and proper behavior of the vecindario, and without question Your Excellency has been informed against it." The *subdelegado* of the province of Yamparáez, Bonifacio Vizcarra, talked about "the need for the vecindario to protect itself and meet against anyone who might try, or had already tried, to stain its proven loyalty, as a whole or in reference to particular accusations from chapetones to Creoles . . . and finally he began to criticize the statements contained in the letter of Your Excellency [the viceroy], trying to convince the vecinos that those expressions were insulting to them and denoted that Your Excellency had been misinformed." When Teniente Asesor Francisco Cano raised the point that all what was being said in the meeting "was seditious and could stir a popular uprising," Ignacio Flores rebuked him by saying that the letter was an irrefutable proof that the viceroy had received information "that went against the People's honor."[85] The cabildo abierto closed with a note of praise for the intendant and his response to the riot whose political connotations were not less apparent than the election of Segovia that had opened it. It was said that all those present "unanimously agreed to thank His Highness [Ignacio Flores] on behalf of the vecindario, and that the cabildo should make his worth known and placed at Your Majesty's [the king] feet and that His Excellency [Viceroy Loreto] should be notified."[86]

Everybody knew by then that Flores's days as intendant of Charcas were numbered.[87]

All must have understood the potential consequences of the collective mobilization of the city, especially its open defiance of the basic premise of colonial government, namely, the unconditional public compliance, although by no means implementation, of royal orders (the famous motto "I obey but do not execute"). It is highly significant that at the end of the cabildo abierto all the participants "pledged there to defend one another against any accusation that might affect the whole community ('el común de la ciudad') or any individual."[88] The royal authorities answered in kind. The audiencia of Charcas and the viceregal court of Buenos Aires condemned in no uncertain terms the collective petition of the vecinos. It was said for instance that the document "provides an exceedingly clear idea of the *defense* it essentially makes of the latest excesses of the plebe."[89] Equally important, the politics of the La Plata patriciate forced them to state as a matter of principle that the vecindario could not speak on behalf of "the whole community" and that this putative collective entity—the city—could not act as a "formal part" in the judicial process that followed the popular uprising.[90] As for the cabildo abierto, it was declared, justifiably so, that the meeting had offered "*to the criticism of the people as a whole a letter which had been addressed only to this council.*"[91] This amounted to nothing less than "exposing to the judgment of a rude and ignorant people the wise letter addressed only to the cabildo by the one [the viceroy] who so worthily represents in these kingdoms the Holy Person of the King Our Lord."[92] The public challenges to Viceroy Loreto was described as a "horrible crime of sedition," "a conspiracy whose only aim has been to implant in the minds of these reckless and ignorant vecinos despicable ideas against the government."[93] At the recommendation of the recently created audiencia of Buenos Aires, Loreto dispatched letters to the councilmen and Ignacio Flores stating his formal "disapproval" of the convocation of a cabildo abierto and the ensuing public debate of his official communication.[94]

The most visible figures of movement would pay dearly for their daring. At the time that the local population was categorically backing the policies of Intendant Ignacio Flores, his removal had already been decided. Two months after the cabildo abierto of October 1785, his successor, Vicente de Gálvez (a protégé of Viceroy Loreto and Minister of the

Indies José de Gálvez) arrived in La Plata with instructions that Flores be escorted by a group of soldiers to Buenos Aires. He remained there under house arrest until his death six months later. Loreto denied him even a single personal audience. In short order, Juan José Segovia suffered the same fate. Forced to travel to the capital of the viceroyalty escorted by a small retinue in order to answer for his role in the 1782 and 1785 riots, he would spend eleven months in isolation in a dungeon. His trial took many years. Segovia had drawn the wrath of the ministers of the audiencia of Charcas and some sectors of the Church when, at Flores's proposal, he had been chosen as head of the Universidad de San Francisco Xavier in early 1786. Sixty-eight of the seventy-five doctors in attendance voted for him.[95] Echoing the double menace posed by the collective mobilization of the urban population—a threat to the traditional social identities of the baroque city and to the new politics of Bourbon centralization—the lawyer was accused of "taking pride in being the *defender of creoles of all qualities*, and proclaiming to be *the tribune of the people and consul of those provinces*."[96] Vicente de Gálvez himself underscored the place of Flores and Segovia in society. Despite his own political alignments, he had to concede that "these individuals are popular among this people."[97] The deposition and arrest of both men became causes célèbres.

It would require a historical reconstruction well beyond the scope of this chapter to make the case that there were strong links between these events and the fact that, after the fall of the Spanish monarchy in 1808, La Plata became the scene of the first open challenges to viceroys' legitimacy and substitution of existing authorities for new government bodies (*juntas de gobierno*). The literature on the Túpac Amaru insurrections has taught us much about why the elites in Upper Peru rejected liberal notions of universal citizenship advocated by the rebel armies coming from the Río de la Plata and New Granada and avoided mobilizing the indigenous peoples. We know relatively little, however, about the process that led to that early outburst of Creole defiance. It is worth recalling, nonetheless, that even in the mid-nineteenth century, according to the historian Gabriel René Moreno, some elderly residents of La Plata still talked about a *before* and an *after* "Segovia's lawsuit."[98] Perhaps it was not so much about Segovia personally as about the dramatic events surrounding his trial. At the very least, the urban conflicts of the early 1780s seem to signal a number of momentous changes: the conformation of a Creole identity rooted in the *patria chica*, the homeland, and ultimately the city and its hinterland, the only organic community inherited from centuries of Spanish rule; the merging of patricians and plebeians into a single "political body" (with all the social and racial stratification of the time); the opposition to Spanish colonialism not by rejecting its cultural and political institutions but because of the systematic exclusion of the American elites from fully participating in those institutions; and the coexistence of a minority of Hispanic and mestizo population with a large majority of indigenous peoples considered barbarians, unredeemable, the other. All these trends would have a very long future in front of them.

## Notes

Research for this article was made possible by funding from Boston College, the Consejo Nacional de Investigaciones Científicas y Técnicas de la Argentina (CONICET), the Escuela de Estudios Hispano-Americanos de Sevilla, the Fundación Antorchas, and the John Carter Brown Library.

1. For an analysis of several aspects of the history of La Plata in the eighteenth century, see Querejazu Calvo, *Chuquisaca*; and Bridikhina, *Sin temor a Dios ni a la justicia real.*

2. See Campbell, *The Military and Society in Colonial Peru*, 158–88.

3. Moreno, *Biblioteca peruana*, 126–27.

4. Thibaud, "La Academia Carolina de Charcas," 40. My emphasis.

5. Querejazu Calvo, *Chuquisaca*, 362. See also Thibaud, "La Academia Carolina de Charcas," 42–47.

6. Moreno, *Biblioteca peruana*, 126. On social and cultural practices of patricians and plebeians in La Plata during this period, see Bridikhina, *Sin temor a Dios ni a la justicia real.* For late colonial Lima and Mexico City, see Estenssoro Fuchs, "La plebe ilustrada," and Voekel, "Peeing on the Palace."

7. Querejazu Calvo, *Chuquisaca*, 384.

8. Bridikhina, "Los honores en disputa."

9. On Ignacio Flores, see Lynch, *Spanish Colonial Administration*, 66–79, 241–46, and 262–64; Guzmán y Polanco, "Un quiteño en el virreinato del Río de la Plata," 159–83; Carrera Andrade, *Galería de místicos e insurgentes*, 69–77; Demélas y Saint-Geours, *Jerusalén y Babilonia*, 70–71.

10. The same applies to the plebe, whose internal racial classifications multiplied to the point where they lost all practical meaning (see, for example, Cope, *The Limits of Racial Domination*, 161–65). For general studies of social relationships in eighteenth-century Spanish American cities, see Romero, *Latinoamérica, las ciudades y las ideas*; Hoberman and Socolow, eds., *Cities and Society in Colonial Latin America*; Hardoy, *Cartografía urbana*

colonial de América Latina y el Caribe; Morse, "El desarrollo urbano de la Hispanoamérica colonial"; and Hünefeldt, "El crecimiento de las ciudades." For the case of Peru, see Flores Galindo, Aristocracia y plebe; and Chambers, From Subjects to Citizens.

11. Rama, La ciudad letrada, 32; Romero, Latinoamérica, las ciudades y las ideas, 85–91.

12. The acting president of the audiencia remembered that already during the indigenous rebellion, as anonymous documents began to appear in the city blaming provincial corregidores and the audiencia for the current state of affairs, "in order to impress the plebeians who made up the [militia] companies, he called his officers and soldiers and made the rounds of the city with them. He praised the Cabildo Secular and the whole vecindario. In this way I was able to eliminate discord between creoles and Spaniards." (Quoted in Querejazu Calvo, Chuquisaca, 385; my emphasis.) See also Lewin, La rebelión de Túpac Amaru, 538–40.

13. A sharp analysis of the double meaning of honor in this society is in Johnson and Lipsett-Rivera, The Faces of Honor, 3–6.

14. Stern, The Secret History, 14.

15. Johnson and Lipsett-Rivera, The Faces of Honor, 8–9.

16. Testimony of Rafael Mena, Archivo General de Indias (hereafter AGI), Charcas, 535.

17. Seed, To Love, Honor, and Obey in Colonial Mexico, 150. See also Lavrín, Sexuality and Marriage in Colonial Latin America; and Chambers, From Subjects to Citizens, 161–80.

18. Clark, "Manhood, Womanhood, and the Politics of Class in Britain," 274.

19. Testimony of Ignacio Valdivieso, AGI, Charcas, 535. My emphasis.

20. Testimony of Nicolás Larrazábal, AGI, Charcas, 535.

21. Testimony of Don Lorenzo, AGI, Charcas, 535.

22. Testimony of Ignacio Valdivieso y Domingo Revollo, AGI, Charcas, 535.

23. Testimony of Don Lorenzo, AGI, Charcas, 535.

24. Testimony of Don Calisto Balda and Blas González, AGI, Charcas, 535.

25. On this incident, see, for example, testimony of alcalde de primer voto Antonio Serrano before oidor Cicerón, August 18, 1785 , AGI, Buenos Aires, 72.

26. Testimony of Domingo Revollo, AGI, Charcas, 535.

27. Testimony of Nicolás Larrazábal, AGI, Charcas, 535. On the importance of avenging public challenges to a person's honor, see Johnson, "Dangerous Words, Provocative Gestures, and Violent Acts." On soldiers' codes of behavior in colonial cities and garrison life, see Marchena Fernández, Ejército y milicias en el mundo colonial americano, 211–72.

28. Testimony of Don Calisto Balda, AGI, Charcas, 535.

29. Testimony of Manuel Oropeza, AGI, Charcas, 535. For a study of urban Indians in La Plata, see Presta, "Devoción cristiana, uniones consagradas y elecciones materiales en la construcción de identidades indígenas urbanas."

30. The fiscal of the Consejo de Indias described León as "a patrician from La Plata." The general prosecutor of La Plata defined him as "a Creole from this city." León is referred to as "Don." AGI, Charcas, 535.

31. Testimony of alguacil mayor del cabildo, Francisco Xavier de Arana, AGI, Charcas, 535. My emphasis.

32. Testimony of *maestre de campo* Francisco Xavier de Arana, AGI, Charcas, 535.

33. Testimony of Nicolás Larrazábal, AGI, Charcas, 535.

34. Testimony of Don Calisto Balda, AGI, Charcas, 535.

35. Ibid.

36. Ibid. My emphasis.

37. Testimony of Nicolás Larrazábal, AGI, Charcas, 535. Emphasis in the original.

38. Testimony of Josef Mariano de León, Charcas, 535. My emphasis.

39. Testimony of Don Juan José Segovia, AGI, Charcas, 535.

40. The close connection between both events was pointed out by the intendant of Potosí and former fiscal of the audiencia of Charcas, Juan del Pino Manrique, who explained that the new riot had stemmed from "an old hatred of that idle, pampered and arrogant plebe to the veteran troops, and *because they were not punished on time for the offenses they committed three years before, this time they have been even more daring.*" (Manrique to the viceroy, Marqués de Loreto, August 16, 1785, AGI, Buenos Aires, 70 n. 2.) My emphasis.

41. The fiscal of the audiencia of Charcas, Domingo Arnaiz de las Revillas, to the viceroy, Marqués de Loreto, August 2, 1785, AGI, Buenos Aires, 70, n.1.

42. On the effect of colonial militias on the formation of casta identities, see Archer, *The Army in Bourbon Mexico*; Campbell, *The Military and Society*; Vinson, *Bearing Arms for His Majesty*.

43. Testimony of the second lieutenant Andrés Núñez Guardabrazo, January 31, 1786, Archivo General de la Nación de Buenos Aires [AGN], IX, Interior, legajo 22, expediente 4. On the causes and characteristics of the riots of 1785, see Lynch, *Administración colonial española*, 226–29.

44. It was said that they were throwing "so many stones that they started to damage the boards [of the doors], and they made a hole in one of them that was almost large enough to let a man through." Fiscal Arnaiz to the viceroy, Marqués de Loreto, August 2, 1785, AGI, Buenos Aires 70, n. 1.

45. Testimony of Juan Antonio Fernández, AGI, Buenos Aires, 72.

46. Ibid. My emphasis.

47. The audiencia to the viceroy, Marqués de Loreto, July 24, 1785, AGI, Buenos Aires, 70, n. 1.

48. Testimony of Juan Antonio Fernández, AGI, Buenos Aires, 72.

49. Gregorio de la Cuesta to the viceroy, Marqués de Loreto, August 1, 1785, AGI, Buenos Aires, no. 1. Emphasis in the original.

50. Testimony of the scribe of the cabildo, Martín José de Terrazas, August 13, 1785, AGI, Buenos Aires, 72. See also Ignacio Flores to the viceroy, Marqués de Loreto, October 15, 1785, AGI, Buenos Aires, 72.

51. Fiscal of the audiencia, Domingo Arnaiz de Revillas, to the viceroy, Marqués de Loreto, August 2, 1785, AGI, Buenos Aires, 70, no. 1.

52. To be considered a vecino in Spanish America, both legally and symbolically, depended less on a person's provenance than on his integration with the community,

reputation, personal networks, and other matters of sociability (Herzog, "La vecindad"). According to Brian Hamnett, "The resident elites included Spaniards and Americans: provenance did not necessarily imply either difference of material interest or any political polarity. The predominance of *American* interests and family connections provided the defining element which distinguished this group from the 'peninsular' elite." Hamnett, "Process and Pattern," 284.

53. Testimony of Gavino de Quevedo Hoyos, May 10, 1786, AGN, IX, Interior, legajo 22, expediente 4.

54. Testimony of teniente asesor, Francisco Cano de la Puerta, August 6, 1785, AGI, Buenos Aires, 72. Testimony of Juan Ventura Avila, October 39, 1786, AGN, IX, Interior, legajo 22, expediente 4. For other examples, see Fiscal Domingo Arnaiz de las Revillas to the viceroy, Marqués de Loreto, August 2, 1785, AGI, Buenos Aires, 70, n. 1.

55. AGN, sala IX, Tribunales, legajo 132, expediente 13.

56. Acta de Acuerdo Extraordinario de la Audiencia, July 24, 1785, AGI, Buenos Aires, 70, n. 1.

57. Fiscal of the audiencia, Arnaiz, to the viceroy, Marqués de Loreto, August 2, 1785, AGI, Buenos Aires, 70, n.1.

58. The Audiencia to Viceroy Loreto, July 24, 1785, AGI, Buenos Aires, 70, n. 1.

59. Quoted in Marchena Fernández, "The Social World of the Military in Peru and New Granada," 58.

60. McFarlane, "The Rebellion of the 'Barrios,'" 250.

61. Guerra, *Modernidad e independencias*, 28.

62. See Kinsbruner, *The Colonial Spanish-American City*, 36–39.

63. Paz, *Sor Juana, or, The Traps of Faith*, 28.

64. McFarlane, "The Rebellion of the 'Barrios,'" 214.

65. Auto del Cabildo, September 20, 1782, AGI, Charcas, 535.

66. Acta del Cabildo Abierto, September 21, 1782, AGI, Charcas, 535.

67. It was said that on an occasion that Segovia gave a speech at the Universidad de Charcas in honor of Ignacio Flores, who had recently been appointed president of the audiencia, the employees were unable to keep out of the main hall the many artisans and workers who wanted to attend the ceremony. An audiencia minister reprimanded university authorities for allowing so many plebeians to be present at such an event. This happened in February 1782, seven months before the attack on the garrison (Gantier Valda, *Juan José de Segovia*).

68. Report by fiscal Domingo Arnaiz, August 20, 1782, AGI, Charcas, 535. My emphasis.

69. "Testimonio del Primer y Segundo expediente sobre los incidentes ocurridos en La Plata," AGI, Charcas 535.

70. On Loreto's policies, see Grieco, *Politics and Public Credit*.

71. Viceroy Marqués de Loreto to Ignacio Flores, August 29, 1785, AGI, Charcas, 433.

72. Ignacio Flores to the viceroy, Marqués de Loreto, September 15, 1785, AGI, Charcas, 433. Note that "patrician unit," for reasons unknown to us, was the name given to a unit of mestizos. As has been said, the only patrician in this unit was the captain, Manuel Allende.

73. AGI, Charcas, 433. It is worth noting again that Loreto's predecessor, the Creole Juán José de Vértiz, had prohibited the *Audiencia* from hearing in matters related to the Indian rebellion of 1780 and had given Ignacio Flores complete jurisdiction over these issues. Likewise, Vertiz accepted that the *cabildo* were in charge of the inquiry into the popular riot of 1782.

74. Fiscal of the Audiencia Arnaiz to the viceroy, Marqués de Loreto, August 2, 1785, AGI, Buenos Aires, 70, n.1. See also testimony of Francisco Cano de la Puerta before the *oidor* Cicerón, August 6, 1785 (AGI, Buenos Aires, 72) and Gregorio de la Cuesta to the viceroy, Marqués de Loreto, August 1, 1785 (AGI, Buenos Aires, 70, n. 1).

75. Antonio Serrano, Juan Antonio Fernández, Diego Ortega y Barrón, Doctor Josef Eustaquio Ponce de León y Cerdeño, Francisco Xavier de Arana, Juan de Mallavia, Francisco de Sandoval, and Joaquín de Artachu to the viceroy, Marqués de Loreto, September 14, 1785, AGI, Buenos Aires, 72.

76. Juan José de Segovia to the intendant of Charcas, Ignacio Flores, AGI, Buenos Aires, 72.

77. Juan José de Segovia to the viceroy, Marqués de Loreto, September 14, 1785, AGI, Buenos Aires, 72.

78. Ignacio Flores to the viceroy, Marqués de Loreto, October 15, 1785, AGI, Buenos Aires, 72. My emphasis.

79. Ibid.

80. Viceroy Marqués de Loreto to the cabildo of La Plata, August 29, 1785, AGI, Buenos Aires, 72. My emphasis.

81. Letter by apoderado José de Arias to the audiencia, October 6, 1785, AGI, Buenos Aires, 72.

82. Ibid.

83. Doctor Francisco Moscoso to fiscal Domingo Arnaiz, October 8, 1785, AGI, Buenos Aires, 72.

84. On the creation of the post of alcaldes de barrio, see Lempériere, "República y publicidad a finales del Antiguo Régimen," 58. For an analysis of the municipal reforms pushed by the Bourbon administration in Lima, see Walker, "Civilize or Control?"

85. All the statements made in the cabildo abierto are taken from Francisco Cano de la Puerta's report to the viceroy, Marqués de Loreto, October 15, 1785, AGI, Buenos Aires, 72.

86. Acta del cabildo, October 7, 1785, AGI, Buenos Aires, 72.

87. For example, a week after the cabildo abierto, Flores said that he would not change his attitude "even if it means I'll be deposed, *as is being announced publicly.*" Ignacio Flores to the viceroy, Marqués de Loreto, October 15, 1785, AGI, Buenos Aires, 72. My emphasis.

88. Doctor Francisco Moscoso to fiscal Domingo Arnaiz, October 8, 1785, AGI, Buenos Aires, 72. It is important to recall that, a few years before, in response to a petition by the cabildo of Buenos Aires to extend Viceroy Pedro de Ceballos's appointment even after a successor had already been named, the Ministro de Indias sent two *regidores* into exile to the Malvinas Islands and ordered that nine other councilmen be barred for seven years (Lynch, *Administración colonial española*, 196–98).

89. Report from fiscal of the audiencia, Domingo Arnaiz, 1October 10, 1785, AGI, Buenos Aires, 72. My emphasis.

90. Report from the *oidor* who was acting as fiscal of the audiencia of Buenos Aires, Palomeque de Céspedes, December 14, 1785, and resolution from the acuerdo extraordinario de Buenos Aires, December 16, 1785, AGI, Buenos Aires, 72.

91. Doctor Francisco Moscoso to fiscal Domingo Arnaiz, October 8, 1785, AGI, Buenos Aires, 72. My emphasis.

92. Francisco Cano de la Puerta to the viceroy, Marqués de Loreto, October 15, 1785, AGI, Buenos Aires, 72.

93. Ibid.

94. Resolution of the acuerdo extraordinario de Buenos Aires, and reports from the viceroy, Marqués de Loreto, to the cabildo of La Plata and to Ignacio Flores, December 16, 1785, AGI, Buenos Aires, 72.

95. Querejazu Calvo, *Chuquisaca*, 445.

96. Moreno, *Biblioteca peruana*, 118.

97. Vicente de Gálvez to Viceroy Loreto, November 15, 1786, and February 15, 1787. AGN, IX, Interior, legajo 22, expediente 4.

98. Moreno, *Biblioteca peruana*, 113–14.

# Conjuring Identities

*Race, Nativeness, Local Citizenship, and Royal Slavery
on an Imperial Frontier (Revisiting El Cobre, Cuba)*

Classifications do not exist only in the empty space of language but in institutions, practices, material interactions with things and other people . . . [People who are classified] can make tacit or even explicit choices, adapt or adopt ways of living so as to fit or get away from the very classifications that may be applied to them.
~Ian Hacking, *The Social Construction of What?*

The *vecinos* [local citizens] of the said *pueblo* [El Cobre], blacks as well as mulattoes, are slaves of His Majesty . . . [S]ince they are slaves they cannot administer ordinary justice . . . [I]t has been a very irregular thing to have allowed them to appoint *alcaldes* [bailiffs].
~Governor Don Pedro Ignacio Ximénez, 1732

The story of El Cobre is very uncertain, not to say fantastic, as it was populated exclusively by Indians and men of color until recently when the riches of its mines attracted more illustrious settlers and even foreign enterprises.
~Report of Governor Don Cayetano de Urbina, 1846

Social identities in early modern Iberian empires were based on a wide range of criteria. Although the importance of the category of race in the formation of these identities has been taken almost for granted, its actual significance has not been sufficiently interrogated. The present volume invites a conversation on the still neglected topic of race with particular reference to the theoretical paradigm of social identity. This linkage reflects one of the interdisciplinary gestures that has marked many fields in the last decades and that, as our editors, Matthew O'Hara and Andrew Fisher, point out in their opening essay, has only begun to influence Latin American colonial historiography. But just as this paradigm begins to inform new work in this field, some scholars have begun to question its utility on different fronts. Rogers Brubaker and Frederick Cooper, among others, would prefer to discard a notion that all too often fails to distinguish between categories and identities.[1] The irreverent title of Ian Hacking's book *The Social Construction of What?* suggests even more disquieting concerns. Widespread allusions to the "socially constructed" character of a motley of things and categories (including "self" or identities) in academic work since the 1970s have often resulted in the trivialization of insights, abstract reifications, formulaic reiterations, oversimplifications, confusions, and misconceptions that sometimes explode in bitter "culture wars" and other ills. Although Hacking's main focus is on the felicitous—and not so felicitous—uses of the social construction claim in general, some of his pointed observations are also applicable to the literature on the social construction of identity. By now a lot of intellectual labor has gone into showing that identities are historically contingent and not essential or given, that they are (at least relatively) fluid and not rigid, that they are imposed but also contested, that they are cultural and social and not natural, even those glossed to seem natural. While initially many of those insights may have seemed fresh and liberating, eventually as they became widespread and normalized they have begun to be taken for granted and have lost much of their force. Alas, such may be the fate of most paradigms once they go mainstream.

While I myself have begun to feel the fatigue of the identity paradigm and its predictable outcomes in much current academic work, I also think that its utility has not been exhausted yet, at least not in the field of colonial Latin American history, especially with regard to race studies. Hacking's admonition (in the epigraph above) that social classifications and categories take shape in "matrices" and through different forms of agency among different sorts of entities betrays a keen historicist and pragmatic stance, one that sets identity construction related queries squarely in the playing field of history in more complex ways. The point is no longer that categories X and Y (racial categories or, in our case, social identities among racialized subjects) are constructed but how, in what kinds of interactions and matrices, and to what effect.[2] In any case, as we open the field of colonial Latin American history to more "identity talk" and to interdisciplinary conversations along this line, we also need to be more discerning regarding what questions are particularly pertinent to our field and histories. This includes reflecting on wrong turns and impasses in the current historiography and the directions that remain to be explored. My own work on the community of royal slaves that emerged in El Cobre, Cuba, during the late seventeenth and eighteenth centuries has been strongly informed by the paradigm of identity making and speaks to some of the theoretical, methodological, and historiographical issues raised by O'Hara and Fisher in their opening essay (and by Hacking on another front).[3]

Overall, one issue that needs to be addressed with greater precision in the historiography as we focus on "race" is the meaning of the category itself, as distinct from the actual system of social labels and their usages. To be sure, the very notion or category of race is fuzzy and its historical development—both in the metropolitan and colonial contexts—still awaits a larger and more sustained investigation. Irene Silverblatt in her recent work, and to a lesser extent in the preface of this volume, for instance, focuses on the emergence of "race thinking" and takes the strong position that race is a modern overdetermined category that came into full being (shall we dare say to the point of "fixity"?) with Iberian expansion and state making in the sixteenth century, while others, including Laura Lewis, argue that "caste" (and not race) was the operative concept in the colonial setting and that it was a more ambiguous and flexible system that combined "inherent differences" with lineage and other social affiliations.[4] The claim needs to be worked out in more nuanced ways not only in Atlantic New World scenarios but further back in time in the Iberian Peninsula (and elsewhere in the Mediterranean), in order to better identify continuities and mutations in the modern notion of race (and caste) in later New World imperial contexts. In any case, the lesser claim that blood ancestry, whether caste-, color-, or race-related (I will bracket the question of their distinctiveness here), became a pervasive criterion of imperial classifications imposing order and hierarchy throughout Iberian New World territories seems indisputable, particularly with reference to the juridical, administrative, and social tripartite system of Spaniard, Indian, and black (but also in relation to their multiple biotic mixes often indexed by the generic term *castas*). Questions remain, however, regarding the *ascendancy* and the practical meanings that these "racial," or protoracial orderings took on in the production of identities throughout colonial space and time—and beyond.[5] Although there is a proliferating literature with its own set of endless debates on racial identities and race relations in modern Latin America (mostly, but not only, on Brazil and Cuba) in the postcolonial period (nineteenth to twenty-first centuries), work on these topics for the colonial period is still sparse.[6]

Notwithstanding the prominence of racialized—or protoracialized—inscriptions in the formation of imperial subjects I want to emphasize in this chapter that race (and its attendant caste) classifications were not the sole categories at play in social life and that their force could be reinforced or attenuated and modulated, if not completely displaced, by their interaction with other categories. In effect, the repertoire of social categories and identifications available to old regime imperial subjects, and for that matter, with some exceptions perhaps, to any subject at any historical moment, was broader and it is the historian's task to identify empirically recurring and significant ones (beyond the other usual suspects of gender or ethnicity). At this point it may be more productive to move beyond issues of racial classification per se and examine broader processes of identity formation among officially racialized subjects including the place of race in the latter's own articulations of collective self. Even as we focus on race we also need to consider whether to talk about "identity," or about interlaced "identities," that is, repertoires of identifications, and the meanings produced by their interactive combination. The notion of weaving or "quilting" categories around "nodal points" of meaning found in some recent identity-related theories may be of some use to guide us into the empirical intricacies at work in colonial historical scenarios as well.[7] This approach is also able to tackle the (implicit and explicit) claims-making dimension of identity questions and struggles that I consider central to this field of studies.

Paradoxically, given the extreme subject position (bordering on a "non-subject" one) that slavery represented, cases of enslavement may be an apposite way to illustrate some aspects of the approach suggested above. Issues of debasement aside, slavery was the most juridically constrained and restricted of imperial classifications, one that at least in principle constituted virtual "social death." In the New World people of African ancestry became closely, even intrinsically, associated to enslaved status and origin. What range of identity options—if any—were available to enslaved subjects of African descent to negotiate their position in Iberian colonial society? In my previous work on El Cobre, I implicitly posed this problem in relation to the "making" of the identity of "royal slavery" in a nonplantation frontier region in eastern Cuba. I studied the process of the negotiation of discursive and practical meaning, including the varied identifications conjured by bonded subjects in that process, with a quasi-ethnographic eye. In that particular historical setting of a frontier Caribbean region, the abstract category of royal slavery came in practice to entail an unprecedented degree of autonomy and de facto freedom that even allowed these enslaved subjects to live as a quasi-corporate pueblo. In the spirit of this volume, I will revisit the case of El Cobre, focusing on the significance of racial categories in the discursive practices related to identity formation and claims making by these imperial bonded subjects, but, as I proposed in the discussion above, I will examine them *in relation* to a broader range of identifications and affiliations. Among the most salient were those related to nativeness (*naturaleza*), Creoleness, indigeneity, *vecindad* (local citizenship), as well as allegiance to the king. I also probe further the bold political claims to freedom, inclusiveness, and local citizenship underlying some of these old regime–based invocations of identity, particularly as they relate to the local institution of the *cabildo* (town council) in the community of El Cobre.

To be sure, the varied reconfigurations of identity that took shape among these imperial bonded subjects almost certainly would not have been possible in plantation settings, perhaps not even in viceregal centers (the agency of subordinate subjects, for one, may not have had as effective outcomes in such contexts). But we still need to know whether dynamics and outcomes akin to those of El Cobre—however unusual these seem to have been—did take shape in analogous regions of empire, in its vast peripheries and frontiers. The prevalence of populations of African descent (despite their invisibility in the historiography outside the classic plantation regions) is patent in the striking profiles that emerge in the maps and tables that Reid Andrews has produced in a recent survey of the region.[8] Research on the various social formations in which these populations participated and the identification categories available to them—in freedom and slavery—throughout different regions and periods needs to be better mapped. As the new field of African diaspora studies gains ground in Latin American history (and begins to form its own subfield of "Afro Latin America"), comparative dimensions become increasingly urgent.

A somewhat different issue that I want to raise in relation to recent trends in the field is the epistemological shift away from the political and economic and into the social and cultural that O'Hara and Fisher note has been taking place since the so-called linguistic turn in the 1970s. I consider this shift not only excessive and problematical but in fact rooted in a false dichotomy between the "material" and the "symbolic" or its supposed analogues, the economy and politics—even political economy—on the one hand and the cultural and social on the other. In my own previous work on El Cobre I attempted to bridge this dissociation by taking what I called a "total" approach to identity making. This approach suggests that practices related to all spheres—so-called material ones and those regarded as purely social and cultural or symbolic—are fundamentally intertwined. For instance, land and labor issues—often relegated to the material production sphere of political economy—also contain deeper layers of meaning fundamentally related to identity making.[9] And while the domain of political economy should by no means be reduced to identity issues and queries, neither should it be impervious to them. Or rather, identity studies would do well to broaden their scope to practices in other productive spheres of life. Such studies become unnecessarily narrow when they restrict their interest to expressive culture and performances, or to the myriad practices of popular culture and religion.

The marginalization of the "political" in colonial Latin American historiography since the linguistic turn has proceeded in other ways too. Although initially this displacement may have represented a healthy and robust reaction against the exclusively political and state-centric approaches of an earlier historiography, for all too long now the new social and cultural histories have eradicated the (colonial) state, as well as political ideologies and discourses from its stories of the past. And yet the state and its juridical, institutional, and discursive apparatuses have an important cultural dimension that is fundamentally involved in the production of identities too (not just in their policing).[10] As I will note later in this chapter, imperial juridical, administrative, and political discourses were also often closely intertwined with social practices and local vernacular cultural discourses in identity making. These imbrications should be probed further rather than eschewed, since they only threaten to disrupt misguided notions of autonomous "authenticity."

But the state and other powerful old regime institutions, such as the Church, also constituted major players in historical settings in more conventionally recognizable ways. They were institutions with their own political projects, logic, interests, and personnel. Although their power was far from absolute (and in some settings perhaps even tenuous), these institutions were part of the context and matrix in which historical agents in colonial Latin America operated, and they should not be cast off from our histories of the colonial past. At the very least their force and legitimacy should be interrogated. State and Church, symbolized in my work by the figures of the "King" and the "Virgin," also occupied a prominent place in my story about identity making among the royal slaves of El Cobre. In fact, while this may not be true for other frontier and peripheral regions in colonial Latin America, one of the most surprising aspects of the case study on El Cobre is the strong presence of the state in its *various* embodiments in this hinterland region of empire and the extent to which its discourses and institutions engaged enslaved subaltern imperial subjects.

Ultimately, even if the hybrid social formation that emerged in this Cuban frontier location were unique to Latin American colonial history, it was produced by bending and stretching the very normative imperial categories, discourses and institutions that generated far more regular and familiar formations throughout the empire. Either way, whether as preview of analogous colonial formations yet to be located in the archive or as a singular case, El Cobre suggests that our historiographical genres need to be opened up to better grasp the paradoxical and hybrid dimensions of social formations and identity making that emerged in the Iberian black Atlantic and more broadly in the New World.[11] In any case, regardless of how sui generis the case of El Cobre turns out to be at the imperial level, the archival record of voices and practices in this community is so rich that it provides a rare opportunity to flesh out the dynamics of identity formation and negotiation among subjects of African descent with keen attention to meaning and ethnographic detail, a task not always possible among subordinate subjects in allegedly more "representative" formations. The localized character of the study also facilitates the examination of identity-making processes among subjects tied to a particular space over a long span of time and across different domains of life.

A few caveats regarding the repertoire of affiliations examined in this chapter are in order. I do not have the space here to explicitly analyze gendered identities among these imperial subjects, although I have done so with some intriguing results elsewhere.[12] The discourses and issues discussed here were gendered in obvious ways particularly given the roles in question (military service, cabildo offices) and those called on to speak on behalf of the community. There is no need to belabor those points except to note that they entailed constructions of masculinity linked to some forms of freedom and even local citizenship. Christian identity was another (often imposed and enforced) significant category in colonial society that also formed part of enslaved and free people of color's repertoire of identifications and which could provide possibilities for claims making.[13] Finally, African categories and ethnicities constituted yet another possible form of identification for people of African descent in colonial society. The royal slaves of El Cobre, however, identified themselves as "Creoles" and did not embrace an African identity, at least not collectively or in the public discourse reflected in the record, so I do not tackle the significance of that identity here (except in some suggestive asides in the endnotes).[14]

### The Emergence of a Pueblo of Creole Royal Slaves: New Hybrid Categories and Identities

In 1670, the Spanish Crown confiscated the copper mines of El Cobre after decades of declining mine production and neglect in the hands of a private contractor. Earlier in the century, these copper mines had constituted a major export enterprise in Spain's American empire, and their production provided copper for the Crown's artillery and its imperial military defense system. The importation of hundreds of African slaves at the turn of the century to work the mines reflected the early insertion of this locality into the circuits of people and goods circulating throughout the Atlantic world. After the mid-1620s, mining production began to decline and the importation of new African slaves also came to an end. At about this time northern European challenges to Spanish hegemony began to escalate with the settlement of islands in the Lesser Antilles during the 1620s and 1630s. This northern European penetration led to a profound transformation of the Caribbean region in a matter of decades. The occupation and settlement of Jamaica after 1655 and decades later the occupation and eventual development of what became Saint Domingue turned eastern Cuba into a strategic frontier zone with a major garrison in the city of Santiago de Cuba. Defense considerations, including the construction of a system of garrisons in key ports throughout the Caribbean and circum-Caribbean region, began to take on a new urgency in Spain's imperial policy. A few decades into the eighteenth century, this multi-imperial Caribbean region took on an even greater prominence due to the valuable plantation commodities produced, exchanged, and circulated legally and illegally through the region. Although the Spanish colonial Caribbean, particularly Cuba, did not become an integral part of this plantation economy until the nineteenth century, its strategic Caribbean location as the "Key to the New World" was paramount to larger imperial projects.

After the deprivatization of the mining jurisdiction took place in the 1670s, some 270 former mining slaves, by then mostly second- and third-generation Creole slaves, became the king's slaves. The practical and ideological meaning of this new category—its so-called social construction—would be negotiated and worked out in subsequent years. By this time the once considerable copper mining enterprise was gone and the royal slaves took on a new significance and valuation primarily for their role in the Crown's imperial defense system. What remained of the old copper works was taken over by its former slaves and turned into an informal local industry of some regional value. The Church also found a new source of value in the community with the emergence of an important Marian shrine in the pueblo. These projects and interests formed part of the wider context in which these imperial subjects negotiated their new position and prerogatives in colonial society.

In 1677 Judge don Antonio de Matienzo received an unusual petition from the royal slaves of El Cobre. The judge, who had been appointed to finalize the state's confiscation of the mining jurisdiction and to dispose of the Crown's new royal slaves, had received orders to sell the royal slaves to interested purchasers or to send able males to work in the royal fortification projects of Havana, constructing the famous defensive walls of that city. The royal orders thus followed conventional understandings of slavery whereby a master could sell or dispose of his slave property as he saw fit. On learning of the king's edict, however, the royal slaves escaped to the nearby mountains, protesting their sale as well as the projected relocation. From the mountains in the vicinity of El Cobre they sent a petition to the acting judge and proceeded to negotiate their eventual stay in El Cobre and their new relation to the Crown, to each other, and to local territory. Generated during that crucial political confrontation with the imperial state, the document provides an invaluable entry point into the new hybrid identity that took shape among these enslaved subjects. While itself the product of a political negotiation, it also illustrates the discursive way that the identity of these royal slaves was negotiated in the first years following the Crown's deprivatization of the mines thereby setting a precedent for the future. In this sense the document constitutes a foundational text.

Although it is not clear who wrote the semiliterate petition, it was allegedly signed by one of the elder royal slaves, Captain Juan Moreno. A few passages tersely illustrate how various categories were inflected and deftly quilted around two major nodal points. Captain Moreno's petition on behalf of "the creole blacks natives of the said mines [of El Cobre] slaves of His Majesty" [negros criollos naturales de dichas minas esclavos que somos de Su Majestad] stated that "the love for our *patria* and our work move us to ask for . . . the mercy of being allowed to stay in our *pueblo*, paying tribute, in whatever manner it is arranged for us while we find [a way to pay] for our freedom [mientras buscamos para nuestra libertad]."[15] This freedom that they would try to buy (as *coartación* or self-purchase) would presumably allow them to select where to live and work.

Moreno intertwined four overlapping categories in his production of the collective subject he represented: blacks, Creoles, "natives [*naturales*] of the mines of [El Cobre]," and "slaves of His Majesty." In quilting together these mostly official categories he subtly inflected their meaning. The first category was a racialized color classification of "blacks" often used indistinctly with the juridical one of "slavery" (so identified with each other and naturalized had those overlapping categories become). Elsewhere in the petition Moreno amplified the color/race category to include "blacks and mulattoes" (*negros y mulatos*) as well. In El Cobre these ubiquitous racial classifications and their variations (*moreno* and *pardo*) as well as those referring to free/slave juridical status appeared consistently in local census and hearth inscriptions, as an intrinsic part of an identity profile in official documents, and in more informal statements such as that of Governor Ximénez in the second epigraph to this chapter.

The primary racial affiliation of the (enslaved) subjects that Moreno represented and spoke for in this petition was blackness, a category produced by descent from African ancestry and slavery that could not be avoided when addressing the state and that was associated with enormous disabilities.

Although the second category, Creole, was a generic identity that referred to birth in the New World and could apply to both enslaved people of African ancestry and people of full Spanish peninsular ancestry (*españoles* or whites), at the time it still constituted a vague claim to a New World insider status with connotations of what may be called "cultural" (or perhaps "ethnic") hybridization. It was a generic category that marked Old World ancestry but also distinction from it, and in the case of slaves it marked a distinction from African birth and identity, one in fact that could also entail some customary entitlements, depending on context and region in the New World.[16] One could ask more generally what kind of entitlements people of African descent, and other sectors of colonial society, claimed in relation to this category when invoking it as an identity. Could New World origin grant them an "inside" status and identity that could become politicized as happened in the case of white Creoles, particularly in the late colonial period? What was the timeline for the development of this politicized identity—if it ever came about—among people of African ancestry elsewhere in colonial Latin America and what did it entail? How did it relate to other categories and identities? In the case of El Cobre, the invocation of this broad identity in the petition, an identity that suggested territorial origin and gestured vaguely toward some hybrid Hispanized culture, did have strong political significance. The most innovative claims made on behalf of this generic Creole subject position, I argue, were intertwined with juridical ones related to local territoriality or nativeness (naturaleza), and community and local citizenship.[17]

The third category mobilized in the petition, "natives of the mines," is more suggestive. It narrowed in this case the Creole category to birth in a particular local territory. This kind of local nativeness does not seem to have been a term commonly applied to slaves, since it usually entailed some local territorial attachments and identity that could suggest birthrights.[18] In this case, however, the local nativeness category was applied to subjects born in a mining district or a *real de minas*. The possible *realengo* (under royal domain or public, nonprivate) character of such a category and its implications for the (redefined) status of these slaves may have been significant in the invocation. It certainly resonates with land and mining claims made in other documents from the time.[19] A century later, as I will discuss subsequently, the affiliations of Creole and natives of the mines underwent yet another kind of hybridization process as they became "indigenized" and in that somewhat different quilting process the community staked out further juridical and political claims.

Finally, in his petition on behalf of his peers, Moreno also invoked the category of "the king's slaves" suggestive perhaps of the new status of the group as enslaved subjects, yet distinct, and privileged subjects, given the status of their powerful master, the king himself, lord over all imperial subjects. Although for some officials the "slave" status of these subjects constituted the defining character of the category that determined who they were, the royal slaves and at times other officials would in turn foreground the "royal" aspect of the affiliation and construe their claims around this feature.[20] That distinction became the basis for disputing the meaning of "royal slavery" in some confrontations with authorities. In fact, the alleged special relationship to the king at times took the character of quasi-vassalage rather than slavery, another term with juridical and political implications that I cannot analyze here.[21]

The most socially, culturally, juridically, and politically loaded formulation in Captain Moreno's petition, however, was the allegation that the black Creole royal slaves, natives of the mines of El Cobre, constituted a pueblo and that El Cobre was their patria. The categories of pueblo and patria overlapped with—and radically qualified—the origin-related categories of Creoleness and natives of the mines. These categories, however, pertained to the discursive field of free (and enfranchised) subjects in the body politic, not of enslaved ones who were in juridical terms located outside the body politic, and their pertinence is still unclear in the case of free subjects of color. In fact, in the case of slaves, the invocation of these categories was not only unprecedented but it constituted a legal incongruence. The claim to a patria chica and to a pueblo constituted a sort of birthright that entitled a subject to live in his or her locality of origin or official residence, a right recognized in the case of freemen but not in the case of slaves.[22] Moreover, a duly constituted pueblo was a form of corporate association and representation in the body politic associated with some sovereignty and citizenship. The petition, then, foregrounded the royal slaves' identity as natives (naturales) of El Cobre their pueblo and patria—while anticipating their status as freedmen and women in the future through a formal process of coartación. Perhaps the most fascinating aspect of this early text was the extent to which it ignored or refused to acknowledge the civil and more radical "social death" entailed by the juridical condition of slavery and the ways in which it subtly inserted these enslaved subjects into the civil polity by adopting discursive categories pertaining to free subjects.[23] Ultimately, by foregrounding affiliations based on origin or nativeness and by emphasizing their relation to the king, Moreno's petition tried to displace or trump the disabilities related to the official categories of race and enslaved status.[24]

Another major, and clearly gender-based, affiliation invoked by Captain Moreno was related to imperial geopolitics and the frontier character of this region. Frontier regions, where defense projects were a state priority, allowed for more flexibility in the configuration of social formations and related identity claims. The incorporation of racially tinged subjects —and at times even enslaved ones—into imperial institutions and defense projects opened new possibilities and venues for making claims on the state. Indeed, central to the profile of El Cobre was the service of male royal slaves as militia soldiers and guards at the port of Guaycabón, and later also as labor power in the construction projects of the imperial fortifications and defense system. Moreno's petition offered the royal slaves' military services "to defend the garrison of [Santiago de] Cuba or any other place," noting that "whenever the opportunity has arisen with some event the governors have remembered to call on us *even though* we are humble black slaves of Our King and Lord [negros humildes esclavos de nuestro Rey y Señor]."[25] The disabilities associated with race *and* overlapping enslaved status were explicitly displaced here by military service of the Crown. Moreno alluded to the unconventional character of the situation in this frontier location by pointing to the precedent of their recruitment and the capacities they had demonstrated *despite* their "humble" (or debased) racial and enslaved status. Bearing arms for His Majesty, in fact, also constituted an important state-sanctioned practice elsewhere in the empire that could help to mitigate the disabilities related to race that marked so many facets of life in the colonial world.[26]

In the case of El Cobre, the significance of these enslaved subjects' military role in this frontier region informed to a great extent the imperial state's accommodating policy toward the community in subsequent years. In 1732, in the midst of another conflict, for instance, the Crown attorney emphasized "the convenience of the conservation and maintenance of that pueblo with slaves and other free *vecinos* [local citizens] because that garrison is frontier with an enemy colony like the Island of Jamaica . . . and there is no doubt that they serve for the defense of the Island."[27] Note, however, that this official pronouncement distinguished between slaves and free vecinos and did not allude to the racial classification of the free local citizens, thereby glossing over the major social and juridical paradoxes that underwrote the formation of this Caribbean frontier community: a community where not only enslaved subjects were local citizens but free citizens were racially tainted subjects. Elsewhere in the empire, racially tainted subjects, even if free, were allegedly excluded from vecino status in the Spanish republics.[28]

In the end, the royal slaves' discursive attempt to insert themselves into the colonial body politic received official recognition. The political agency and mobilization through marronage that underwrote Moreno's petition turned the controversial discursive claims of the text into a historical reality as the royal slaves won the collective concession to stay in El Cobre as a community. In fact, although most of the royal slaves of Captain Moreno's and subsequent generations never purchased their juridical freedom, they were nonetheless able to become a corporate pueblo and to negotiate a series of social, economic, and political concessions associated with that communal formation. In the next two or three decades they obtained a collective land concession that enabled them to live as a semipeasant and (informal) mining community. Four militia companies were also organized in the pueblo. Most surprisingly of all, however, the community acquired a cabildo, a controversial institution linked to their pueblo status whose important political implications will be examined in the next section. All in all, by 1773 El Cobre had grown into an important pueblo on the island with some 1,320 inhabitants of whom 64 percent were still royal slaves, 2 percent were personal slaves of villagers, and 34 percent were free people of African descent, mostly manumitted descendants or relatives of royal slaves.[29]

Once the community had consolidated into a pueblo, a new vernacular category and identity emerged among these imperial subjects that echoed some and overwrote other categories mobilized and interwoven in Moreno's petition. Significantly, the collective identity of *cobreros* (natives of El Cobre) referred exclusively to local origin and community bonds and did not mark juridical distinctions between free and royal slave members of the community. In this sense the vernacular identity of cobreros not only denied the primacy of the state's juridical status classifications but elided them altogether while focusing exclusively on local nativeness. To be sure, nativeness, just like vecindad or local citizenship, was also a juridical category, but one which entailed other prerogatives and lines of affiliation.

### The Local Cabildo: A Political and Racial Predicament

With the years, the most controversial issue that emerged in relation to El Cobre was the existence and legitimacy of the local cabildo. Cabildos were institutions of municipal self-government that operated in duly constituted pueblos, towns and cities in the Republics of Spaniards and Indians. While the actual power of cabildos in the colonial world varied through place and time, their autonomous and representative civil character, to the extent they ever had it, had been eroded to insignificance by the late seventeenth century, particularly in the Republic of Spaniards. Yet they remained powerful markers of social distinction. These colonial institutions of local self-governance were more vibrant in the Republic of Indians and were strongly defended by communities, although they were also the source of much local conflict and factionalism. Since there is still little research on existing black pueblos, and racial and social exclusions precluded people of African descent from holding those positions in the Republic of Spaniards or Indians, little is known about the cabildo's significance with regard to subjects of African descent.

The controversial and contentious character of the cabildo, especially among enslaved subjects who despite their formation as a community had no place in the body politic and thus no representative, corporate, or local citizenship rights, did not escape some royal authorities. In 1732 Governor Ximénez, an official unusually intent on dismantling the customary prerogatives that this community had acquired throughout the decades, noted that "the *vecinos* of the said *pueblo* [El Cobre], blacks as well as mulattoes, are slaves of His Majesty . . . [S]ince they are slaves they cannot administer ordinary justice, because it has been a very irregular thing to have allowed them to appoint *alcaldes* [bailiffs], that is some *mayorales* [overseers] to subject the others, because since they are many it is necessary to have someone to order them, and particularly to be in charge of appointing the [corvee labor] squadrons of those who come to the construction works [in the fortifications] . . . and they are not mayorales either because they have not been appointed by their master but by their own will."[30] Although in the 1670s there were individual *capitanes*, alcaldes, and *mandadores* operating in El Cobre (recall the slave Captain Juan Moreno above) it is not clear when these ranks mutated into a full-fledged cabildo. At least by 1709 there was already a cabildo of royal slaves—rather than one of the free of color—operating in the community, the existence of which confirms the extended concessions that the cobreros obtained in the years following the founding petition of 1677. In El Cobre, the imperial state also had four local militias companies and had organized its male royal slaves into a corvee labor system similar to the *repartimientos* of corporate Indian communities elsewhere in the empire.

To Governor Ximénez, the institutions and entitlements that had become customary among these royal slaves defied the proper legal and political order of things in the empire. He decried the cabildo, particularly because it allowed enslaved alcaldes to serve as magistrates of the first instance, a marker, in principle, of some degree of sovereignty. That disturbing sovereignty was manifested as well in the royal slaves' possession of a (collective) will deployed in the election of their own (male) officials, a political act that contrasted with the passivity and subjection entailed by the master's right to appoint labor overseers at his will. Ximénez's critique underscored the incompatibility of the slave juridical status of these subjects with any other category that could attenuate its practical meaning. He found the concessions made to this community of royal slaves excessive and he took it upon himself to dismantle the aberrations that he found operating in this hybrid formation. And yet, paradoxically, Ximénez invoked racial categories to refer to the vecinos of El Cobre, as if free black local citizens electing their own black officials would not have constituted an anomaly per se.[31]

Ximénez's attempts to restore the proper colonial order of things met with strong political resistance from not only the royal slaves but also from other sectors of colonial society, including the Church. The dramatic conflict that consumed the community and other sectors of colonial society during more than a decade of Ximénez's tenure points to the politics that had to be deployed to negotiate, defend, or for that matter destabilize the meaning attached to identities. During these years and on many occasions throughout the late seventeenth and eighteenth centuries the cobreros engaged in varying forms of political mobilization common among other subordinate subjects in Old Regime societies, including petitioning, litigation, flight, and even work stoppages in defense of prerogatives linked to their own understandings of their hybrid identity.

But if Governor Ximénez's protestation aptly reveals the (official) logic underwriting the institution of the cabildo in colonial society and the kind of subjects associated with it, the following passages allow us to witness the rearticulation of that institutional logic and the ways in which its discursive and political limits could be contested or expanded by imperial subjects, in this case enslaved and racially disabled ones. The significance of the cabildo for the royal slaves of El Cobre was deftly encapsulated in the memory of an event still alive in the pueblo some twenty-five years after its occurrence. In a representation directed to the captain general of the island during the clashes with Ximénez in the 1730s, the royal slaves recalled that around 1709, once the Audiencia of Santo Domingo's judge Chirino had arrived in Santiago to investigate the royal slaves' accusations and grievances against the then Governor Canales, "the said Don Nicholas Chirino called the regidores [of El Cobre] . . . and once in his presence His Highness ordered that they take a seat in the benches of the cabildo of the said city [Santiago de Cuba] with the title of regidores given to them in the name of both Majesties. And in view of those honors they thanked the said gentleman while excusing themselves from taking those seats that he offered them because of *nuestra pobreza y color quebrado* [our poverty and tainted blood]. And His Highness told them to occupy the seats by an order of Our Lord and Master."[32] The event recalled in this memorial was nothing less than an act that had allegedly legitimated the cobreros' cabildo. The memory was anchored in a simplified version of the hegemonic imperial discourse of royalism whereby a king's emissary, an audiencia judge, authorized the community's cabildo "in the name of both Majesties." Thus, the imperial state was centrally inscribed in these subjects' sense of self and in this old memory of a key event in their past. The irregular basis of that cabildo was suggested in this episode not so much by the local officials' slave status as by their racial and class standing: "our poverty and tainted blood." Not only did the king's judge acknowledge the cobreros' right to office despite their tainted blood and their impoverished condition or class; by ordering them to sit in the very benches of the capital city's cabildo, he allegedly recognized the equality in status between the officers in El Cobre and those in the eastern city of Santiago de Cuba. That was a decidedly radical memory that spoke to the cobreros' sense of identity in the present.

The details of the episode constituted a dramatic (if utopian) rendition of the alleged honor and even citizenship status that a cabildo body granted upon its officials, and by extension to the community and local citizens (vecinos) it represented. In this memory, the institution did not merely constitute a symbolic expression of local and communal identity, although it was that too. The cabildo's power and "magic" lay as well in the social honor and political value it conferred on the group's collective self, despite the impurity of their blood and other social "deficiencies" attributed to their kind. In this long-standing memory, royal recognition of their cabildo may have even implied a recognition of the royal slaves' freedom, their juridical status as *natives* and *citizens*, and more radically, the equality of their cabildo with others in the Republic of Spaniards.

A memorial filed many years later, in 1792, when the royal slaves of El Cobre went to court to defend their right to exist as a pueblo and to make a claim for collective freedom, articulated more explicitly the theoretical significance of the cabildo institution in the Spanish empire's political and legal discursive order. The juridically based passage resonates with the significance that the royal slaves had implicitly given to the cabildo in the story of the past discussed above and recalled in a memorial produced half a century before. That reverberation of meaning in different discursive sites points to the overlapping relation between vernacular and juridical discourses. The attorney, Don Simón de Echenique, argued that

> The population of Santiago del Cobre was therefore composed of free individuals who had houses, land plots, livestock . . . They constituted a parish and paid tithes . . . [and] they formed a municipal body. They governed themselves. In short, *aside from their civil freedom as vassals [of the king], they enjoyed as well a political one* . . . This constituted a political right [*posesión política*] that supersedes [*supera*] the civil one because it favors all as a body and the civil one only protects each one

individually. The former, since it is the principal and is more extensive, subsumes unto itself the other one as accessory. Therefore even if there had really been enslaved people [in the community] they would have been reputed free given the existence of the municipal body in which they were encompassed.[33]

The passage made an important distinction between two kinds of freedom. Although the degree of self-governance allowed in an absolute polity was decidedly minimal, a collectively represented body or a corporation suggested a more extensive notion of political citizenship in Spanish legal theory while civil liberty entailed only individual freedom and property rights. Moreover, as Ximénez had earlier pointed out, the supposedly representative character of the cabildo embodied the political exercise of a collective "will." Furthermore, according to the cobreros' own imaginings, such a capacity to exercise the will and express sovereignty conferred equality to corporate groups despite the presence of strong hierarchies of race, lineage, and class, as if the political and civil discursive order trumped or annulled the juridical and customary restrictions of the limpieza de sangre regime. But notions about civil and political rights in the imperial polity intersected and clashed with those based on racial thinking or purity of blood and its social orderings. Not all (civil) free subjects in the imperial polity could aspire to political freedom—or citizenship—as that entitlement would have profoundly disrupted established social hierarchies.

But what about Indians? Could they exercise political freedom despite their racial and social "deficiencies"? Indigenous subjects were located in a separate republic or polity—the Republic of Indians—with its own limited sovereignty and general subordinate status to the Spanish polity as a conquered or subjected people. The political rights allowed to Indians as a separate people and their colonially configured corporate communities did not directly impinge on the hierarchies of the Spanish polity itself. Their republic was a jurisdiction underwritten by a different logic. Black subjects and castas (racially mixed subjects)—and Indians who fled the jurisdiction of the Indian republic—on the other hand, were located in the Spanish republic and constituted parts of its internal racial hierarchies. The existence of nonwhite corporate pueblos with cabildo institutions under the jurisdictional space of the Spanish republic meant the conferral of political rights—with the consequent implication of some general equality—to racially "defective" subordinate groups within the Spanish polity.

Because of black subjects' inherent association with slavery and servitude, and thus with a deep-rooted stain difficult if not impossible to erase, they could not possess a political freedom that implied sovereignty, the exercise of political will, and the power to execute ordinary justice. Although they could have individual civil freedom, it seemed incongruous to officials such as Ximénez to have blacks and castas exercise political freedom alongside or, even worse, over españoles/whites. In fact, blacks apparently could not exercise it in the imperial body polity even within their own racial group since they had no special juridical standing.[34] Some of these issues writ large would be addressed later in the debates of the Cortes of Cádiz in 1812, in Latin America's independence struggles, and in postcolonial societies in the region.[35]

This intertwined juridical, political, and social logic may be a reason why Governor Cayetano (see the third epigraph to this chapter) mistakenly conflated Indians and people of color in his uncertain memory of former times in El Cobre. In fact, the category and figure of "the Indian," at times as an actual historical referent but more often as trope, also had a presence in the cobreros' social memory and at times it also played a role in the construction of their own identity in ways that speak to the issues discussed above.[36] A vernacular story about three caciques relates how the cobreros became the natives, holders and preservers of ancient Indian land through conquest and royal intervention. The quasi-legendary narrative constituted a discursive construction of the royal slaves' and cobreros' rights to land, territory, and corporate identity by "indigenizing" their rights and their position in the colonial body politic. When asked about the origins of El Cobre, the cobrero Sánchez reported to the royal scribe that "[El Cobre's] first beginning and foundation had been three Indian cacique brothers: one had his home in Baracoa and his name was Coa, the other was named Cuba and lived there [Santiago de Cuba], and the third lived in the village of El Cobre and his name was Cobe. He had given up [se rindió? se vendió?] himself with the greatest humility during the Conquest without it being even necessary to fire a shot. He [Sánchez] mentioned the lands that the Cacique Cobe had owned at the time and [said] that His Majesty had given them as a mercy to the Pueblo of El Cobre and its naturales [the cobreros]."[37] After conquering and subjugating the cacique Cobe and taking his land, the chimerical figure of the king (the imperial state), a ubiquitous presence in so many "past and present" stories in this community and more generally in the political imaginary of the Old Regime, granted that territory to his imperial subjects, the cobreros. As a simple royalist story, not unlike that of the visiting judge legitimizing the cobreros' cabildo, the figure of the king here had the power to take and give land, to alter the social order, to reward his own slaves or vassals, to allow and legitimize an implicitly "anomalous" situation such as that of slaves (or even people of African descent) constituting a corporate community, and to turn them into the heirs of indigenous territory and rights. Yet the story is in fact more complex in the way it portrays the subject position of the cobreros as analogous to that of Indians in the Republic of Indians. It is also quite sophisticated in the way it triangulates the transfer of rights to land between the king and indigenous and black (enslaved) subjects or cobreros (the new natives of El Cobre).

The king did not so much transfer the rights to the territory of the subjected Lord Cobe and his people to his slaves/vassals—the cobreros— as grant the latter the subject position and rights of Indians in the colonial polity. Note that the rights to the conquered land were transferred in the story to a colonial corporate entity and to the natives of that pueblo, and that the cobreros were ambiguously portrayed as "natives" (naturals) of the pueblo. There is also an apparently paradoxical detail in the story that is significant: the conquest of the cacicazgo took place without resistance. Informing this whole episode of a vernacular story was the juridical basis that underwrote the constitution of the special colonial jurisdiction of the Republic of Indians. This jurisdiction was created to protect the rights of subjected nations. Subjection without resistance, in effect, entitled the subjected to retain—or to be granted—some rights in the imperial polity including possession of their land and a limited sovereignty. Thus the territory of Cobe's cacicazgo was transformed into the colonial entity of a corporate pueblo (El Cobre), an entity subject to the jurisdictional regime of the Indian republic. In other words, this is a story about the cobreros' rights to land, to community, and to local sovereignty (in the form of the cabildo). The narrative fused the cobreros' local "nativeness" to El Cobre with the colonial rights of Indians as "original natives" (*naturales originarios*) of their territory gesturing to yet another kind of hybridization.

Moreover, by tracing the name of "El Cobre" to the cacique "Cobe" the story sidestepped the pueblo's foundation as a Spanish copper-mining settlement where the cobreros had once been "regular," privately owned slaves. It also elided the cobreros' status as royal slaves with claims to the land and the resources of a real de minas jurisdiction that was discussed earlier in this chapter. Instead, the narrative grounded the origins and boundaries of the cobreros' imagined local community in the ancient past of precolonial history. By way of this story of the past, the cobreros discursively took the place of Indian subjects in the body polity of the present. The diachronic continuity of El Cobre from an ancient Indian cacicazgo to a black colonial corporate community also suggested a synchronic spatial analogy between these two groups in the eighteenth century's colonial present since there were actually two corporate Indian communities in the environs of this village of royal slaves (Jiguaní and El Caney). Although a juridical logic imbued the vernacular story of the three caciques, the cobreros also made use of the Indian trope to construe their hybrid colonial position concretely in terms analogous to those of contemporary Indian communities.

It is significant that this story was related to a royal official in 1792, precisely at the time when the status of the mining jurisdiction, and of the royal slaves, was the subject of litigation in Madrid. The cobreros at the time were contesting an earlier decision of the Crown to reprivatize the jurisdiction and return it to the heirs of the previous contractors. That dictate would have meant a restoration of the status quo ante the confiscation of the mines in 1670, a brutal transformation of the royal slaves into private slaves and the dissolution of the centenarian community. The invocation of the three caciques story, and its attempt to imbricate *nativeness* to El Cobre with *indigeneity* and its rights, constituted an alternate discursive strategy to legitimize the cobreros' hybrid juridical and social formation then under siege. More generally, the story also points to the protean character of the Indian trope in colonial society—and in some regions, alas, to this day—and its significance in the construction of various multilayered identities among "non-Indian" subjects.[38]

To conclude, the case of El Cobre serves as a reminder that when focusing on populations of African descent and the "construction" of their identities in the Spanish colonial world, historians of colonial Latin America—and those of the African diaspora in this region of the Atlantic world—should also be attentive to the broader colonial institutions, categories, and imaginaries through which their subjects were shaped and shaped themselves. I have argued here that, aside from casta and race, imperial understandings of nativeness related to local patriotism, indigeneity, Creoleness, vecindad (local citizenship), allegiance to the king, religion, and yes, also class, constituted salient frames of reference and categories for thinking and contesting identities, even in the more restricted case of enslaved or free subjects of African descent. In fact, these affiliations inflected and interacted with the categories of imperial racial ordering in various ways throughout different periods and locations (albeit never completely obliterating racial ones). "Africanness" (in its various manifestations) was, of course, also part of the repertoire of sanctioned and unsanctioned affiliations available to racialized subjects in colonial society, albeit a thorny one given that it was often tantamount to foreignness, outsider status, enslavement, and other negative associations (such as barbarism and paganism) that could result in further stigmatization, exclusion, and even persecution. Much work remains yet to be done regarding the deployments of "African" (or neo-African) identity, particularly in terms of how it could be quilted with other categories that would enable the assertion of claims in colonial and later in postcolonial settings.[39]

*Epilogue: Transition to Colonial Modernity*

By 1800, after a prolonged litigation in Madrid, the pueblo's paradoxical status was resolved by the juridical concession of collective freedom and corporate status. Thereafter the community of El Cobre would constitute a corporate "villa" or town (rather than a pueblo) with local citizens (vecinos) who had usufruct rights to family plots and common land, and a cabildo (or later an *ayuntamiento*). The cobreros had finally won official recognition of their civil freedom and some political freedom (albeit not equality) within the absolutist imperial polity. Yet by the late 1820s the tide had turned against them once more. British mining enterprises obtained concessions to exploit the mines of El Cobre and "more illustrious settlers" began to arrive (see the third epigraph to this chapter). Proposals to "whiten" the town through new settlement policies were in circulation while African slaves were imported in massive numbers to work the mines in the pueblo and the coffee plantations of surrounding regions. All in all, liberal state policies, transnational mining forces, new global configurations, and new stakeholders in the region—the new forces of colonial "modernity"—led to the cobreros' erosion of political freedom and by the 1840s to the dismantling of the corporate black community. In 1841 Captain General Don Gerónimo de Valdés wrote: "Lately some occurrences have given me the opportunity to disband an Ayuntamiento of people of color [in El Cobre] unique in its kind and the scandal of this island."[40] Valdés's commentary was provoked by the unsettling sight of racialized subjects of African descent in the possession of political freedom and local citizenship rather than merely civil freedom, particularly alongside the new "more illustrious" white settlers. Overall, the possibilities for political freedom among racialized subjects of African descent in the island had become more intractable with the general development of slave plantation society, the advent of colonial modernity, and increasing imperial political repression in Cuba.

Whatever the cobreros' efforts to resist the advent of colonial modernity locally may have been, these seem to have lacked political teeth since they lost control of their community to white Creoles and foreign miners after the 1830s. Thereafter, even the memory of an earlier black Creole community with a corporate status became uncertain, at least in official memory. We still lack documentation from the nineteenth century that could allow us to follow up on the transformations that took place among old-time cobreros faced with the arrival of hundreds of African slaves, Creole white settlers, Spaniards, foreign (British) white workers, and by the late 1850s even Chinese indentured servants. We do not know if and how old identities were contested and renegotiated at this time, particularly in relation to race, or by what political means this may have happened. Neither do we know what side the cobreros took in the anticolonial wars that flared in El Cobre and eastern Cuba during the last decades of the late nineteenth century nor how they would have construed their alliances in that context. The silence is unfortunate. It is particularly at frustrating moments like this, when the voices of subordinate subjects (regardless of their mediated character) cannot be found in the archival record, that paradigm fatigue gives way to a fuller appreciation of the possibilities and utility—not to say the beauty—of identity studies in all their textural and textual depth.

## Notes

The first epigraph can be found on page 31 of *The Social Construction of What?* The second epigraph was drawn from Gov. Pedro de Ximénez, Santiago de Cuba, December 24, 1732, "Expediente bancos iglesia," f. 642–42v, Archivo General de Indias-Santo Domingo 451; the third, from Report of Gov. Cayetano de Urbina, Santiago de Cuba, February 1846, Archivo Histórico Nacional-Ultramar 463(2).

1. See the discussion by O'Hara and Fisher in this volume; Brubaker and Cooper, "Beyond 'Identity.'"

2. I hasten to add that our questions and formulations need not all be cast in the metalanguage of identity theory, although the concept of identity has spilled over to nonacademic spheres where it has taken its own life in the kind of "looping effect of human [or interactive] kinds" that Hacking—as philosopher and historian—is particularly interested in investigating. See Hacking, especially 31–34, 58–59.

3. Díaz, *The Virgin, the King and the Royal Slaves of El Cobre*.

4. Silverblatt, *Modern Inquisitions*; Lewis, *Hall of Mirrors*, 4–5, 22–24; Wade, *Race and Ethnicity in Latin America*, 5–9, 25–30.

5. Douglas Cope found that race did not have primacy at least among the lower orders in Mexico City, among whom he found a vague notion of "plebeianness" to predominate, albeit race did seem to be a dominant criterion in marriage choices. The tripartite system, however, was basically "fixed," although the middle categories were more blurred and "fluid." It is, however, clear that the latter stand for different forms of biotic "mix" even if the exact proportions are understandably unclear. Cope, *The Limits of Racial Domination*. See also Wade, *Race and Ethnicity in Latin America*, 25–30.

6. For the modern period the specialized bibliography is by now extensive. For a historical survey of the literature, see Andrews' *Afro-Latin America*. For the colonial period, the literature is much more limited. Specifically for Cuba, the classic monograph is still Martínez-Alier, *Marriage, Class and Colour in Nineteenth-Century Cuba*. More recently there is Helg, *Our Rightful Share*; and Ferrer's *Insurgent Cuba*. All of the latter studies, however, focus on the nineteenth century and on modern Cuban plantation society and its aftermath.

7. Torfing, *New Theories of Discourse*; Laclau, *The Politics of Rhetoric*; Holstein and Gubrium, *The Self We Live By*. These works stress the importance of identity repertoires used by people, discourses embedded in identity narratives that people deploy in everyday life, and particularly nodal or quilting points and master signifiers that sustain or anchor the identity meaning in "signifying chains." These approaches shed light on the historical material I analyze in more commonsensical language. See Pablo Vila's use of these concepts in *Crossing Borders, Reinforcing Borders* and more recently in *Border Identifications*.

8. As late as 1800 people of African descent constituted majorities not only in Brazil (67 percent) and Cuba (54 percent) but elsewhere throughout Spanish America in present-

day Venezuela (61 percent), Puerto Rico (56 percent), Spanish Santo Domingo (66 percent), Panama (66 percent) and they had a significant numerical presence in places such as Colombia (39 percent, with majorities in some regions), Argentina (37 percent), and Costa Rica (16 percent). Andrews, *Afro-Latin America*, 41.

9. Díaz, *The Virgin, the King and the Royal Slaves of El Cobre*, especially chaps. 6, 8, and 9.

10. Corrigan and Sayer, *The Great Arch.*

11. I use the concept of "hybridization" in ways that go beyond the usual understanding related to the emergence of new biotic or culturally hybrid/"mestizo" subjects and identities. Rather than employ the term exclusively in a cultural and social sense, I push the concept into the realm of institutional formations, juridical categories, and political discourses, including their vernacular manifestations.

12. Díaz, "Of Life and Freedom in the (Tropical) Hearth"; Díaz, "Mining Women, Royal Slaves." See also Díaz, *The Virgin, the King and the Royal Slaves of El Cobre*, particularly 86–89, 166–78, 189–91, 232–54, 276–83.

13. I examine those processes in great detail in Díaz, *The Virgin, the King and the Royal Slaves of El Cobre*, chaps. 4 and 5. See also a condensed version in Díaz, "The Virgin of Charity of El Cobre." For contemporary examples, see my website on El Cobre, Cuba, http://humweb.ucsc.edu/elcobre.

14. For the transformation from African to Creole slaves see Díaz, *The Virgin, the King and the Royal Slaves of El Cobre*, chap. 1. Early naming practices in this community may point to some African identifications even among Creole slaves, 21–22, 41–53.

15. Petition of Captain Juan Moreno, Santiago del Prado, July 13, 1677, fols. 454–55v, Archivo General de Indias-Santo Domingo [hereafter AGI-SD] 1631 (my emphasis). For the entire document, see http://humweb.ucsc.edu/elcobre.

16. African birth, in turn, had different categorical affiliations: *bozal*, *etiope*, or *nación*, with specific distinctions regarding area of provenance in Africa, for instance, Congo, Angolan, Mina.

17. How Creoleness as a form of nativeness could affect identity status in different regions of the New World for people of African descent still awaits new studies or historical ethnographies. Identity formation for white Creole subjects in Spanish America is much better understood. I have not seen the category Creole for subjects of African ancestry applied in metropolitan contexts. The category for the equivalent situation was *ladino*. These distinctions and their usages merit further scrutiny.

18. Additional linguistic research is needed elsewhere in the empire to answer this question with more certainty.

19. Díaz, *The Virgin, the King and the Royal Slaves of El Cobre*, chap. 2, especially 59–65.

20. The *Siete Partidas* made only a brief reference to the juridical distinction of royal slavery in its statutes on slavery but basically it did not set them apart as a separate category. The distinction was highlighted in practice only in some locations, such as in El Cobre.

21. In her book *Defining Nations*, Tamar Herzog points to the political and juridical significance of "vassalage to the King" in terms of rights and prerogatives based on one

sense of political community in early modern Spain, which could overlap or contrast with other understandings of community based on nativeness (naturaleza) and citizenship (vecindad) in local communities (especially 68–70, 91–93, 133–34). The royal slaves of El Cobre seemed to invoke both identities and their attendant rights and obligations.

22. On the understandings of nativeness, citizenship, and foreignness in early modern Spain and Spanish America (in the Republic of Spaniards), see Herzog, *Defining Nations*; on the construction of naturaleza and a community of natives, see 68–76, 94–97, 105–10.

23. On the concepts of "social death" and "natal alienation" that underwrote slavery, see Patterson, *Slavery and Social Death*, especially 1–14.

24. The discourse for political rights and citizenship based on the nodal point of nativeness (natal origin, birthright, and love for the patria community) embodied in the affiliation to pueblo and patria was echoed in the late nineteenth century by that of the birthrights granted by the "Cuban patria" or "Cubanness." In the ideology propounded by Jose Martí and other modern nineteenth-century patriots, these later claims also trumped, in principle, racial distinctions and their related disabilities.

25. Petition of Captain Juan Moreno, July 13, 1677, AGI-SD 1631 (my emphasis).

26. The Crown made extensive use of the free population of African descent in its defense projects elsewhere in the empire by establishing militias of morenos and pardos with their own officers in New Granada, Mexico, Río de la Plata, and Cuba, among other locations. See Vinson, *Bearing Arms for His Majesty*. Elsewhere in the empire, as in Florida and Santo Domingo, some pueblos of black freedmen were created for imperial defense too. See Landers, "Gracia Real de Santa Teresa de Mose." For others see Díaz, *The Virgin, the King and the Royal Slaves of El Cobre*, 351, n. 7.

27. Crown attorney's summary, Madrid, June 3, 1732, AGI-SD 493.

28. Herzog, *Defining Nations*, 48, 52–55. This generalization may merit further systematic research, since Herzog's study focused on Spaniards.

29. Family census of El Cobre, 1773, AGI-SD 1628.

30. Gov. Pedro de Ximénez, Santiago de Cuba, December 24, 1732, "Expediente bancos iglesia," f. 642–42v, AGI-SD 451.

31. This is an interesting issue in need of further clarification since, as already mentioned, elsewhere in colonial Spanish America free subjects of African descent were allegedly excluded from the category of *vecindad*. See Herzog, *Defining Nations*, 48, 52–55.

32. Memorial of the cobreros to Captain General Juan Francisco Güemes y Horcacitas, ca. 1734, "Autos 1735," f. 658–665, AGI-SD 451. The document is available in the "Voices" section at http://humweb.ucsc.edu/elcobre.

33. Representation of Don Simón de Echenique on behalf of the Natives and Vecinos of El Cobre, Madrid, March 12, 1793, AGI-SD 1627 (my emphasis).

34. Free people of African ancestry could have a limited self-governance or sovereignty in other kinds of corporations with racialized constituencies such as battalions in the militias of color, in Christian black lay brotherhoods or *cofradías*, and in the African *cabildos de nación* (not to be confused with the cofradías). The operation of African

cabildos still awaits more extended study. The classic work is Ortiz, "Los cabildos afrocubanos." Some new glimpses into these associations and their self-governance appear in Childs, *The 1812 Aponte Rebellion in Cuba and the Struggle against Atlantic Slavery*, 95–119. For black brotherhoods in Brazil, see the chapter by Dantas in this volume.

35. Herzog, *Defining Nations*, 141–63, 186–88; Helg, *Liberty and Equality in Caribbean Colombia, 1770–1835*, especially 237–48.

36. A foundational story about the apparition of the Virgin of Charity related by a royal slave and recorded in 1688 also made use of the Indian trope. See Díaz, *The Virgin, the King and the Royal Slaves of El Cobre*, chap. 4, especially 102–7.

37. Testimony of Francisco Sánchez, El Cobre, ca. April 8, 1790, Cuaderno 6, AGI-SD 1629.

38. Perhaps the most radical and iconic spin of this trope is found in the case of Haiti where people with a strong black identification and a clear memory of their African descent took on the indigenous name of the island for their postcolonial nation. In doing so they constructed themselves as the heirs, successors, and avengers of the original natives of the land. See Geggus, *Haitian Revolutionary Studies*, especially chap. 11, 205–20. Contemporary black communities in Colombia hold social memories of multiple caciques, Indians and blacks, albeit with differing interpretations. See Rojas Martínez, *Si no fuera por los quince negros*. Perhaps the best-known case of "non-Indians" invoking the Native American trope occurred among white Creoles in seventeenth- and eighteenth-century Mexico. See Pagden, "Identity Formation in Spanish America"; and Cañizares-Esguerra, *How to Write the History of the New World*. For an account of the problematic way in which the Indian trope has been and still is utilized in the Dominican Republic to construct national (and individual) identities, see Fischer, *Modernity Disavowed*, part 2.

39. Particularly promising lines of research, for instance, are the previously mentioned African cabildos de nación and their prerogatives, including those of association, self-governance, possession of property, cultural expression. Another more interesting situation would be the later combination of African cultural affiliation with different kinds of political rights including citizenship claims throughout Latin America.

40. Captain General don Gerónimo de Valdés to the secretary of state and government of Ultramar, Havana, September 28, 1841. AGN-Ultramar 4631.

# Indigenous Citizenship

*Liberalism, Political Participation, and Ethnic Identity
in Post-Independence Oaxaca and Yucatán*

According to the Mexican national state, there were no more indigenous people in the country after 1824. "Indigenousness," liberals argued, was nothing more than a juridical construct of colonialism standing in the way of the establishment of political equality, equal opportunity, and economic advance. The new institutions of independent Mexico in theory erased ethnic distinctions; whatever cultural and economic vestiges remained would soon fade away. Yet indigenous people certainly did not disappear after independence, nor did Mexicans cease to acknowledge their existence. State officials referred to them often as they reported on the travails of daily governance, and indigenous people identified themselves as such when speaking and writing about their situation, their needs, and their difficulties. Despite national rhetoric, "indigenousness" continued to have real, practical meanings in Mexico's social and economic worlds.

One oft-stated explanation of this contradiction is that the official elimination of the category of "indigenous" simply had no effect on politics, that throughout much of the nineteenth century the weakness of the national state, a lack of will on the part of officials, and a generalized desire on the part of the nonindigenous elite to maintain the basic colonial structures of power combined to negate any stated intention of breaking down ethnic distinctions in the interest of political equality. To the extent that liberalism did break down ethnic distinctions, scholars have argued, it did so only in destructive ways. Liberal policies, especially the privatization of land, actively eliminated the privileges and protections that had shielded indigenous people from the harshest effects of poverty and exploitation during the colonial era. Indigenous identity remained—because indigenous people were treated as inferior—but the safety net that ethnic distinction had represented during the colonial era disappeared. "Indigenous" was no longer a useful political identity but merely an increasingly subordinated cultural one.[1]

This chapter argues, by contrast, that indigenous identity persisted in Mexico, not just in a cultural but perhaps most importantly in a political sense. The narrative about liberalism outlined above, while there is much about it that is true, is inadequate to explain this. Liberal policies and politics were not ignored; they had to be confronted, by both the state and by indigenous people, and this confrontation profoundly affected the development of local political cultures and practices. And liberalism did not affect indigenous people in a uniformly negative manner. All of the Mexican states had to respond to national demands for institutional change aimed at replacing corporate privilege with near universal individual citizenship. Yet the people in those states, nonindigenous and indigenous alike, approached this project from varied circumstances, and it was their choices that would determine precisely what the new system looked like on the ground. What Mexicans in the states of Oaxaca and Yucatán did with the challenges of Mexican liberalism—and the very different results their responses had for both the meanings of "indigenous" and the lives of indigenous people—is the subject of this chapter. In these heavily indigenous states, the elimination of the colonial category of "indio" posed a particular challenge. The institutional choices made as each state developed its own constitutional structures became a crucial arena for the reimagining of indigenousness, as states sought ways to retain crucial elements of colonial structures while both incorporating and taking advantage of the requirements of the new liberal system.

A key site for this endeavor was the organization of town government. Indigenous people had, throughout the colonial era, chosen their own distinctly indigenous councils, the *cabildos* or *repúblicas de indios*, which had served as both instruments of local government and representatives of indigenous communities to the Spanish Crown.[2] Beginning with the liberal Spanish constitutional experiment that commenced in 1812, the official disappearance of local government based on ethnic distinctions was a foregone conclusion. But on the ground, the lines between the old and new systems would not be so clear. Both Spanish constitutionalism and the Mexican federalism that followed put great stock in the encouragement of municipal self-administration, vastly extending the number of cities, towns, and villages that could elect governing bodies.[3] These new councils were intended to facilitate the political participation of new citizens and to counteract the authoritarianism of centralized authority. As such, they were in theory very different from the colonial repúblicas; they were elected not just by indigenous people but by the male population regardless of ethnicity; they were not intended to serve a representative but merely an administrative function; and they were intended to reflect the desires of individual citizens, not of the commons. In practice, however, the colonial and liberal councils could look quite similar. They were both chosen locally, even if in different ways. They had similar duties and responsibilities. And most importantly, they were both based on the all-important notion of local autonomy.[4]

The maintenance of an autonomous sphere of local activity in which the state could not interfere had long been a major component of Spanish governance of indigenous people. Tristan Platt, in his study of indigenous villages in Bolivia, identified a "pact of reciprocity," a tacit agreement in which indigenous people agreed to pay tribute to the colonial state in exchange for land.[5] A broader definition of this pact would substitute "autonomy" for "land"; autonomy could include issues of land tenure, but it also encompassed any issue that touched on control over local affairs. It meant freedom not just to own land but also to choose how that land would be distributed and used. It meant latitude in methods of choosing local officials. It meant that the state would not interfere unduly in modes of social hierarchy and social control within the villages. And it meant freedom not just from Spanish interference but also from interference from other indigenous villages and villagers. Conversely, indigenous people agreed not just to pay tribute but, in general, to recognize the authority of the state and submit to its demands. Indigenous people and representatives of the state did not always agree about the precise terms of the pact, but their relationship was profoundly shaped by it.

Mexican liberalism threatened this arrangement because it rejected the possibility that a particular ethnic group could have a special relationship with the state. But liberalism too promoted a notion of municipal autonomy, however different, and it would be difficult to effect a complete transformation from one kind of autonomy to the other. In places like Oaxaca and Yucatán, where the challenge of governing a majority indigenous population was central to any political action, the difficulty would be particularly acute.

In these two states, the new systems of governance that developed after independence reflected both genuine attempts to comply with new requirements and significant continuities from the colonial era. Mexican liberalism posed a shared challenge across the nation yet allowed for significant variation on the local level, so that the elements of the old and new emerged in unique combination in each state. This interpretation has crucial significance for our understanding of the continuing attempts of the Mexican national state to define and determine the content of liberalism. The transformation of ethnic categories was at the center of that ongoing national project. The actual negotiation of their content, however, occurred locally, as both states and new citizens attempted to address the dissonance between national ideals and entrenched local realities. In the end, this process produced a system—or, rather, systems —that, while in and of themselves dynamic, were remarkably resistant to the unifying intentions of national reform.

At the start of the nineteenth century, 90 percent of Oaxaca's 600,000 residents were indigenous, while in Yucatán, out of nearly 389,000, the indigenous population stood at approximately 70 percent.[6] Among these people, precolonial notions of group identity and of distinctions between groups persisted, especially in Oaxaca, which was home to fifteen or more linguistic groups (Yucatán's indigenous population was exclusively Maya). Yet in both places, colonial policies of ethnic distinction meant that all these people *also* understood themselves to be members of an indigenous population with a unique relationship to government. The two states, then, shared the circumstance of a significant majority of indigenous people who actively thought of themselves as such.

Oaxaca's indigenous population, however, was not only proportionally larger; it was also geographically separate from the nonindigenous population, which was concentrated in Oaxaca City and some larger towns. Although larger towns and cities could have significant indigenous populations, very few small towns had significant numbers of nonindigenous residents.[7] Further, it was in the many small and largely indigenous towns that the vast majority of the state's economic production took place. The production and processing of the state's two leading commodities—cotton and cochineal dye—was largely in the hands of indigenous people while their marketing was in the control of nonindigenous individuals.[8] Yucatán's indigenous population was not only proportionally smaller but also less geographically isolated from nonindigenous people. Although in much of the eastern peninsula nonindigenous people were few and far between, by the end of the eighteenth century, in the state's most accessible regions, significant numbers of them lived in the countryside and rural towns. This constituted a dramatic change from the previous two centuries. Yucatán has no precious metals and a climate and land ill suited to the production of most European crops; for much of the colonial era, in the words of Nancy Farriss, it was the "periphery of a periphery."[9] The Maya population produced no single product similar to cochineal that could be marketed by nonindigenous people. Nonindigenous people thus had no compelling reason to be in the countryside, and the net effect was the striking isolation of indigenous Yucatecans. But late in the colonial era, nonindigenous entrepreneurs had begun to experiment with new enterprises, especially the raising of cattle, which brought them into previously indigenous places. Not only did indigenous people now share their municipal space with nonindigenous townspeople but they often found themselves both in competition for land and forced to sell their labor. By 1800, substantial numbers of indigenous people worked on landed estates, either in addition to their own agricultural production or full time.[10]

In 1824, then, when legislators in the two states confronted the prospect of accommodating new liberal institutions, they faced a problem that was in some ways similar. Both Oaxaca and Yucatán remained places where autonomous indigenous towns dominated the political landscape, and thus both state legislatures faced a fundamental problem of governability. It was difficult for a nonindigenous minority to control an indigenous majority, especially where the economy rested on their production, their land, or their labor. Official ethnic distinctions that delineated the rights and privileges of each group had long been essential to such control; by buttressing the pact of reciprocity, they had promoted government legitimacy. For both Oaxacan and Yucatecan legislators, it was clear that simply to remove those distinctions now would be to court disaster.

At the same time, the differences between the two states would have far-reaching effects. If in both places the erasure of ethnic distinctions held obvious dangers for the nonindigenous population, under some circumstances, it could also be appealing. In Oaxaca, for the most part, it was not. The elimination of juridical ethnic identity seemed neither urgent nor workable, as few nonindigenous people saw an alternative to a system of autonomous indigenous production and nonindigenous marketing that, although in depression at independence, had created great wealth through most of the colonial period.[11] In Yucatán, by contrast, where the colonial economy had not been able to extract as many resources from the indigenous villages, the prospect of the expansion of nonindigenous utilization of indigenous land and labor was enticing. Among the nonindigenous elite, it had created what Howard Cline called "a climate of opinion saturated by the spirit of enterprise."[12] If erasing ethnic distinctions could free up that land and labor by removing indigenous people's exclusive claims to such resources, a judicious attempt to do so held a great deal of appeal.

These differences were manifested immediately in the choices that the two state legislatures made in their construction of municipal government. Liberalism demanded the replacement of the indigenous repúblicas de indios with local bodies elected by the population without ethnic distinction. Both Oaxaca's and Yucatán's state legislatures honored this requirement in their constitutions and accompanying laws. In Oaxaca, the constitutional congress legislated the creation of two kinds of councils. In towns that had at least three thousand inhabitants, the residents would elect "ayuntamientos," while in smaller settlements the councils, with essentially the same duties, would be called "repúblicas."[13] This approach was replicated in Yucatán, where larger towns would elect ayuntamientos and smaller ones would choose "juntas municipales."[14] But in Yucatán another element was added to the mix. Here, in the words of the congressman who proposed it, "for the collection of the established taxes, and only for this objective," the república de indios was written back into the law.[15]

Both of these systems retained the basic distinction between the political participation of indigenous and nonindigenous people while *also* honoring the requirements of the new liberal institutions. In Oaxaca, the ethnic distinction was implicit. Towns smaller than three thousand were usually almost entirely indigenous. If the retention of the colonial name for their councils were not enough to indicate the intention of the laws to reinforce the political segregation of the population, the law providing for the exceptional granting of ayuntamientos to smaller towns was. If a town with fewer than three thousand inhabitants could prove that it had sufficient "enlightenment or industry," "measured principally according to the number of their vecinos who can read or write," it could be allowed to elect an ayuntamiento. This requirement eliminated the large majority of indigenous citizens, standing in for an explicit expression of ethnic preference.[16] With some exceptions, the demographic peculiarities of Oaxaca allowed for ethnic distinctions to be made geographically, between towns, without violating the terms of liberal law. In Yucatán, geographical distinction of this type was not possible, as there was a significant nonindigenous presence in "indigenous" towns. Thus, the state legislature chose to make an explicit ethnic distinction *within* those towns. Indigenous people would elect their own repúblicas. But because they would *also* have the opportunity to vote in elections for the new town councils, here, too, the terms of the new institutions were honored.

What the two systems shared, then, was the intention of making the new liberal institutions compatible with the continuation of ethnic distinctions that were theoretically antithetical to them but that served an indispensable role in local administration. In both states, indigenous people would be allowed to exercise the prerogatives of the new universal citizenship, voting not only for town councils but for state and national representatives as well. But at the same time, they would participate in a system in which their contact with the government came most often through institutions—the repúblicas—that were understood to be uniquely indigenous. Both states, then, had created out of their quandary at independence a new set of ideas and institutions that might be called "indigenous citizenship." Indigenous people had, in theory, all the rights of any citizen, regardless of ethnicity. But alongside this, built into the institutions, was a set of assumptions about them *as indigenous*. Tellingly, Yucatán's new indigenous councils were not called "repúblicas de indios" but rather "repúblicas de *indígenas*." This new term—which both indigenous and nonindigenous people came to use almost immediately in both places—constituted a new category that had no strict juridical definition but remained central to indigenous people's relationship to the state.

The implications of "indigenous citizenship" for indigenous people's interests in practice would, however, depend in large part on the intentions that had sparked its creation in the first place. In Oaxaca, the system essentially reproduced the status quo. In Yucatán, by contrast, the system was designed to promote change. The universally elected council in most Oaxacan towns was synonymous with the república and was therefore to be indigenous. In Yucatán, by separating the new council from the república, the legislature had virtually guaranteed it to be *nonindigenous*, providing a foothold for nonindigenous administration in indigenous villages. Yucatecan legislators felt themselves obligated to retain the república because they feared that the nonindigenous authorities could not effectively collect taxes, but beyond that they did not intend the república to govern.[17] This was, as Terry Rugeley has noted, a reinterpretation of the república that severely limited its scope.[18] In Oaxaca, then, ethnic differentiation was intended in at least one sense to keep indigenous villagers autonomous; in Yucatán, it was intended to make them less so.

And yet, indigenous people themselves could challenge these intentions in the way that they engaged and used the new institutions. Here again, there is much that the two states shared. In both places, indigenous people ably navigated their unique dual citizenship. They made claims based on both their old and new political identities, insisting simultaneously on their right to participate in universal politics and on their unique political privileges as indigenous people. In Yucatán, indigenous people could complain, as did the villagers of Xcupilcacab in 1832, that interference with their votes in universal town council elections "scorned the will of the majority of the inhabitants of the pueblo."[19] They could insist, as did the people of Tibolón when threatened with the loss of their junta, that they knew "how to esteem to a high degree [their] precious rights and . . . seek to avoid that they be ignored and trampled in the coming elections."[20] At the same time, though, they consistently stressed the limits of the reach of the juntas into certain aspects of indigenous people's lives, especially those that interfered with their direct relationship with the state government. And in Oaxaca, the villagers of the barrio of La Ciénaga could demand a council in the terms of both federalism and tradition. They wrote that elections in their town would not be "opposed to the system of established government" but were instead "very much in conformity with that in which each numerous population distant from another has its independent and free government." But they also claimed the right to a council because it was "the custom, as thus it will conform to justice and the public good and [the good] of our barrio."[21] Indigenous people in both places quickly assessed the situation and were able to make claims based on both their universal and their unique indigenous citizenships.

This last case, however, also suggests some of the differences that indigenous people confronted in the two institutional environments. The government official advising in the case of La Ciénaga proved receptive to the town's arguments, writing that "in every free Government and principally in the federal, the citizens have the right to be governed by themselves, so that they can attend to their interests." Here, he used the language of federalism. But like the villagers, he also appealed to customary distinctions, writing that villagers could not "attend to their interests" when "they are governed by outside authorities, as frequently happens in populations of indigenous people."[22] Not only was this Oaxacan official willing to recognize the ethnic distinction but he also expressed the opinion that indigenous people needed special protection. A similar admission would be hard to come by in Yucatán, since such protection would interfere with the economic goals of much of the population. Indeed, one crucial difference between the nature of ethnic distinctions in the two states would be the willingness of state officials to play the game according to the rules that indigenous people demanded.

This difference would become much more apparent as national politics forced state governments to adapt to rapidly changing institutional requirements. In Mexico as a whole, federalism would be replaced by centralism in late 1835 and would return in 1846. In Yucatán in particular, the swings would be even more dramatic, as the state drifted in and out of the Mexican union and experimented locally with different forms of government. Yucatecans experienced a brief centralist interim from 1829 to 1831, followed by the return of federalism and the shift back to centralism with the rest of Mexico in 1835. 1841 brought renewed Yucatecan independence under a federalist constitution, and the state would remain essentially independent until the outbreak of the Caste War in 1847 forced its return to the fold.

All these changes in government meant changes in local municipal structures. Under centralism, most villages would lose the right to elect their own local administrative bodies. National law stated that the only towns that would continue to elect local councils would be the state capitals, other towns with at least eight thousand inhabitants, and port towns of at least four thousand. In all other places, *jueces de paz* (justices of the peace) would govern, "proposed by the subprefect, named by the prefect, and approved by the governor."[23] Yucatán had put a similar system into effect in 1829 and would do so again in 1836.[24] Oaxaca began the process of replacing repúblicas with appointed jueces by mid-1837.[25]

These new municipal structures worked to counteract village autonomy on a number of fronts, eliminating elections, limiting local control over village finances, and making jueces in the smallest villages dependent on larger towns.[26] What is more, in Oaxaca in particular, the new laws had a distinctly ethnic dimension. The ideal juez de paz would be literate, hold some property, and have at least some education; he would, in short, be an "hombre de bien," and nonindigenous. Because the indigenous council had persisted in Oaxaca as the sole local authority, the institution of appointed jueces not only threatened autonomy; it also threatened a particularly *indigenous* autonomy. None of this was lost on those most directly concerned. As one Oaxacan town official put it in 1841, "Since the Constitution of 1836 was promulgated the pueblo has lost its rights."[27]

The fact that these words were written by an appointed juez de paz himself, however, says much about the ultimate nature of the changes in Oaxaca. Oaxacan villagers confronted the potentially drastic shift with relative equanimity, reflecting both the way that indigenous people insisted on particular privileges and the way officials responded. Villagers expected that autonomy was part of their bargain with the state, and officials were well aware of this. The government thus faced serious limitations on its ability to effect change. The replacement of indigenous authorities with nonindigenous jueces was, first, a practical problem; men fitting the above description were hard to come by in Oaxacan villages. When they did try to find them, it could produce lamentable results. Officials occasionally appointed men who did not actually reside in the town in question and who were thus usually unacceptable to the villagers. Such men could face serious difficulties; the newly appointed juez of Yxcatlán, for instance, complained that he was unable to do his job "because the pueblo is of pure indígenas whose language is unknown to me."[28] Even indigenous candidates could spark protest. In Santiago Plumas in 1838, the outgoing local administration objected to the appointment of Juan Santiago, who not only did not live in the village but was widely known as a *vago*—an unemployed and unrooted individual—"because he does not pay the contribution nor is he written in the catalog or list of the Municipality."[29] And when government officials chose younger men who had not adequately fulfilled the traditional duties necessary for holding higher posts, some townspeople could react angrily.[30]

Such situations exacerbated both factionalism within the villages and conflict between villagers and the state. When they occurred, however, they often compelled officials to reinterpret centralist municipal law so that in key ways it replicated its predecessor, thus preventing similar conflicts in the future. When villagers rejected unacceptable candidates, they forced officials to name the people that the villagers requested. In the end, the majority of jueces in centralist Oaxaca were, in the words of one official in Teotitlán, "unfortunate indígenas," and, in the eyes of the villagers, usually the men that they wanted.[31] In practice, these men governed much like the repúblicas had, down to collaboration with a larger group, as is evidenced by the easy slippage between the words themselves in villagers' correspondence; townspeople often described themselves as having a "juez and república."[32] Of course, there was not necessarily unanimity among the villagers, and the change in national institutions could translate into real shifts of power within the towns. But in the end it was more common than not for villagers to reach agreements that presented a united face to the state.[33]

Not only would this process of negotiation allow for the replication of the federalist system—and by extension the continuation of crucial colonial practices—it could also lead to the *expansion* of rights, because, in practice, more towns could have jueces de paz than had had repúblicas under the old rules. For settlements that were either attached to larger towns or not yet incorporated, the centralist laws provided, for the first time, a local administrator unique to their community. And because villagers were so successful in remaking the juez into a replication of the república, they saw this as an opportunity to rise to the rank of pueblo. By the end of the centralist period, the juez de paz, a potentially intrusive imposition, became a sought-after privilege.[34] In 1844, the law changed again in such a way as to make the jueces even more important, limiting them to cabeceras and replacing them with less powerful *jefes* or *agentes de policía*. Right away, the towns moved to counteract the effects of the new law, rushing to request jueces de paz between 1844 and 1845, citing the difficulty posed by travel to the cabeceras, their capacity to govern themselves, and their history of doing so. Success was not guaranteed, but it was certainly a possibility.[35] The flexibility of the state is evident in a case from October 1844, when the government granted the request of the town of Concepción Buena Vista for a juez de paz, putting four other towns under its jurisdiction. This set off a flurry of activity, as each of the subject towns claimed to be more deserving of a juez. Eventually, the original single juzgado became three.[36]

In Oaxaca, then, both villagers and officials responded to the potential threat that centralism posed by negotiating. Villagers quickly learned the avenues by which they could gain concessions, and officials proved willing in many cases to grant them. Despite the fact that centralism by its very nature attacked the autonomy of the pueblos, the new system became a tool for protecting and even enhancing that autonomy. In the process, the largely unspoken ethnic distinction that was at the heart of Oaxacan local politics stayed intact.

Centralism proved much more conflictual in Yucatán, and much more corrosive of the notion of ethnic distinction. On the surface, this seems surprising, as the particularities of Yucatecan municipal structures suggest that indigenous people would not be greatly affected by the change. Jueces de paz replaced not the repúblicas but rather the juntas municipales, which had, after all, never been indigenous institutions to begin with. The repúblicas de indígenas continued, in practice, to be sanctioned by the state and retained their obligation to collect taxes. But, in fact, the switch to jueces de paz caused considerable dissatisfaction, especially among indigenous people.

The problem lay in the fact that centralism undermined a vital distinction that federalism had upheld. Under federalism, the law had established an "absolute inhibition" against the participation of alcaldes, ayuntamientos, and juntas municipales in the collection of either religious or secular taxes, both of which were supervised by the state.[37] In theory, this seems to have been because of a concern that municipal authorities would abuse tax collection and foment discord among indígenas.[38] It most likely also reflected the worry that indigenous people would not be willing to submit taxes to men outside their own communities—the reason for the reestablishment of the repúblicas in the first place. But in practice this clear distinction served the all-important purpose of establishing a direct line between the state government and the indigenous communities. It was through the management of taxes, above all, that the government of Yucatán continued to negotiate the pact of reciprocity with indigenous Yucatecans.

Centralism did not replicate the "absolute inhibition." Unlike juntas municipales, which were locally elected administrative institutions, jueces de paz were appointed and thus officially representatives of the state. As such, they were not only allowed but also obligated to make sure that tax collection went smoothly. Although repúblicas were still the official tax collectors, jueces de paz increasingly involved themselves in the process. Often, the jueces' involvement came in the form of demands for labor service. Jueces were responsible for arranging periodic labor drafts on state projects such as roads or pest control. After 1831, villagers began to complain that the officials were also arranging for townspeople to perform service on private projects specifically as compensation for tax debt. When the indigenous villagers of Cholul, for instance, complained in 1831 that their juez was forcing them to work illegally on labor projects in the city of Izamal, they claimed that they had in fact paid their taxes and owed nothing to the state.[39] Similarly, the juez of the coastal town of Chicxulub arranged for the indigenous villagers to perform farm work, claiming that the cacique's ineptitude at collecting religious taxes made some compensatory arrangement necessary. When eighty villagers gathered to protest, the juez jailed the cacique and most members of the república.[40]

To make matters worse, villagers increasingly found that the government was now less willing to step in to mitigate the abuses of local officials. Yucatán's unique institutional arrangements potentially preserved the colonial notion of the special obligation of the state to protect the indigenous population. Under federalism, indigenous people could realistically assume that the government accepted this obligation, forging the notion that it was completely compatible with liberalism. Thus, even under centralism, indigenous communities continued to stress their belief that the governor in particular had this role. As a group of indígenas from Quelul complaining about compensatory labor service put it in a petition to the governor, "Excellent Sir, for all classes of private service you should preside and mediate . . . between the parties; without this prerequisite no one can be compelled or rewarded . . . to ignore this would be to trample upon the sacred rights of liberty so recommended by the laws."[41] And in Yaxkukul in 1838, villagers accusing their juez of intimidating and perhaps killing a local woman in the context of a property dispute expressed their certainty that the governor would intervene, insisting that their pueblo "breathes . . . the air of liberty."[42] But increasingly the government did not answer these calls. Thus the frustration of a group of villagers from a small town near Motul who found it difficult to get justice against the abusive "alcalde" of their town. Appeals the cacique and república had made to various government officials had all gone unanswered.[43]

The fundamental difference between Oaxaca and Yucatán lay not in the two states' willingness to implement institutions; both states diligently followed the dictates of centralist law regarding municipal structures. Nor did it lie in the reaction of indigenous people; both indigenous populations were quick to identify the problems with centralism and to demand a reinterpretation. Rather, it lay in the leverage that those indigenous people actually had with the state, and the spirit in which nonindigenous officials approached the situation. The colonial notion of the obligation of the state to protect indigenous people, present in both places at independence, did not survive the first half of the nineteenth century in equal measure. In Oaxaca, officials may often have been derisive about the state's indigenous citizens, claiming that they "did not want to be enlightened," that they were "little inclined to work," and that, when serving as municipal officers, they were "generally . . . all useless."[44] But when it came to supporting villagers' claims to particular state consideration, they often spoke the same language as their indigenous constituents. After a drought in 1831, for example, when the departmental governor José María Pando asked the state governor to "extend his paternal protection toward these indígenas,"[45] he was echoing indigenous people's claims about the government's long-understood obligation to be flexible.

The Yucatecan state was much less willing to play this role. It was not entirely *unwilling*; it would be a mistake to equate the interests of the state entirely with the interests of the nonindigenous entrepreneurs who were seeking access to indigenous villagers. In fact, the Yucatecan state faced conflicting pressures from various parties—indigenous people, entrepreneurs, and more "traditional" nonindigenous landholders—and their response was often to try to preserve the status quo. Certainly, the stated intent of the retention of the república was not to provide indígenas with a representative voice but merely to provide for more efficient collection of taxes. But because taxes were at the center of the relationship to the government, in practice, the legislation had given indigenous people a direct representative voice that bypassed the other councils and helped to keep the peace until the late 1840s. That the government was not quick to allay the effects of the change to centralism, however, suggests that it did not share indigenous people's fundamental assumptions about what being indigenous ought to mean, even in a liberal society, or at least that it would allow other more pressing concerns to override it. In the end, faced with fiscal crisis and tempted by the potential of indigenous lands to alleviate it, the state betrayed its pact with indigenous Yucatecans, allowing for the alienation of indigenous holdings with a momentous decree in 1841.[46] Though the complete story is beyond the scope of this chapter, all these events contributed to the eventual collapse of government legitimacy among many indigenous people, and the beginning of the Caste War in 1847.


What Oaxacans and Yucatecans did with national liberal institutions was very different and resulted in very different local political cultures with divergent consequences for the relationship between the state and indigenous people. They reached these points by undergoing processes that were in many ways similar. Mexico's radical first federalism offered a great deal of flexibility in local affairs, but it was not infinitely flexible. Oaxacan and Yucatecan legislators faced a similar challenge. The very "illiberal" colonial practice of distinguishing politically between indigenous and nonindigenous people had long been at the heart of the stability of local politics. But now the juridical distinction that had supported this stability was no longer an institutional option. This meant that each state, as it devised new institutions, had to find a way to reconcile the essentially irreconcilable, and each state did exactly that.

As a whole, the narrative about liberalism discussed at the outset of this chapter cannot explain both the Oaxacan and Yucatecan experiences. Yet at first glance, each of the two cases does seem to bear out the claims of one part of the narrative. The assertion that liberal institutions made little difference to ethnic distinction seems to fit best in Oaxaca, where the basic parameters of colonial economic and political structures did remain intact. But even if those structures did not change, liberalism nevertheless became deeply imbricated in local political culture. Oaxacans, both indigenous and not, understood the institutions they lived with to be simultaneously traditional and liberal. As then governor Benito Juárez, soon to become famous as a liberal reformer, remarked in 1848, "Since before the establishment of the federal system, the pueblos of the state have had the democratic custom of electing their functionaries for themselves." Under the institutions of federalism, he continued, "The pueblos have recovered not only their ayuntamientos and repúblicas, but also the right to elect them in conformity with their ancient customs."[47] Juárez easily conflated pre- and postconquest municipal institutions and freely expressed the compatibility of "democracy" and "ancient customs," and his statements here are quite representative across the broad spectrum of Oaxacan society in the first half of the nineteenth century, especially among the local officials who had to actually govern.

When liberalism as nationally construed made an appearance in Oaxaca in the form of national reform, its potential effects were limited by this convergence. The Ley Lerdo of 1856, which legislated the privatization of communally held land, was intended to strike at the heart of indigenous autonomy and to promote once and for all the erasure of ethnic distinction. A thorough implementation of this law would have had a tremendous effect in Oaxaca, with its majority indigenous population holding the majority of land in common. And indeed, villagers protested, arguing that their lands were too scarce to subdivide all of them among all the villagers, and that, for as long as they could remember, they had rotated usufruct rights in recompense for revolving community duties. This system would collapse if all land were permanently subdivided.[48] And once again, Oaxacan officials agreed.

One departmental governor, for instance, was concerned that the allocation of land to private individuals, "even if these are themselves vecinos" (that is, townspeople), would have detrimental effects on the communities that he supervised. This governor took a radical step, suspending all land alienation in his department, seemingly confirming the narrative about national liberalism's limited implementation.[49] But, crucially, this is not how *most* Oaxacans, either villagers or officials, dealt with this threat to their livelihoods and to their ability to govern. In fact, the Ley Lerdo was not ignored in Oaxaca, and most Oaxacans did not refuse to carry it out; on the contrary, there was a tremendous amount of litigation surrounding the ownership of land after 1856, initiated by villagers, small-holders, and hacendados alike. Yet in the end, indigenous people continued to control much of their land as indigenous communities.[50] In the documents left behind from this flurry of activity, the language and logic of private property coexisted with the language and logic of communal property, just as the language of liberalism coexisted with the language of custom. What officials and villagers shared was a common commitment to finding a way to implement the law without causing fundamental disruptions. For officials, this meant being open to "illiberal" forms of property holding with deep roots in both precolonial and colonial society; for villagers, it meant being open to "liberal" ones. In effect, "liberalism"—in the form of the Ley Lerdo—failed to have its intended impact in Oaxaca because liberalism had so successfully become a part of local political culture. The structures of government and society in Oaxaca in 1856 were in crucial ways replications of pre-independence forms and ideologies. And yet most Oaxacans understood them to be products of the new system as well. Liberal reform would have limited effects on colonial practices in a place that was, in the minds of both the state and citizens, *already* liberal.[51]

So Oaxaca does not entirely bear out the claims of a narrative in which liberalism was simply ignored. But what of Yucatán? Here, surely, is a prime example of the assertion that liberalism, by succeeding in its goals of separating indigenous people from their communal lands, removed the protections afforded by ethnic distinctions and turned indigenous people into an oppressed minority. A glance at Yucatán in the later nineteenth century, when the number of indígenas residing on landed estates had risen to 75 percent, and when those workers were heavily indebted and living in virtual prisons, seems to bear this out.[52] Yet Yucatán's complete adherence to this narrative is undermined by the anomaly of the Caste War. First, it would not be entirely accurate to say that liberalism *caused* the massive conflagration that began in 1847. As in Oaxaca, Yucatecans had built a local liberalism in the years before that. Unlike Oaxaca, the elements of that local liberalism did not work together smoothly. Attempts to rename the colonial as liberal succeeded only partially here. But it is clear that indigenous Yucatecans, like indigenous Oaxacans, accepted, embraced, and used the notion of liberalism, sometimes successfully, to advance their interests in relation to the state. When in 1841 and beyond the government made it clear that it would not listen to those arguments, indigenous people's reaction was not just to the betrayal of the colonial pact but *also* to the betrayal of indigenous understandings of Yucatecan *liberalism*. In the end, Yucatán's indigenous villagers lost much of their land not as a result of the national reform but rather in the process of the reconstruction of the state after the Caste War, when the elite pushed an economic agenda that stressed both the needs of the export economy and the dangers of indigenous autonomy. By that time, the notion of "liberalism" belonged almost entirely to the elite, and their version of it resisted the political incorporation of indigenous people under any circumstances. But the rise of this new Yucatecan liberalism is only understandable in the context of the failure of an earlier local liberal political culture that indigenous people participated in, and that was categorically similar to the one that prevailed in Oaxaca.

The effects of the introduction of liberal administration in Mexico on what it meant to be indigenous were by no means preordained. Responses to the challenges posed by liberalism neither erased ethnic identities nor left them unchanged. And the practice of liberalism neither brought indigenous people fully into an undifferentiated political community nor utterly excluded them from it. Before independence, ethnic identity—and in particular indigenousness—was a crucial aspect of politics. The fact that it was so deeply imbricated in both the theory and practice of governance meant that after independence, it would inevitably continue to be so. But politics and governance had changed, and both indigenous and nonindigenous people would be faced with the task of fitting old notions of ethnic difference into new political and legal frameworks that in and of themselves altered the way that ethnicity worked. In both Oaxaca and Yucatán, indigenous and nonindigenous people did just this, devising often creative—and sometimes destructive—solutions to the problems that their situations presented. That things turned out so differently in the two states certainly suggests that this process could produce very different political systems, and very different notions of the role of ethnicity in politics. But a closer look also reveals what was shared. In both places, the attempt to reconcile liberal universalism and indigenous particularity was a—perhaps *the*—central concern of local politics. In the years to come, a reformist and transformative national liberalism would come face to face with the variety of ways in which Mexicans had already met this challenge.

*Notes*

I would like to thank the panelists and audience at the Latin American Studies Association conference in 2004 for their comments on an earlier version of this essay, especially Emilio Kourí for inviting me to participate. The essay is part of a larger study of state-indigenous relations in Oaxaca and Yucatán, and I am particularly grateful to Jeremy Adelman, Peter Guardino, and David Freund for their readings of this work.

1. These narratives are often found together and can be used in the service of very different arguments; for two examples, see Stein and Stein, *The Colonial Heritage of Latin America*, 160–62 and Bonfil Batalla, *México Profundo*, 94–107.

2. These councils represented both continuity with earlier administrative forms and changes wrought by particular Spanish introductions. For Yucatán, see Restall, *The Maya World*, 51–83. For Oaxaca, see Terraciano, *The Mixtecs of Colonial Oaxaca*, 182–97, and Romero Frizzi, *El sol y la cruz*, 121–28. See also Haskett, *Indigenous Rulers*, especially 27–85.

3. Cunniff, "Mexican Municipal Electoral Reform"; Annino, "Cádiz y la revolución territorial de los pueblos mexicanos."

4. On the origins of Spanish municipal reform, see Castro, *La revolución liberal y los municipios españoles*; on the participation of American deputies at the Spanish Cortes, see Rieu-Millan, *Los diputados americanos en las Cortes de Cádiz*. For discussions of the hybrid nature of Mexican liberalism, see Guerra, "El soberano y su reino"; Annino, "Ciudadanía 'versus' gobernabilidad republicana en México"; and the essays in Rodríguez O., ed., *The Divine Charter*.

5. Platt, *Estado boliviano y ayllu andino*, 40.

6. For Oaxaca, see Sánchez Silva, *Indios, comerciantes y burocracia en la Oaxaca poscolonial*, 48. The number for Yucatán is derived from local statistical documents compiled for 1802–11 by Farriss, *Maya Society under Colonial Rule*, appendix 1, "The Population of Yucatán," 397–98.

7. Chance, *Race and Class in Colonial Oaxaca*, 145, 151, 156; Romero Frizzi, *El sol y la cruz*, 208; and Taylor, "Town and Country in the Valley of Oaxaca," 76.

8. Sánchez Silva, *Indios, comerciantes y burocracia en la Oaxaca poscolonial*, 96–104; Chance, *Conquest of the Sierra*, 29.

9. Farriss, *Maya Society under Colonial Rule*, 30–33.

10. Patch, *Maya and Spaniard in Yucatan*, 138–50; Farriss, *Maya Society under Colonial Rule*, 366–375.

11. Sánchez Silva, *Indios, comerciantes y burocracia en la Oaxaca poscolonial*, 87–110; 217–18. The attitude of the Oaxacan elite toward their system is perhaps best manifested in their response to the abolition, in 1786, of the *repartimiento*, the institution that facilitated the extraction of cotton and cochineal from the communities. Although the reform was intended in large part to promote the freer circulation of goods, nonindigenous Oaxacans objected, as they saw it as a threat to their ability to profit from indigenous production. Hamnett, *Politics and Trade in Southern Mexico*, 122–26; 128–31. See also Ibarra, *Clero y política en Oaxaca*, 64–69.

12. Cline, "The 'Aurora Yucateca' and the Spirit of Enterprise in Yucatán," 32. See also García Quintanilla, "En busca de la prosperidad y la riqueza," 93–97.

13. "Constitución particular del Estado de Oaxaca," January 10, 1825, 42–58; "Se prescriben las condiciones necesarias para el establecimiento de ayuntamientos y repúblicas en los pueblos del estado," January 25, 1825; and "Ley que arregla el gobierno económico de los departamentos y pueblos del estado," March 13, 1825, *Colección de leyes y decretos del estado libre de Oaxaca*, 106–9; 206–212.

14. "Sobre el régimen económico y juntas municipales del estado," September 20, 1824, *Colección de leyes . . . de Yucatán*, 1:310–18.

15. *Gaceta de Mérida*, no. 92, June 2, 1824, congressional session of May 28, 1824; "Sobre Repúblicas de indígenas," July 26, 1824, *Colección de leyes . . . de Yucatán*, 1:277–80.

16. "Se prescriben las condiciones . . ."

17. See the testimony of deputy Juan N. Rivas, *Gaceta de Mérida*, no. 14, October 14, 1823, congressional session of September 25, 1823.

18. Rugeley, *Yucatán's Maya and the Origins of the Caste War*, 94.

19. "Información producida por el alcalde de Hopelchén, por designación del Gobernador, sobre los hechos ocurridos con motivo de las elecciones del pueblo de Xcupilcacab," February 11, 1832, Archivo General del Estado de Yucatán (AGEY), Poder Ejecutivo (PE), Gobernación (G), box 10, vol. 4, exp. 8.

20. "Representación de varios vecinos del pueblo de Tibolón, pidiendo que dicho pueblo tenga junta municipal o de lo contrario sea agregado al de Sotuta," December 11, 1832, AGEY, PE, G, box 17, vol. 5, exp. 15.

21. Fernando de León to governor of Centro, December 22, 1846, Archivo General del Estado de Oaxaca (AGEO) , Gobernación (G), Gobierno de los Distritos (GD), Centro.

22. Governor of Centro, December 29, 1846, AGEO, G, GD, Centro.

23. "Leyes Constitucionales," in Tena Ramírez, ed., *Leyes fundamentales de México 1808–1982*, 243–44.

24. I have been unable to locate the actual laws from the "illegitimate" insurgent administration of 1829–31, but it is clear from evidence from the villages that this was essentially the system instituted. See, for example, "Proposición de ternas para la designación de Jueces de Paz y procuradores de los pueblos de Pisté y Chichimilá," AGEY, PE, G, box 16, vol. 2, exp. 48.

25. José María Parada, July 11, 1837, AGEO, G, GD, Jamiltepec, Jueces de Paz.

26. "Reglamento provisional para el gobierno interno de los Departamentos," March 20, 1837, in Dublán and Lozano, eds., *Legislación mexicana*, 3:323–38.

27. Juez de Paz of Santa Catarina Yxtepeji, September 28, 1841, AGEO, G, GD, Villa Juárez, Subprefectura de Villa Alta. On the intentions of centralist law regarding local government, see Guardino, *Peasants, Politics, and the Formation of Mexico's National State*, 98–103.

28. Manuel María Callejas, January 24, 1846; subprefect of Tuxtepec, June 24, 1846, AGEO, G, GD, Tuxtepec, Subprefectura de Teotitlán.

29. "Propuesta en terna para el nombramiento de Jues de Paz . . . ," December 4, 1838; Gaspar Martínez to Juez de Paz of Santiago Plumas, December 19, 1838; Corporación Municipal of Santiago Plumas to prefect of Teposcolula, December 27, 1838, Instituto Nacional de Antropología e Historia (INAH), Archivo Histórica en Micropelícula (AHM), Oaxaca (O), Archivo del Juzgado de Teposcolula (AJT), roll 31; and Tribunal Superior de Justicia, April 13, 1841, AGEO, G, GD, Centro.

30. This phenomenon is documented extensively for Villa Alta in Guardino, *The Time of Liberty*, 241–248.

31. José Mantecón to secretario del despacho, March 16, 1840, AGEO, G, GD, Teotitlán.

32. Juez and República to prefect, January 21, 1840, AGEO, G, GD, Teposcolula; Pedro Santiago to departmental governor, July 9, 1840, AGEO, G, GD, Huajuapan.

33. Guardino, *The Time of Liberty*, 243–45; 270.

34. See, for instance, Carrizola to prefect of Teposcolula, February 18, 1839, INAH, AHM, O, AJT, roll 31; Escribano nacional público for República of San Francisco Yucucundo, October 31, 1838; "Padrón de almas del Pueblo de Yucucundo"; Ramón Martínez Zurita, November 10, 1838; prefect of Teposcolula to subprefect of Nochistlán, March 8, 1839; José Miguel to governor, April 1, 1839; cura of Peñoles, April 11, 1839; Martínez Zurita, April 16, 1838; Ramón Villegas to governor, February 2, 1840; Manuel Contreras, May 2, 1840; Ramón Villegas, July 1, 1840; AGEO, G, GD, Teposcolula; Junta Departamental, November 4, 1840, AGEO, G, GD, Centro.

35. For some successes and failures, see Manuel Torres, Máximo Guzmán, Rosalino Contreras, and Luciano Zárate to subprefect of Juchitán, September 11, 1845; subprefect

of Juchitán, September 12, 1845; AGEO, G, GD, Juchitán, subprefectura de Tehuantepec; prefect of Teposcolula, August 9 and September 8, 1844, AGEO, G, GD, Teposcolula, Juzgado de Paz; jefe de policía de Capulalpán, March 10, 1845, AGEO, G, GD, Centro; Francisco Franco, April 11, 1845, AGEO, G, GD, Villa Alta, Policía; Francisco Franco to secretario del despacho, February 14, 1845, AGEO, G, GD, Villa Alta, Juzgados de Paz.

36. Prefect of Teposcolula, October 4, 1844, AGEO, G, GD, Teposcolula, Juzgados de Paz; Vicente Rodríguez, jefe de policía of Plumas, to departmental governor, November 30, 1844, AGEO, G, GD, Centro; Común de San Miguel Astatla, November 29, 1844, AGEO, G, GD, Teposcolula, Coixtlahuaca; Benigno Rojas, October 4, 1844; prefect from subprefect to governor, December 26, 1844, AGEO, G, GD, Teposcolula, Juzgado de Paz; Asamblea Departamental, January 3, 1845, AGEO, G, GD, Centro. This process of seeking increased autonomy from other indigenous villages strongly echoes colonial trends in which pueblos sought to be named "cabeceras," or head towns, rather than subject villages. See Dehouve, "The 'Secession' of Villages in the Jurisdiction of Tlapa," and Lockhart, The Nahuas after the Conquest, 47–58. For the Mixteca, see Terraciano, The Mixtecs of Colonial Oaxaca, 131.

37. "Que arregla el cobro de la contribución personal," November 23, 1833, in Aznar Pérez, ed., Colección de leyes, 1:147–49; "Sobre el cobro de obvenciones," October 22, 1825, in Aznar Pérez, ed., Colección de leyes, 2:44–47.

38. "Sobre el cobro de obvenciónes."

39. "Averiguación promovida por queja de los indígenas de Cholul, contra el Juez de Paz de Conkal, por violentarlos a desempeñar trabajos en las milpas del subdelegado, del cura y las suyas propias," August 4, 1831, AGEY, PE, Justicia (J), box 23, vol. 3, exp. 13; "Averiguación promovida por queja de vecinos del pueblo de Cholul, contra Marcelo Martín, juez de paz de Conkal, por tenerlos en prisión," AGEY, PE, J, vol. 3, exp. 14.

40. "Diligencias para la averiguación de unos hechos que se atribuyen al Juez de Paz del pueblo de Chicxulub contra el cacique y justicias de aquel pueblo," July 20, 1831, AGEY, PE, J, box 23, vol. 3, exp. 12.

41. "Representación de los indios del pueblo de Quelul, acusando a Bernardino Jimenez, Juez de Paz de dicho pueblo, por obligarlos a torcer caña en condiciones injustas," AGEY, PE, G, box 16, vol. 3, exp. 20; "Averiguación promovida por queja de República de Indígenas del pueblo de Quelul, partido de Peto, contra el Juez de paz de Ichmul, por forzarlos a repartimientos y trabajos que consideran abusivos," April 16, 1831, AGEY, PE, J, box 23, vol. 3, exp. 9.

42. "Sumaria promovida por Pedro Nolasco May y otros vecinos de Yaxkukul contra Luis Silveira, Juez de Paz de dicho pueblo, por abuso de autoridad," March 1–May 2, 1838, AGEY, Justicia, Penal, box 9, exp. 24.

43. "Representación de varios vecinos de la jurisdicción de Motul contra el alcalde Timoteo Bolio, por abuso de autoridad," April 25, 1837, AGEY, PE, G, box 19, vol. 9, exp. 20.

44. Ygnacio José Ortega, "Notas ó Adiciones al Plan Estadístico," April 12, 1830, AGEO, G, GD, Juchitán; José Mantecón, governor of Teotitlán, September 1837, AGEO, G, GD,

Teotitlán; José Mantecón to secretario del Superior Gobierno del Departamento, September 30, 1836, Teotitlán, Acontecimientos.

45. José María Pando to secretario del gobierno del estado, July 8, 1831, AGEO, G, GD, Zoochila, Comunicados.

46. "Sobre enagenación de terrenos baldíos," April 5, 1841, in Aznar Pérez, ed., *Colección de leyes*, 2:116–18.

47. Benito Juárez, "Exposición al soberano congreso al abrir sus sesiones, julio 2 de 1848," 159–61.

48. Ayuntamiento of Juchitán, April 6, 1858, AGEO, G, GD, Juchitán; Auxiliares of San Blas, Santa María, Guichivere, San Gerónimo, Lavorio, Jalisco, San Jacinto, Diagaveche, Cerrito, Lioza, and Totonilco to governor of Tehuantepec, September 12, 1857, AGEO, G, GD, Tehuantepec.

49. Governor of Huajuapan to Secretario del Despacho Universal del Estado, August 1, 1856, AGEO, G, GD, Huajuapan.

50. One early account claimed that as late as 1910, 99.8 percent of Oaxacan heads of family lacked individual private property (McBride, *The Land Systems of Mexico*, 146). Although this number is perhaps exaggerated, more recent research has borne out the basic observation that communal landholding remained extensive, and that capitalist agriculture, even though it did advance significantly in some parts of Oaxaca in the nineteenth century, did not significantly alter that fact. Garner, *La revolución en la provincia*, 25–39; Cassidy, "Las haciendas oaxaqueñas en el siglo XIX," 292–323.

51. This assessment, based on my research into the very earliest responses to the Ley Lerdo in the late 1850s, is reinforced by the findings of Jennie Purnell and Francie R. Chassen-López for the latter part of the nineteenth century, when the vast majority of land cases were adjudicated. Purnell, "Citizens and Sons of the *Pueblo*," 220–28; Chassen-López, *From Liberal to Revolutionary Oaxaca*, 88–105.

52. Patch, *Maya and Spaniard in Yucatan*, 150; Joseph, *Revolution from Without*, 27; Katz, "Labor Conditions on Haciendas in Porfirian Mexico," 18–19; Wells, *Yucatán's Gilded Age*, 151–58; and Joseph, "Rethinking Mexican Revolutionary Mobilization," 140–46.

# Conclusion

In January 1719, Mexico City authorities arrested three artisans for robbing several hundred pesos' worth of cash and clothing from a wealthy merchant's store. They quickly identified the ringleader, a weaver named Francisco de Ledesma—better known to his friends as Francisco Franco. He called himself a Spaniard, though the jailer had some doubts: "going by his color, hair, and the knowledge of [his fellow] workers, he is a mulatto."[1] After a lengthy trial, Francisco was found guilty and sentenced to eight years' labor in a sweatshop (*obraje*). His lawyer objected, claiming that Spaniards could not legally suffer forced labor. The court, however, dug through its records and uncovered forty-three cases of Spaniards condemned to obrajes between 1689 and 1721. Ironically, the investigator himself questioned the "Spanish" status of several of these prisoners, citing as an example one Francisco Necasio, whose assigned master had "not taken him for a Spaniard, but for a *mestizo*, which he was."[2] The court nonetheless maintained its position, emphasizing the class issue: those who could not pay for their crimes with money had to pay with their bodies. Labor in obrajes had never carried the stain of infamy; besides, those condemned were typically artisans who could continue their professions in these workshops. What could be more suitable? This legal dispute eventually reached the Council of the Indies, but before it could be resolved, the case took a surprising final twist. A Spaniard appeared who gave Francisco yet another surname (de la Hoya Moro) and another identity: an escaped slave "of the Turkish nation" who should be returned to his owners.[3]

One is tempted to ask: who was this mystery man, anyway? But that may be the wrong question. As the essays in this volume demonstrate, understanding identity in colonial Latin America is seldom straightforward. In particular, the authors challenge any notion of identity as something obvious or transparent, stable or permanent. We can begin with the imperial setting itself. Colonization and its attendants—warfare, disease, and exploitation—massively disrupted existing social boundaries, undermining (to a greater or lesser extent) accepted hierarchies, introducing new identities (such as "Indian" and "Christian"), and even creating new ethnic groups (the Yaquis of modern-day Sonora are an excellent example).[4] Moreover, the invading Spaniards introduced a new biological dynamic. European and African migrants mingled with native populations to produce a bewildering and (from the Spanish viewpoint) threatening diversity. Colonial elites attempted to impose some order on this runaway process by identifying supposedly discrete groups (such as "mestizos" and "mulattoes") and by situating them in a racial hierarchy that historians know as the *sistema de castas*. The *sistema* of course placed Spaniards in the dominant position, with those of mixed ancestry (*castas*) in the middle, and Indians and blacks at the bottom. Spaniards posited these categories as natural and inevitable, but forcing this conceptual grid on social reality proved a strain. In practice, the sistema de castas actually permitted considerable flexibility both in defining social difference and in regulating interethnic relations. It would be misleading to treat "caste" as the equivalent of "race." Laura Lewis reminds us that Spaniards reserved the term *raza* for those with "Jewish and Moorish 'blood'—an immutable and undesirable substance." Caste also "linked racial quality to blood or ancestry" but "seems to have been less [emotionally] charged"; it dictated the basic nature of people (Indians were weak, blacks were aggressive) without determining their entire character.[5] While Spanish colonizers never hesitated to issue blanket condemnations of their inferiors, in their daily lives they judged the worthiness of castas on a case-by-case basis. They willingly traded with and loaned money to prominent mulatto merchants, and they also aided casta clients in a variety of ways, including acting as character witnesses in petitions and law suits. Elites never regarded non-Spaniards as their equals, but the two groups interacted in dynamic and nuanced contexts, rather than in a simple structure of dominance and subordination. Maneuvering within the interstices of the colonial system, imperial subjects could attempt to forge their own identities.

Historians can catch only glimpses of such self-fashioning. As Andrew Fisher and Matthew O'Hara emphasize, our access to subaltern experience and consciousness is highly mediated. We encounter ordinary people at extraordinary moments: when they petition the Crown, when they stand before the Inquisition, when they become involved in criminal proceedings, or when they celebrate key moments in the life cycle (baptisms, marriages, and burials). At these "contact points," the social actors' views are contained within and constrained by elite frameworks. Parish registers, for example, are a vital source for data on ethnicity: but do they reflect the parishioners' own declarations, the priests' judgments, or a mixture of both? Inquisitors and judges shaped plebeian testimony in a variety of ways. Eighteenth-century Mexico City courts often insisted that indigenous testimony be taken in Nahuatl, even when the witnesses spoke good Spanish—an instance of colonial categorization trumping objective conditions and common sense.[6] Furthermore, the courts dictated the entire process, deciding which questions to ask and which answers were acceptable and enforcing these strictures through displays of symbolic power, backed by the threat of institutionalized violence.

Yet for all these advantages, colonial tribunals encountered all too many Francisco Francos, persons of indeterminate name and lineage. These cases represented more than an occasional glitch in the system. Elites understood that plebeians consciously manipulated their racial status. As Pedro Alonso O'Crouley, an eighteenth-century Spanish visitor to Mexico, put it, "Many pass as Spaniards who know in their hearts they are mulattoes."[7] O'Crouley assumed, as did most inquisitors, judges, and priests, that racial labels had prescriptive force, that the Spanish conception of "caste" was hegemonic. Everyone possessed a "real" identity, a true nature—even if this could not be established definitively. He, and other elites, shied away from the more disquieting possibility that caste identity was inherently unstable. But Inquisition records, for example, show that time and again witnesses disagreed about a defendant's racial status, not because they were poor observers but because they employed various—sometimes conflicting—criteria. "Mestizo" and "mulatto" meant different things to different people. Multiple "symbolic markers," ranging from the mundane (hair length) to the transcendent (Christian spirituality), "competed . . . for primacy."[8] Subalterns could not ignore the official classifications, but they could rework their content. What the records show us, then, is how imperial subjects chose to position themselves socially and culturally, how they strategically used the available racial ideologies and categories to shape the public presentation of their identities.

All of our authors stress the dynamic interaction between individuals and the state. Racial identities could evolve rapidly in response to changing royal policy (see the discussion in Ann Twinam's chapter). Moreover, the state itself was neither static nor monolithic. If, as Irene Silverblatt insists, Spain was creating a "modern" bureaucracy in the sixteenth and seventeenth centuries,[9] the task remained far from complete. The "imperial gaze" was still fragmented, and colonials encountered—and attempted to play off—multiple levels of the imperial system.

Every royal subject had the right to appeal to the Crown. Certainly the king's orders did not always prevail in the colonial world, in part because they tended to be sweeping, imperative statements that had to be reinterpreted to suit local conditions. Yet they served as powerful (if sometimes double-edged) weapons in any bureaucratic dispute. But how to win the Crown's favor? Three of our readings show how indigenous lords, royal slaves, and black and mulatto confraternities creatively reshaped their collective identities to strengthen their appeals. Jeremy Mumford's illuminating study of sixteenth-century Peru suggests the tension between native and imported concepts of difference. For Andeans, the notion of "lordship" crosscut ethnic divisions, and the local rulers (*kurakas*) maintained the crucial lord/commoner social boundary well after the conquest. As Mumford notes, the Spanish—strangers in a strange land—needed the expertise of these Andean elites to extract Peru's wealth. So they acknowledged the kurakas' legitimacy as "natural lords" and granted them the honorific title "don," something that eluded many conquistadors. But the kurakas sought more than merely the continuation of their pre-Columbian status. In a new, fluid environment, they competed with Spanish *encomenderos* for power. They actively adopted the trappings of Spanish privilege, including coats of arms, horses, and royal titles. Most strikingly, they offered Philip II an enormous bribe—more than equal to the encomenderos' similar effort—to recognize them as a permanent Peruvian aristocracy. In the end, this attempt to make themselves the "dukes and counts of Peru" by leveraging their middleman status, their access to both Spanish and indigenous culture, failed. The kurakas' hybrid conception of lordship ran headlong into a colonialist ideology which affirmed that all Indians were inferior to Spaniards and needed the paternal care of priests and royal officials. The new governor, Lope de Castro, stripped native lords of their right to bear Spanish arms and ride horses and established Indian municipal governments along Spanish lines (complete with town councils, or *cabildos*) to undermine their authority. He did not fully succeed: the kurakas quickly came to dominate town governance, making it their new power base. The kurakas "preserved hereditary succession" and continued to act as native lords into the late eighteenth century, though they ruled over shrunken domains. Moreover, their elite status became submerged in a broader, regnant Indian identity.[10]

But if the colonized peoples of the Andes and Mesoamerica had to recognize that they were now "Indians"—at least when dealing with government bureaucracies—they do not seem to have internalized this label. In native language records, terms like "indio" or "indígena" almost never appeared.[11] Instead, indigenous peasants gave their allegiance to the very corporate communities that the Spanish had initiated or reorganized. These towns, usually incorporating a saint's name and celebrating the Christian ritual calendar (though often in very distinct ways), provided a highly localized sense of ethnic identity, which in some places persisted deep into the twentieth century. In Guatemala, during the 1970s, knowledgeable observers could still pinpoint a Maya woman's town of origin from the intricate designs woven into her *huipil*.[12] The community also became the chief vehicle for interacting with Spanish authorities. Town councils petitioned for the removal of offensive priests, confirmation of land titles, relief from debt and labor burdens, or remission of tribute levies. If legal appeals did not bring satisfaction, riots served as another, albeit risky, negotiating tactic.

The corporate community, then, proved a useful mechanism for defending locally defined rights and interests. In seventeenth- and eighteenth-century Cuba, a group of slaves used it as a model for attaining de facto liberty. When the mines of El Cobre closed in 1670, the slaves found themselves transferred from private to crown ownership. Like the Andean kurakas, their status was in flux, and they seized the opportunity to negotiate with royal officials. Their request was more modest than the kurakas' but in some ways more remarkable because of their apparently illegitimate position: should property even dare to speak? Yet as María Elena Díaz notes, they drew upon multiple identities, calling themselves "blacks," "Creoles," and "natives of the mines," as well as "slaves of His

Majesty." The petitioners brought these categories together through their daring assertion that El Cobre was their homeland, their *patria*. They were not mere transients or dislocated people but a community with roots in this specific location—and even a foundation myth that "grounded the origins and boundaries of [this] imagined local community in the ancient past of pre-colonial history." In effect, they opened up an autonomous space by "indigenizing" themselves, by claiming the status and privileges of peasant *pueblos* (indeed, they actually acquired a cabildo). Their cause had an undeniable logic. As the king's special subjects, they eagerly served their royal master through construction work and, especially, military service—the equivalent of the Indians' *repartimiento* or *mita* (rotating labor draft). But to carry out these tasks, they needed a resource base, rights to the land that would sustain them. Only a formally acknowledged, secure patria would allow them to be good husbands, fathers, soldiers, and Christians as they (and surely the Crown) desired. This is the most extraordinary example in our entire collection of how imperial subjects (a particularly apt term in this case) could reinterpret colonial categories for their own benefit. Like indigenous peasants, they forged a local, communal identity: *cobreros*. By focusing attention on their "native" and "Creole" qualities (and by providing genuine services to the Crown in an exposed frontier region) the cobreros successfully equated themselves with self-governing Indian pueblos. This enabled them to override the distinction between the two republics and to "mitigate the disabilities related to race that marked so many facets of life in the colonial world."

Mariana Dantas charts a somewhat different collective struggle in eighteenth-century Minas Gerais, where preto, crioulo, and pardo confraternities sought to carve out their own autonomous space for worship and social interaction. These religious brotherhoods offered people of color a rare chance for both mutual support and community outreach. Even so, the brothers had to tread with care, for they faced considerable suspicion, and threats of intervention, from other *mineiros*. Dantas acknowledges that they "employed several categories of self-identification" including "property holders, heads of households, and persons of honor." Yet among our authors she places the most stress on "structure" as opposed to "agency." In her account, the racial hierarchy is a palpable presence, something that people of color must perforce acknowledge and take into their calculations. Thus, pardo women pursued relationships with white men to improve their status and life chances, but hypergamous marriages proved rare. By the second half of the eighteenth century, Minas Gerais was no longer a frontier region; the era of social fluidity, if it ever existed, had passed. In fact, Minas Gerais now had more slaves than Bahia, a major sugar-producing province in the Brazilian northeast, where African slavery had first emerged as a dominant institution. The deeply ingrained, inescapable division between Portuguese slaveholders and enslaved Africans perhaps rendered racial boundaries more rigid; certainly nonwhites, including freed-men and women, continued to be strongly associated with slaves and suffered many of the same restrictions.

Yet they did not remain passive victims. In fact, the confraternities' strategies echoed those of the cobreros. First, they turned their weakness—their lowly racial status—into a strength. The same labels used to demean them "could be internalized as parameters of a collective identity." Cultivating such an identity meant excluding whites from membership, but in other regards it promoted an expanded sense of social responsibility, as the confraternities purchased the freedom of enslaved brothers and took on welfare and public services. In this way, the brotherhoods could argue that their exclusivity and desire for a degree of independence (by founding their own churches, for example) actually benefited the wider community. Second, people of color appealed directly to the Crown. Much like the cobreros, they presented themselves as "loyal vassals" and as established residents of specific towns, who performed vital economic tasks. But while the cobreros elided their links to Africa, the mineiro petitioners chose to foreground race. In fact, the members of one brotherhood petitioning the queen presented themselves as deserving of her "attention and favors" precisely "*because* of their racial identity" (emphasis mine). The confraternities, operating within a restrictive terrain, attempted to transform race into a means of empowerment—at the cost of reinforcing the captaincy's social divisions.

As Dantas points out, such collective strategies coexisted with other, more flexible ones, often pursued by individuals who aimed at circumventing or transcending their inferior standing. In the closing decades of the colonial era, a small number of mulattoes and pardos adopted this approach, petitioning the Spanish Crown for a royal decree (*gracias al sacar*) that would make them legally "white." The king, of course, represented the ultimate source of justice in the Hispanic world. Everyone, as

Ann Twinam notes, accepted his right and capacity to alter his subjects' status: just as the monarch could confer nobility, he could remedy the "defect" of African ancestry. Moreover, he could do this at a single stroke. I have argued elsewhere that "passing" usually marked a long-term adjustment in castas' social networks.[13] The gracias al sacar greatly accelerated this process, allowing upwardly mobile castas to clear the final, formal barriers that kept them (and their children) out of prestigious occupations and higher education.

Yet these whitening decrees met increasing resistance, especially in Venezuela. Racial labels, as always, had multiple meanings and existed in multiple contexts. Twinam highlights the distinction between "Hispanic traditions" and American "variants." Venezuela, a major beneficiary of the expanding Atlantic economy, had come to rely on African slavery more than any other region in Spanish America. As in Brazil, this may have heightened awareness of racial boundaries. Venezuelan Creoles apparently came to regard slave descent as a permanent, indelible stain: admittance of pardos to elite institutions became, in their minds, simply intolerable. Facing such discrimination, pardo petitioners began to readjust their self-presentation. They drew increasing attention to color as a means of categorization and attempted to demonstrate that their families had experienced a genuine process of "whitening" over generations. Like the confraternity brothers of Minas Gerais, they downplayed their threat to the racial hierarchy, but through different means: instead of embracing a collective racial identity, they distanced themselves from other castas. They were exceptional rather than representative. Venezuelan elites were not mollified and consistently frustrated the mobility even of successful petitioners. Unsurprisingly, the *obedezco pero no cumplo* formula triumphed. Royal decrees were filtered through bureaucrats on the ground; in the end, the most important negotiations over racial identity took place within the colonies.

Officials in Spain could believe that "the king counts more than blood" and change the racial label of a transatlantic subject by fiat. But American Spaniards could not afford to be cavalier about the social categorization that underwrote their dominance. The colonial distribution of power—in Cynthia Radding's words, the "stark inequalities of entitlement and privilege"—depended on a clear distinction between victors and vanquished, rulers and ruled, superiors and inferiors. We have already seen how

Spanish officials beat back the kurakas' desire to share governance of Peru. More generally, the "two republic" model attempted to cement the conquest dichotomy of Spaniard and Indian. Yet it soon ran aground on its own contradictions. As previously mentioned, colonization often had a destabilizing effect, even where the Spaniards' physical presence was comparatively weak. In the borderland regions studied by Radding, disease, exploitation, missionary efforts—and the population movements they prompted—fragmented native communities and reassembled them in novel configurations. When Spanish observers tried to apply fixed labels to this ever-shifting kaleidoscope, the mismatch between external categorization and internal subjectivity reached acute proportions. Official counts are at best misleading: "the same people may appear in different ethnic garments," or conversely, different people may receive the same ethnic designation. Even the most basic and supposedly unambiguous category—"Indian"—took on new, complex dimensions. In Sonora, parish priests differentiated between *indios de pueblo* and the oddly named *indios laboríos y otras castas*. Were the latter Indians or not? They might be glossed as "mestizos," but Radding argues that we are dealing less with ethnic or racial distinctions than with "class differences of locality and social status."

Frontiers are perhaps a special case; the fluidity that marked initial colonization elsewhere tended to persist for decades or centuries in the borderlands, where a weakened state had only a limited ability to reorganize social space. If nothing else, Indians could migrate beyond imperial boundaries. But as Jane E. Mangan demonstrates in her chapter, Spaniards did not completely control identity formation even in the indigenous heartland. Potosí saw the introduction of a market economy that transformed the social landscape and opened up new opportunities—including new ways to generate wealth—for some indigenous people. Most notably, indigenous women quickly moved into this emerging economic sector. At one level, this seems a natural development. "Native Andean items dominated the market" and female venders "worked hand in hand with the . . . kurakas" to funnel goods (such as coca) to indigenous consumers. By the 1570s, however, more individualized retailers, known as *regatones*, had arrived upon the scene. Spaniards always found the presence of "shameless" women in public venues troubling; among other things, they feared that social intercourse would lead to sexual misbehavior. The regatones, though, proved especially disturbing because of their aggressive and (in official eyes) antisocial behavior: they purchased goods and illegally resold them at higher prices.

What is striking here is the development of an identity largely based on a specific activity—marketing—rather than on overtly racial markers. Though condemned by the authorities, the regatones crafted a mode of being that transcended ethnic boundaries, for it attracted non-Indian women as well. Some mestizas began to adopt indigenous dress, consume indigenous foods, and even join indigenous confraternities. They became "mestizas en habito de india," seemingly embracing downward ethnic mobility. But while this label expressed Spanish concern, it probably had little negative impact on those so designated. Immersion in the indigenous social and cultural milieu may indeed have proved beneficial, giving them the connections and know-how to become successful traders. Thus, the market environment which the Spaniards engendered helped to create new social categories that defied the logic of Hispanic "racial thinking."

Mangan shows that Spanish observers often used material culture as a stand-in for "racial" difference. They distinguished, for example, between "Spanish" and "Indian" dress (even though the latter, toward the end of the sixteenth century, had incorporated many European elements). David Tavárez also sees "visual and contextual readings" as a key method for ascribing ethnic identity, while adding two others: institutional adjudications and personal strategizing. However, his main point is that caste labels such as "mestizo" or "mulatto," however defined, failed to capture the self-identity of subalterns. Tavárez draws upon three Inquisition cases from seventeenth-century Mexico in which accused "castas" claimed to be "Indians" (evidently to escape the Inquisition's jurisdiction). In all three instances, investigations to determine the defendants' "true" status confronted confusing and contradictory evidence. Comparing personal traits, parish records, and the testimony of neighbors and acquaintances yielded no consensus. How should we understand this failure? Tavárez acknowledges the now standard view that plebeians had ambiguous, fragmentary, and easily manipulated identities but goes beyond this to suggest that racial labels may simply not have possessed much significance in their lives: "daily survival was not directly tied to one's public casta identification." Their self-declarations occurred in a coercive context. Just as, in physics, experimental design determines whether electrons register as waves or particles, so the defendants' confrontation with the Inquisition forced them to choose a single label, to make a "public or legal pronouncement that clarified" their status. The Inquisition itself seemed to recognize the limitations of its methods; unable to categorize the accused securely, the tribunal dropped all three inquiries.

The instability of colonial identities also extended to the "Spanish" classification. Over time, differences emerged between Spaniards from the homeland (*peninsulares*) and those born and raised in the New World (Creoles). The peninsulares generally read Creole distinctiveness as inferiority. They decried the Creoles' suspect racial background, intellectual and moral shallowness, ostentation in dress and speech, avid consumption of pernicious American products (such as tobacco and chocolate), and immodest sexual behavior.[14] In the eighteenth century, criollo pretensions to rule over castas and Indians came under increasing fire. Spain's Bourbon dynasty launched an interventionist campaign to reassert royal authority in the colonies. This went much further than the controversial whitening of a few pardos. The Crown systematically sought to undermine competing power holders, including the Church and the Creole aristocracy.

Sergio Serulinkov's chapter shows how imperial politics—that is, short-term policies and events, as opposed to structural forces—could rapidly alter social identities. In late eighteenth-century La Plata (modern-day Sucre), relations between city residents and the colonial state became increasingly problematic. Higher taxes certainly played a role, though mainly as one aspect of a larger pattern: the Crown's apparent disregard for traditional rights and privileges. The townspeople had shed their blood defending La Plata against the massive indigenous uprising of 1780–81; royal officials, instead of rewarding them, installed Spanish soldiers and disbanded the heroic local militia. The soldiers' violence and sexual abuses made them seem like "an occupation army, governed by rules of behavior and legal privileges of their own." An infuriated populace struck back by rioting. Although these *tumultos* targeted soldiers, they had a broader "native son" flavor that caused frightened peninsulares to seek refuge in city churches. In the aftermath, Creole elites lent no support to the armed representatives of royal authority. They admitted the rioters had been misguided but they respected their desire for "justice" and refused to single out anyone for prosecution. The cabildos abiertos they summoned only reaffirmed the city's solidarity, effectively setting it in opposition to the colonial government. Political events had shattered the social hierarchy by breaking open the ethnic category at the top: "Spaniards." An unmistakable rift opened up between peninsulares and Creoles; the latter, glossing over both racial and class boundaries, forged an alliance with the castas. The city itself would now become the focus of collective identity. As Serulinkov points out, this collapse of the *sistema de castas* could occur because urban residents came to define themselves against both the Indians, the traditional "other," and the colonial state that had humiliated the Creole patricians, rubbing their noses in their inferiority as colonials.

La Plata's short-lived interethnic coalition foreshadowed independence-era alliances, as Creoles like Bolívar recruited people of color into revolutionary armies. In Mexico, an agreement between the Creole general Agustín de Iturbide and the casta insurgent Vicente Guerrero unified anti-royal forces and doomed Spanish rule. The new country's triumphant leaders then took the next logical step: under the influence of liberal and nationalist ideologies, they abolished racial labels altogether. From this point on, all the land's inhabitants would be "Mexicans." Like the Bourbons before them, liberals in Mexico and elsewhere would show special interest in assimilating the (former) Indians into the national mainstream. The complex interplay between liberalism and the "Indian problem" has been a central feature of politics in Mesoamerica and the Andes ever since. Karen Caplan's chapter discusses the beginning of this process, focusing on the contrasting outcomes in two Mexican states: Oaxaca and Yucatán.

The national government could not, of course, eliminate Mexico's colonial heritage in one fell swoop; instead, liberals envisioned a more gradual transition. They continued to recognize the distinctiveness of Indian communities but incorporated them through the concept Caplan refers to as "indigenous citizenship." She remarks that "indigenous people had, in theory, all the rights of any citizen . . . But alongside this . . . was a set of assumptions about them *as indigenous*" that affected the privileges they received. Indians could potentially have the best of both worlds, invoking their rights as active citizens while retaining some of their special, protected colonial status. However, their success in asserting this dual identity, and in pressing their claims, largely depended on local power configurations. Indigenous/state relations differed sharply in Oaxaca and Yucatán. Simply put, Oaxacan leaders had economic incentives to preserve the autonomy of indigenous pueblos, whereas in Yucatán, Creole elites foresaw great benefits in a more intense exploitation of Maya land and labor. Therefore, a modus vivendi soon emerged in Oaxaca that reconciled indigenous traditions with liberalism. Even after a centralist government achieved power, indigenous leaders gained appointments as justice of the peace, the key political post at the community level, and they maintained a collaborative style of governance that stretched back to the colonial epoch. By contrast, the Yucatecan Maya lacked economic leverage, so government officials had less reason for good will, tolerance, and negotiation. The indigenous/state compact ruptured, resulting in a bitter and bloody caste war.

The essays in this collection range over two continents and more than three hundred years and focus on many different social actors, from Andean lords to marginalized castas, from Creole elites to pardo slaves. One of the fascinating aspects of the colonial encounter is that the confluence of Europeans, Indians, and Africans created new peoples and a new sociocultural environment. Yet we can no longer view mestizaje as a mechanism that more or less automatically generated novel racial identities—the view enshrined in eighteenth-century casta paintings, where a Spaniard and an Indian produce a mestizo, a Spaniard and a mestizo a castizo, and so on.[15] All the authors present racial and ethnic classifications as highly problematic and variable, rather than as relatively stable categories of belonging. The persistence of specific racial labels masked the underlying dynamism of identity formation in colonial Latin America. Subalterns constantly negotiated their status with the representatives of the state: inquisitors, judges, corregidores, governors, and even the monarch. The very complexity of imperial governance allowed for multiple sites of contention and manipulation. Of course, colonials could seldom afford (and may rarely have wished) to mount open challenges to royal authority or dominant ideologies, such as patriarchy. Yet they could still pursue their own agendas. Our authors build upon a generation of "history from the bottom up," but they avoid reducing "agency" to "resistance." Indeed, perhaps the most common strategy described in this volume consisted of creative adaptation. Andean kurakas forging a hybrid model of legitimate rule; cobreros claiming a pueblo and a patria; mestizas turning into regatones to inhabit an indigenous economic niche; castas taking on diffuse and slippery cultural markers; Creole elites rejecting alliances with peninsulares—all these people drew upon, reinterpreted, or subverted colonial categories to carve out more satisfactory identities for themselves. The essays document this creativity while also situating it within the limitations imposed by colonial oppression. Along the way, they bring their protagonists vividly to life, as individuals and small groups, caught at moments of self-definition, struggling with difficult choices. As such, they help us see how imperial subjects understood and experienced their world.

*Notes*

1. Archivo General de las Indias (Seville), México, legajo 673, January 14, 1719.

2. Ibid., July 1, 1722.

3. Ibid., October 17, 1721.

4. See Hu-DeHart, *Missionaries, Miners, and Indians*.

5. Lewis, *Hall of Mirrors*, 23–24.

6. See, for example, Archivo del Ex-Ayuntamiento de la Ciudad de México, Rastros y Mercados, vol. 3728, exp. 6.

7. Quoted in Carrera, *Imagining Identity in New Spain*, 14.

8. Bennett, *Africans in Colonial Mexico*, 82.

9. Silverblatt, *Modern Inquisitions*.

10. For the "shrinking web" of Andean social relations, see Spalding, *Huarochirí*, 168–208. For the "failed partnership" between Maya elites and the colonial state in Yucatán, see Farriss, *Maya Society under Colonial Rule*, 96–103.

11. This has been clearly established by James Lockhart and his students. See, for example, Lockhart, *The Nahuas after the Conquest*, 8.

12. Annis, *God and Production in a Guatemalan Town*, 118–20.

13. Cope, *The Limits of Racial Domination*, 83–84.

14. On the relationship between Creoles and peninsulares in Spanish America, see Pagden, "Identity Formation in Spanish America."

15. For the most detailed and sophisticated treatment of this genre, see Katzew, *Casta Paintings*.

# Bibliography

Abercrombie, Thomas A. "La perpetuidad traducida: Del 'debate' de la perpetuidad a Taqui Oncoy y un movimiento comunero peruano." In *Incas e indios cristianos: Elites indígenas e identidades cristianas en los Andes coloniales*, edited by Jean-Jacques Decoster. Cuzco: Centro de Estudios Regionales Andinos Bartolemé de Las Casas, 2002.

Adorno, Rolena. *Guaman Poma: Writing and Resistance in Colonial Peru*. Austin: University of Texas Press, 1986.

Aguiar, Marcos Magalhães de. "A Evolução da vida associativa em minas colonial e a cociabilidade confrarial negra." *Anais da Sociedade Brasileira de Pesquisa Histórica* 21 (2002): 225–36.

Aguirre Beltrán, Gonzalo. *Cuijla: Esbozo etnográfico de un pueblo negro*. 2nd ed. Mexico City: Fondo de Cultura Económica, 1989.

———. *La población negra de México: Estudio etnohistórico*. 2nd ed. Mexico City: Fondo de Cultura Económica, 1972 [1946].

Almeida, Angela Mendes de. *O gosto do pecado: Casamento e sexualidade nos manuais de confessores dos séculos XVI e XVII*. Rio de Janeiro: Editora Rocco, 1992.

Althouse, Aaron. "Contested Mestizos, Alleged Mulattos: Racial Identity and Caste Hierarchy in Eighteenth-Century Pátzcuaro, Mexico." *The Americas* 62, no. 2 (2005): 151–75.

Amit, Vered. "An Anthropology without Community?" In *The Trouble with Community: Anthropological Reflections on Movement, Identity, and Collectivity*, edited by Vered Amit and Nigel Rappaport. London: Pluto Press, 2002.

Anderson, Perry. *Lineages of the Absolutist State*. London: NLB, 1974.

Anderson, Rodney. "Race and Social Stratification: A Comparison of Working Class Spaniards, Indians and Castas in Guadalajara, Mexico in 1821." *Hispanic American Historical Review* 68, no. 2 (1988): 209–43.

Andrews, George Reid. *Afro-Latin America, 1800–2000*. Oxford: Oxford University Press, 2004.

Andrien, Kenneth J., and Rolena Adorno, eds. *Transatlantic Encounters: Europeans and Andeans in the Sixteenth Century*. Berkeley: University of California Press, 1991.

Annino, Antonio. "Cádiz y la revolución territorial de los pueblos mexicanos, 1812–1821." In *Historia de las elecciones en Iberoamérica, siglo xix: De la formación del espacio político nacional*, edited by Antonio Annino. Mexico City: Fondo de Cultura Económica, 1995.

——. "Ciudadanía 'versus' gobernabilidad republicana en México: Las orígenes de un dilema." In *Ciudadanía política y formación de las naciones: Perspectivas históricas de América Latina*, edited by Hilda Sabato. Mexico City: El Colegio de Mexico, Fideicomiso Historia de las Américas, and Fondo de Cultura Económica, 1999.

Annis, Sheldon. *God and Production in a Guatemalan Town*. Austin: University of Texas Press, 1987.

Antonil, André João. *Cultura e opulência do Brazil por suas drogas e minas*. São Paulo: Editora Itatiaia, 1982.

Archer, Christon I. *The Army in Bourbon Mexico, 1760–1810*. Albuquerque: University of New Mexico Press, 1977.

Ares Queija, Berta. "Mestizos en hábito de indios: ¿Estrategias transgresoras o identidades difusas?" In *Passar as fronteiras: Actas do ii Colóquio Internacional sobre mediadores culturais séculos xv a xviii (Lagos-Outubro 1997)*, edited by Rui Manuel Loureiro and Serge Gruzinski. Lagos: Centro de Estudos Gil Eanes, 1999.

Arrom, Silvia Marina. "Introduction: Rethinking Urban Politics in Latin America before the Populist Era." In *Riots in the Cities: Popular Politics and the Urban Poor in Latin America, 1765–1910*, edited by Silvia Mariana Arrom and Servando Ortoll. Wilmington, Del.: SR Books, 1996.

Arzáns de Orsúa y Vela, Bartolomé. *Historia de la Villa Imperial de Potosí*, edited by Lewis Hanke y Gunnar Mendoza. 3 vols. Providence, R.I.: Brown University Press, 1965.

Assadourian, Carlos Sempat. " 'La gran vejación y destruición de la tierra': Las guerras de sucesión y de conquista en el derrumbe de la población indígena del Perú." In *Transiciones hacia el sistema colonial andino*. Lima: Instituto de Estudios Peruanos, 1994.

——. "Los señores étnicos y los corregidores de indios en la conformación del Estado colonial." In *Transiciones hacia el sistema colonial andino*.

Aubert, Guillaume. " 'The Blood of France': Race and Purity of Blood in the French Atlantic World." *William and Mary Quarterly* 61, no. 3 (2004): 439–78.

Áznar Pérez, Alonso, ed. *Colección de leyes, decretos, órdenes, o acuerdos de tendencia general del poder legislativo del estado libre de Yucatán*. 3 vols. Mérida: Imprenta del Editor, 1849–51.

Bakewell, Peter. *Miners of the Red Mountain: Indian Labor in Potosí, 1545–1650*. Albuquerque: University of New Mexico Press, 1984.

Balibar, Etienne, and Immanuel Wallerstein. *Race, Nation, Class: Ambiguous Identities*. London: Verso, 1991.

Bandera, Damián de la. "Relacion general de la disposición y calidad de la provincia de Guamanga . . . [1557]." In *Relaciones geográficas de Indias, Perú*, vol. 1, edited by Marcos Jiménez de la Espada. Madrid: Ministerio de Fomento, 1965.

Barbosa, Waldemar de Almeida. *Dicionário da terra e da gente de Minas*. Belo Horizonte: Arquivo Público Mineiro, 1985.

Barr, Juliana. *Peace Came in the Form of a Woman: Indians and Spaniards in the Texas Borderlands*. Chapel Hill: University of North Carolina Press, 2007.

Barragán Romano, Rossana. "¿Indios de arco y flecha? Entre la historia y la arqueología de las poblaciones del norte de Chuquisaca (siglos XV–XVI)*. Sucre: Antropólogos del Surandino, Inter-American Foundation, 1994.

Barth, Fredrik. "Boundaries and Connections." In *Signifying Identities: Anthropological Perspectives on Boundaries and Contested Values*, edited by Anthony P. Cohen. London: Routledge, 2000.

———. "Enduring and Emerging Issues in the Analysis of Ethnicity." In *The Anthropology of Ethnicity: Beyond "Ethnic Groups and Boundaries,"* edited by Hans Vermeulen and Cora Govers. Amsterdam: Het Spinhuis, 1994.

———. Introduction. In *Ethnic Groups and Boundaries: The Social Organization of Cultural Difference*, edited by Fredrik Barth. Boston: Little, Brown, 1969.

Behar, Ruth. "Sexual Witchcraft, Colonialism, and Women's Powers: Views from the Mexican Inquisition." In *Sexuality and Marriage in Colonial Latin America*, edited by Asunción Lavrin. Lincoln: University of Nebraska Press, 1989.

Bendle, M. F. "The Crisis of 'Identity' in High Modernity." *British Journal of Sociology* 53, no. 1 (2002): 1–18.

Bennett, Herman L. *Africans in Colonial Mexico: Absolutism, Christianity, and Afro-Creole Consciousness, 1570–1640*. Bloomington: Indiana University Press, 2003.

———. "Lovers, Family and Friends: The Formation of Afro-Mexico, 1580–1810." Ph.D. dissertation, Duke University, 1993.

Bergad, Laird. *Slavery and the Demographic and Economic History of Minas Gerais, Brazil, 1720–1888*. New York: Cambridge University Press, 1999.

Bhabha, Homi K. *The Location of Culture*. New York: Routledge, 1994.

Bicalho, Maria Fernanda. *A cidade e o império: O Rio de Janeiro no século XVIII*. Rio de Janeiro: Civilização Brasileira, 2003.

Biernacki, Richard. *The Fabrication of Labor: Germany and Britain, 1640–1914*. Berkeley: University of California Press, 1995.

Bonfil Batalla, Guillermo. *México Profundo: Reclaiming a Civilization*. Translated by Philip A. Dennis. Austin: University of Texas Press, 1996.

Borges, Célia Maia. *Escravos e libertos nas Irmandades do Rosário: Devoção e solidariedade em Minas Gerais, séculos XVIII e XIX*. Juiz de Fora: Editora UFJF, 2005.

Boschi, Caio César. *Os leigos e o poder: Irmandades leigas e política colonizadora em Minas Gerais*. São Paulo: Editora Ática, 1986.

Bourdieu, Pierre. *The Logic of Practice*. Translated by Richard Nice. Stanford, Calif.: Stanford University Press, 1990.

———. *Outline of a Theory of Practice*. Translated by Richard Nice. New York: Cambridge University Press, 1977.

Boxer, Charles C. R. *The Golden Age of Brazil, 1695–1750: Growing Pains of a Colonial Society*. Berkeley: University of California Press, 1962.

———. *The Portuguese Seaborne Empire, 1415–1825.* New York: A. A. Knopf, 1969.

Boyer, Richard E. *Lives of the Bigamists: Marriage, Family and Community in Colonial Mexico.* Albuquerque: University of New Mexico Press, 1995.

———. "Negotiating *Calidad:* The Everyday Struggle for Status in Mexico." *Historical Archaeology* 31, no. 1 (1997): 64–73.

Brading, David A. *Miners and Merchants in Bourbon Mexico, 1763–1810.* New York: Cambridge University Press, 1971.

Bridikhina, Eugenia. "Los honores en disputa: La identidad corporativa de la elite administrativa colonial charqueña (siglos XVII–XVIII)." Paper presented at the Sexto Congreso Internacional de Etnohistoria, Buenos Aires, November 22–25, 2005.

———. *Sin temor a Dios ni a la justicia real: Control social en Charcas a fines del siglo XVIII.* La Paz: Instituto de Estudios Bolivianos, 2000.

Brooks, James F. *Captives and Cousins: Slavery, Kinship and Community in the Southwest Borderlands.* Chapel Hill: University of North Carolina Press, 2002.

Brubaker, Rogers, and Frederick Cooper. "Beyond 'Identity.'" *Theory and Society* 29, no. 1 (2000): 1–47.

Brubaker, Rogers, Mara Loveman, and Peter Stamatov. "Ethnicity as Cognition." *Theory and Society* 33, no. 1 (2004): 31–64.

Bucholtz, Mary. "From Mulatta to Mestiza: Passing and the Linguistic Reshaping of Ethnic Identity." In *Gender Articulated: Language and the Socially Constructed Self*, edited by Kira Hall and Mary Bucholtz. New York: Routledge, 1995.

Burns, Kathryn. "Gender and the Politics of Mestizaje: The Convent of Santa Clara in Cuzco, Peru." *Hispanic American Historical Review* 78, no. 1 (1998): 5–44.

Caballero, Lucas. *Relación de las costumbres y religión de los indios manasicas.* Edited by Manuel Serrano Sanz. Madrid: Librería General de V. Suárez, 1933 [1706].

Cahill, David. "Colour by Numbers: Racial and Ethnic Categories in the Viceroyalty of Peru, 1532–1821." *Journal of Latin American Studies* 26, no. 2 (1994): 325–46.

———. "The Long Conquest: Collaboration by Native Andean Elites in the Colonial System, 1532–1825." In *Technology, Disease and Colonial Conquests, Sixteenth to Eighteenth Centuries: Essays Reappraising the Guns and Germs Theories*, edited by George Raudzens. Leiden: Brill, 2001.

———. "Taxonomy of a Colonial 'Riot': The Arequipa Disturbances of 1780." In *Reform and Insurrection in Bourbon New Granada and Peru*, edited by John Fisher, Allan Kuethe, and Anthonly McFarlane. Baton Rouge: Louisiana State University Press, 1990.

Cajías de la Vega, Fernando. *Oruro 1781: Sublevación de indios y rebelión criolla.* 2 vols. La Paz: CEPA, 2005.

Campbell, Leon. *The Military and Society in Colonial Peru, 1750–1810.* Philadelphia: American Philosophical Society, 1978.

Cañizares-Esguerra, Jorge. *How to Write the History of the New World: Histories, Epistemologies, and Identities in the Eighteenth-Century Atlantic World.* Stanford, Calif.: Stanford University Press, 2001.

Carrasco, Pedro. "Indian-Spanish Marriages in the First Century of the Colony." In *Indian Women of Early Mexico*, edited by Susan Schroeder, Stephanie Wood, and Robert Haskett. Norman: University of Oklahoma Press, 1997.

Carrera, Magali Marie. *Imagining Identity in New Spain: Race, Lineage and the Colonial Body in Portraiture and Casta Paintings*. Austin: University of Texas Press, 2003.

Carrera Andrade, Jorge. *Galeria de místicos e insurgentes: La vida intelectual del Ecuador durante cuatro siglos (1555–1955)*. Quito: Casa de la Cultura Ecuatoriana, 1959.

Carroll, Patrick. *Blacks in Colonial Veracruz: Race, Ethnicity and Regional Development*. Austin: University of Texas Press, 1991.

Cassidy, Thomas J. "Las haciendas oaxaqueñas en el siglo xix." In *Lecturas históricas del estado de Oaxaca*, vol. 3, *Siglo xix*, edited by María de los Ángeles Romero Frizzi. Mexico City: Instituto Nacional de Antropología é Historia and Gobierno del Estado de Oaxaca, 1990.

Castro, Concepción de. *La revolución liberal y los municipios españoles*. Madrid: Alianza Editorial, 1979.

Chamberlain, Robert S. "The Concept of the 'Señor Natural' as Revealed by Castilian Law and Administrative Documents." *Hispanic American Historical Review* 19, no. 2 (1939): 130–37.

Chambers, Sarah C. *From Subjects to Citizens: Honor, Gender and Politics in Arequipa, Peru, 1780–1854*. University Park: Pennsylvania State University Press, 1999.

Chance, John K. *Conquest of the Sierra: Spaniards and Indians in Colonial Oaxaca*. Norman: University of Oklahoma Press, 1989.

——. *Race and Class in Colonial Oaxaca*. Stanford, Calif.: Stanford University Press, 1978.

Chance, John K., and William B. Taylor. "Estate and Class: A Reply." *Comparative Studies in Society and History* 21, no. 3 (1979): 434–42.

——. "Estate and Class in a Colonial City: Oaxaca in 1792." *Comparative Studies in Society and History* 19, no. 4 (1977): 454–87.

Chassen-López, Francie R. *From Liberal to Revolutionary Oaxaca: The View from the South: Mexico 1867–1911*. University Park: Pennsylvania State University Press, 2004.

Chaves, Cláudia Maria das Graças. *Perfeitos negociantes: Mercadores das minas setecentistas*. São Paulo: Annablume, 1999.

Childs, Matt. *The 1812 Aponte Rebellion in Cuba and the Struggle against Atlantic Slavery*. Chapel Hill: University of North Carolina Press, 2006.

Clark, Anna. "Manhood, Womanhood, and the Politics of Class in Britain, 1790–1845." In *Gender and Class in Modern Europe*, edited by Laura L. Frader and Sonya O. Rose. Ithaca, N.Y.: Cornell University Press, 1996.

Cleaton, Christin Ellen. "Caciques into Indios: The Spanish Imperial Project in the First Generation after Conquest." Ph.D. dissertation, suny Stony Brook, 2005.

Clendinnen, Inga. "'Fierce and Unnatural Cruelty': Cortés and the Conquest of Mexico." *Representations* 33 (1991): 65–100.

Cline, Howard F. "The 'Aurora Yucateca' and the Spirit of Enterprise in Yucatán." *Hispanic American Historical Review* 28, no. 1 (1948): 30–60.

Cohen, Anthony. *Self-Consciousness: An Alternative Anthropology of Identity*. New York: Routledge, 1994.

———. *The Symbolic Construction of Community*. New York: Routledge, 2000 [1985].

*Colección de documentos inéditos relativos al descubrimiento, conquista y colonización de las posesiones españolas en América y Oceanía, sacados en su mayor parte del Real Archivo de Indias*. 42 vols. Madrid: Impr. de M. Bernaldo de Quirós, 1864–89.

*Colección de leyes, decretos y órdenes del augusto congreso del estado libre de Yucatán*. 2 vols. Mérida: Tipografía de G. Canto, 1896.

*Colección de leyes y decretos del estado libre de Oaxaca*. Oaxaca: Imprenta del Estado en el Ex-Obispado, 1879.

Combès, Isabelle. *Ethno-Historias del Isoso: Chané y chiriguanos en el Chaco boliviano (siglos XVI al XX)*. La Paz: IFEA, PIEB, 2005.

Cope, R. Douglas. *The Limits of Racial Domination: Plebeian Society in Colonial Mexico City, 1660–1720*. Madison: University of Wisconsin Press, 1994.

Cornblit, Oscar. *Power and Violence in the Colonial City: Oruro from the Mining Renaissance to the Rebellion of Tupac Amaru (1740–1782)*. New York: Cambridge University Press, 1995.

Corrigan, Philip, and Derek Sayer. *The Great Arch: English State Formation as Cultural Revolution*. Oxford: Basil Blackwell, 1985.

Cosamalón Aguilar, Jesús. *Indios detrás de la muralla: Matrimonios indígenas y convivencia inter-racial en Santa Ana (Lima, 1795–1820)*. Lima: Pontificia Universidad Católica del Perú, 1999.

Costa, Iraci del Nero da, and Francisco Vidal Luna. *Minas colonial: Economia e sociedade*. São Paulo: Livraria Pioneira Editora, 1973.

Cotta, Francis Albert. "Para além da desclassificação e da docilização dos corpos: Organização militar nas Minas Gerais do século XVIII." *Mneme: Revista de Humanidades* 2, no. 3 (2001), http://www.cerescaico.ufrn.br.

Cramaussel, Chantal. "De como los españoles clasificaban a los indios: Naciones y encomiendas en la Nueva Vizcaya Central." In *Nómadas y sedentarios en el norte de México: Homenaje a Beatriz Braniff*, edited by Marie-Areti Hers, José Luis Mirafuentes, and María de los Dolores Soto. Mexico City: Universidad Nacional Autonónoma de México, 2000.

———. *Poblar la frontera: La provincia de Santa Bárbara en Nueva Vizcaya durante los siglos XVI y XVII*. Zamora: El Colegio de Michoacán, 2006.

Cuello, José. "Racialized Hierarchies of Power in Colonial Mexican Society: The *sistema de castas* as a Form of Social Control in Saltillo." In *Choice, Persuasion, and Coercion. Social Control on Spain's North American Frontiers*, edited by Jesús F. de la Teja and Ross Frank. Albuquerque: University of New Mexico Press, 2005.

Cunniff, Roger. "Mexican Municipal Electoral Reform, 1810–1822." In *Mexico and the Spanish Cortes, 1810–1822: Eight Essays*, edited by Nettie Lee Benson. Austin: University of Texas Press, 1966.

Cutter, Charles R. *Protector de indios in Colonial New Mexico, 1659–1821.* Albuquerque: University of New Mexico Press, 1986.

D'Altroy, Terence N. "Transitions in Power: Centralization of Wanka Political Organization under Inka Rule." *Ethnohistory* 34, no. 1 (1987): 78–102.

Dantas, Mariana L. R. "Inheritance Practices among Individuals of African Origin and Descent in 18th-Century Minas Gerais, Brazil." In *The Faces of Freedom: The Manumission and Emancipation of Slaves in Old World and New World Slavery*, edited by Marc Kleijwegt. Leiden: Brill, 2006.

Davis, David Brion. *The Problem of Slavery in Western Culture.* Ithaca, N.Y.: Cornell University Press, 1966.

de Asúa, Miguel, and Roger French. *A New World of Animals: Early Modern Europeans on the Creatures of Iberian America.* Burlington, Vt.: Ashgate, 2005.

Dean, Carolyn. *Inka Bodies and the Body of Christ: Corpus Christi in Colonial Cusco, Peru.* Durham, N.C.: Duke University Press, 1999.

Deeds, Susan M. *Defiance and Deference in Mexico's Colonial North: Indians under Spanish Rule in Nueva Vizcaya.* Austin: University of Texas Press, 2003.

——. "Double Jeopardy: Indian Women in Jesuit Missions of Nueva Vizcaya." In *Indian Women of Early Mexico*, edited by Susan Schroeder, Stephanie Woods, and Robert Haskett. Norman: University of Oklahoma Press, 1997.

——. "Subverting the Social Order: Gender, Power, and Magic in Nueva Vizcaya." In *Choice, Persuasion, and Coercion: Social Control on Spain's North American Frontiers*, edited by Jesús F. de la Teja and Ross Frank. Albuquerque: University of New Mexico Press, 2005.

Degler, Carl N. *Neither Black nor White: Slavery and Race Relations in Brazil and the United States.* New York: Macmillan, 1971.

Dehouve, Danièle. "The 'Secession' of Villages in the Jurisdiction of Tlapa (Eighteenth Century)." In *The Indian Community of Colonial Mexico: Fifteen Essays on Land Tenure, Corporate Organizations, Ideology and Village Politics*, edited by Arij Ouweneel and Simon Miller. Amsterdam: CEDLA, 1990.

Demélas, Marie-Danielle, and Yves Saint-Geours. *Jerusalén y Babilonia: Religión y política en el Ecuador, 1780–1880.* Quito: Corporación Editora Nacional, 1988.

"Descripción de la villa y minas de Potosí: Año de 1603." In *Relaciones geográficas de indias: Peru*, edited by Marcos Jiménez de la Espada and José Urbano Martínez Carreras. Vols. 183–185 of *Biblioteca de autores españoles desde la formación del lenguaje hasta nuestros días*. Madrid: Ediciones Atlas, 1965.

Díaz, María Elena. "Freedom in the (Tropical) Hearth: El Cobre, 1709–1773." In *Beyond Bondage: Free Women of Color in the Americas*, edited by David Barry Gaspar and Darlene Clark Hine. Urbana: University of Illinois Press, 2004.

——. "Mining Women, Royal Slaves: Copper Mining in Colonial Cuba, 1670–1780." In *Mining Women: Gender in the Development of a Global Industry, 1700–2000*, edited by Laurie Mercier and Jaclyn Viskovatoff. New York: Palgrave Macmillan, 2006.

——. "Rethinking Tradition and Identity: The Virgin of Charity of El Cobre." In *Cuba,* the Elusive Nation: Interpretations of National Identity, edited by Damián J. Fernandez and Madeline Cámara Betancourt. Gainesville: University of Florida Press, 2000.

———. *The Virgin, the King and the Royal Slaves of El Cobre: Negotiating Freedom in Colonial Cuba, 1670–1780*. Stanford, Calif.: Stanford University Press, 2000.

Díaz Rementería, Carlos J. *El cacique en el virreinato del Perú: Estudio histórico-jurídico.* Seville: Universidad de Sevilla, Departamento de Antropología y Etnología de América, 1977.

Diez de San Miguel, Garci. *Visita hecha a la provincia de Chucuito por Garci Díez de San Miguel en el año 1567.* Lima: Casa de la Cultura, 1964.

Di Meglio, Gabriel. "Un nuevo actor para un nuevo escenario: La participación política de la plebe urbana de Buenos Aires en la década de la Revolución (1810–1820)." *Boletín del Instituto de Historia Argentina y Americana "Dr. Emilio Ravignani"* 24 (2001): 7–42.

Dobyns, Henry F., Paul H. Ezell, Alden W. Jones, and Greta S. Ezell. "What Were Nixoras?" *Southwestern Journal of Anthropology* 16, no. 2 (1960): 230–68.

Dublán, Manuel, and José María Lozano, eds. *Legislación mexicana, ó colección completa de las disposiciones expedidas desde la independencia de la república.* 34 vols. Mexico City: Imprenta del Comercio, á Cargo de Dublán y Lozano, Hijos, 1876–1904.

Dupeyron, Guy Rozat. *Indios imaginarios e indios reales en los relatos de la conquista de México.* Mexico: Tava Editorial, 1993.

Dym, Jordana. " 'Our Pueblos, Fractions with No Central Unity': Municipal Sovereignty in Central America, 1808–1821." *Hispanic American Historical Review* 86, no. 3 (2006): 432–66.

Earle, Timothy K. *How Chiefs Come to Power: The Political Economy in Prehistory.* Stanford, Calif.: Stanford University Press, 1997.

Elkins, Stanley. *Slavery: A Problem in American Institutional and Intellectual Life.* Chicago: University of Chicago Press, 1959.

Eltis, David. *The Rise of African Slavery in the Americas.* New York: Cambridge University Press, 2000.

Escobari de Querejazu, Laura. "Conformación urbana y étnica en las ciudades de La Paz y Potosí durante la colonia." *Historia y Cultura* 18 (1990): 43–77.

Espinoza Soriano, Waldemar. "El memorial de Charcas: 'Crónica' inédita de 1582." *Cantuta, Revista de la Universidad Nacional de Educación* (1969): 117–52.

———. "Los huancas, aliados de la conquista: Tres informaciones inéditas sobre la participación indígena en la conquista del Perú." *Anales Científicos de la Universidad Nacional del Centro del Perú* 1 (1972): 9–407.

———. "Reducciones, pueblos, y ciudades." In *Pueblos y culturas de la Sierra Central del Perú*, edited by Duccio Bonavia and Rogger Ravines. Lima: Cerro Pasco, 1972.

Estenssoro Fuchs, Juan Carlos. "La plebe ilustrada: El pueblo en las fronteras de la razón." In *Entre la retórica y la insurgencia: Las ideas y los movimientos sociales en los Andes, Siglo XVIII*, edited by Charles Walker. Cuzco: Centro de Estudios Regionales Andinos Bartolomé de las Casas, 1995.

Faria, Sheila de Castro. *A colônia em movimento: Fortuna e família no cotidiano colonials.* Rio de Janeiro: Editora Nova Fronteira, 1998.

Farriss, Nancy M. *Maya Society under Colonial Rule: The Collective Enterprise of Survival.* Princeton, N.J.: Princeton University Press, 1984.

Fernández de Palencia, Diego. *Primera y segunda parte de la historia del Peru.* Edited by Juan Pérez de Tudela Bueso. Vols. 164–65 of *Biblioteca de autores españoles desde la formación del lenguaje hasta nuestros días.* Madrid: Ediciones Atlas, 1963 [1571].

Ferrer, Ada. *Insurgent Cuba.* Chapel Hill: University of North Carolina Press, 1999.

Few, Martha. *Women Who Lead Evil Lives: Gender, Religion and the Politics of Power in Colonial Guatemala.* Austin: University of Texas Press, 2002.

Fields, Barbara J. "Whiteness, Racism, and Identity." *International Labor and Working-Class History* 60, no. 1 (2001): 48–56.

Figueiredo, Luciano R. A. *O avesso da memória: Cotidiano e trabalho da mulher em Minas Gerais no século XVIII.* Rio de Janeiro: José Olympio, 1993.

———. *Barrocas famílias: Vida familiar em Minas Gerais no século XVIII.* São Paulo: Hucitec, 1997.

———, ed. *Códice Costa Matoso.* Belo Horizonte: Fundação João Pinheiro, Centro de Estudos Históricos e Culturais, 1999.

Fischer, Sibylle. *Modernity Disavowed: Haiti and the Cultures of Slavery in the Age of Revolution.* Durham, N.C.: Duke University Press, 2004.

Flint, Valerie I. J. *The Imaginative Landscape of Christopher Columbus.* Princeton, N.J.: Princeton University Press, 1992.

Florentino, Manolo. *Em costas negras: Uma história do tráfico de escravos entre a África e o Rio de Janeiro.* São Paulo: Cia. das Letras, 1997.

Flores Galindo, Alberto. *Aristocracia y plebe: Lima 1760–1830 (estructura de clases y sociedad colonial).* Lima: Mosca Azul Editores, 1984.

Fragoso, João Luis. *Homens de grossa aventura: Acumulação e hierarquia na praça mercantil do Rio de Janeiro.* São Paulo: Civilização Brasileira, 1998.

Frazier, E. Franklin. *The Negro Family in the United States.* Chicago: University of Chicago Press, 1939.

Freyre, Gilberto. *The Masters and the Slaves.* Translated by Samuel Putnam. New York: A. A. Knopf, 1946.

Furtado, Júnia Ferreira. *Chica da Silva e o contratador dos diamantes: O outro lado do mito.* São Paulo: Companhia das Letras, 2003.

———. *Homens de negócio: A interiorização da metrópole e do comércio nas minas setecentistas.* São Paulo: Hucitec, 1999.

Ganson, Barbara. *The Guaraní under Spanish Rule in the Río de la Plata.* Stanford, Calif.: Stanford University Press, 2003.

Gantier Valda, Joaquín. *Juan José de Segovia.* Sucre: Banco Nacional de Bolivia, 1989.

García Canclini, Néstor. *Consumers and Citizens: Globalization and Multicultural Conflicts.* Translated by George Yúdice. Minneapolis: University of Minnesota Press, 2001.

————. *Hybrid Cultures: Strategies for Entering and Leaving Modernity.* Translated by Christopher L. Chiappari and Silvia L. López. Minneapolis: University of Minnesota Press, 1995.

García Martínez, Bernardo. *Los pueblos de la Sierra de Puebla: El poder y el espacio entre los indios del norte de Puebla hasta 1700.* Mexico City: Colegio de México, 1987.

García Recio, José María. *Análisis de una sociedad de frontera, Santa Cruz de la Sierra en los siglos XVI y XVII.* Seville: Diputación Provincial de Sevilla, 1988.

García Quintanilla, Alejandra. "En busca de la prosperidad y la riqueza: Yucatán a la hora de la independencia." In *Los lugares y los tiempos: Ensayos sobre las estructuras regionales del siglo XIX en México*, edited by Alejandra García Quintanilla and Abel Juárez. Mexico City: Editorial Nuestro Tiempo for COMESCO, Universidad Veracruzana, and Universidad Autónoma de Nuevo León, 1989.

Garcilaso de la Vega, El Inca. *Royal Commentaries of the Incas and General History of Peru.* Translated by Harold Livermore. 2 vols. Austin: University of Texas Press, 1966.

Garner, Paul H. *La Revolución en la provincia: Soberanía estatal y caudillismo en las montañas de Oaxaca (1910–1920).* Mexico City: Fondo de Cultura Económica, 1988.

Garrett, David Townsend. *Shadows of Empire: The Indian Nobility of Cusco, 1750–1825.* New York: Cambridge University Press, 2005.

Gauderman, Kim. *Women's Lives in Colonial Quito: Gender, Law, and Economy in Spanish America.* Austin: University of Texas Press, 2003.

Geertz, Clifford. *The Interpretation of Cultures.* New York: Basic Books, 1973.

Geggus, David P. *Haitian Revolutionary Studies.* Bloomington: Indiana University Press, 2002.

Gerhard, Peter. *A Guide to the Historical Geography of New Spain.* Rev. ed. Norman: University of Oklahoma Press, 1993.

Gibson, Charles. *The Aztecs under Spanish Rule: A History of the Indians of the Valley of Mexico, 1519–1810.* Stanford, Calif.: Stanford University Press, 1964.

Gibson, Charles, ed. *The Spanish Tradition in America.* New York: Harper and Row, 1968.

Giddens, Anthony. *Central Problems in Social Theory.* Berkeley: University of California Press, 1979.

————. *The Constitution of Society: Outline of the Theory of Structuration.* Berkeley: University of California Press, 1984.

Glave, Luis Miguel. *Trajinantes: Caminos indígenas en la sociedad colonial, siglos XVI–XVII.* Lima: Instituto de Apoyo Agrario, 1989.

Gleason, Philip. "Identifying Identity: A Semantic History." *Journal of American History* 69, no. 4 (1983): 910–31.

Goldschmidt, Eliana Maria Rea. *Casamentos mistos: Liberdade e escravidão em São Paulo colonial.* São Paulo: Annablume, 2004.

Goldwert, Marvin. "La lucha por la perpetuidad de las encomiendas en el Perú virreinal, 1550–1600." *Revista Histórica* 22–23 (1955–56, 1958–59): 350–60, 207–20.

Góngora, Mario. *El estado en el derecho indiano: Época de fundación (1492–1570).* Santiago: Universidad de Chile, Instituto de Investigaciones Historico-Culturales, 1951.

Gotkowitz, Laura. "Trading Insults: Honor, Violence, and the Gendered Culture of Commerce in Cochabamba, Bolivia, 1870s–1950s." *Hispanic American Historical Review* 83, no. 1 (2003): 83–118.

Gouvea, Maria de Fátima Silva. "Milícias." In *Dicionário do Brasil Colonial, 1500–1808*, compiled by Ronaldo Vainfas. Rio de Janeiro: Editora Objetiva, 2000.

Greenleaf, Richard E. "Historiography of the Mexican Inquisition: Evolution of Interpretations and Methodologies." In *Cultural Encounters: The Impact of the Inquisition in Spain and the New World*, edited by Mary Elizabeth Perry and Anne J. Cruz. Berkeley: University of California Press, 1991.

——. *Inquisición y sociedad en el México colonial*. Madrid: J. Porrúa Turanzas, 1985.

——. "The Inquisition and the Indians of New Spain: A Study in Jurisdictional Confusion." *The Americas* 22, no. 2 (1965): 138–66.

——. "The Mexican Inquisition and the Indians: Sources for the Ethnohistorian." *The Americas* 34, no. 3 (1978): 315–44.

——. *The Mexican Inquisition of the Sixteenth Century*. Albuquerque: University of New Mexico Press, 1969.

Grieco, Viviana L. "Politics and Public Credit: The Limits of Absolutism in Late Colonial Buenos Aires." Ph.D. dissertation, Emory University, 2005.

Gruzinski, Serge. *The Conquest of Mexico: The Incorporation of Indian Societies into the Western World, 16th–18th Centuries*. Translated by Eileen Corrigan. Cambridge, Mass.: Polity Press, 1993.

——. *Images at War: Mexico from Columbus to "Blade Runner" (1492–2019)*. Translated by Heather MacLean. Durham, N.C.: Duke University Press, 2001.

——. *L'Aigle et la sibylle: Fresques indiennes du Mexique*. Paris: Imprimerie Nationale, 1994.

——. *The Mestizo Mind: The Intellectual Dynamics of Colonization and Globalization*. Translated by Deke Dusinberre. New York: Routledge, 2002.

Guaman Poma de Ayala, Felipe. *Nueva corónica y buen gobierno*. Edited by John Murra and Rolena Adorno. Translated by Jorge Urioste. Mexico City: Siglo xxi, 1980.

Guardino, Peter. *Peasants, Politics, and the Formation of Mexico's National State: Guerrero, 1800–1857*. Stanford, Calif.: Stanford University Press, 1996.

——. *The Time of Liberty: Popular Political Culture in Oaxaca, 1750–1850*. Durham, N.C.: Duke University Press, 2005.

Guerra, Francois-Xavier. *Modernidad e independencias: Ensayos sobre las revoluciones hispánicas*. Madrid: Editorial MAPFRE, 1992.

——. "El soberano y su reino: Reflexiones sobre la génesis del ciudadano en América Latina." In *Ciudadanía política y formación de las naciones: Perspectivas históricas de América Latina*, edited by Hilda Sabato. Mexico City: El Colegio de México, Fideicomiso Historia de las Américas, Fondo de Cultura Económica, 1999.

Guevara Gil, Armando. "Los caciques y el señorío natural en los Andes coloniales (Perú, siglo xvi)." In *xiii Congreso del Instituto Internacional de Historia del Derecho Indiano 2*. San Juan: Asamblea Legislativa de Puerto Rico, 2003.

Guilarte, A. M. *El régimen señorial en el siglo XVI*. Valladolid: Universidad de Valladolid, 1962.

Gutiérrez, Ramón A. *When Jesus Came, the Corn Mothers Went Away: Marriage, Sexuality, and Power in New Mexico, 1500–1846*. Stanford, Calif.: Stanford University Press, 1991.

Guzmán y Polanco, Manuel de. "Un quiteño en el virreinato del Río de la Plata. Ignacio Flores, Presidente de la Audiencia de Charcas." *Boletín de la Academia Nacional de la Historia* 53 (1980): 159–83.

Hacking, Ian. *The Social Construction of What?* Cambridge, Mass.: Harvard University Press, 1999.

Hale, Charles R. "Does Multiculturalism Menace? Governance, Cultural Rights and the Politics of Identity in Guatemala." *Journal of Latin American Studies* 34, no. 3 (2002): 485–524.

Hamnett, Brian R. *Politics and Trade in Southern Mexico, 1750–1821*. New York: Cambridge University Press, 1971.

———. "Process and Pattern: A Re-examination of the Ibero-American Independence Movements, 1808–1826." *Journal of Latin American Studies* 29, no. 2 (1997): 279–328.

Hanke, Lewis. "Un festón de documentos lascasianos." *Revista Cubana* 16 (1941): 150–211.

Hardoy, Jorge Enrique. *Cartografía urbana colonial de América Latina y el Caribe*. Buenos Aires: Grupo Editor Latinoamericano, 1991.

Harris, Marvin. *Patterns of Race in the Americas*. New York: Walker, 1964.

Hartmann, Roswith. "Mercados y ferias prehispánicos en el area andina." *Boletín de la Academia Nacional de Historia (Quito)* 54, no. 118 (1971): 214–35.

Haskett, Robert. *Indigenous Rulers: An Ethnohistory of Town Government in Colonial Cuernavaca*. Albuquerque: University of New Mexico Press, 1991.

Hastorf, Christine Ann. "One Path to the Heights: Negotiating Political Inequality in the Sausa of Peru." In *The Evolution of Political Systems: Sociopolitics in Small-Scale Sedentary Societies*, edited by Steadman Upham. New York: Cambridge University Press, 1990.

Hastorf, Christine A., Timothy K. Earle, Herbert E. Wright Jr., Lisa LeCount, Glenn Russell, and Elise Sandefur. "Settlement Archaeology in the Jauja Region of Peru." *Andean Past* 2 (1989): 81–130.

Helg, Ailene. *Liberty and Equality in Caribbean Colombia*. Chapel Hill: University of North Carolina Press, 2004.

———. *Our Rightful Share: The Afro-Cuban Struggle for Equality, 1886–1912*. Chapel Hill: University of North Carolina Press, 1995.

Herskovitz, Melville Jean. *The Myth of the Negro Past*. New York: Harper and Brothers, 1941.

———. *The New World Negro: Selected Papers in Afroamerican Studies*. Bloomington: Indiana University Press, 1966.

Herskovitz, Melville Jean, and Frances S. Herskovitz. *Rebel Destiny: Among the Bush Negroes of Dutch Guiana*. New York: McGraw-Hill, 1934.

Herzog, Tamar. *Defining Nations: Immigrants and Citizens in Early Modern Spain and Spanish America*. New Haven, Conn.: Yale University Press, 2003.

——. "Private Organizations as Global Networks in Early Modern Spain and Spanish America." In *The Collective and the Public in Latin America: Cultural Identities and Political Order*, edited by Luis Roniger and Tamar Herzog. Portland, Ore: Sussex Academic Press, 2000.

——. "La vecindad: Entre condición formal y negociación continua. Reflexiones en torno a las categorías sociales y las redes personales." *Anuario del Instituto de Estudios Histórico-Sociales* 15 (2000): 123–31.

Higgins, Kathleen J. *"Licentious Liberty" in a Brazilian Gold-Mining Region: Slavery, Gender, and Social Control in Eighteenth-Century Sabará, Minas Gerais*. University Park: Pennsylvania State University Press, 1999.

Higgins, Nicholas P. *Understanding the Chiapas Rebellion: Modernist Visions and the Invisible Indian*. Austin: University of Texas Press, 2004.

Hoberman, Louisa Schell, and Susan Migden Socolow, eds. *Cities and Society in Colonial Latin America*. Albuquerque: University of New Mexico Press, 1986.

Holanda, Sérgio Buarque de. *História da civilização brasileira: A época colonial*. São Paulo: Difel, 1985.

Holstein, James A., and Jaber F. Gubrium. *The Self We Live By: Narrative Identity in a Postmodern World*. New York: Oxford University Press, 2000.

Hu-DeHart, Evelyn. *Missionaries, Miners, and Indians: Spanish Contact with the Yaqui Nation of Northwestern New Spain, 1533–1820*. Tucson: University of Arizona Press, 1981.

Hünefeldt, Christine. "El crecimiento de la ciudades: Culturas y sociedades urbanas en el siglo XVIII latinoamericano." In *Historia General de América Latina*, vol. 4. Edited by Enrique Tandeter. Madrid: Ediciones UNESCO/Editorial Trota, 2000.

Ibarra, Ana Carolina. *Clero y política en Oaxaca: Biografía del Doctor José de San Martín*. Serie Dishá. Oaxaca: Instituto Oaxaqueño de las Culturas, Universidad Nacional Autónoma de México, and Fondo Estatal para la Cultura y las Artes, 1996.

Israel, Jonathan. *Race, Class and Politics in Colonial Mexico, 1610—1670*. London: Oxford University Press, 1975.

Izquierdo Martín, Jesús. *El rostro de la comunidad: La identidad del campesino en la Castilla del Antiguo Régimen*. Madrid: Consejo Económico y Social, Comunidad de Madrid, 2001.

Jackson, Robert H. *Race, Caste, and Status: Indians in Colonial Spanish America*. Albuquerque: University of New Mexico Press, 1999.

Jackson, Robert H., and Erick Langer. *The New Latin American Mission History*. Lincoln: University of Nebraska Press, 1995.

Jaffary, Nora E., ed. *Gender, Race and Religion in the Colonization of the Americas*. Burlington, Vt.: Ashgate, 2007.

Jenkins, Richard. *Foundations of Sociology: Towards a Better Understanding of the Human World*. New York: Palgrave, 2002.

———. *Social Identity*. New York: Routledge, 2002.

Jiménez de la Espada, Marcos, ed. *Relaciones geográficas de Indias, Perú*. Vol. 183–85. Madrid: Ministerio de Fomento, 1965.

Johnson, H. B. "Portuguese Settlement, 1500–1580." In *Colonial Brazil*, edited by Leslie Bethel. New York: Cambridge University Press, 1987.

Johnson, Lyman L. "Dangerous Words, Provocative Gestures, and Violent Acts: The Disputed Hierarchies of Plebeian Life in Colonial Buenos Aires." In Johnson and Lipsett-Rivera, eds., *The Faces of Honor*.

Johnson, Lyman L., and Sonya Lipsett-Rivera, eds. *The Faces of Honor: Sex, Shame, and Violence in Colonial Latin America*. Albuquerque: University of New Mexico Press, 1998.

Jones, Kristine L. "Comparative Raiding Economies: North and South." In *Contested Ground: Comparative Frontiers on the Northern and Southern Edges of the Spanish Empire*, edited by Donna Guy and Thomas E. Sheridan. Tucson: University of Arizona Press, 1998.

Joseph, Gilbert M. "Rethinking Mexican Revolutionary Mobilization: Yucatán's Seasons of Upheaval, 1909–1915." In *Everyday Forms of State Formation: Revolution and the Negotiation of Rule in Modern Mexico*, edited by Gilbert M. Joseph and Daniel Nugent. Durham, N.C.: Duke University Press, 1994.

———. *Revolution from Without: Yucatán, Mexico, and the United States, 1880–1924*. Durham, N.C.: Duke University Press, 1988.

Kamen, Henry. *The Spanish Inquisition: A Historical Revision*. New Haven, Conn.: Yale University Press, 1998.

Karasch, Mary. "Suppliers, Sellers, Servants and Slaves." In *Cities and Society in Colonial Latin America*, edited by Louisa Schell Hoberman and Susan M. Socolow. Albuquerque: University of New Mexico Press, 1986.

Katz, Friedrich. "Labor Conditions on Haciendas in Porfirian Mexico: Some Trends and Tendencies." *Hispanic American Historical Review* 54, no. 1 (1974): 1–47.

Katzew, Ilona. *Casta Painting: Images of Race in Eighteenth-Century Mexico*. New Haven, Conn.: Yale University Press, 2004.

Keen, Benjamin. *The Aztec Image in Western Thought*. New Brunswick, N.J.: Rutgers University Press, 1971.

Kellogg, Susan. "Depicting *Mestizaje*: Gendered Images of Ethnorace in Colonial Mexican Texts." *Journal of Women's History* 12, no. 3 (2000): 69–92.

———. "The Woman's Room: Some Aspects of Gender Relations in Tenochtitlan in the Late Pre-Hispanic Period." *Ethnohistory* 42, no. 4 (1995): 563—77.

Kiddy, Elizabeth W. "Ethnic and Racial Identity in the Brotherhoods of the Rosary of Minas Gerais, 1700–1830." *The Americas* 56, no. 2 (1999): 221–52.

King, James F. "The Case of José Ponciano de Ayarza: A Document on *Gracias al Sacar*." *Hispanic American Historical Review* 24, no. 3 (1944): 440–51.

Kinsbruner, Jay. *The Colonial Spanish-American City: Urban Life in the Age of Atlantic Capitalism*. Austin: University of Texas Press, 2005.

Klein, Herbert. "The Colored Militia of Cuba: 1568–1868." *Caribbean Studies* 6, no. 2 (1966): 17–27.

———. *Slavery in the Americas: A Comparative Study of Virginia and Cuba*. Chicago: University of Chicago Press, 1967.

Konetzke, Richard, ed. *Colección de documentos para la historia de la formación social de hispanoamérica, 1493–1810*. 5 vols. Madrid: Consejo Superior de Investigaciones Científicas, 1953.

Kraay, Hendrik. *Race, State, and Armed Forces in Independence-Era Brazil: Bahia, 1790s-1840s*. Stanford, Calif.: Stanford University Press, 2001.

Kuethe, Allan J. "The Status of the Free-Pardo in the Disciplined Militias of New Granada." *Journal of Negro History* 56, no. 2 (1971): 105–15.

Kuznesof, Elizabeth. "Ethnic and Gender Influences on 'Spanish' Creole Society in Colonial Spanish America." *Colonial Latin American Review* 4, no. 1 (1995): 153–76.

Laclau, Ernesto. *The Politics of Rhetoric*. Colchester: University of Essex, 1998.

Laclau, Ernesto, and Chantal Mouffe. *Hegemony and Socialist Strategy: Towards a Radical Democratic Politics*. Translated by Winston Moore and Paul Cammack. London: Verso, 1985.

Lamadrid, Enrique R. *Hermanitos Comanchitos: Indo-Hispanic Rituals of Captivity and Redemption*. With photographs by Miguel A. Gandert. Albuquerque: University of New Mexico Press, 2003.

Landers, Jane. "Gracia Real de Santa Teresa de Mose: A Free Black Town in Spanish Colonial Florida." *American Historical Review* 95, no. 1 (1990): 9–30.

Langer, Erick D. "Missions and the Frontier Economy: The Case of the Franciscan Missions among the Chiriguanos, 1845–1930." In *The New Latin American Mission History*, edited by Erick Langer and Robert H. Jackson. Lincoln: University of Nebraska Press, 1995.

Langer, Erick D., and Elena Muñoz, eds. *Contemporary Indigenous Movements in Latin America*. Wilmington, Del.: SR Books, 2003.

Lara Cisneros, Gerardo. *El cristianismo en el espejo indigena: Religiosidad en el occidente de la Sierra Gorda, siglo XVIII*. Mexico City: Instituto Nacional de Antropologia e Historia, 2002.

Larson, Brooke. *Colonialism and Agrarian Transformation in Bolivia, Cochabamba, 1550–1900*. Durham, N.C.: Duke University Press, 1998 [1988].

Larson, Brooke, and Olivia Harris with Enrique Tandeter, eds. *Ethnicity, Markets, and Migration in the Andes: At the Crossroads of History and Anthropology*. Durham, N.C.: Duke University Press, 1995.

Las Casas, Bartolomé de. *Obras escogidas de fray Bartolomé de las Casas*. Vols. 95, 96, 105, 106, 110. Edited by Juan Pérez de Tudela. Madrid: Biblioteca de Autores Españoles, 1957–58.

*Las Siete Partidas del sabio rey D. Alfonso el nono*. Madrid: Joseph Thomas Lucas, 1758.

Lavrin, Asunción. *Sexuality and Marriage in Colonial Latin America*. Lincoln: University of Nebraska Press, 1989.

Lemoine, Ernesto. *Valladolid-Morelia 450 años: Documentos para su historia (1537–1828)*. Morelia: Morevallado, 1993.

Lempériere, Annick. "República y publicidad a finales del antiguo régimen (Nueva España)." In *Los espacios públicos en Iberoamérica: Ambigüedades y problemas, Siglos XVIII–XIX*, edited by Francois-Xavier Guerra and Annick Lempériere. Mexico City: F.C.E., 1998.

Leonard, Irving. *Books of the Brave: Being an Account of Books and of Men in the Spanish Conquest and Settlement of the Sixteenth-Century World*. Berkeley and Los Angeles: University of California Press, 1992 [1949].

Levillier, Roberto. *Don Francisco de Toledo, supremo organizador del Perú: Su vida, su obra (1515–1582)*. 3 vols. Madrid: Espasa-Calpe, 1935–40.

Levillier, Roberto, ed. *Gobernantes del Perú, cartas y papeles, siglo XVI: Documentos del Archivo de Indias*. 14 vols. Madrid: Sucesores de Rivadeneyra, 1921–26.

Lewin, Boleslao. *La rebelión de Túpac Amaru y los orgínes de la independencia de Hispanoamérica*. Buenos Aires: Sociedad Editora Latino Americana, 1967.

Lewin, Linda. "Natural and Spurious Children in Brazilian Inheritance Law from Colony to Empire: A Methodological Essay." *The Americas* 48, no. 3 (1992): 351–96.

Lewis, Laura. *Hall of Mirrors: Power, Witchcraft, and Caste in Colonial Mexico*. Durham, N.C.: Duke University Press, 2003.

Lewkowicz, Ida. "As mulheres mineiras e o casamento: Estratégias individuais e familiares nos séculos XVIII–XIX." *História* 12 (1993): 13–28.

Lizarraga, Fray Reginaldo de. *Descripción breve de toda la tierra del Perú, Tucumán, Río de la Plata y Chile*. Edited by Mario Hernández Sánchez-Barb. In vol. 216 of *Biblioteca de autores españoles desde la formación del lenguaje hasta nuestros días*. Madrid: Ediciones Atlas, 1968.

Lockhart, James. "Double Mistaken Identity: Some Nahua Concepts in Postconquest Guise." In *Of Things of the Indies: Essays Old and New in Early Latin American History*. Stanford, Calif.: Stanford University Press, 1999.

———. "Encomienda and Hacienda: The Evolution of the Great Estate in the Spanish Indies." *Hispanic American Historical Review* 49, no. 3 (1969): 411–29.

———. *The Nahuas after the Conquest: A Social and Cultural History of the Indians of Central Mexico, Sixteenth through Eighteenth Centuries*. Stanford, Calif.: Stanford University Press, 1992.

———. *Spanish Peru, 1532–1560: A Colonial Society*. Madison: University of Wisconsin Press, 1968.

———. *Spanish Peru, 1532–1560: A Social History*. 2nd ed. Madison: University of Wisconsin Press, 1994.

———. "A Vein of Ethnohistory: Recent Nahuatl-Based Historical Research." In *Nahuas and Spaniards: Postconquest Central Mexican History and Philology*. Stanford, Calif.: Stanford University Press, 1991.

Lohmann Villena, Guillermo. *El corregidor de indios en el Perú bajo los Austrias*. Madrid: Ediciones Cultura Hispánica, 1957.

Loveman, Mara. "Is 'Race' Essential?" *American Sociological Review* 64, no. 6 (1999): 891–98.

Luengo Múñoz, Manuel. "Sumaria noción de las monedas de Castilla e Indias en el siglo XVI." *Anuario de Estudios Americanos* 7 (1950): 326–66.

Luna, Francisco Vidal. *Minas Gerais: Escravos e senhores: Análise da estrutura populacional e econômica de alguns centros mineratórios, 1718–1804*. São Paulo: IPE/USP, 1981.

Lutz, Christopher H. *Santiago de Guatemala, 1541–1773: City, Caste and the Colonial Experience*. Norman: University of Oklahoma, 1994.

Lynch, John. *Spanish Colonial Administration, 1782–1810: The Intendant System in the Viceroyalty of the Río de la Plata*. New York: Greenwood Press, 1969.

Mallon, Florencia. *Peasant and Nation: The Making of Postcolonial Mexico and Peru*. Berkeley: University of California Press, 1995.

Mangan, Jane E. *Trading Roles: Gender, Ethnicity, and the Urban Economy in Colonial Potosí*. Durham, N.C.: Duke University Press, 2005.

Mannarelli, María Emma. *Private Passions and Public Sins: Men and Women in Seventeenth-Century Lima*. Translated by Sidney Evans and Meredith D. Dodge. Albuquerque: University of New Mexico Press, 2007.

Manrique, Nelson. *Vinieron los sarracenos: El universo mental de la conquista de Américas*. Lima: DESCO, 1993.

Maravall, José Antonio. *Poder, honor, y élites en el siglo XVII*. Madrid: Siglo XXI; Lima: Ediciones Flora Tristán, 1994.

Marchena Fernández, Juan. *Ejército y milicias en el mundo colonial americano*. Madrid: Editorial MAPFRE, 1992.

——. "The Social World of the Military in Peru and New Granada: The Colonial Oligarchies in Conflict, 1750–1810." In *Reform and Insurrection in Bourbon New Granada and Peru*, edited by John Fisher, Allan Kuethe, and Anthony McFarlane. Baton Rouge: Louisiana State University Press, 1990.

Martin, Cheryl English. *Rural Society in Colonial Morelos*. Albuquerque: University of New Mexico Press, 1985.

Martínez, María Elena. "The Black Blood of New Spain: *Limpieza de Sangre*, Racial Violence, and Gendered Power in Early Colonial Mexico." *William and Mary Quarterly* 61, no. 3 (2004): 479–520.

——. "Religion, Purity, and 'Race': The Spanish Concept of Limpieza de Sangre in Seventeenth-Century Mexico and the Broader Atlantic World." Working Paper #00019, International Seminar on the History of the Atlantic World, Harvard University, 2000.

Martínez Cereceda, José L. *Autoridades en los Andes: Los atributos del señor*. Lima: Pontificia Universidad Católica del Perú, 1995.

Martinez-Alier, Verena. *Marriage, Class and Colour in Nineteenth-Century Cuba: A Study of Racial Attitudes and Sexual Values in a Slave Society*. New York: Cambridge University Press, 1974.

Matienzo, Juan de. *Gobierno del Perú.* Edited by Guillermo Lohmann Villena. Paris: Institut Français d'Etudes Andines, 1967 [1567].

Maxwell, Kenneth. *Pombal, Paradox of the Enlightenment.* New York: Cambridge University Press, 1995.

Maybury-Lewis, David, ed. *The Politics of Ethnicity: Indigenous People in Latin American States:* Cambridge, Mass.: Harvard University Press, 2002.

McAlister, Lyle N. "Social Structure and Social Change in New Spain." *Hispanic American Historical Review* 43, no. 3 (1963): 349–70.

McBride, George McCutchen. *The Land Systems of Mexico.* New York: American Geographical Society, 1923.

McCaa, Robert. "Calidad, Class, and Marriage in Colonial Mexico: The Case of Parral, 1788–1790." *Hispanic American Historical Review* 64, no. 3 (1984): 477–501.

McCaa, Robert, Stuart Schwartz, and Arturo Grubessich, "Race and Class in Colonial Latin America: A Critique." *Comparative Studies in Society and History* 21, no. 3 (1979): 421–33.

McFarlane, Anthony. "The Rebellion of the 'Barrios': Urban Insurrection in Bourbon Quito." In *Reform and Insurrection in Bourbon New Granada and Peru,* edited by John Fisher, Allan Kuethe, and Anthony McFarlane. Baton Rouge: Louisiana State University Press, 1990.

McKinley, P. Michael. *Pre-Revolutionary Caracas: Politics, Economy, and Society, 1777–1811.* New York: Cambridge University Press, 1985.

Melville, Elinor G. K. *A Plague of Sheep: Environmental Consequences of the Conquest of Mexico.* New York: Cambridge University Press, 1994.

Mendiburu, Manuel de. *Diccionario histórico-biográfico del Perú.* 12 vols. 2nd ed. Lima: Imprenta "Enrique Palacios," 1931–35 [1874–80].

Menegus Bornemann, Margarita. "El gobierno de los indios en la Nueva España, siglo XVI: Señores or cabildo." *Revista de Indias* 59, no. 217 (1999): 599–617.

Metcalf, Alida C. *Family and Frontier in Colonial Brazil: Santana de Parnaíba, 1580–1822.* Berkeley: University of California Press, 1992.

——. *Go-Betweens and the Colonization of Brazil, 1500–1600.* Austin: University of Texas Press, 2005.

Mignolo, Walter D. *The Darker Side of the Renaissance: Literacy, Territoriality, and Colonization.* Ann Arbor: University of Michigan Press, 1995.

——. *The People of Quito, 1690–1810: Change and Unrest in the Underclass.* Greenwood, Conn.: Westview Press, 1994.

Minchom, Martin. "La economia subterranea y el mercado urbano: Pulperos, 'indias gateras' y 'recatonas' del Quito colonial (siglos XVI–XVII)." In *Memorias del Primer Simposio Europeo sobre Antropología del Ecuador,* compiled by Segundo E. Moreno Yánez. Quito: Ediciones Abya-Yala, 1985.

——. *The People of Quito, 1690–1810: Change and Unrest in the Underclass.* Greenwood, Conn.: Westview Press, 1994.

Mintz, Sidney W., and Richard Price. *The Birth of African-American Culture: An Anthropological Perspective.* 2nd ed. Boston: Beacon Press, 1992.

Montané Martí, Julio César. "De *nijoras* y 'españoles a medias.'" In *xv Simposio de Historia y Antropología de Sonora*. Hermosillo, Mexico: Universidad de Sonora, 1991.

Moreno, Gabriel René. *Biblioteca peruana: Notas bibliográficas inéditas*. Vol. 3. Edited by Rene Danilo Arze Aguirre y Alberto M. Vázquez. La Paz: Fundación Humberto Vázquez-Machicado, 1996.

Moreno de los Arcos, Roberto. "New Spain's Inquisition for Indians from the Sixteenth to the Nineteenth Century." In *Cultural Encounters: The Impact of the Inquisition in Spain and the New World*, edited by Mary Elizabeth Perry and Anne J. Cruz. Berkeley: University of California Press, 1991.

Mörner, Magnus. *La corona española y los foráneos en los pueblos de indios de América*. Stockholm: Almquist and Wiksell, 1970.

——. "Economic Factors and Stratification in Colonial Spanish America with Special Regard to Elites." *Hispanic American Historical Review* 63, no. 2 (1983): 335–69.

——. "The History of Race Relations in Latin America: Some Comments on the State of Research." *Latin American Research Review* 1, no. 3 (1966): 17–44.

——. *Race Mixture in the History of Latin America*. Boston: Little, Brown, 1967.

Morse, Richard M. "Claims of Political Tradition." In *New World Soundings: Culture and Ideology in the Americas*. Baltimore: Johns Hopkins University Press, 1989.

——. "El desarrollo urbano de la Hispanoamérica colonial." In *Historia de América Latina*, vol. 3, edited by Leslie Bethell. Barcelona: Editorial Crítica, 1990.

——. "The Multiverse of Latin American Identity, c. 1920-c.1970." In *Latin America since 1930: Ideas, Culture and Society*. Vol. 10 of *The Cambridge History of Latin America*, edited by Leslie Bethell. New York: Cambridge University Press, 1995.

Moxó, Salvador de. *Feudalismo, señorío y nobleza en la Castilla medieval*. Madrid: Real Academia de la Historia, 2000.

Mulvey, Patricia A. "Slave Confraternities in Brazil: Their Role in Colonial Society." *The Americas* 39, no. 1 (1982): 39–68.

Murra, John V. "Aymara Lords and Their European Agents at Potosí." *Nova Americana* 1, no. 1 (1978): 231–44.

——. "El control vertical de un máximo de pisos ecológicos en la economía de las sociedades andinas." In *Formaciones económicas y políticas del mundo andino*. Lima: Instituto de Estudios Peruanos, 1975.

——. *The Economic Organization of the Inka State*. Greenwich, Conn.: JAI Press, 1980 [1956].

——. "Litigation over the Rights of 'Natural Lords' in Early Colonial Courts in the Andes." In *Native Traditions in the Postconquest World*, edited by Elizabeth Hill Boone and Tom Cummins. Washington, D.C.: Dumbarton Oaks, 1998.

Nader, Helen. *Liberty in Absolutist Spain: The Habsburg Sale of Towns, 1516–1700*. Baltimore: Johns Hopkins University Press, 1990.

——. *The Mendoza Family in the Spanish Renaissance, 1350–1550*. New Brunswick, N.J.: Rutgers University Press, 1979.

Nash, Gary B. "The Hidden History of Mestizo America." In *Sex, Love, Race: Crossing*

*Boundaries in North American History*, edited by Martha Hodes. New York: New York University Press, 1999.

Nazzari, Muriel. "Concubinage in Colonial Brazil: The Inequalities of Race, Class and Gender." *Journal of Family History* 21, no. 2 (1996): 107–24.

———. *Disappearance of the Dowry: Women, Families, and Social Change in São Paulo, Brazil (1600–1900)*. Stanford, Calif.: Stanford University Press, 1991.

Nirenberg, David. *Communities of Violence: Persecution of Minorities in the Middle Ages*. Princeton, N.J.: Princeton University Press, 1996.

Nishida, Mieko. "Manumission and Ethnicity in Urban Slavery: Salvador, Brazil, 1808–1888." *Hispanic American Historical Review* 73, no. 3 (1993): 361–91.

Nordenskiöld, Erland. *Exploraciones y aventuras en Sudamérica*. Translated by Gudrun Birk and Angel E. García. La Paz: Apoyo Para el Campesinado Indígena del Oriente Boliviano, 2001.

Numhauser, Paulina. *Mujeres indias y señores de la coca: Potosí y Cuzco en el siglo XVI*. Madrid: Catédra, 2005.

Núñez Cabeza de Vaca, Alvar. *Comentarios de Alvar Núñez Cabeza de Vaca, adelantado y governador de Rio de la Plata, escritos por Pedro Hernández, escribano y secretario de la provincia*. 5th ed. Madrid: Espasa-Calpe, 1971.

———. *Relación*. In *Alvar Núñez Cabeza de Vaca: His Account, His Life, and the Expedition of Pánfilo de Narváez*, vol. 1, edited by Rolena Adorno and Patrick Charles Pautz. Lincoln: University of Nebraska Press, 1999.

Ocaña, Fray Diego de. *Un viaje fascinante por la América hispana del siglo XVI*. Edited by Fray Arturo Álvarez. Madrid: Studium, 1969.

Odriozola, Manuel de, ed. *Documentos históricos del Peru en las épocas del coloniaje despues de la conquista y de la independencia hasta la presente*. 10 vols. Lima: Tip. de A. Alfaro, 1863–77.

O'Gorman, Edmundo. *La invención de América: El universalismo de la cultura de Occidente*. Mexico City: Fondo de Cultura Económica, 1958.

O'Phelan Godoy, Scarlett. *Kurakas sin sucesiones: Del cacique al alcalde de indios (Peru y Bolivia 1750–1835)*. Cuzco: Centro de Estudios Regionales Andinos Bartolomé de las Casas, 1997.

———. *Rebellions and Revolts in Eighteenth Century Peru and Upper Peru*. Cologne: Oohlau, 1985.

———. *Un siglo de rebeliones anticoloniales: Perú y Bolivia, 1700–1778*. Cuzco: Centro de Estudios Bartolomé de las Casas, 1988.

Ortiz, Fernando. "Los cabildos afrocubanos." In *Ensayos etnográficos: Fernando Ortiz*. Havana: Editorial de Ciencias Sociales, 1984 [1921].

Ortner, Sherry. "Subjectivity and Cultural Critique." *Anthropological Theory* 5, no. 1 (2005): 31–52.

———. "Theory in Anthropology since the Sixties." *Comparative Studies in Society and History* 26, no. 1 (1984): 126–66.

O'Toole, Rachel Sarah. "Inventing Difference: Africans, Indians, and the Antecedents of 'Race' in Colonial Peru (1580s–1720s)." Ph.D. diss., University of North Carolina, Chapel Hill, 2001.

Pagden, Anthony. *The Fall of Natural Man: The American Indian and the Origins of Comparative Ethnology.* New York: Cambridge University Press, 1982.

———. "Identity Formation in Spanish America." In *Colonial Identity in the Atlantic World, 1500–1800,* edited by Nicholas Canny and Anthony Pagden. Princeton, N.J.: Princeton University Press, 1987.

Paiva, Eduardo F. *Escravidão e universo cultural na colônial: Minas Gerais, 1716–1789.* Belo Horizonte: Editora da UFMG, 2001.

———. *Escravos e libertos nas Minas Gerais.* São Paulo: Annablume, 1995.

Pallares, Amalia. *From Peasant Struggles to Indian Resistance: The Ecuadorian Andes in the Late Twentieth Century.* Norman: University of Oklahoma Press, 2002.

Paredes Martínez, Carlos. "Grupos étnicos y conflictividad social en Guayangareo-Valladolid, al inicio de la época colonial." In *Lengua y etnohistoria purépecha: Homenaje a Benedict Warren,* edited by Carlos Paredes Martínez. Mexico City: Centro de Investigaciones y Estudios Superiores en Antropología Social (CIESAS), 1997.

Patch, Robert W. *Maya and Spaniard in Yucatan, 1648–1812.* Stanford, Calif.: Stanford University Press, 1993.

Patterson, Orlando. *Slavery and Social Death: A Comparative Study.* Cambridge, Mass.: Harvard University Press, 1982.

Paz, Octavio. *Sor Juana, or, The Traps of Faith.* Translated by Margaret Sayers Peden. Cambridge, Mass.: Harvard University Press, 1988.

Pease, Franklin. *Curacas, reciprocidad y riqueza.* Lima: Pontificia Universidad Católica del Perú, 1992.

Pereña Vicente, Luciano. "La pretensión a la perpetuidad de las encomiendas del Perú." In *Estudios sobre política indigenista española en América.* Vol. 2. Valladolid: Universidad de Valladolid, 1976.

Perry, Mary Elizabeth. *Gender and Disorder in Early Modern Seville.* Princeton, N.J.: Princeton University Press, 1990.

Pinto, Virgílio Noya. *O ouro brasileiro e o comércio Anglo-Português.* São Paulo: Companhia Editora Nacional/MEC, 1979.

Platt, Tristan. *Estado boliviano y ayllu andino: Tierra y tributo en el norte de Potosí.* Lima: Instituto de Estudios Peruanos, 1982.

———. " 'Without Deceit or Lies': Variable *Chinu* Readings during a Sixteenth-Century Tribute-Restitution Trial." In *Narrative Threads, Accounting and Recounting in Andean Khipu,* edited by Jeffrey Quilter and Gary Urton. Austin: University of Texas Press, 2002.

Postero, Nancy Grey, and León Zamosc, eds. *The Struggle for Indigenous Rights in Latin America.* Brighton: Sussex Academic Press, 2004.

Powers, Karen Vieira. *Andean Journeys: Migration, Ethnogenesis, and the State in Colonial Quito.* Albuquerque: University of New Mexico Press, 1995.

———. *Women in the Crucible of Conquest: The Gendered Genesis of Spanish American Society, 1500–1600.* Albuquerque: University of New Mexico Press, 2005.

Pratt, Mary Louise. *Imperial Eyes: Travel Writing and Transculturation.* New York: Routledge, 1992.

Presta, Ana María. "Devoción cristiana, uniones consagradas y elecciones materiales en la construcción de identidades indígenas urbanas: Charcas, 1550–1659." *Revista Andina* 41 (2005): 109–30.

Presta, Ana María, ed. *Espacio, etnias, frontera: Atenuaciones políticas en el sur del Tawantinsuyu, siglos XV–XVIII.* Sucre: Antropólogos del Surandino, 1995.

Puente Brunke, José de la. *Encomienda y encomenderos en el Perú: Estudio social y político de una institución colonial.* Seville: Excma. Diputación Provincial de Sevilla, 1992.

Puente Luna, Jose Carlos de la. "What's in a Name? An Indian Trickster Travels the Spanish Colonial World (Jeronimo Limaylla, Peru)." Master's thesis, Texas Christian University, 2006.

Purnell, Jennie. "Citizens and Sons of the *Pueblo:* National and Local Identities in the Making of the Mexican Nation." *Ethnic and Racial Studies* 25, no. 2 (2002): 213–37.

Querejazu Calvo, Roberto. *Chuquisaca, 1539–1825.* Sucre: Imprenta Universitaria, 1987.

Racine, Matthew T. "Service and Honor in Sixteenth-Century Portuguese North Africa: Yahya-u-Ta'fuft and Portuguese Noble Culture." *Sixteenth Century Journal* 32, no. 1 (2001): 67–90.

Radding, Cynthia. *Entre el desierto y la sierra: Las naciones o'odham y tegüima de Sonora, 1530–1840.* Mexico City: Centro de Investigaciones y Estudios Superiores en Antropología Social (CIESAS), 1995.

———. *Landscapes of Power and Identity: Comparative Histories in the Sonoran Desert and the Forests of Amazonia from Colony to Republic.* Durham, N.C.: Duke University Press, 2005.

———. "Voces chiquitanas: Entre la encomienda y la misión en el oriente de Bolivia (siglo XVIII)." *Anuario del Archivo y Biblioteca Nacionales de Bolivia* (1997): 123–38.

———. *Wandering Peoples: Colonialism, Ethnic Spaces, and Ecological Frontiers in Northwestern Mexico, 1700–1850.* Durham, N.C.: Duke University Press, 1997.

Rama, Angel. *La ciudad letrada.* Montevideo: Arca, 1995.

Ramenofsky, Ann F., Michael K. Church, and Jeremy Kulisheck. "Investigating Differential Persistence of Pueblo Populations: A Landscapes Approach." Paper presented at the Tenth Southwest Symposium, Las Cruces, New Mexico, January 14, 2006.

Ramírez, Susan. "Exchange and Markets in the Sixteenth Century: A View from the North." In *Ethnicity, Markets, and Migration in the Andes: At the Crossroads of History and Anthropology,* edited by Brooke Larson and Olivia Harris with Enrique Tandeter. Durham, N.C.: Duke University Press, 1995.

———. *To Feed and Be Fed: The Cosmological Bases of Authority and Identity in the Andes.* Stanford, Calif.: Stanford University Press, 2005.

———. *The World Turned Upside Down: Cross-Cultural Contact and Conflict in Sixteenth-Century Peru.* Stanford, Calif.: Stanford University Press, 1996.

Ramos, Donald. "Community, Control, and Acculturation: A Case Study of Slavery in Eighteenth-Century Brazil." *The Americas* 42, no. 4 (1986): 419–51.

———. "Marriage and the Family in Colonial Vila Rica." *Hispanic American Historical Review* 55, no. 2 (1975): 200–255.

Rappaport, Joanne, and David Gow. "The Indigenous Public Voice: The Multiple Idioms of Modernity in Native Cauca." In *Indigenous Movements, Self-Representation, and the State,* edited by Kay B. Warren and Jean E. Jackson. Austin: University of Texas Press, 2002.

Restall, Matthew. "A History of the New Philology and the New Philology of History." *Latin American Research Review* 38, no. 1 (2003): 113–34.

———. *The Maya World: Yucatec Culture and Society, 1550–1850.* Stanford, Calif.: Stanford University Press, 1997.

———. *Seven Myths of the Spanish Conquest.* Oxford: Oxford University Press, 2003.

Restall, Matthew, ed. *Beyond Black and Red: African-Native Relations in Colonial Latin America.* Albuquerque: University of New Mexico Press, 2005.

Rieu-Millan, Marie Laure. *Los diputados americanos en las Cortes de Cádiz (igualdad o independencia).* Madrid: Consejo Superior de Investigaciones Científicas, 1990.

Rodríguez O., Jaime E., ed. *The Divine Charter: Constitutionalism and Liberalism in Nineteenth-Century Mexico.* Lanham, Md.: Rowman and Littlefield, 2005.

Rodríguez Prampolini, Ida. *Amadises de América: La hazaña de Indias como empresa caballeresca.* 2nd ed. Caracas: Centro de Estudios Latinoamericanos Rómulo Gallegos, 1977.

Rodríguez Salgado, Mia. *The Changing Face of Empire: Charles V, Philip II and Habsburg Authority, 1551–1559.* New York: Cambridge University Press, 1988.

———. "Christians, Civilised and Spanish: Multiple Identities in Sixteenth-Century Spain." *Transactions of the Royal Historical Society* 8 (1998): 233–51.

Rodulfo Cortés, Santos. *El regimen de "las gracias al sacar" en Venezuela durante el periodo hispánico.* 2 vols. Caracas: Italgráfica, 1978.

Rojas Martinez, Axel A. *Si no fuera por los quince negros: Memoria colectiva de la gente negra de Tierradentro.* Popayán: Editorial Universidad del Cauca, 2004.

Romano, Ruggiero. "Entre encomienda castellana y encomienda indiana: Una vez más el problema del feudalismo americano (siglos XVI–XVII)." *Anuario Instituto de Estudios Histórico-Sociales* 3 (1988): 11–39.

Romero, José Luis. *Latinoamérica, las ciudades y las ideas.* Buenos Aires: Siglo Veintiuno Editores, 1976.

Romero Frizzi, María de los Angeles. *El sol y la cruz: Los pueblos indios de Oaxaca colonial.* Mexico City: Centro de Investigaciones y Estudios Superiores en Antropología Social (CIESAS) and Instituto Nacional Indigenista (INI), 1996.

Rugeley, Terry. *Yucatán's Maya and the Origins of the Caste War.* Austin: University of Texas Press, 1996.

Russell-Wood, A. J. R. *Fidalgos and Philantropists: The Santa Casa de Misericórdia of Bahia, 1550–1755.* Berkeley: University of California Press, 1968.

———. *Slavery and Freedom in Colonial Brazil.* Oxford: Oneworld, 2002.

Saeger, James Schofield. *The Chaco Mission Frontier: The Guaycurúan Experience.* Tucson: University of Arizona Press, 2000.

Salomon, Frank. *Native Lords of Quito in the Age of the Incas: The Political Economy of North Andean Chiefdoms*. New York: Cambridge University Press, 1986.

Sánchez Silva, Carlos. *Indios, comerciantes y burocracia en la Oaxaca poscolonial, 1786–1860*. Oaxaca: Instituto Oaxaqueño de las Culturas, Fondo Estatal para la Cultura y las Artes, and Universidad Autónoma Benito Juárez de Oaxaca, 1998.

Santillán, Hernando de. "Relación del origin, descendencia política y gobierno de los Incas." In *Tres relaciones de antigüedades peruanas*, edited by Marcos Jiménez de la Espada. Madrid: Ministerio de Fomento, 1879.

Scarano, Julita. *Devoção e escravidão: A Irmandade de Nossa Senhora do Rosário dos Pretos no distrito diamantino no século XVIII*. São Paulo: Nacional, 1975.

Schatzki, Theodore R., Karin Knorr Cetina, and Eike von Savigny, eds. *The Practice Turn in Contemporary Theory*. New York: Routledge, 2001.

Schwartz, Stuart B. "Brazilian Ethnogenesis: *Mestiços, Mamelucos*, and *Pardos*." In *Le Nouveau Monde, mondes nouveaux: L'expérience américaine*, edited by Serge Gruzinski and Nathan Wachtel. Paris: Éditions Recherche sur les Civilisations, 1996.

———. "New World Nobility: Social Aspirations and Mobility in the Conquest and Colonization of Spanish America." In *Social Groups and Religious Ideas in the Sixteenth Century*, edited by Miriam Usher Chrisman and Otto Grundler. Kalamazoo: Western Michigan University, 1978.

———. *Sugar Plantations in the Formation of Brazilian Society: Bahia, 1550–1835*. New York: Cambridge University Press, 1985.

Schwartz, Stuart B., ed. *Implicit Understandings: Observing, Reporting, and Reflecting on the Encounters between Europeans and other Peoples in the Early Modern Era*. New York: Cambridge University Press, 1994.

Schwartz, Stuart B., and Frank Salomon. "New Peoples and New Kinds of People: Adaptation, Readjustment, and Ethnogenesis in South American Indigenous Societies (Colonial Era)." In *The Cambridge History of the Native Peoples of the Americas*, Vol. 3, Pt. 2, edited by Frank Salomon and Stuart B. Schwartz. New York: Cambridge University Press, 1999.

Scott, James. *Seeing Like a State: How Certain Schemes to Improve the Human Condition Have Failed*. New Haven, Conn.: Yale University Press, 1998.

Seed, Patricia. "The Social Dimensions of Race: Mexico City, 1753." *Hispanic American Historical Review* 62, no. 4 (1982): 569–606.

———. *To Love, Honor, and Obey in Colonial Mexico: Conflicts over Marriage Choice, 1574–1821*. Stanford, Calif.: Stanford University Press, 1988.

Seed, Patricia, and Philip F. Rust, "Estate and Class in Colonial Oaxaca Revisited." *Comparative Studies in Society and History* 25, no. 4 (1983): 703–10.

Sewell, William H. "A Theory of Structure: Duality, Agency, and Transformation." *American Journal of Sociology* 98, no. 1 (1992): 1–29.

Sheridan, Cecilia. *Anónimos y desterrados: La contienda por el "sitio que llaman de Quayla," siglos XVI–XVIII*. Mexico City: Centro de Investigaciones y Estudios Superiores en Antropología Social (CIESAS), 2000.

Sicroff, Albert A. *Los estatuos de limpieza de sangre: controversias entre los siglos xv y xvii*. Madrid: Taurus Ediciones, 1985.

Silverblatt, Irene. *Modern Inquisitions: Peru and the Colonial Origins of the Civilized World*. Durham, N.C.: Duke University Press, 2004.

———. *Moon, Sun and Witches: Gender Ideologies and Class in Inca and Colonial Peru*. Princeton, N.J.: Princeton University Press, 1987.

Silva, Maria Beatriz Nizza da. *História da família no Brazil colonial*. Rio de Janeiro: Editora Nova Fronteira, 1998.

———. *Sistema de casamento no Brasil colonial*. São Paulo: Companhia Editora Nacional, 1984.

Soares, Mariza de Carvalho. *Devotos da cor: Identidade étnica, religiosidade e escravidão no Rio de Janeiro, século xviii*. Rio de Janeiro: Civilização Brasileira, 2000.

———. "Mina, Angola e Guiné: Nomes d'África no Rio de Janeiro setecentista." *Tempo* 6 (December 1998): 73–93.

Solórzano Pereira, Juan de. *Política indiana*. 5 vols. Madrid: Compañía Ibero-Americana de Publicaciones, 1972 [1648].

Souza, Juliana Beatriz Almeida de. "Viagens do rosário entre a Velha Cristandade e o Além-Mar." *Estudos Afro-Asiáticos* 23, no. 2 (2001): 1–17.

Spalding, Karen. *Huarochirí: An Andean Society under Inca and Spanish Rule*. Stanford, Calif.: Stanford University Press, 1984.

———. "Kurakas and Commerce: A Chapter in the Evolution of Andean Society." *Hispanic American Historical Review* 53, no. 4 (1973): 581–99.

———. "Social Climbers: Changing Patterns of Mobility among the Indians of Colonial Peru." *Hispanic American Historical Review* 50, no. 4 (1970): 645–64.

Spores, Ronald. *Mixtec Kings and Their People*. Norman: University of Oklahoma Press, 1967.

Stavig, Ward. *The World of Túpac Amaru: Conflict, Community, and Identity in Colonial Peru*. Lincoln: University of Nebraska Press, 1999.

Stein, Stanley J., and Barbara H. Stein. *The Colonial Heritage of Latin America: Essays on Economic Dependence in Perspective*. New York: Oxford University Press, 1970.

Stern, Steve J. "Feudalism, Capitalism, and the World-System in the Perspective of Latin America and the Caribbean." *American Historical Review* 93, no. 4 (1988): 829–72.

———. *Peru's Indian Peoples and the Challenge of Spanish Conquest: Huamanga to 1640*. 2nd ed. Madison: University of Wisconsin Press, 1993.

———. *The Secret History of Gender: Women, Men, and Power in Late Colonial Mexico*. Chapel Hill: The University of North Carolina Press, 1995.

Stoler, Ann Laura, and Frederick Cooper. "Between Metropole and Colony: Rethinking a Research Agenda." In *Tensions of Empire: Colonial Cultures in a Bourgeois Word*, edited by Ann Laura Stoler and Frederick Cooper. Berkeley: University of California Press, 1997.

Suárez Fernández, Luis. *Nobleza y monarquía: Entendimiento y rivalida: El proceso de construcción de la corona española*. Madrid: Esfera de los Libros, 2003.

Sweet, James H. "The Iberian Origins of American Racist Thought." *William and Mary Quarterly* 54, no. 1 (1997): 143–66.

———. *Recreating Africa: Culture, Kinship, and Religion in the African-Portuguese World, 1441–1770.* Chapel Hill: University of North Carolina Press, 2003.

Swidler, Ann. "Culture in Action: Symbols and Strategies." *American Sociological Review* 51, no. 2 (1986): 273–86.

Tannenbaum, Frank. *Slave and Citizen: The Negro in the Americas.* New York: Vintage Books, 1946.

Tavárez, David. "Idolatry as an Ontological Question: Native Consciousness and Juridical Proof in Colonial Mexico." *Journal of Early Modern History* 6, no. 2 (2002): 114–39.

———. "La idolatría letrada: Un análisis comparativo de textos clandestinos rituales y devocionales en comunidades nahuas y zapotecas, 1613–1654." *Historia Mexicana* 49, no. 2 (1999): 197–252.

———. "The Passion according to the Wooden Drum: The Christian Appropriation of a Zapotec Ritual Genre in New Spain." *The Americas* 62, no. 3 (2006): 413–44.

Taylor, William B. "Town and Country in the Valley of Oaxaca." In *Provinces of Early Mexico: Variants of Spanish American Regional Evolution*, edited by Ida Altman and James Lockhart. Los Angeles: UCLA Latin American Center Publications, 1976.

Tena Ramírez, Felipe, ed. *Leyes fundamentales de México, 1808–1982.* 11th ed. Mexico City: Editorial Porrúa, 1982.

Terraciano, Kevin. *The Mixtecs of Colonial Oaxaca: Ñudzahui History, Sixteenth through Eighteenth Centuries.* Stanford, Calif.: Stanford University Press, 2001.

Thibaud, Climent. "La Academia Carolina de Charcas: Una 'escuela de dirigentes' para la Independencia." In *El siglo XIX: Bolivia y América Latina*, compiled by Rossana Barragán, Dora Cajías y Seemin Qayum. La Paz: Muela del Diablo Editores, 1997.

Thornton, John. *Africa and Africans in the Making of the Atlantic World, 1400–1800.* 2nd ed. New York: Cambridge University Press, 1998.

Tomichá Charupá, Roberto. "La encomienda en Santa Cruz de la Sierra (1751–1753): El caso de los chiquitos Eugenio y Jacinto Manabí." *Anuario del Archivo y Biblioteca Nacionales de Bolivia* (2004): 749–94.

———. *La primera evangelización en las reducciones de Chiquitos, Bolivia, 1691–1767: Protagonistas y metodología misional.* Cochabamba: Universidad Católica Boliviana, 2002.

Torfing, Jacob. *New Theories of Discourse: Laclau, Mouffe and Žižek.* New York: Oxford University Press, 1999.

Trelles Aréstegui, Efraín. *Lucas Martínez Vegazo: Funcionamiento de una encomienda peruana inicial.* Lima: Pontificia Universidad Católica del Perú, 1982.

Twinam, Ann. "The Etiology of Racial Passing: Constructions of Informal and Official 'Whiteness' in Colonial Spanish America." In *New World Orders: Violence, Sanction, and Authority in the Early Modern Americas.* Philadelphia: University of Pennsylvania Press, 2005.

———. "Padres blancos, madres pardas: Género, familia y las estrategias de ascenso en América Colonial." Paper delivered at the Association of European Historians of Latin America, Castellón, Spain, September 2005.

———. "Pedro de Ayarza: The Purchase of Whiteness." In *The Human Tradition in colonial Latin America*, edited by Kenneth Andrien. Wilmington, Del.: Scholarly Resources Press, 2002.

———. "Playing the 'Gender Card': Imperial Bureaucrats, Petitioners, and Gracias al Sacar Legitimations and Whitenings." Paper delivered at the Rocky Mountain Council of Latin American Studies, Phoenix, February 2003.

———. *Public Lives, Private Secrets: Gender, Honor, and Illegitimacy in Colonial Spanish America.* Stanford, Calif.: Stanford University Press, 1999.

Van Young, Eric. "Conflict and Solidarity in Indian Village Life: The Guadalajara Region in the Late Colonial Period." *Hispanic American Historical Review* 64, no. 1 (1984): 55–79.

———. "The Cuautla Lazarus: Double Subjectives in Reading Texts on Popular Collective Action." *Colonial Latin American Review* 2, no. 1–2 (1993): 3–26.

———. "The New Cultural History Comes to Old Mexico." *Hispanic American Historical Review* 79, no. 2 (1999): 211–47.

Vega, Andres de. "La descripción que se hizo en la provincia de Xauxa [1582]." In *Relaciones geográficas de Indias, Perú*, edited by Marcos Jiménez de la Espada. Vol. 1. Madrid: Ministerio de Fomento, 1965.

Vila, Pablo. *Border Identifications: Narratives of Religion, Gender and Class on the U.S./Mexico Border.* Austin: University of Texas Press, 2005.

———. *Crossing Borders, Reinforcing Borders: Social Categories, Metaphors and Narrative Identities in the U.S.-Mexico Border.* Austin: University of Texas Press, 2000.

Vinson, Ben III. *Bearing Arms for His Majesty: The Free-Colored Militia in Colonial Mexico.* Stanford, Calif.: Stanford University Press, 2001.

———. "Estudiando las razas desde la periferia: Las castas olvidadas del sistema colonial mexicano (lobos, moriscos, coyotes, moros y chinos)." In *Pautas de convivencia étnica en la América Latina colonial (Indios, negros, mulatos, pardos y esclavos)*, edited by Juan Manuel de la Serna Herrera. Mexico City: Universidad Nacional Autónoma de México, 2005.

Viqueira, Juan Pedro. "Una fuente olvidada: El Juzgado Ordinario Diocesano." In *Las fuentes eclesiásticas para la historia social de México*, edited by Brian Connaughton and Andrés Lira. Mexico City: UAM-Iztapalapa and Instituto Mora, 1997.

Voekel, Pamela. "Peeing on the Palace: Bodily Resistance to Bourbon Reforms in Mexico City." *Journal of Historical Society* 5, no. 2 (1992): 183–208.

Wachtel, Nathan. *The Vision of the Vanquished: The Spanish Conquest of Peru through Indian Eyes, 1530–1570.* New York: Barnes and Noble, 1977.

Wade, Peter. *Race and Ethnicity in Latin America.* Sterling, Va.: Pluto Press, 1997.

Walker, Charles F. "Civilize or Control? The Lingering Impact of the Bourbon Reforms." In *Political Cultures in the Andes, 1750–1950*, edited by Nils Jacobsen and Cristóbal Aljovín de Losada. Durham, N.C.: Duke University Press, 2005.

Wallerstein, Immanuel. "The Construction of Peoplehood: Racism, Nationalism, Ethnicity." *Sociological Forum* 2, no. 2 (1987): 373–88.

Weber, David J. *Bárbaros: Spaniards and Their Savages in the Age of Enlightenment*. New Haven, Conn.: Yale University Press, 2005.

Weinstein, Barbara. "Buddy, Can You Spare a Paradigm? Reflections on Generational Shifts and Latin American History." *The Americas* 57, no. 4 (2001): 453–66.

Wells, Allen. *Yucatán's Gilded Age: Haciendas, Henequen, and International Harvester, 1860–1915*. Albuquerque: University of New Mexico Press, 1985.

Wightman, Ann W. *Indigenous Migration and Social Change: The Forasteros of Cuzco, 1570–1720*. Durham, N.C.: Duke University Press, 1990.

Williams, Eric. *Capitalism and Slavery*. Chapel Hill: University of North Carolina Press, 1944.

Wolf, Eric R. "Perilous Ideas: Race, Culture, People." *Current Anthropology* 35, no. 1 (1994): 1–7.

Wolff, Inge. *Regierung und Verwaltung der kolonialspanischen Städte in Hochperu, 1538–1650*. Cologne: Böhlau-Verlag, 1970.

Wood, Stephanie. *Transcending Conquest: Nahua Views of Spanish Colonial Mexico*. Norman: University of Oklahoma Press, 2003.

Zabálburu, Francisco de, and José Sancho Rayon, eds. *Nueva colección de documentos inéditos para la historia de España y sus Indias*. Madrid, 1894–96.

Zavala, Silvio A. *La encomienda indiana*. Madrid: Imprenta Helénica, 1935.

Zemella, Mafalda. *O abastecimento da capitania das Minas Gerais no século XVIII*. São Paulo: Hucitec, 1990.

Zmora, Hillay. *Monarchy, Aristocracy, and State in Europe, 1300–1800*. New York: Routledge, 2001.

# Contributors

KAREN D. CAPLAN is an assistant professor of Latin American history at Rutgers University, Newark. She is the author of *Local Liberalisms: Mexico's Indigenous Villagers and the State, 1812–1857* (forthcoming from Stanford University Press).

R. DOUGLAS COPE is an associate professor of history at Brown University. He studies the creation and development of multiethnic societies in Mexico, paying particular attention to the experience of the urban poor.

MARIANA L. R. DANTAS is an assistant professor of history at Ohio University. She is the author of *Black Townsmen: Urban Slavery and Freedom in the Eighteenth-Century Americas.*

MARÍA ELENA DÍAZ, an associate professor of history at the University of California, Santa Cruz, is the author of *The Virgin, the King and the Royal Slaves of El Cobre: Negotiating Freedom in Colonial Cuba, 1670–1780.* Díaz's current research examines the topics of slavery and freedom, legal, political, and religious cultures, and social identities in eastern Cuba during the late colonial and postcolonial periods.

ANDREW B. FISHER, an assistant professor of history at Carleton College, has published on topics related to indigenous collective identity and the interethnic relations among the rural poor in colonial Mexico. He is currently developing both of these themes in a book-length study of the tierra caliente of western Mexico, which spans the late fifteenth through early nineteenth centuries.

JANE E. MANGAN, a historian of the colonial Andes, is the Malcolm Overstreet Partin Assistant Professor of History at Davidson College. She is the author of *Trading Roles: Gender, Ethnicity and the Urban Economy in Colonial Potosí* and is currently at work on a project titled "Transatlantic Obligations: Legal and Cultural Constructions of Family in the Sixteenth-Century Iberian World."

JEREMY RAVI MUMFORD is a member of the Michigan Society of Fellows. He works on the history of the colonial Andes and on the comparative history of indigenous people in the Americas.

MATTHEW D. O'HARA is an assistant professor of history at the University of California, Santa Cruz. He is the author of *A Flock Divided: Race, Religion, and Politics in Mexico (1749–1857)*, forthcoming from Duke University Press.

CYNTHIA RADDING is a professor of history at the University of New Mexico. Her scholarship focuses on the intersection of ethnohistory and environmental history, with comparative perspectives on imperial borderlands in the Americas, as is illustrated by her two recent books, *Wandering Peoples* and *Landscapes of Power and Identity*.

SERGIO SERULNIKOV, a researcher at the Consejo Nacional de Investigaciones Científicas y Técnicas de la Argentina (CONICET), teaches Latin American history at Universidad de San Andrés, Argentina, and Boston College. His recent publications include *Subverting Colonial Authority: Challenges to Spanish Rule in Eighteenth-Century Southern Andes* and "The Politics of Intracommunity Land Conflict in the Late Colonial Andes," *Ethnohistory* vol. 55, no. 1.

IRENE SILVERBLATT is a professor of cultural anthropology and history at Duke University and the author of *Modern Inquisitions: Peru and the Colonial Origins of the Civilized World* and *Moon, Sun, and Witches: Gender and Class in Inca and Colonial Peru*.

DAVID TAVÁREZ, who holds a joint PhD in anthropology and history from the University of Chicago, is an assistant professor of anthropology at Vassar College and is currently finishing an analysis of indigenous responses to idolatry eradication projects in Central Mexico. His publications include articles in *Historia Mexicana, Ancient Mesoamerica, The Americas, Journal of Early Modern History, Colonial Latin American Review,* and eight book chapters.

ANN TWINAM, a professor of history at the University of Texas at Austin, is the author of *Public Lives, Private Secrets: Gender, Honor, Sexuality and Illegitimacy in Colonial Spanish America* and "Women and Gender in Colonial Latin America" published in the American Historical Association series *Women and Gender History in Global Perspective*. She is currently finishing a monograph titled "Erasing the 'American Defect': Mulatos and the Purchase of Whiteness in Colonial Spanish America."

# Index

Bourdieu, Pierre, 32n21

Boyer, Richard, 83

Brazil, 26

brotherhoods, 129–36, 223n34, 254–55; corporate actions and responsibilities of, 133–35; racial differentiation of, 133–34; among slaves, 130–35, 139n37

Brubaker, Rogers, 19–21, 27, 36n59, 142, 144, 161n4, 198

bureaucratic practices. *See* institutional practices

Caballero Calderón, Manuel, 150, 157

Caballero Carranza, Manuel, 147

*cabecera* governance, 246n36

Cabeçón, Cristóbal, 98n12

*cabildo* governance, 51; of El Cobre's royal slaves, 210–19, 223n34; in Oaxacan and Yucatecan communities, 226–27, 243n2; in rebellious La Plata, 167–68, 183–89

*cacique*, 57n25

Cagigal, Juan Manuel de, 157

*calidad, qualidade*, 81, 144–45; of free blacks, 26, 121, 125–29; in marriage decisions, 125–29, 138n25, 254–55; of *pardos* and *mulatos*, 148–49; variability in, 11–12, 33n34, 93, 97. *See also* blood

Cámara of the Indies, 141–43, 150, 159–60

Camorlinga, Diego, 103–4, 106–9

Cañas, Francisco Xavier de, 176–78

Cano, Francisco, 185–86, 188

*capitanias donatárias* (land grants), 137n6

Caplan, Karen, 3, 28–29, 53

Caribbean region, 204–5

Carrera, Lope de, 86

casta system. *See sistema de castas*

Caste War of Mexico, 234, 239, 242

Castilian aristocracy, 43, 46, 56n1

Castillo, Felipe del, 89

Castillo, Gaspar del, 89

*castizo* category, 12, 33n27, 81

Castro, Lope de, 49–53, 253

categories of difference. *See* racial categorization

category of race, 199–200, 221n5

Catholic Church, x, 2, 203; El Cobre's slave *cabildo* and, 213; idolatry challenged by, 90–93, 95, 99–100nn27–29, 111; inquisitorial jurisdiction of, 25, 87, 90–97, 99n19, 100n36, 258–59; Jesuit missions of, 102, 109–11, 257–58; lay brotherhoods of, 129–36; pure blood defined by, 146

Cayetano de Urbina, Governor, 197, 216

Chambillas, Diego, 70

Chance, John K., 33n34

*chapetón* category, 181

Charcas, 25, 101–13

Charles V of Spain, 42, 44

Chassen-López, Francie R., 247n51

children: civil status of, 3–4, 155–56; of mixed heritage, 72–73; petitions of legitimacy by, 149; of unmarried couples, 128–29

Chiquitos lowlands, 104–7, 113n3

Chirino, Nicholas, 213–14

*cholo* category, 74, 169, 171. *See also mestizo/mestiço* category

Christianity. *See* Catholic Church

Cieza de Léon, Pedro, 61, 68

citizenship, 27; of El Cobre's royal slaves, 210, 214, 219, 223n24; in indigenous Mexican communities, 231–32, 244n18

civil jurisdiction, 87

clean blood, xi, 5–7, 31n16, 144–47, 149, 162n16

Cline, Howard, 230

*cobreros. See* El Cobre (Cuba) community of royal slaves

coca, 65, 68

cochineal dye, 229

El Cobre (Cuba) (*cont.*)

service of, 209; origin tropes of, 216–18, 224n38; petition for freedom by, 205–11, 222nn20–21; pueblo formation of, 210–11; self-administered government (*cabildo*) of, 211–20

encomenderos: legal protections of, 102–4; Peruvian perpetuity controversy and, 39–45, 49, 52, 56n1, 56n9, 56n13, 252–53; in Potosí's markets, 65–66

*encomienda*, 43–44, 46–47, 102, 104–11

*español* category, ix, 81, 172. *See also* Creole/*criollo*/*crioulo* category; *peninsular* category; whiteness

Esquivel, Thomás de, 103

Estrada, Francisco de, 98n12

ethnic identity: descent as basis for, 81, 97n1; of indigenous marketers of Potosí, 64, 67–69, 77, 78n5; of Peruvian *mestizos*, 71–72

ethnicity, as term, 7–9, 97n1

ethnogenesis, 102, 106–13

Evaristo de Jesus Borbua, Juan, 150

Farriss, Nancy, 229

Fernández, Tomás, 150

Fisher, Andrew, 198, 199, 202, 250–51

Flores, Antonio, 158

Flores, Ignacio, 170, 179, 181, 185–90, 194n67, 195n73, 195n87

Franco, Francisco, 249

Frazier, E. Franklin, 34n45

free blacks of Minas Gerais district, 3, 26, 254–55; collective negotiations of identity by, 129–36; legal complaints of, 115–16, 122–23; marriage practices of, 123–29, 138n22, 138n25; racial categories of, 115, 120–23, 136n1; self-identification of, 115–17, 122–23, 129; slave ownership by, 126, 138n27; slavery associated with, 117–22; taxation of, 120–21

Gallegos, Diego de, 157

Gálvez, José de, 182, 190

Gálvez, Vicente de, 189–90

Ganson, Barbara, 107

Garavaglia, Juan Carlos, 107

García Recio, José María, 107

*gateras* (indigenous market women), 24, 61, 63, 78n22; clash with expected roles of, 62, 77n3; ethnic labeling of, 67–69, 71–72, 77, 78n5; individual agency of, 68; *mestizas en habito de india*, 62, 71–76, 77, 258; *pallas* (indigenous noblewomen), 62, 64, 68, 74; *regatones* (indigenous hucksters), 62, 69–71, 257–58; Spanish merchants and, 66–67, 69, 76; Spanish regulation of, 76–77; taxation and tribute arrangements of, 65–66, 68, 71–72, 79n23

Geertz, Clifford, 18–19

Gembuel, Francisco, 95

gender: in divisions of labor, 110–11, 114n19, 209; in militia service, 209–10; in slavery contexts, 3–4, 204, 209. *See also* women

*genízaro* groups, 108

Giddens, Anthony, 21

Girón, Francisco Hernández, 41, 47, 50

gold mining, 115, 117–20, 137nn6–7

Gómez de Tagli, Juan, 85

Gotkowitz, Laura, 74

*gracias al sacar* whitening petitions, 141–43, 147–51, 161nn2–3, 162n7, 255–56

Greenleaf, Richard, 98n9

Groot, Pedro, 150

group membership. *See* collective identities

Guacrapaucar, Carlos, 48, 51, 52

Guacrapaucar, Felipe, 39, 48, 53–54

Guacrapaucar, Gerónimo, 41, 45–48, 49, 52

Guaman Poma de Ayala, Felipe, 1, 4

Guerrero, Vicente, 260
Guimarães, Francisca Ferreira, 125

Hacking, Ian, 197, 198, 221n2
Hernández, Baltazar, 85, 89–90
Hernández, Francisco, 83–90, 94–95,
    98n9, 98n16, 100n38
Herskovitz, Melville, 34n45
Herzog, Tamar, 222n21
Hispanicization, 63, 73
historical scholarship: of institutional in-
    teraction, 22–23, 36n68, 37n70; of ra-
    cial ideologies, 10–15, 32n27, 33n34,
    33nn37–38, 34nn43–45; of social
    identity, 15–23, 34n47, 36n59,
    36nn67–68, 37n70, 197–99, 201–2,
    221n2, 221nn6–8; total approach to
    identity making, 200–204, 221n7
honor, 4, 55–56, 116, 124–25, 172–75, 214
hybridity, 7–8, 15, 31n17; of El Cobre's
    royal slaves, 204–11, 222n11, 253–54;
    of indigenous borderland populations,
    109–11, 257–58; of Peru's indigenous
    aristocracy, 41, 54–55, 252–53; total
    approach to identity making, 200–
    204, 221n7

identity, 7–9, 19–20. See also social iden-
    tity
idolatry, 90–93, 95, 99–100nn27–29
illegitimacy, 72, 149
Incas: Jauja valley conquered by, 45–47;
    in uprising plot of 1565, 49–50
indias gateras. See gateras
indigenous peoples, 1–2; aristocratic
    kurakas of Peru, 23–24, 39–56, 57n25,
    252–53; borderland hybrid groups of,
    101–13, 257–58; colonial creation of,
    6; communal lands of, 103–4, 240–
    42, 247nn50–51; dual subjecthood or
    citizenship of, 93–97, 231–32; en-
    slavement of, 104–8; ethnic distinc-

tions among, 64; ethnogenesis of, 102,
    106–13; idolatry rituals of, 90–93, 95,
    99–100nn27–29; intermarriage of, 3–
    4, 30n3, 30n5, 63; jurisdiction of iden-
    tity of, 87, 90–91, 93, 95–97, 99n19;
    Mexican identities challenged by,
    225–43, 260–61; pacts of reciprocity
    of, 28–29, 46–48, 50, 227, 237; politi-
    cal sovereignty of, 4–5, 51–54, 215–
    18; Potosí's market women, 24, 61–77,
    257–58; traditional dress (acsu) of, 62,
    72–77, 98n6, 253; witchcraft of, 111
indio category, ix, 7, 11–12, 81, 110,
    226, 253
indios laboríos category, 110, 257
Inquisition, 25, 87, 90–97, 99n19,
    100n36, 258–59
institutional practices: in borderland
    areas, 102, 109–11, 257–58; Bourbon
    centralization, 167–69, 190, 205, 259–
    60; census-taking, 102; contact points
    of, 12, 21–23, 30, 36nn67–68, 37n70,
    47, 142, 202–3; legal jurisdiction of
    casta, 87, 90–91, 96, 141–61, 252;
    Mexico's liberalized governance, 225–
    47, 260–61; regulation of Potosí
    women marketers, 76–77; taxes and
    tributes, 65–66, 68, 71–72, 79n23,
    102, 118–19, 230; Two Republic sys-
    tem, 4–5, 53, 256–57; whitening peti-
    tions, 26–27, 141–61, 161nn2–3,
    162n7, 255–56. See also Catholic
    Church; colonial practices; local gov-
    ernance; racial categorization; sistema
    de castas
Islam, 146
Iturbide, Agustín de, 260

Jamaica, 204–5
Jauja valley of Peru, 41, 45–51. See also
    perpetuity controversy
Jenkins, Richard, 17, 36n59

indigenous borderland populations, 109–11, 257–58; in Potosí's indigenous women's market, 62–64, 69, 71–77, 258; self-labeling of, 83–90; social status of, 72–73

Mexias Bejarano, Diego, 151–54, 158–60

Mexico, 28–29, 225–29, 232, 235–36, 238, 243, 260–61; Caste War of 1847, 234, 239, 242; indigenous peoples taxed in, 230–31, 237, 239; Ley Lerdo of 1856, 240–41, 247nn50–51; liberalized national governance of, 233–34; origin tropes in, 224n38. *See also* Inquisition; Oaxaca and Yucatán regions

militias: of El Cobre, 209–10; of La Plata, 180–82, 186–87, 194n72

Minas Gerais (Brazil) district, 3, 26, 116, 254–55; gold mining in, 115, 117–20, 137nn6–7; land grants in, 118, 137nn6–7; lay brotherhoods of, 129–36, 139nn37–38; marriage practices in, 123–29, 138n22, 138n25; slavery in, 117–22, 126. *See also* free blacks of Minas Gerais district

mining industry: copper, 204–5, 218, 219–20; gold, 115, 117–20, 137nn6–7; silver, 64–67, 69, 76, 102; slavery in, 117–20, 204–5

Mintz, Sidney, 34n45

Mónica, María, 84–85

Montemayor, Alonso de, 65–66

Monterroso, Tomás de, 99n28

Moorish blood, 146, 250

Moreno, Gabriel René, 169

Moreno, Juan, 204–11

*morisco* catetgory, 33n37

Mörner, Magnus, 10–11, 32n27

*mulatto/mulato* category, 4, 81, 90–93, 98n8, 109, 138n26, 161n1, 251; *calidad* of birth in, 148–49; color and appearance in, 153–58; establishment of, 144–46; occupational limitations of,

147, 152–53; slavery as marker of, 152–53, 163n53; whitening petitions and, 141–43, 147–61

multinodular model of identity, 9

Mulvey, Patricia, 139n37

Mumford, Jeremy, 23–24, 252

Murcia, Juan de, 89

Murra, John, 66

Nader, Helen, 55

*naturaleza*, 82, 94, 144–45, 147, 149, 161n2, 162n12, 201, 222n21, 223n22. *See also calidad/qualidade*

Navajos, 108

Necasio, Francisco, 249

*negro* category, ix, 7, 11, 81, 109, 112, 206

New Christians, xi

New Spain: *encomenderos* of, 52, 102; social identity in, 101–13

Nicolasa Garces, María, 158

Nicolasa Juana, 90–93, 95

*nijoras* (servant class), 108

*nobleza*, 145, 162n12, 172

Oaxaca and Yucatán regions, 28–29, 227, 243; *cabecera* governance in, 236, 246n36; centralized appointments in, 234–39, 245n24; common lands in, 240–42, 247nn50–51; demographics of, 228–29; dual citizenship in, 231–33, 244n18; economic basis of, 229–30; indigenous categories eliminated in, 225–26, 230; local structures of, 226, 230–32, 240, 243n2, 244n18; taxation in, 230, 236–37, 239

*obedezco pero no cumplo*, 189, 256

Ocaña, Diego de, 73, 75

occidentalism, x–xi

O'Crouley, Pedro Alonso, 251

O'Hara, Matthew, 197–98, 199, 202, 250–51

Old Christians, xi

Orduña, Diego de, 88

origin, 81, 207–9, 216–18, 224n38. *See also* blood; *sistema de castas*

Ortner, Sherry, 34n47

Our Lady of Mercy and Saint Benedict brotherhood, 131

Our Lady of the Rosary brotherhood, 130–36, 139nn37–38

Palla, Catalina, 68

*pallas* (indigenous noblewomen), 62, 64, 68, 74

Pando, José María, 238–39

*pardo* category, 81, 115, 121–23, 129–35, 136n1, 138n26, 161n1; *calidad* of birth in, 148–49; color and appearance in, 153–58; establishment of, 144–46; occupational limitations of, 147, 152–53; slavery as marker of, 152–53, 163n53; social mobility of, 158–59, 164n78; whitening petitions and, 141–43, 147–61

Pardo Guild of Caracas, 159, 164n65

passing, 10, 12, 94–95, 147, 162n22

*patria* category, 208–9

patronage networks, 13

Payco, Juana, 75–76, 79n31

Paz, Joseph Luis, 145, 150, 154

Paz, Octavio, 183

Pellicel Aberrucia, Melchora, 98n15

*peninsular* category, 181, 193n52, 259. *See also español* category; whiteness

Peralta, Petronila, 150, 157

perpetuity controversy, 23–24, 252–53; contact point of labor and capital in, 47; indigenous aristocracy in, 39–41, 44–51, 52–56, 56n1, 57n25; new political structures of, 40–41, 43–44, 51–52; Spanish *encomenderos* in, 39–45, 49, 52, 56n1, 56n9, 56n13; uprising plot of 1565, 49–50

Peru. *See gateras*; perpetuity controversy

Peti, Josef, 176–78, 181, 184

phenotype, 6–7. *See also* blood

Philip II of Spain, 1, 4, 42, 44, 49, 252

Philip III of Spain, 149

Pizarro, Francisco, 47

Platt, Tristan, 28–29, 227

*plebe* category, 191n10

political culture, ix–xii, 2–5, 23

*Politics* (Aristotle), 50–51

Ponciano de Ayarza, Joseph, 148, 150, 157

Portugal, 125

practice theory, 21–22

Pratt, Mary Louise, 36n67

Presta, Ana María, 107

*preto* category, 115, 121, 123, 129–35, 136n1

Price, Richard, 34n45

*pueblo* category, 208–11, 257

pure blood (*limpieza*), xi, 5–7, 31n16, 144–47, 149, 162n16

Purnell, Jennie, 247n51

quilting, 200, 221n7

race thinking, 81, 97n3, 199, 221n5

racial categorization, 32n27, 33n34, 221n5; bureaucratic practice of, xi, 2–5, 6, 10–12, 14–15, 62; color in, 153–56; in contemporary cases, 95–96; of El Cobre's royal slaves, 27–28, 199–200; of free blacks in Minas Gerais district, 115, 120–23, 136n1; holistic determination of, 171–72; intermediate categories in, 3–4, 81, 144–51, 250; overdetermination of race thinking and, 81, 97n3, 199; by phenotype, 6–7; of Potosí's *mestizos en habita de india*, 71–77; renegotiation of, 13–14, 34n43, 82–97, 149–61, 200–202; self-understanding and, 20–23; as social distilling, 20–21; terminology of, 7–9, 31n17, 32nn20–24, 112; Two Republic system and, 4–5, 53, 256–57; whitening petitions and, 141–51, 161nn2–3, 162n7, 164n65, 255–56. *See also* blood; ethnic identity; hybridity; *sistema de castas*; social identity

racial ideologies: historical scholarship of, 10–15, 32n27, 33n34, 33nn37–38, 34nn43–45, 221n5; Wallerstein's world system and, 6, 32n24

Radding, Cynthia, 25, 256–57

Ramírez, Bernardo, 141–43, 154, 158

reciprocal relationships, 28–29; between central and local governments, 237; between colonizers and native peoples, 3, 227; in Peruvian alliances, 46–48, 50

*repartimiento* (forced labor) system, 102, 108, 212, 244n18, 254

*república de españoles* governance, 223n22

*repúblicas de indígenas* governance, 231–32, 236–37, 244n18

*repúblicas de indios* governance, 215, 217, 226, 230–31, 243n2. *See also* indigenous peoples; institutional practices

Rey, Joesph, 150

Ribera, Antonio de, 39, 41–44, 51, 56n13

Roca, Lorenzo de la, 104–6

Rojas, Francisco, 83–90, 94–95, 98n9, 100n38

Rugeley, Terry, 232

Sá, Manuel Dias de, 124–25

Sá, Maria Francisco de, 124–25

Saeger, James, 107

Saint Domingue, 205

Saint Elisbão and Our Lady of the Rosary, 133

Salazar de Mejía, Francisco de, 69

Salomon, Frank, 73, 77

Santa María, Pablo de, 149

São Gonçalo García brotherhood, 134–35

Schwartz, Stuart, 73, 77

Seed, Patricia, 12, 82, 173

Segovia, Juan José, 185–90, 194n67

Seide, Andrés Manuel de, 145–46

self-understanding, 20–21

Serulnikov, Sergio, 27

Sewell, William, 21–22

*Siete partidas*, 145, 222n20

Silverblatt, Irene, 36n68, 81, 97, 97n3, 199, 252

silver mining, 64–67, 69, 76, 102

*sistema de castas*, 10, 32n27, 72, 199–200, 250, 253; abandoned children, 155–56; *calidad* (social condition), 11–12, 26, 33n34, 81, 93, 97; *crianza* (upbringing), 90–93; establishment of, 143–51; identification processes of, 82–83; individual negotiations with, 82–97, 97n3, 98n8, 99n19, 100n33, 141–44, 251–52, 258–59; *lenguaje* (language) and, 93, 97; relaxation of, 167; visual readings of casta and, 82, 91–93, 98n6, 251, 258–59. *See also* blood

slaves, slavery, 26; African identities of, 204, 219, 222n16; Aristotle's rationale of, 50–51, 55; black ownership of, 126, 138n27; *capitação* tax on, 118–21, 137n10; citizenship options of, 210, 214–15, 219, 223n24; economic diversification of, 119–20; in *encomiendas*, 104–11; gender imbalances of, 3–4; historical scholarship on, 14, 34n45; intermarriage of, 120; lay brotherhoods and, 130–35, 139n37, 223n34; local autonomy in El Cobre of, 27–28, 199–220, 222nn20–21, 253–54; manumission rates, 117, 120, 134; in Minas Gerais district of Brazil, 117–22, 126; in mining industries, 117–20, 204–5, 219–20; racial basis of, 5–6; royal, 201. *See also* blacks; *pardo* category

social distilling, 20–21

social identity, ix–xii, 3–5, 13; boundary

social identity (*cont.*)

definition in, 16–18; collective formation of, 17, 21, 27–28, 36n59, 129–35, 253–55; contact points in, 21–23, 30, 36nn67–68, 47, 142; dynamic nature of, x, xii, 1–2, 15–23, 93–97, 249–53, 261–62; El Cobre slaves' interactive formations of, 199–220, 253–54; of free blacks of Minas Gerais, 115–36, 254–55; historical scholarship on, 15–23, 34n47, 36n59, 36nn67–68, 37n70, 197–99, 201–2, 221n2, 221nn6–8; in imperial borderlands, 101–13, 257–58; individual agency and subjectivity in, 15, 18–19, 35n47, 36n59, 100n33, 141–44, 158–59, 164n65; in La Plata, 169–73, 182–91, 259–60; *lenguaje* and *calidad*, 11–12, 26, 33n34, 81, 93, 97; in marriage decisions, 125–29, 138n25, 254–55; as nexus of categorization and self-understanding, 20–23; styles and values internalized in, 54–55; terminology of, 7–9, 19–20, 31n17, 32nn20–24, 112; total approach to identity making, 200–204, 221n7. *See also* racial categorization

Soto, Antonia de, 114n19

Soto Cabeçón, Juis de, 84

Spain, x–xi, 2, 5, 6–7, 40, 255–56; Bourbon imperial policies in, 167–69, 190, 205, 259–60; Castilian aristocracy in, 43, 46; constitutional government in, 226–27; *encomenderos* of the New World, 39–45, 65–66; municipal structures in, 27–28, 52; *naturaleza, limpieza,* and *calidad* in, 145–51, 162n16; purity of blood edicts in, 145–47. *See also* Catholic Church; colonial practices; *sistema de castas*

Spalding, Karen, 45

stained blood, xi–xii, 4

Stern, Steve J., 6, 47, 172–73

Stoler, Ann, 153

Sweet, James H., 34n45

Tannenbaum, Frank, 34n45

Taquima, Madalena, 70–71

Tavárez, David, 7, 24–25, 258–59

taxes and tributes, 65–66, 102; *capitação* on slaves, 118–21, 137n10; of free blacks, 120–21; in Mexico's indigenous communities, 230, 237, 239; of Potosí's market women, 68, 71–72, 79n23

terminology, 7–9, 24–25, 31n17, 32nn20–24, 112

Thibaud, Clément, 169

Thornton, John, 34n45

Toledo, Francisco de, 53

Torres y Portugal, Fernando de, 70

total approach to identity making, 200–204, 221n7

traditional dress (*acsu*), 62, 72–77, 98n6, 257

translation, 7–8

Túpac Amaru rebellion, 27, 167–69, 171, 178–79, 182–84, 190

Twinam, Ann, 3, 26–27, 81, 252, 256

Two Republic system, 4–5, 53, 256–57

Universidad de San Francisco Xavier, 169, 171, 190

uprisings: in La Plata, 175–82, 192n12, 193n40, 193n44; Túpac Amaru rebellion, 27, 167–69, 171, 178–79, 182–84, 190

urban culture: Creoles of La Plata, 27, 167–91, 259–60; Iberian municipal practices, 27–28, 76–78; Potosí's indigenous social hierarchies, 24, 61–77; renegotiations of casta in, 82–97

Valdés, Gerónimo de, 220

Valenzuela brothers, 148, 157

Valiente, Alonso, 98n15

*vecino* category, 181, 183, 193n52, 210, 223n31

Vértiz, Juan José de, 170, 185, 187, 195n73

Villa Imperial de Potosí. *See gateras* (indigenous market women)

Villavicencio, Diego Xaimes Ricardo, 90–93, 99–100nn28–29, 100n36

Vinson, Ben, 158, 164n78

Viscama, Juana, 69

Vivero, Rodrigo de, the Younger, 85, 89, 98n15

Vizcarra, Bonifacio, 188

Wade, Peter, 8

Wallerstein, Immanuel, 6, 32n24

Wankas of Peru, 41, 45–46. *See also* perpetuity controversy

whiteness, 26–27, 161n4; *calidad* of, 148–49; color and appearance in, 153–58; *gracias al sacar* petitions for whitening, 141–43, 147–51, 161nn2–3, 162n7, 255–56; *naturaleza* and *limpieza* of, 144–46, 149; passing, 10, 12, 94–95,

147, 162n22; title of "don" and, 158; Venezuelan renegotiations of, 151–61, 164n65, 256. *See also* Creole/*criollo*/*crioulo* category; *español* category; *peninsular* category

Williams, Eric, 5–6

witchcraft, 111

Wolf, Eric, 14

women: *cholas*, 74; gender-based power and, 173–75; intermarriage of, 3–4, 30n3, 30n5, 63, 72, 120; racially based abuse of, 115; social hierarchies in Potosí market, 24, 61–77, 257–58; Spanish-born, 72; traditional dress of, 62, 72–77. *See also* marriage practices

Ximénez, Pedro Ignacio, 197, 211–16

Xocoiotl, Clara, 85

Yahya-u-Ta'fuft, 55

*yanaconas*, 61, 77n2

Yanes, Nicolas Francisco, 157–58

Ynaso, Juan, 69

Yucatán. *See* Oaxaca and Yucatán regions

ANDREW B. FISHER is an assistant professor
in the Department of History at Carleton College.

MATTHEW D. O'HARA is an assistant professor
in the Department of History at the University of
California, Santa Cruz.

Library of Congress Cataloging-in-Publication Data
Imperial subjects : race and identity in colonial Latin America / Andrew B. Fisher and
Matthew D. O'Hara, eds. ; foreword by Irene Silverblatt.
p. cm. — (Latin America otherwise)
Includes bibliographical references and index.
ISBN 978-0-8223-4401-8 (cloth : alk. paper)
ISBN 978-0-8223-4420-9 (pbk. : alk. paper)
1. Identity (Psychology)—Latin America—History. 2. Latin Americans—Ethnic
identity. 3. Latin America—History—To 1830. I. Fisher, Andrew B., 1970– II.
O'Hara, Matthew D. (Matthew David), 1970– III. Series: Latin America otherwise.
F1408.3.I57 2009
305.80098—dc22    2008051101